Syntactic Gradience

For Geri, Emma, and Milena

Syntactic Gradience

The Nature of Grammatical Indeterminacy

BAS AARTS

OXFORD

UNIVERSITY PRESS

OXFORD
UNIVERSITY PRESS

Great Clarendon Street, Oxford OX2 6DP

Oxford University Press is a department of the University of Oxford.
It furthers the University's objective of excellence in research, scholarship,
and education by publishing worldwide in

Oxford New York

Auckland Cape Town Dar es Salaam Hong Kong Karachi
Kuala Lumpur Madrid Melbourne Mexico City Nairobi
New Delhi Shanghai Taipei Toronto

With offices in

Argentina Austria Brazil Chile Czech Republic France Greece
Guatemala Hungary Italy Japan Poland Portugal Singapore
South Korea Switzerland Thailand Turkey Ukraine Vietnam

Oxford is a registered trade mark of Oxford University Press
in the UK and in certain other countries

Published in the United States
by Oxford University Press Inc., New York

British Library Cataloguing in Publication Data
Data available

Library of Congress Cataloging in Publication Data
Data available

Typeset by SPI Publisher Services, Pondicherry, India
Printed in Great Britain
on acid-free paper by
Biddles Ltd., King's Lynn, Norfolk

ISBN 978–0–19–921926–1 (HB)
        978–0–19–921927–8 (PB)

1 3 5 7 9 10 8 6 4 2

Contents

Abbreviations   xi
Acknowledgements   xiii

1 Introduction   1

Part I Theoretical Background   7

2 Categorization in Linguistics   9

2.1 Introduction   9
2.2 The classical philosophical tradition of categorization   11
2.3 The linguistic tradition: early grammarians   14
2.4 Twentieth-century approaches to linguistic categorization   17
    2.4.1 Bloomfield and American structuralism   17
    2.4.2 Transformational grammar   18
    2.4.3 Generative Semantics   23
    2.4.4 Descriptive grammar   25
    2.4.5 Cognitive approaches   26
    2.4.6 Functional-typological and discourse typological
          linguistics   30
    2.4.7 Other frameworks: Phrase Structure Grammar and
          Construction Grammar   32

3 Grammatical Gradience   34

3.1 Introduction   34
3.2 Notions of gradience in ancient and modern philosophy   35
3.3 The linguistic tradition: early grammarians   38
3.4 Twentieth-century approaches to gradience   39
    3.4.1 The post-Bloomfieldians and Bolinger   39
    3.4.2 Firth and Halliday   42
    3.4.3 Transformational Grammar   43
    3.4.4 Generative Semantics   52
    3.4.5 Logical approaches to linguistic vagueness: the Prague
          school, Zadeh, and Ross   58
    3.4.6 Descriptive grammar   62
    3.4.7 Cognitive approaches   68

3.4.8 Functional-typological and discourse-typological
          linguistics   71
3.4.9 Optimality Theory   72
3.4.10 Probability Theory   73
3.4.11 Other frameworks: Phrase Structure Grammar,
          Word Grammar, Lexical-Functional Grammar, and
          Construction Grammar   75
3.5 Two types of gradience   79

4 Gradience and Related Notions   80

4.1 Introduction   80
4.2 Serial relationship   80
4.3 Syntactic mixing: mergers   83
4.4 Multiple analysis and reanalysis   86
4.5 Gradience and Prototype Theory   87
4.6 Gradience and Markedness Theory   90

Part II Gradience in English: Case Studies   95

5 Subsective Gradience   97

5.1 SG within word classes   97
    5.1.1 Verbs   98
    5.1.2 Nouns   101
    5.1.3 Adjectives   105
    5.1.4 Prepositions   107
5.2 SG within phrases   111
5.3 SG within clauses   117
5.4 SG in grammar   121

6 Intersective Gradience   124

6.1 IG between word classes   124
    6.1.1 Gradience between pre-head elements within
              noun phrases   124
        6.1.1.1 Determinatives and pronouns   125
        6.1.1.2 Determinatives and adjectives   125
        6.1.1.3 Determinatives and adverbs   127
        6.1.1.4 Adjectives and nouns   129
        6.1.1.5 Adjectives and adverbs   136
    6.1.2 Gradience between verbs and other word classes   138
        6.1.2.1 Verbs and adjectives   138
        6.1.2.2 Verbs and nouns   143

6.1.2.3 Verbs and prepositions/conjunctions 145
6.1.2.4 Verbs and adverbs 149
6.1.3 Further cases 150
6.1.3.1 Adverbs, prepositions, and conjunctions 150
6.1.3.2 Adverbs and nouns 155
6.1.3.3 Adjectives and prepositions 156
6.2 IG between phrases 158
6.2.1 Adjective phrases and noun phrases 158
6.2.2 Adjective phrases and prepositional phrases 160
6.2.3 Noun phrases and prepositional phrases 161
6.3 IG in grammar 162

7 Constructional Gradience 164
7.1 Introduction 164
7.2 A brief history of the notion 'construction' 164
7.2.1 Structuralism and Transformational Grammar 164
7.2.2 Descriptive grammar 166
7.2.3 Cognitive Linguistics 167
7.2.4 Constructionist frameworks 168
7.3 The notion 'construction' 170
7.4 Constructional Gradience 171
7.4.1 Subsective Constructional Gradience (SCG) 171
7.4.1.1 Pseudoclefts 172
7.4.1.2 Constructions involving subject–auxiliary inversion (SAI) 173
7.4.1.3 Verb + NP and Verb + NP + NP constructions 173
7.4.1.4 Transitive constructions 174
7.4.1.5 The possessive construction 175
7.4.1.6 Complex prepositions 176
7.4.1.7 The passive gradient 178
7.4.2 Intersective Constructional Gradience (ICG) 180
7.4.2.1 Genitival constructions 180
7.4.2.2 Taylor's possessive constructions gradient 181
7.4.2.3 Coordination and subordination 182
7.4.2.4 Verb complementation: monotransitive, ditransitive, and complex transitive constructions 185
7.4.2.5 Complements and adjuncts 186
7.4.2.6 Syntactic blends and fusions 187

7.5 Constructional Gradience in grammar   192
   7.5.1 Vague meaning   193
   7.5.2 'Too much' meaning   194
   7.5.3 'Too little' meaning   195
7.6 A purely syntactic approach to constructions   196

Part III Formalization   199

8 Modelling Syntactic Gradience   201

8.1 Introduction   201
8.2 Vagueness, representations, and gradience   202
   8.2.1 Eliminating vagueness by looking more closely:
          apparent sameness   203
   8.2.2 Eliminating vagueness by looking more closely:
          apparent differences   203
   8.2.3 Determinatives: a further case of apparent sameness?   204
8.3 A formalization of Subsective Gradience and Intersective
     Gradience   205
   8.3.1 Subsective Gradience   205
   8.3.2 Intersective Gradience   207
8.4 Some applications   208
   8.4.1 SG in the adjective class   209
   8.4.2 IG between verbs and nouns: the English gerund   210
   8.4.3 IG between verbs and adjectives   214
   8.4.4 IG between adjectives and prepositions: *near* and *like* 215
   8.4.5 Complementizers and prepositions   219
   8.4.6 Constructions: V + NP + [*to*-infinitive] vs.
          V + [NP + *to*-infinitive]   222
8.5 The present account vs. the Aristotelian and 'Sorites' models 223
8.6 The syntactic properties of the categories   225
   8.6.1 How can we be sure to identify all the relevant
          properties, and are all the properties equally important? 225
   8.6.2 How can we know that a particular property
          is an independent one and not merely a variant
          of an already identified property?   227
   8.6.3 Is it indeed the case that the syntactic properties
          that characterize a particular form class are unique
          to that class?   227

8.6.4 Is it true that an element belonging to a particular
class can converge on at most one other word
class in any one syntactic configuration?   228
8.7 'True hybridity'   228
8.8 The nature of grammatical categories   234
8.9 The contiguity of grammatical categories   235
8.10 Conclusion   241

References   243
Index   265

Abbreviations

A(P)	adjective (phrase)
Acc	accusative
Adj(P)	adjective (phrase)
AdvP	adverb phrase
AgrP	agreement phrase
AVM	Attribute Value Matrix
CCH	Contingent Category Hypothesis
CCxG	Cognitive Construction Grammar
CFC	Complete Functional Complex
CG	Constructional Gradience
COMP	complementizer (position)
CP	complementizer phrase
CxG	Construction Grammar
D(et)	determiner/determinative
DP	determiner phrase
FF	formal features
FLOB	*Freiburg-Lancaster/Oslo-Bergen Corpus*
GB	Government and Binding Theory
GC	Governing Category
GPSG	Generalized Phrase Structure Grammar
GS	Generative Semantics
H	head
HFC	Head Feature Convention
HPSG	Head-driven Phrase Structure Grammar
I(P)	inflection (phrase)
ICE-GB	*British component of the International Corpus of English*
ICG	Intersective Constructional Gradience
IG	Intersective Gradience
LFG	Lexical Functional Grammar
MT	Markedness Theory

N(P)	noun (phrase)
NegP	negative phrase
NGP	Nominal Gerund Phrase
Obj	object
OED	*Oxford English Dictionary*
OO/O2	direct object
OT	Optimality Theory
P(P)	preposition(al) (phrase)
Poss	possessive
P&P	Principles and Parameters Theory
PRO	pronominal anaphor
PT	Prototype Theory
Q	embedded questions
RCxG	Radical Construction Grammar
SAI	subject–auxiliary inversion
SCG	Subsective Constructional Gradience
SG	Subsective Gradience
SR	serial relationship
Subj	subject
SV	Subject–Verb
SVO	Subject–Verb–Object
SVOA	Subject–Verb–Direct Object–Adjunct
SVOC	Subject–Verb–Direct Object–Object Complement
SVOO	Subject–Verb–Indirect Object–Direct Object
TG	Transformational Grammar
TP	tense phrase
UCH	Universal Category Hypothesis
UCxG	Unification Construction Gramar
UG	Universal Grammar
V(P)	verb (phrase)
VFORM	verb form
VGerPs	Verbal Gerund Phrases
WG	Word Grammar
WXDY	What's X doing Y construction

Acknowledgements

Some of the material in this book was presented in talks, lectures, and seminars in various places, to wit Bonn, Busan, Edinburgh, Granada, Jaén, Lancaster, Manchester, Munich, Oxford, Roehampton, Seoul, and Zürich. I would like to thank the audiences there for valuable feedback. I also wish to thank students at UCL and at the Universities of Zürich and Jaén for useful discussions. I have received comments on (parts of) this book from the following colleagues and friends: Flor Aarts, Valerie Adams, Philippe Blache, Noël Burton-Roberts, Bernard Comrie, Bill Croft, David Denison, Liliane Haegeman, Martin Haspelmath, Dick Hudson, Evelien Keizer, Guilio Lepschy, Robert Munro, Terttu Nevailanen, Carita Paradis, Gergana Popova, Jean-Philippe Prost, Mariangela Spinillo, John Taylor, Tim Waller, Wim van der Wurff and a number of anonymous readers commissioned by OUP. Thanks are also due to John Davey at OUP for his keen interest in this book and for his support, to Kim Allen, my copy editor, and to Tim Waller for his meticulous proofreading. I'm immensely grateful to all these people, whose input has improved the book in many respects. As always, for any remaining errors I alone should be held to account. Parts of this book have appeared in a different form elsewhere, namely as Aarts (2004a, 2004b, 2006). I'm grateful to the publishers of these articles for permission to reprint them.

This book is dedicated, with much love, to my wife Geri and to my two daughters Emma and Milena.

BAS AARTS

University College London
August 2006

Cleopatra

What was he, sad or merry?

Alexas

Like to the time o'th'year between the extremes
Of hot and cold, he was nor sad nor merry.

Cleopatra

O well-divided disposition! Note him,
Note him, good Charmian, 'tis the man; but note him!
He was not sad, for he would shine on those
That make their looks by his; he was not merry,
Which seemed to tell them his remembrance lay
In Egypt with his joy; but between both.
O heavenly mingle! Be'st thou sad or merry,
The violence of either thee becomes,
So does it no man else. Met'st thou my posts?

William Shakespeare, *Antony and Cleopatra*, I.5.
(The New Penguin Shakespeare, Edited by Emrys Jones)

1

Introduction

Does one grain make a heap? Obviously not. Do two grains make a heap? No. Do one hundred grains make a heap? Yes. Where should one draw the line?

(Eubulides' Paradox of the Sorites, ca. 400 BC)

Eubulides of Megara's celebrated Paradox of the Sorites (or Heap) brings to the fore the problems we face in setting up boundaries in the world around us: when can we call a collection of grains a heap? When we have one or ten or fifty? Is there a cut-off point such that a certain number of grains of sand form a heap, but n–1 grains do not? What about a man with three hairs; is he bald? What if he has one thousand hairs? And again, is there a point at which we can say 'a man with n hairs is bald, but a man with $n+1$ hairs is not'? Similarly, if we line up the Mona Lisa in the Louvre with ninety-nine faithful copies that differ only minutely from each other, such that the original painting ML is virtually indistinguishable from ML+1, and ML+1 is virtually indistinguishable from ML+2 etc., can we then identify a particular painting in the line-up where we must say, 'this painting bears no resemblance to the Mona Lisa'?[1] Philosophers have often struggled with the problem of delimitation, and with the setting-up of boundaries. Aristotle held that the categories which we use to class the phenomena in the world around us are hard and inviolable, but others have long recognized that they may not be as clearly delimited as Aristotle made them out to be, and that we have to recognize boundary fluidity between taxonomic constructs.

This book is about drawing lines in the domain of grammar and about boundary vagueness. In linguistics the term *gradience* is often used to designate this phenomenon. An early book on gradience (Bolinger 1961a) illustrated the phenomenon in the acoustic domain. Continuous phenomena have received progressively more attention in a number of domains of language study, notably sociolinguistics (Labov 1973; Hudson 1996), psycholinguistics (Rosch and

---

[1] The last two illustrations are variants of the Sorites Paradox, called the Paradox of the Bald Man and the Mona Lisa Paradox. There are many other versions of the paradox; see e.g. Chatterjee (1994: 153f.), Williamson (1994).

Mervis 1975; Rosch *et al.* 1976; Rosch 1978), semantics (Coates 1983; Fuchs and Victorri 1994; Wierzbicka 1989, 1990, 1996), typological linguistics (Croft 1991, 2001), functional/typological linguistics (Givón 1986, 2001), and cognitive linguistics (Lakoff 1987*a*; Langacker 1987, 1991; Geeraerts 1989; Taylor 2003; Ungerer and Schmid 1996; Cruse and Croft 2004). For a collection of influential writings from a variety of different perspectives, see Aarts *et al.* (2004). Studies of categorization can be found in the collections of Corrigan, Eckman and Noonan (1989) and Tsohatzidis (1990). Many of these studies have in general been concerned with the cognitive mechanisms of categorizing three-dimensional objects. Thus Labov's well-known study on drinking vessels investigated the question of what are the defining characteristics of cups, and at which point a particular drinking vessel would more adequately be named a mug. For scholars such as Taylor the central concern is to study 'the meanings of linguistic forms, and the categorization of the world which a knowledge of these forms entails' (Taylor 2003: xii). Much less attention has been paid to gradient phenomena in the more narrowly defined domain of syntax, although there are exceptions, see for example Quirk *et al.* (1985) and Taylor (2003).

This book grew out of a feeling of discomfort with not only the views of the radical categorizationalists, that is to say most linguists working in formal syntactic frameworks, but also with those of eclectic linguists for whom anything goes, with a 'gradience-is-everywhere' perspective. Among the latter group are a number of descriptive grammarians, as well as many linguists working in discourse-based, cognitive, and typological frameworks. I share with the formal syntacticians a belief that syntax is autonomous, and that in setting up categories of grammar we should first and foremost look at the distributional facts. Semantic and pragmatic considerations are of secondary importance. However, I am unhappy with their unyielding views about categorization, and I am also uncomfortable with a degree of disingenuousness on their part when the facts of language are often ignored, and when they are guilty of sneaking in hybridity or gradient phenomena through the back door. The GB/P&P (Government and Binding Theory/Principles and Parameters Theory) notion of a 'prepositional complementizer' is a case in point in sentences such as *I want (for) John to leave*, where *for* is a complementizer because it functions to introduce a subordinate complement clause, but, unlike any other complementizer, it must also be able to assign Case, hence the hybrid label. There are other examples, as we will see.

The views of linguists who regard continuous phenomena in language as given are not seldom equally unsatisfactory. What often happens is that gradience is posited when elements of language are difficult to categorize or in some ways resemble each other, and we end up with descriptions that are replete with unwarranted continuities. As an example of this, consider the cline between imperatives and declaratives below, from Givón (1986: 96):

Do it!	= Most prototypical imperative
You might as well do it.	
I suggest that you do it.	
It would be nice if you did it.	
It would be nice if it were done.	
It needs to be done.	= Most prototypical declarative

Givón claims that this gradient is functionally *and* structurally motivated, with reference to such notions as 'the power/authority relation between speaker and hearer', 'speaker urgency in getting something done', etc. I have difficulty in seeing how these sentences shade into each other syntactically. Descriptive grammars, Quirk *et al.* (1985) among them, are also prone to falling into the gradience trap. In this book I will argue that if we eliminate imprecise descriptions, gradience is diminished or sometimes even disappears.

In the history of linguistics oppositions like the one signalled above are of course not new. There have been a number of controversies in which the views of nomothetically inclined linguists, who feel that languages are orderly, rule-based systems, are pitted against the opinions of those who think languages are inherently flexible entities that are not (exclusively) susceptible to blind and indiscriminate applications of rules. Thus in antiquity the analogists—Aristotle among them—stressed the regularities in language and its propensity for order and systematicity, while the anomalists pointed out the 'messiness' of language. (See Robins 1990: 21f. and Seuren 1998: 23–7 for discussion.) In the nineteenth century there were heated disagreements between those who subscribed to the Neogrammarian manifesto that all sound laws are exceptionless and linguists who felt that such thinking was too dogmatic. The recently deceased philosopher Zeno Vendler captured the controversy beautifully when he said to a colleague 'Well, for you, Tom, language is a neo-classical garden; but for me, it is a jungle.'[2] At the present time, in expressing their views on gradience, linguists are instrumental in history repeating itself. Yet again we encounter a tension between scholars of different persuasions who have little patience for the views of others. However, as we will see in Chapter 3, there are signs that the two 'camps' mentioned above are less firmly entrenched than they have been for the last few decades. I consider this a positive development. Because this development

---

[2] From a website dedicated to Vendler after his death: www.phil.ucalgary.ca/people/vendler.

is so recent, the reasons for the rapprochement are not yet clear. Maybe it is the waning of Chomsky's influence, or the realization that some sort of compromise between the two positions is possible, as I will be arguing here.

The aim of this book is to study the phenomenon of gradience in close detail, limiting the scope to English and to syntax. I will only deal with the notion of gradience conceived of as 'categorial indeterminacy', and not with what is arguably an entirely separate manifestation of gradience, namely indeterminacy in the area of acceptability/grammaticality judgements (see Fanselow *et al.* 2006 for a collection of wide-ranging articles with this perspective), although this type of gradience will be discussed to some extent in Chapter 3. Among the problems I will investigate are the following: What exactly is gradience, and how do we recognize gradient phenomena? Are there 'diagnostics' for establishing the existence of gradience? Is gradience an undifferentiated phenomenon? It is often claimed that it is pervasive in grammar (see e.g. Langacker 1987: 18), but is this really so? How pervasive is it? For example, while some elements in particular contexts may be said to be in a gradient relationship with each other (e.g. verbs and adjectives), there never appears to be gradience between, say, sentences and adjectives. Is gradience a grammatical phenomenon, or merely a by-product of performance, as has recently been argued? The answer to this last question has implications for the question of whether or not gradience should play a role in theoretical grammar. Are theoreticians right in insisting on a degree of idealization to describe the world around us (see e.g. Chomsky 1995: 7)? How does gradience relate to such notions as (syntactic) blend (Bolinger 1961*b*), cline (Halliday 1961: 248–9), serial relationship (Quirk 1965), and squish (Ross 1972: 316, 1973*a*: 98, 1974: 113)? Are they perhaps all (instantiations of) the same thing?

The position I will be arguing for is that gradience is an undeniable property of grammar, whether the latter is conceived as a mental construct in the Chomskyan sense or as a representational system, that is as a systematic and idealized representation of mentally constituted language in the shape of a description or model of that mental reality. Having said this, to my mind it is incumbent on linguists to eliminate gradience where it comes about as a result of sloppy description. This can be done by successively falsifying grammatical descriptions that contain various degrees of gradience. We can, however, never hope to eliminate categorial vagueness from grammar altogether. I will argue for what might be called 'constrained indeterminacy'.

In this book I will attempt to be more precise about the vague phenomenon of gradience. I will distinguish two types of category fluidity. One type I will call *Subsective Gradience* (SG). It is an intra-categorical phenomenon which allows members of a class to display the properties of that class to varying degrees. The second type is called *Intersective Gradience* (IG). This is an inter-categorical phenomenon which comes about when two form classes 'converge' on each other. I will argue that while the two types of gradience are grammatically real, IG is not as widespread as is often claimed.

In an effort to pin down the notion of gradience, I will devise a formalization of SG and IG, using a number of case studies, mainly from English. The formalism makes use of morphosyntactic tests to establish whether an item belongs to a particular class or to a 'bordering' one by weighing up the form class features that apply to the item in question. I will defend the view that a midway position between the Aristotelian and the cognitivist conceptions of categorization is to be preferred, by allowing for gradience in the grammar, but nevertheless maintaining sharp boundaries between categories. The ideas put forward in this book have wider implications for the study of language, in that they address the problem posed by the existence of a tension between generally rigidly conceived linguistic concepts and the continuous phenomena they describe.

The remainder of this book is structured as follows. The next two chapters have a partly parallel structure. In Chapter 2 I will look at the concept of categorization, focusing on how it has been dealt with over time in linguistics. Chapter 3 also has an historiographical aim: it discusses the history of the notion of vagueness in philosophy and the concept of gradience in linguistics. Here I will also elaborate on the notions of SG and IG introduced above. Chapter 4 deals with linguistic concepts related to gradience, such as serial relationship, markedness and the like. Chapters 5–7 discuss gradience between different types of grammatical form classes: word classes, phrases, clauses, and constructions. The final chapter critically assesses the notion of gradience, and returns to a number of case studies presented in Chapters 5–7. It will tie the book together by describing the formalism mentioned above more explicitly.

Part I
Theoretical Background

2

Categorization in Linguistics

Any object Δ that you choose to take either falls under the concept Φ or does not fall under it; *tertium non datur.*

(Frege 1903/1997: 259)

All grammars leak.

(Sapir 1921/1957: 38)

2.1 Introduction

Categorization in its most general sense can be seen as a process of systematization of acquired knowledge. Each time we come across something new in our worlds—concrete entities, as well as abstract concepts—we try to accommodate it by assigning it to some category or other. This phenomenon is especially common in early childhood when children progressively acquaint themselves with the world around them. However, knowledge systematization in fact occurs throughout the lives of all human beings. Conceived of in this way, as knowledge systematization, categorization is a cognitive process which allows human beings to make sense of the world by carving it up, in order for it to become more orderly and manageable for the mind. As such, it has important implications for a wide range of disciplines, among them anthropology, philosophy, sociology, psychology, and science in general. As a brief example of how categorization has been seen to operate in the field of medicine, consider the way the medical world dealt with the AIDS phenomenon. When it was first encountered, the illness had to be made sense of, especially in relation to other illnesses and their known symptoms. In other words, the disease had to fit into a taxonomy of illnesses; it had to be *categorized.* The first thing scientists noted was that AIDS was something that had never been encountered before. This is a kind of 'negative categorization'. Then, as research progressed, it was established that AIDS is caused by a virus called HIV. At each stage, new facts led to a new way of systematizing our knowledge of AIDS. What is important to stress here is that knowledge systematization refers to the way we 'position' that knowledge in relation to our knowledge of related notions and concepts. To a considerable degree categorization is the imposition of a meta-reality on the world which involves a good deal of idealization. The problem in slicing up reality into chunks is that we do not want the chunks to be too large, nor do we want them to be too small: regarding the world as an undifferentiated continuous mass is not productive, nor is compartmentalization into infinitesimal categories.

In linguistics, too, categorization is of paramount importance. Language in its spoken form is no more than a stream of sounds, and traditionally linguistics has been concerned with the mapping of these sounds onto meaning. This process is mediated by syntax, which is concerned with the segmentation of linguistic matter into units, namely categories of various sorts, and groupings of one or more of these categories into constituents. In present-day linguistics, it is safe to say, no grammatical framework can do without categories, however conceived. All working linguists recognize one set or other of word classes and relational categories, be they innate or not. It is for this reason that categorization is of central concern to the study of language. Indeed, for the American linguist Labov '[i]f linguistics can be said to be any one thing it is the study of categories: that is, the study of how language translates meaning into sound through the categorization of reality into discrete units and sets of units' (1973: 342).

Categorization is no trivial matter. As Lyons (1968: 270) notes, 'there is very little consistency or uniformity in the use of the term "category" in modern treatments of grammatical theory': different linguists have used wider or narrower definitions of what they regard as linguistic categories. For some, the categories of language are the word classes. For others, tense, mood, person, number, etc. are also categories. Categorization raises a variety of problems, mostly having to do with the determination and delimitation of class membership. For example, on grounds of elegance and economy, in setting up a system of parts of speech, ideally the number of postulated categories is maximally restricted. A more commodious system leads to generalizations being missed, and flies in the face of Occam's razor, in that entities are multiplied beyond necessity. Throughout the history of grammar writing, from antiquity onwards, the problem of setting up an adequate system of parts of speech has been paramount. For the Greeks the noun and the verb were primary. Adjectives were regarded by Plato and Aristotle as verbs, but as nouns by the Alexandrians and later grammarians (Lyons 1968: 323). There was some debate as to whether or not there should be a separate class of participles, which have both verbal and nominal characteristics (Robins 1990: 39). In the two centuries or so leading up to 1800 the deliberations of English grammarians resulted in 56 different systems of parts of speech (see Michael 1970: 521–9, 1987: 344). In present-day grammatical frameworks there is still a great deal of discussion about issues of classification, as we will see. This chapter will look at a number of approaches to categorization. In the next section I will discuss the classical philosophical tradition and its pervasive influence on linguistics up to the present, moving on to the linguistic tradition in Section 2.3. Twentieth-century approaches to categorization will be explored in Section 2.4. I will present a more or less comprehensive historiographical overview of what has been said on categorization, without pursuing a particular ideological line of thought.

2.2 The classical philosophical tradition of categorization

The word *category* (from Greek *katēgoria*) derives from Aristotle (Störig 1959/ 1985, I: 167), and originally meant 'statement'. Perhaps the oldest ideas on categorization were those of Aristotle, as expounded in his *Metaphysics* and *Categories*. Aristotle held that a particular entity can be defined by listing a number of necessary and sufficient conditions that apply to it (these are the *symbebēkóta*, mentioned in Robins 1990: 39). This view has been referred to as the classical, scholastic or Aristotelian theory of categorization (Lakoff 1987*a*: 6; Taylor 2003: 20).[1] As an example, consider Aristotle's well-known definition of *man* as a 'two-footed animal':

Therefore, if it is true to say of anything that it is a man, it must be a two-footed animal; for this was what 'man' meant; and if this is necessary, it is impossible that the same thing should not be a two-footed animal; for this is what 'being necessary' means—that it is impossible for the thing not to be. It is, then, impossible that it should be at the same time true to say the same thing is a man and is not a man. (*Metaphysics*, IV, 4, 1589)

Associated with this view is what has been called the *all-or-none* principle of categorization, or the Law of the Excluded Middle (Ross 1974: 111; Langacker 1987: 16; Taylor 2003: 21), which holds that something must be either inside or outside a category, that is a particular entity must be either a man or not a man, it cannot be something in between.[2] In the classical model categories have clear boundaries and their members have equal status (Wittgenstein 1953/1958, part I: paragraphs 67–71; Rosch 1978: 35; Lakoff 1987*a*: 16–17; Corrigan 1989: 10; Taylor 2003: 21–2).

---

[1] Another term that has been used is the *criterial-attribute model* (Langacker 1987: 16).

[2] Strictly speaking, we should distinguish between the Law of the Excluded Third and the Law of the Excluded Middle, as argued in Seuren (1998: 318–19). The former allows only two truth values, whereas the latter disallows gradations between truth values, however many there are.

As has often been observed by many writers, the influence of the classical theory of categorization has been pervasive and long-lasting. Taylor (2003: 78) points to the Bible (specifically the Book of Genesis, which discusses the species) and formal education as possible factors for the continuing popularity of Aristotelian categorization in linguistics, whereas Michael attributes the 'hardening of categories' to the fact that

> [o]ur whole conception of grammar for a vernacular has been deeply and, it may be argued, disastrously influenced by the fact that it was formed before there was any science of language. The hardening of categories, the increasing autonomy of logic and rhetoric, and the lack of any science of language, forced on grammar a preoccupation with the classification and analysis of words alone. (Michael 1970: 490)

Murphy (2002: 26) suggests that the classical theory was popular due to its ties with traditional logic. All these factors may well have played a role, but perhaps more important are a number of further factors. One is that allowing for the converse of strict categorization, that is, imprecision and/or vagueness, goes against what science is all about: the elimination of doubts and uncertainties about the world in the pursuit of truth. In other words, vagueness is simply not respected in the scholarly world.[3] Another factor is the observation that the classical theory is a *simple* model which stipulates clear criteria for establishing membership of a particular category. Furthermore, as we have seen, clearly delineated categories enable us to bring (a semblance of) order to the anarchic diversity of the world around us. Allowing for gradience is *prima facie* not an attractive option because it potentially opens the floodgates to a mass of uninterpretable and unclassifiable phenomena, a point also made by Michael. A final possible explanation for the popularity of classical categorization is that it seems to be in tune with a strong human propensity to see the world as being structured in terms of discrete entities.

Of the nineteenth-century philosophers who were influenced by Aristotle's strict categorization, Gottlob Frege stands out. Frege, one of the founders of modern logic, had little time for vagueness and insisted on sharp delimitation. Writing about concepts in his *Grundgesetze der Arithmetik*, he states that:

> The law of the excluded middle is really just another form of the requirement that the concept should have a sharp boundary. Any object Δ that you choose to take either

---

[3] As Wittgenstein (1953/1958: 42; §88) lamented: ' "Inexact" is really a reproach, and "exact" is praise. And that is to say what is inexact attains its goal less perfectly than what is more exact' (quoted in Chatterjee 1994: 1). Of course, the opposition precise/vague is a recognizable bone of contention for linguists working in academic departments of language and literature, where the linguists chide their literary colleagues for pseudo-scientific wishy-washy thinking, while the latter regard the work of their linguistic colleagues as 'cold' and precluding flexible creativity.

falls under the concept Φ or does not fall under it; *tertium non datur*. (Frege 1903/1997: 259)

Frege denied that vague concepts can have a role to play in logic. Wittgenstein's views were diametrically opposed to those of Frege; they will be discussed in the next chapter.

Early in the twentieth century, Bertrand Russell held that 'logic takes us nearer to heaven than most other studies' (1923/1996: 65), and for him, as for Wittgenstein later, all language is vague. He argued that vagueness is not so much a property of the world, but of our *representation* of it:

Apart from representation, whether cognitive or mechanical, there can be no such thing as vagueness or precision; things are what they are, and there is an end of it. Nothing is more or less what it is, or to a certain extent possessed of the properties which it possesses. (Russell 1923/1996: 62)

This amounts to saying that ontic vagueness does not exist, and is reminiscent of Wittgenstein's dictum 'Die Welt ist alles, was der Fall ist' ('The world is all that is the case') (1921/1981: 31). Dummett (1975/1996: 111) makes a related point when he says that the question of whether the world itself might be vague is not actually an intelligible one.

Russell's article contains a noteworthy statement:

The law of the excluded middle is true when precise symbols are employed, but it is not true when symbols are vague, as, in fact, all symbols are. (Russell 1923/1996: 62)

If all symbols are vague, there can be no such thing as a 'precise symbol'. It then follows that the Law of the Excluded Middle is not true, and can never apply to any symbols at all. This would be a desirable conclusion in view of Russell's claim that vagueness is a concept that can only be applied to representations, as symbols are representations *par excellence*.

Russell allows for degrees of vagueness. A Sorites-type notion like 'bald' is clearly vague, but so are concepts like 'metre', which are defined relative to a benchmark located somewhere in the world. In the case of the metre it is the distance between two marks on a rod at a certain temperature in Paris. However, the marks on the rod cannot be indicated with precision, so Russell argues, and temperature can never be measured exactly. Therefore even the concept 'metre' is vague, but to a lesser degree than 'bald'.

Another tenet of Russell's paper is that vagueness is something that can be manipulated. One of his examples involves two glasses of water which are identical to the eye, but in fact one of them contains typhoid bacilli. If we use a microscope the vagueness disappears, and we can see that one of the glasses is contaminated. Maps are also vague as representations of whatever they represent, but we can get closer and verify how accurate our representation is. The point he is making is that vagueness is a proximity problem: the closer you get, the more it disappears.

2.3 The linguistic tradition: early grammarians

Turning now to categorization in the study of language, there has been a long tradition of classifying the elements of language into groupings of units, such as word classes, phrases, and clauses. Indeed, for grammarians the concern has always been to set up a taxonomy of the linguistic elements of particular languages, and to describe how they interrelate. Linguistic categorization, especially as far as the word classes are concerned, has been heavily influenced by the thinking of Aristotle, who stressed the disjunctive nature of language:

Of quantities some are discrete, others continuous; and some are composed of parts which have position in relation to one another, others are not composed of parts which have position. Discrete are number and language. (*Categories*, 6, p. 8)

Aristotle's views on categories harmonize with his stance in the debate in antiquity on *analogy* versus *anomaly* (Robins 1990: 21f.; Seuren 1998: 23–7). Adherents of the former—Aristotle among them—stressed the regularities in language and its propensity for order and systematicity, while adherents of the latter pointed out the 'messiness' of language. Robins (1990: 21f.) notes that the Greek ideas on analogy/anomaly were mostly handed down by the Roman author Varro, and speculates that he may have misrepresented the opposition as having been a confrontational one between writers, rather than a situation in which different ideas on the two views co-existed.

The early Greek grammarians were the first to propose the notion of 'part of speech' (μέρος λόγου), and the first system, by Dionysius Thrax (ca. 100 BC), has survived in various incarnations to the present day, with tweakings by a number of grammarians, among them Varro (116–27 BC), Apollonius Dyscolus (ca. 110–175 AD), Donatus (ca. 310–363 AD), and Priscian (ca. 500 AD).

For the medieval period Ian Michael distinguishes three types of grammars (1970: 12–22): literary grammars, logical grammars, and speculative grammars. The first group are mostly based on the literary perspective of the work of Donatus and Priscian, while the second group draws on the logical aspects of the work of these grammarians. The speculative grammars written by the so-called Modistae (ca. 1200–1350) were concerned with the relationship between language, thought, and the world. R. H. Robins writes:

Speculative grammar was the product of the integration of the grammatical descrip-tion of Latin as formulated by Priscian and Donatus into the system of scholastic philosophy. Scholasticism itself was the result of the integration of Aristotelian philosophy, at the hands of such thinkers as St Thomas Aquinas, into Catholic theology.... In the context of scholasticism, the mere description of Latin, as laid down by Priscian and Donatus, was considered inadequate, however useful it might be paedagogically. This change in the conception of the proper objectives of higher level grammatical studies came about gradually, as did the terminology in which speculative grammar was set out. Commentators had already begun to go further than straightforward elucidation and exegesis, and the view was now expressed that Priscian had not delved deeply enough into his subject in merely describing the language, but should have investigated the underlying theory and the justification for the elements and categories that he employed. (Robins 1990: 84–5)

There is no space here for a full account of the work of speculative grammar-ians (see especially Covington 1984), suffice it to say that they are generally credited with being the first to formulate a theory of grammar incorporating categories of grammar called *modes*.

Renaissance scholars reacted against speculative grammar 'as being philo-sophically tedious, educationally undesirable, and couched in a barbarous degeneration of the Latin language' (Robins 1990: 122). As has been chronicled by Robins, the period was characterized by a greater attention to languages other than Greek and Latin (e.g. Arabic and Hebrew) and by the writing of grammars of vernacular and exotic languages. These descriptions were increasingly written without slavish recourse to Latin and Greek models, and began to adopt principles of description still in use today, such as drawing on distributional evidence, as in the work of Petrus Ramus. As far as the categories of grammar were concerned, these too were described in terms of the language under investigation, although this sometimes led to simplistic views, witness the citation below from William Bullokar:

As English hath few and short rules for declining of words, so it hath few rules for joining of words in sentence or in construction. (Bullokar 1586: 53; cited in Michael 1987: 324)

But later there was also evidence of original thinking. Thus, whereas in the tradition the articles were generally not regarded as a word class in their own right—Latin does not have them—the playwright Ben Jonson in his English grammar of 1640 recognized them as a separate class (Robins 1990: 133). Other interesting treatments of grammatical categories can be found at the close of the eighteenth century in the works of James Burnett Lord Monboddo (1774), J. Horne Tooke (1786), Henry St John Bullen (1797), H. Groombridge (1797), and Lovechild (pseudonym of Lady Eleanor Fenn; 1798). Each of these authors defended systems of word classes that contained only two or three elements. (See Ian Michael's systems 51, 55, and 56; 1987: 269f.)

Up to roughly 1800 the study of grammar, at least in England, was mostly concerned with word-based grammatical categories, that is, the parts of speech. Some grammarians displayed a perhaps somewhat lackadaisical attitude to the word classes:

I have adopted the usual distribution of words into *eight classes*, in compliance with the practice of most *Grammarians*; and because, if any number, in a thing so arbitrary, must be fixed upon, this seems to be as comprehensive and distinct as any. (Priestley 1761: 2)

Others often struggled with the uncertainties of how to delineate word classes. In early grammars we therefore find classes with double labels, such as 'pronoun adjective' and 'noun adjective'. For further discussion, see Michael (1970) and Spinillo (2004). Michael (1970: 141f., 274, 443f.) surmises that the reason for the uncertainties had to do with the fact that grammarians were asking the wrong kinds of questions:

That these uncertainties were not understood by the early grammarians is another consequence of the fact that they had not yet distinguished between formal, structural and syntactic criteria.... Any considerable variations can fairly be regarded as evidence of instability.... Their question is 'What is a participle?'. It could not yet be, 'How, and for what purposes, shall we classify such-and-such a feature?'. It followed, therefore, that 'where to put' the participle could be, for the writer, a fairly unimportant matter.... The diversity of systems is evidence of the grammarians' discomfort, which expressed itself in the only way it could: by shifting the elements in the scheme uneasily round and round. (Michael 1970: 274)

As for syntax, there was not much concern with grammatical functions (GFs), such as subject, object, etc. (Michael 1970).[4]

The opposition empiricism vs. rationalism (or apriorism) became prominent as a component of the beginnings of scientific thinking from the later Renaissance onwards. The former stressed the value of observation, while the latter valued reason. The dialectic between empiricists and rationalists also played a role in linguistics. In the nineteenth century strict methodological thinking was in evidence amongst the *Junggrammatiker* (also known as the Neogrammarians). Working in Leipzig, these linguists held that all sound laws are exceptionless. Taking such a stance as a working hypothesis encourages

---

[4] It is an interesting question whether or not these too should be regarded as categories. One point of view is that only form classes can be set up as categories. However, to the extent that they can be given a purely structural definition in terms of a number of criterial attributes, GFs clearly also qualify as categories (as argued, e.g., by Huddleston 1984: 51).

one to look for recalcitrant data that disprove it. On the basis of such data one then either modifies the hypothesis or explains the problematic data in some other way, as Karl Verner did when he discovered what turned out to be only apparent exceptions to Grimm's Law ('Verner's Law'). Leskien, one of the Neogrammarians, wrote in 1876 'If one admits optional, contingent, and unconnected changes, one is basically stating that the object of one's research, language, is not amenable to scientific recognition' (quoted in Robins 1990: 203). Neogrammarians were also adherents of the *Stammbaumtheorie* developed by August Schleicher, which is characterized by discrete categories of language groups, in contradistinction to the adherents of the *Wellentheorie* (wave theory). Most work in modern linguistics now applies the Popperian methodology described above as a matter of course. What is interesting about the Neogrammarian manifesto (and indeed, the analogy/anomaly controversy mentioned earlier) is that it caused an opposition of theory/idealization vs. empiricism/flexibility, much in the way the notion of gradience was to do in the century that followed.

2.4 Twentieth-century approaches to linguistic categorization

2.4.1 *Bloomfield and American structuralism*

For a twentieth-century pre-structuralist linguist such as Bloomfield, categories are *form classes* (1933: 146). Thus: '[l]arge form-classes which completely subdivide either the whole lexicon or some important form-class into form-classes of approximately equal size, are called categories' (1933: 270). The parts of speech are cited as examples of form classes, as are number, gender, case, and tense.

[I]n any one form-class, every form contains an element, the *class meaning*, which is the same for all forms of this form-class. Thus, all English substantives belong to a form-class, and each English substantive, accordingly, has a meaning, which, once it is defined for us (say, as 'object'), we can attribute to every substantive form in the language. (Bloomfield 1933: 146)

Bloomfield allows for a certain degree of fluidity of classification in remarking that '[f]orm-classes are not mutually exclusive, but cross each other and overlap and are included one within the other, and so on' (1933: 269). Trask (1999: 279–80) notes that with the exception of Fries, Gleason, and Hockett, American structuralists were not very interested in the parts of speech. As is well-known, the post-Bloomfieldians developed a rigorous—some would say dogmatic—methodology which incorporated 'discovery procedures', a strict separation of linguistic levels, etc. An all-or-none view of categorization was very much a part of that methodology. A typically unyielding and orthodox Aristotelian view was propounded by Martin Joos some twenty years after Bloomfield in a passage worth citing at length:

The linguistic categories, then, are absolutes which admit of no compromise. They correspond roughly to favorite categorizations in the real world, and it is widely held that every community subdivides the phenomena in the real world according to the categories of its language, rather than the reverse. But the correspondence between the discrete categories of the language and the continuous phenomena of the real world is not and cannot be precise. Our reaction, as linguists, to this situation, is very simple: all phenomena, whether popularly regarded as linguistic (such as the tone of anger in an utterance) or not, which we find we cannot describe precisely with a finite number of absolute categories, we classify as non-linguistic elements of the real world and expel them from linguistic science. Let sociologists and others do what they like with such things—we may wish them luck in their efforts to describe them precisely in their own terminology, but no matter whether they describe them with discrete categories or not, for us they remain vague, protean, fluctuating phenomena—in a word, they represent that 'continuity' which we refuse to tolerate in our own science. (Joos 1957: 351)

This is as strong an expression of the *Principium Exclusi Tertii* as one can get! It is probably the post-Bloomfieldian concern with a strict methodology and strongly worded statements like the one above regarding continuous phenomena in language that had the most influence on linguistic thinking in the second half of the twentieth century. As we will see in the next section and chapter, dissenting voices started to be heard in the 1960s.

2.4.2 *Transformational grammar*

Newmeyer (2000: 221) points out that all approaches to generative grammar are algebraic in nature. This naturally has consequences for the ways in which the elements of generative grammar are viewed. From the point of view of categorization, a mathematical approach results in an all-or-none view of category membership. It also results in the fact that the theory of language adopted is a model, a point made by Pollard and Sag, working in the HPSG (Head-Driven Phrase Structure Grammar) framework:

In any mathematical theory about an empirical domain, the phenomena of interest are *modelled* by mathematical structures, certain aspects of which are conventionally understood as corresponding to observables of the domain. The theory itself does not talk directly about the empirical phenomena; instead, it talks about, or is *interpreted by*, the modelling structures. Thus the predictive power of the theory arises from the conventional correspondence between the model and the empirical domain. (Pollard and Sag 1994: 6; emphasis in original)

Of course, *any* description of a language, mathematical, descriptive or otherwise, is a model, and can be viewed as a representation of the mental system that language constitutes.

In early generative linguistics the principal categories (word classes, phrases, etc.) were taken for granted. There is no discussion in, for example, Chomsky (1957) addressing the problem of which form classes the proposed grammar should recognize. McCawley (1982: 176) laments that in TG '[n]ot only is there no generally accepted conception of syntactic category, but it is difficult to find *any* explicit statements of what it is for two things to belong to the same syntactic category'. Chomsky (1965: 65–6) distinguishes *formatives* (subdivided into lexical and grammatical items) and *category symbols* (e.g. NP, N, VP, V, etc.). The grammatical formatives and the category symbols are assumed to belong to a universal set.

The establishment of *cross-categorial generalizations* as part of the X-bar theory of syntax (Chomsky 1970) was an attempt to capture the similarities between the major categories N, V, A, and P. X-bar syntax allows for at least three categorial levels: the lexical level (X^0), the bar level (X') and the phrasal level (XP). Bar level categories can be motivated through the use of such anaphoric elements as *one* in a sentence such as (1):

(1)   I like the small medieval painting, but not the big one.

Here *one* refers back to the string *medieval painting*, which is clearly less than a full phrase but more than a lexical element.

In his 1970 paper Chomsky also introduces the notion of *syntactic features* [$\pm$N;$\pm$V], which were used to define the syntactic categories, 'thereby eliminating "syntactic category" as a notion of theoretical significance' (Newmeyer 1986: 153). Thus nouns are taken to be [$+$N, $-$V], verbs are [$-$N, $+$V], adjectives are [$+$N, $+$V], and prepositions are [$-$N, $-$V]. Transformations may not change one category into another (the 'lexicalist hypothesis'). In more recent work Chomsky designates FF(LI) as the set of formal features (FF) of a lexical item (LI) (1995: 231). Syntactic features allow for the specification of 'supercategories' (Jackendoff 1977: 31f.; Radford 1988: 147). Thus, [$+$N] comprises nouns and adjectives, [$-$N] comprises verbs and prepositions, [$+$V] comprises verbs and adjectives, while [$-$V] denotes nouns and prepositions. In turn these supercategories allow for specific generalizations to be made; for example, one can say that the [$-$N] categories verb and preposition allow for complements in the form of a noun phrase. Notice that all the features mentioned above are binary, imposing an either/or choice. Baker (2003: 2) notes that Chomsky's feature theory 'is widely recognized to have almost no content in practice. The feature system is not well integrated into the framework as a whole, in that there are few or no principles that refer to these features or their values.'

We find a different feature system in Jackendoff (1977: 32f.). For him the categories N and V carry the feature [+Subj], while A and P are [−Subj]. In addition V and P are assigned the feature [+Obj] because they can take a complement, while N and A are [−Obj].

As noted, TG recognized only the major word-level categories noun, verb, adjective, and preposition, a situation that persisted into later frameworks. However, in recent work Baker offers a new approach to the word classes. For him verbs are predicates, labelled [+V], a feature which is to be interpreted as 'takes a specifier'. In other words, verbs are lexical items that license subjects.[5] Nouns are conceived of as referential elements which carry [+N] as their only feature. Adjectives are defined negatively as elements that are neither verbs nor nouns. Baker further argues that adpositions (prepositions and post-positions) should be reanalysed as functional categories, and are not part of the word class system (2003: 20f.).

The status of such elements as adverbs has been largely ignored (although see Jackendoff 1977: 32f.; Emonds 1987; Radford 1988). As we will see presently, complementizers received their own position with an associated maximal projection in phrase markers, but whether they should be regarded as word classes in their own right is not at all obvious (Hudson 1995, 2000a). Follow-ing Bresnan (1970, 1972), in *Lectures on Government and Binding* (Chomsky 1981) the topmost level in a sentence carried the categorial label S′ (S-bar), which had the nodes COMP and S as its immediate constituents. Although bar levels are supposed to be intermediate between phrase level (double bar) projections and lexical (zero-level) projections, S′ was regarded as an excep-tional maximal projection. In Chomsky (1986a) both COMP and S received their own maximal projections, labelled CP and IP, respectively, headed by C and I. Later versions of Chomskyan theory split open the I-node (the *Split INFL Hypothesis*, cf. Pollock 1989), thus creating a number of so-called *functional categories*, for example Agreement Phrase (AgrP), Tense Phrase (TP), Negative Phrase (NegP), etc. (See below for further discussion of functional categories.)

Let us take a closer look at the category C. This generative innovation, first proposed in Rosenbaum (1967), actually represented a bit of an anomaly. On the one hand this category is clearly lexical, as it can contain such elements as *that, whether, if,* and *for.* On the other hand it is functional (in the present-day sense of that term, see below) in that it can act as a landing site for elements

---

[5] Nouns and adjectives can also take subjects, but need a mediating 'Pred' node to be able to do so.

that move successive-cyclically and for preposed auxiliary verbs. It is always projected, even if it remains empty. Hudson (1995: 50) signals further problems, and rejects both the category of complementizer and the associated phrase marker position.

In more recent theoretical frameworks such as Chomsky's Principles and Parameters/Minimalist Program nouns and verbs are regarded as innate (cf. Jackendoff 1994: 81).[6] In addition to the conventional categories, or *substantive categories* as they are called in Chomsky (1995: 6),[7] P&P/Minimalism assumes the existence of so-called *empty categories* and abstract *functional categories*. An example of the former is the trace, an element of grammar which is left behind after movement, much like a footstep in the sand, for example in the following structure: *Jim$_i$ was sacked t$_i$*. In this passive sentence the subject *Jim* is assumed to derive from the position marked by the trace. The subscript 'i' indicates coreferentiality. The categorial status of the trace depends on the category of the displaced element. In the example above it is a noun phrase. Chomskyan theory recognizes a whole host of different kinds of empty elements. Apart from traces there are 'big PRO' (a 'pronominal anaphor' which occurs in control structures, e.g. *I persuaded him$_i$ [PRO$_i$ to go]*) and 'little pro' (a phonetically null pronoun which occurs in the subject position of most of the Romance languages, e.g. *pro deseo comprar dos libros* (Spanish for 'I want to buy two books')). The term

---

[6] Or at least universal. This seems to be a position that is held more widely, even though it is not uncontroversial, see e.g. Robins (1952: 293–4), Lyons (1977: 429). Aarsleff (1982: 167) notes that

the Port-Royal Grammar had assumed that some word classes—such as those of the noun and the verb—were primary in relation to other classes, which were only abbreviations or convenient substitutes for the former, as most of the pronouns were for nouns. These latter classes had therefore been 'invented' to fulfill those functions.

Cf. also Trask:

[I]t appears that nouns and verbs are the only word-classes that anybody wants to defend universal status for. The universality of nouns and verbs was affirmed by Sapir, queried by Whorf, and denied by Hockett, mainly on the basis of the Wakashan and Salishan languages of the Pacific Northwest of North America. But further work on these languages, perhaps most notably by Bill Jacobsen, has called Hockett's interpretation severely into question. And Paul Schachter, in his article in the 1985 Shopen volumes entitled *Language Typology and Syntactic Description*, asserts firmly that, on the basis of the evidence currently available, we may safely conclude that recognizable and distinguishable classes of nouns and verbs do indeed appear in all spoken languages. (Trask 1998)

See also Chomsky (1965: 65–6), mentioned above, and Trask (1999). Croft (1991: 37, 42f.) notes that it has been claimed for a small minority of languages that the distinction between noun and verb cannot be made.

[7] Chomsky (1965) takes these to be N, V, A, and Particle (see also Emonds 1985: 14). The most common set of core word classes adopted is N, V, A, and P. Adverbs are not usually recognized as being a core word class, on the grounds that they are positional variants of adjectives (cf. e.g. Emonds 1985: 13 fn. 1, and especially 162).

'empty category' is strictly speaking misleading and a misnomer. The reason is that these categories are only empty in the sense that they cannot be perceived physically and have no lexical semantic content.

Abstract functional categories came very much into vogue in the 1990s. The first to be proposed was 'I' (for Inflection), together with its associated phrasal projection IP (Chomsky 1986*b*), formerly 'S'. As we saw above, later additions include Tense/TP, Agr/AgrP, Neg/NegP, and many others (see e.g. Ouhalla 1991). Like the empty categories, in most cases functional categories cannot be perceived, although they can act as hosts for linguistic material. For example, in P&P-theory the I-node is said to accommodate modal verbs, if present in a sentence, and, as we have seen, the complementizer node 'C', if unfilled by an overt complementizer, can act as a landing site for preposed auxiliary verbs in interrogative structures. For a critique of the notion of functional category, see Hudson (1995, 2000*a*).

In a sense, empty and functional categories are a continuation of the classical tradition, in that they can be defined by listing a number of necessary and sufficient conditions. Thus, in P&P-theory *wh*-traces receive a thematic role, and are assigned abstract Case, while NP-traces receive a thematic role, but are *not* assigned Case. However, leaving aside work in morphology, on the whole the positing of empty categories and abstract functional categories constitutes a significant departure from the tradition of linguistic categorization. For the first time categories are admitted into the system of grammar which are actually inaudible and invisible (except at abstract levels of representation).[8]

Principles and Parameters theory also makes use of what we might call *second order categories*. One example is the *Governing Category* (GC). GCs play a role in the Binding Theory which deals with the distribution of pronouns, anaphors, and referential expressions. Without going into this in too much detail, let us look at one or two examples. In the sentence *Mark likes himself* the anaphorical element *himself* must be bound in its GC, which is a domain in which it is governed (by e.g. a verb) and has access to a suitable subject expression to which it can be bound. In this particular example the GC is the whole sentence. In *Eric thinks that Andy likes him* the pronominal element *him* must not be bound to *Andy*, but may be bound to *Eric*. Its GC is the subordinate clause.

Emonds (1985: 162) makes use of what he calls *disguised lexical categories*. They consist of frequently used and semantically underdetermined members of the lexical categories, and belong to closed subclasses which he refers to as

---

[8] Of course, traditional grammar has always allowed for implied elements (such as e.g. the Direct Object in *I was reading*), and for ellipsis (as in e.g. *Alison will go to the fireworks, but Nick won't*), but it will be clear that this is an entirely different phenomenon.

'grammatical nouns, verbs, adjectives and prepositions'. Examples of grammatical verbs are such items as *be, have, get, do, go, come, let,* and *make* (and possibly *want* and *say,* 1985: 169). Other verbs simply belong to the open class of verbs. (Auxiliary verbs are not included in either of the groups; they are regarded as VP-Specifiers, i.e. nonlexical categories.) It is interesting to note that Emonds chooses to create subcategories within the lexical categories, rather than create new categories altogether. Although no gradience between the grammatical lexical categories and the contentful ones is posited, the use made by Emonds of the term *disguised* lexical category does suggest a shading within lexical categories from more open members to more grammaticalized ones. In other words, there appears to exist a cline of openness within lexical categories. In Emonds (2001) grammatical heads are called *semi-lexical heads*.

Culicover (1999) departs from the generative tradition by suggesting that the *Universal Category Hypothesis* (UCH) should be abandoned in favour of the *Contingent Category Hypothesis* (CCH). 'On this alternative scenario, the learner presumably has to compare all of the words of the language with one another, form hypotheses about which of them function in a similar way, and on the basis of these similarities determine what the categories are' (1999: 37). The language learner initially acquires categories on the basis of conceptual notions, for example words that denote objects are categorized as nouns (the *Conceptual Principle*). Later this process needs to be relaxed, because languages contain abstract nouns that do not denote objects. This is when the process of *Formal Categorization* comes into play, which assigns elements to categories on the basis of their morphosyntactic properties.

Although constraining the grammatical apparatus has always been one of the methodological guiding principles of TG, it was not always practised. This was a problem in early TG, which the generative semanticists tried to address (see Section 2.4.3), and also in later versions. As we have just seen, there was a veritable explosion of functional categories in the last two decades of the last century. This seems to have been rather a retrograde development, reminiscent of the explosion of transformations in the 1960s.

The classical categories are perhaps best regarded as *idealizations*, which are arguably necessary in order to make sense of reality. I will return to this point in Section 3.4.3.

2.4.3 *Generative Semantics*

Newmeyer (1986: 82), writing on the rise of the Generative Semantics movement, notes that one of the earliest signs of discontent with Chomsky's 1965 *Aspects* model came with the presentation of a paper by Paul Postal in which he argued that adjectives should really be reclassified as verbs (see also Lakoff 1970). This interest in categorization remained a key concern amongst the generative semanticists, and further proposals for the conflation of categories were made. Harris (1993: 108) has observed that the attempts to reduce the inventory of categories 'became something of a program'. Examples of the type of reasoning employed by generative semanticists to reduce the number of categories are Ross's proposal that adjectives are noun phrases (Ross 1969*a*), and his proposal to streamline the category of verbs, by suggesting that auxiliaries are really main verbs (Ross 1969*b*).[9] Harris has chronicled the apotheosis of the generative semantic application of Occam's razor:

Postal's reductionist campaign [gathered] a good deal of steam—adjectives were re-analyzed as deep verbs, adjective phrases disappeared at deep structure, some nouns were also deep verbs, prepositions and conjunctions were deep verbs, prepositional phrases dissolved at deep structure, tenses were deep verbs, quantifiers were deep verbs, articles arose transformationally, the verb phrase dissolved at deep structure—and abstract syntax arrived at a convenient little core of deep categories: NPs, Vs, and Ss. There were noun phrases, verbs, and sentences at deep structure and every other category was introduced transformationally. [footnote omitted] (Harris 1993: 115)

Newmeyer furthermore observes that

[i]n the late 1960s, the generative semanticists began to realize that as the inventory of syntactic categories became more and more reduced, those remaining bore a close correspondence to the categories of symbolic logic. The three categories whose existence generative semanticists were certain of in this period—sentence, noun phrase, and verb—seemed to correspond directly to the proposition, argument, and predicate of logic. (Newmeyer 1986: 100)

McCawley (1998: 192f.) builds on this early work and proposes 'that to every logical category there corresponds a fuzzy syntactic category having semantic, internal syntactic, and external syntactic dimensions, and ... I will identify S, Det, and Conj as being the syntactic counterparts of the logical categories of proposition..., quantifier, and (logical) conjunction.' NP too is a fuzzy category (in the sense of Rosch 1978). I will return to his notion of fuzzy NPs in Chapter 5. Earlier McCawley (1977/1982: 184) had argued for a conception of grammar in which syntactic category labels are merely shorthands for combinations of factors to which syntactic phenomena are sensitive.

---

[9] This issue was picked up later in a debate between the British linguists Rodney Huddleston and Frank Palmer (cf. Huddleston 1974, 1976*a*, 1976*b*; Palmer 1979, 1987, 1990). See also Emonds (1976), Pullum (1976), Pullum and Wilson (1977), Radford (1976), Warner (1993), and Chapter 5 for discussions and elaborations of this idea. The first modern descriptive grammar to describe auxiliaries as main verbs is Huddleston and Pullum *et al.* (2002), some thirty years after Ross's proposal.

Much has been written on the collapse of the Generative Semantic movement. Interestingly, in McCawley's view the conception of syntactic categories was part of the reason for the undoing of Generative Semantics (GS):

The one part of GS theory that can plausibly be implicated in the demise of the GS community is the GS treatment of syntactic categories, which is one of the few parts of GS theory that any prominent GS-ists have subsequently recanted (McCawley 1977, 1982) ... Coincidentally, the radical revisions that interpretive semanticists were making in their versions of generative syntactic theory included the adoption of the 'X-bar' conception of syntactic categories, which identified two of the factors that affect the syntactic behavior of a linguistic unit, namely, the difference between a word unit and a phrasal unit, and the part of speech of the unit or of its head. Once a descriptive framework was available that allowed linguistic generalizations to be stated in terms of those factors, considerable progress was made in the analysis of the many syntactic phenomena in which those factors play a role.

No important tenets of GS rule out the adoption of a conception of syntactic categories as defined by these factors *in addition to* logical categories, and indeed a conception of syntactic categories as reducible to those and other factors (with logical category being merely one of several factors that influence a unit's syntactic behavior) is adopted in McCawley (1977, 1982) and subsequent works. However, in the 1960s and early 1970s, an assumption shared by GS-ists and interpretive semanticists impeded GS-ists from adopting such a conception of categories, namely the assumption that syntactic categories must remain constant throughout derivations: a word (with a determinate part of speech) that replaced a complex of semantic material (thus, a unit not having a part of speech) could not differ in category from the replaced unit and thus parts of speech could not be part of the category system. (McCawley 1996: 168)

2.4.4 *Descriptive grammar*

Descriptive linguists on the whole follow the ancients in their categorization of linguistic elements into classes. The Aristotelian either/or-tradition is evident in the frequent use of categorial oppositions such as those below:

lexical/grammatical
full/empty
open/closed
variable/invariable

Notice that the first of these is close to the generative lexical/functional category distinction. Crystal (1967: 30–41) discusses the problems these dichotomies pose in detail, and concludes that 'these four pairs of terms are not as valuable or as fundamental as has been implied by the frequency of their use, and are of very little relevance for word classification, as the resultant divisions are too general and ill-defined' (1967: 40–1). For criticism of the open/closed distinction, see Hudson (2000a: 28f.).

As for the traditional parts of speech, they have at times been regarded as troublesome. In the early part of the twentieth century Jespersen criticized the 'sham' definitions of the word classes 'in which it is extremely easy to pick holes' (1924: 58), although later he confidently asserted that although precise definitions were difficult 'the classification itself rarely offers occasion for doubt' (1933: 66). In any case for Jespersen '[a] great many English words may, if considered isolatedly (as parts of "language"), belong to more classes than one; but in each particular application (in "speech") they can only belong to one, and it is generally easy to determine which one' (1909–1949, VII: 41, 1924: 62). Note the hedge 'generally', though. In the second half of the century, grammarians have been keen to stress that categorial boundaries are not always clear-cut: 'there are numerous places in the grammar where it is necessary to recognise categories with a clear prototypical core but a some-what fuzzily delimited periphery. . . . [S]ome measure of indeterminacy may arise over the delimitation of non-prototypical instances' (Huddleston 1984: 72). In Quirk *et al.* (1985), unlike in their earlier 1972 work, boundary fluidity is also stressed: '[g]rammar is to some extent an indeterminate system. Categories and structures, for example, often do not have neat boundaries' (1985: 90). Quirk *et al.* chide grammarians who are 'tempted to overlook such uncertainties, or to pretend that they do not exist' (ibid.). Finally, Huddleston and Pullum *et al.* (2002) contains detailed discussions of borderlines between categories, and offers criteria for establishing which are the central members of the word classes.

I return to the treatment of gradient phenomena in Modern Descriptive Grammar in the next chapter.

2.4.5 *Cognitive approaches*

Langacker (1987) has the following to say about grammatical categories:

Counter to received wisdom, I claim that basic grammatical categories such as **noun, verb, adjective,** and **adverb** are semantically definable. The entities referred to as nouns, verbs, etc. are symbolic units, each with a semantic and a phonological pole, but it is the former that determines the categorization. All members of a given class share fundamental semantic properties, and their semantic poles thus instantiate a single abstract schema subject to reasonably explicit characterization. (Langacker 1987: 189)

Thus, a noun is regarded as a symbolic entity whose semantic characteristic is that it instantiates a schema, referred to as [THING]. Verbs designate processes, whereas adjectives and adverbs are said to designate atemporal relations (Langacker 1987: 189).[10]

Cognitive linguists have been vociferous in rejecting the classical categories, and instead allow for members of categories to be more or less typical exemplars of the category in question. The most typical member of a category is then called a *prototype*. The following passage by the semanticist John Lyons foreshadows these views:

The thesis that will be maintained here is that the semantic, or ontological, part of the traditional definitions of the parts-of-speech define for each part-of-speech, not the whole class, but a distinguished subclass of the total class. Each such semantically defined subclass is focal within the larger class in much the same way that, according to the Berlin and Kay [(1969)] hypothesis..., a particular area within the total area denoted by a colour term is focal. (Lyons 1977: 440)

With regard to category boundaries, cognitive linguists have argued that they cannot be sharply delimited. In the words of Langacker:

[Another] dimension of the discreteness issue concerns the propriety of positing sharp distinctions between certain broad classes of linguistic phenomena, thereby implying that the classes are fundamentally different in character and in large measure separately describable. The nondiscrete alternative regards these classes as grading into one another along various parameters. They form a continuous spectrum (or field) of possibilities, whose segregation into distinct blocks is necessarily artifactual. (Langacker 1987: 18)

Langacker points out that gradience is a pervasive phenomenon.

Cognitive linguists do not reject Aristotelian categories altogether. The membership of so-called *natural kind categories* which contain natural real-world entities, such as, for example, animals, are at least partly determined by the nature of the entities to be classified. For example, a fish is categorized as such because of its biological make-up. Natural kind terms are indexical, and natural kind categories have clear boundaries, but prototype effects can show up inside them (Taylor 2003: 47f., 67f.; though see Lakoff 1987*a*: 169f. for discussion). By contrast, *nominal kind categories* (Schwartz 1980; Pulman 1983: 154f.) seem to be part of a superimposed artificial taxonomy and contain man-made entities. Their membership is determined by criterial attributes. As a result, they can have fuzzy boundaries. Taylor (2003) gives *toy* and *vehicle* as examples. Schwartz (1980: 182) mentions *pencil, bottle,* and *chair.* See also Wierzbicka (1990: 355–6). A similar distinction between natural kinds and nominal kinds seems to have

---

[10] Outside cognitive grammar there have been other semantic approaches to grammar; see e.g. Dixon (1991/2005), Wierzbicka (1996).

been made by John Wilkins in the late seventeenth century. He distinguished between

[s]uch things as subsist by themselves, or which (according to the old Logical definition) *require a subject of inhesion*. (Wilkins 1668/1968: 26; emphasis in original)

Inhesion refers to inherent qualities. See Salmon (1979: 111) for discussion.

In cognitive linguistics use is made of so-called *levels of categorization* (Rosch *et al.* 1976; Taylor 2003: 48f.). Three levels are distinguished: a superordinate level, a basic level, and a subordinate level.[11] The basic level is the one that is most directly relevant to the notion of prototype. Examples given by Rosch *et al.* (1976: 388) include those shown in Table 2.1. For Rosch *et al.*:

Segmentation of experience occurs to form basic levels which maximize the differentiability of categories. For categories of *concrete* objects, basic objects are the most general classes at which attributes are predictable, objects of the class are used in the same way, objects can be readily identified by shape, and at which classes can be imaged. Basic objects should generally be the most useful level of classification. Universally, basic object categories should be the basic classifications made during perception, the first learned and first named by children, and the most codable, most coded, and most necessary in the language of any people. (Rosch *et al.* 1976: 435)

Cognitive linguists have concerned themselves mostly with the classification of concrete entities. Lakoff has argued that attention must also be paid to other types of categories, including linguistic ones:

TABLE 2.1 Levels of categorization

Superordinate level	Basic level	Subordinate level
Fruit	Apple	Delicious apple; Mackintosh apple etc.
	Peach	Freestone peach; Cling peach etc.
	Grapes	Concord grapes; Green seedless grapes etc.
Tool	Hammer	ball-peen hammer, claw hammer etc.
	Saw	hack hand saw, cross-cutting hand saw
	Screwdriver	Phillips screwdriver, regular screwdriver

Source: Rosch *et al.* (1976: 388)

---

[11] As so often, many ideas that have become commonplace in certain branches of linguistics—and are sometimes claimed to have been used there first—can be found in the work of Jespersen. For example, regarding apples he notes that '*apple* is abstract in comparison with any individual apple that comes within our ken, and so is *fruit* to an even higher degree' (1924: 63).

[M]ost of the discussion of categorization within the philosophical, psychological, and anthropological literature is focused on concrete objects—plants, animals, artifacts, people. It is important that the focus be enlarged to include categories in nonphysical domains. The nonphysical domains—emotions, language, social institutions, etc.—are perhaps the most important ones for the study of mind. Since the conceptual structure of such domains cannot be viewed as merely a mirror of nature, the study of such domains may thus provide a clearer guide to the workings of the mind. (Lakoff 1987a: 180)

Lakoff emphasizes the importance of studying linguistic categories by observing that '[l]inguistic categories are among the kinds of abstract categories that any adequate theory of the human conceptual system must be able to account for' (ibid.). Lakoff's book, however, does not concern itself very much with what we might call grammatical categorization *sensu stricto*, for example with the classification of words into word classes, word class boundaries, etc. At the end of the book there are three sizeable case studies, one on the concept of anger, the second on the word *over*, and the third on *there*-constructions in English. But in effect these are really *semantic*, not syntactic, studies. For example, there is no discussion, in the chapter on *over*, of the *categorial differences* between the different instantiations of this word in sentences such as *I peered over the wall; Could you hand over that book?; We all went over*. In the introductory section to the case studies Lakoff says that *over* 'is basically a preposition, but it can also function as an adverb, a prefix, a particle, and a predicate adjective', but we learn nothing more about this. In fact, even this statement is unsatisfactory, because lexical items do not *function* as adverbs, prefixes, particles, or predicate adjectives, they *are* adverbs, prefixes, particles, or predicate adjectives.

Cruse (1992: 108) suspects that 'cognitive linguistics will eventually have to make its peace with "classical" categories, and structuralist notions such as lexical relations and semantic components, rather than treating them as enemies to be repudiated at all costs; perhaps they can be incorporated in a way analogous to that in which Einstein's theory of relativity incorporated, rather than repudiated, Newtonian physics.' Along similarly reconciliatory lines Steven Pinker (1999: 275f.) has suggested that the mind employs Wittgensteinian 'family resemblance categories' in learning irregular verbs, but uses Aristotelian categories for learning regular verbs (cf. also Bybee and Moder 1983). Members of the first type of category must be memorized, while members of the second type of category are subject to rules.

The facts about verbs and the facts about concepts converge to suggest that the human mind is a hybrid system, learning fuzzy associations and crisp rules in different subsystems. Most of the recent models of human categorization in cognitive psychology (which are designed to capture people's speed and accuracy when learning artificial categories in the lab) are built out of two parts: a pattern associator for categories based on families of similar exemplars, and a rule selector for categories based on rules. The psychologists were forced to these hybrid models because with some categories subjects quickly figure out a rule (such as 'rectangles that are taller than they are wide'), whereas with other categories subjects go by their gut feelings, memorizing some of the examples and classifying the new ones according to how similar they are to the memorized ones. No model that uses a single mechanism to capture people's behavior with every kind of category does as well as the hybrid models. (Pinker 1999: 279)

2.4.6 *Functional-typological and discourse typological linguistics*

Like the cognitivists, functional grammarians also subscribe to a more flexible approach to categorization, and make use of prototypes, which allow for a core and a periphery. Givón (1984: 51f., 2001: 49f.) recognizes four word classes: noun, verb, adjective, and adverb. (Prepositions are conspicuously absent.) Nouns typically denote 'concrete, physical, compact entities made out of durable, solid matter, such as "rock", "tree", "dog", "person" etc.'. Verbs are lexicalizations of 'experiential clusters denoting rapid changes in the state of the universe. These are prototypically *events* or *actions*'. Nouns, verbs, and adjectives can be ordered on what Givón calls the *time–stability scale*, with nouns and verbs at the two extremes. See Thompson (1988) for criticism of Givón's scale, to which I will return in Chapter 3. As for the properties of the categories themselves, for Givón '[n]on-discreteness in language is...not an alternative to discrete categories, but rather its complement in a complex hybrid system' (1995: 13). The classical categories are thus not rejected, but are seen instead as complementary to fuzzy-edged classes. Givón gives up 'unfettered' gradience and fuzziness, and even 'does penance' for earlier sins:

Aristotle has not been alone in his worry about the no-man's-land between categoriality and flux. In the early formative decade of the functional-typological renaissance, say 1967 to 1977, there were perfectly good reasons why many of us would have wanted to view non-discreteness as an alternative to the Generative love affair with discrete categories. Following Ross (1972, 1973[*b*]) and Lakoff (1973[*a*]), we began to discover the less-than-categorial aspects of grammar. But as is often the case in the context of rebellion (intellectual or otherwise), excess tends to breed counter-excess, as opposing camps strive for maximal differentiation within a limited space. Thus, the extreme Platonic categoriality of the Generative dogma pushed us, in the early 1970s, into an equally dogmatic extreme. Ultimately though, trading one reductive dogma for another is a bad strategy in science. It was a lousy gambit when Chomsky (1959) insisted that we choose between his dogmatic innatism and Skinner's equally dogmatic stimulus–response. And it hasn't improved with age. (Givón 1995: 12)

Givón suggests that there is a distinction between what he calls *automated processing* and *attended processing* which may be important in such a way that core members of a category are the most frequent and are processed rapidly and automatically, while peripheral members are much less common and may require contextual clues before they can be fully interpreted. He suggests that there exists a *fallacy of categorial impurity*, inspired by the classical conception of categories, formulated as follows:

Categories that exhibit any overlap at all cannot be distinct, but rather must be contiguous sub-sections of the same category. (Givón 1995: 14)

He goes on to say that this 'apparent logical conundrum' can be resolved if we recognize categories with prototype structures, and if we adopt the distinction between automated and attended processing. In Givón (1986) an argument is put forward for regarding prototypes as being a compromise between Platonic and Wittgensteinian approaches to categorization.

In schematic form overlapping categories look as shown in Figure 2.1 (Givón 1995: 14; see also Givón 1986: 81, 2001: 31f.):

In a number of papers in the 1980s Hopper and Thompson (1980, 1984, 1985) argued that grammatical categories are lexicalizations of certain salient discourse functions. Under this view, nouns are lexicalizations of 'discourse manipulable participants', while verbs are lexicalizations of 'reported events' (Hopper and Thompson 1984: 703). Thompson (1988) argues that adjectives, or Property Concept Words, as she calls them, share verbal and nominal features in the languages of the world.

[G]iven that Property Concept Words share the *predicating* function with *Verbs*, and the *referent-introducing* function with *Nouns*, this sharing of both verbal and nominal *functions in discourse* provides an explanation for the fact that Property Concepts will

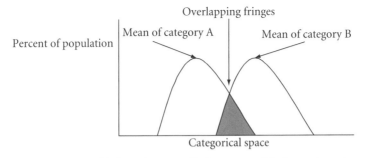

FIGURE 2.1 Distributional balance between distinctness and indeterminacy in natural categories

sometimes be categorized with morpho-syntactic properties similar to those of Verbs, and sometimes with morpho-syntactic properties similar to those of Nouns, while sometimes, since they are neither prototypical Nouns nor prototypical Verbs, they are categorized as a separate lexical category of Adjective. (Thompson 1988: 181; emphasis in original)

In this framework not all elements of a particular form class have equal status. Prototypical members of a class have particular semantic properties, but more important for their status as prototypes is their discourse role. Thus a generic noun like *tigers* in *tigers are dangerous* is deemed less centrally a noun than tigers in *these tigers are dangerous*. The word *tigers* in the former example is nonreferential, while in the latter example it singles out a particular set of identifiable tigers. Prototypical members of categories are predicted to display a greater potential for morpho-syntactic variation (e.g. in showing number, tense, and other distinctions).

Croft (1991) attempts to define syntactic categories universally using language-internal and language-external criteria, where the internal criteria are conceived as being structural in nature, involving markedness and prototypes, while external criteria are semantic/pragmatic in kind (1991: 37). For Croft there exist *peripheral* or *intermediate categories* (1991: 23, 133) such as numerals (cf. Comrie 1981: 101f.), which are of relevance synchronically, and *transitory categories*, which are diachronically intermediate. An example of the latter are auxiliary verbs (Croft 1991: 142f.). He suggests that transitory categories are not involved in propositional functions such as predication or modification, but result from certain unstable universal processes and display 'a cline of grammatical behavior rather than a prototypical core' (1991: 144). As an overall conclusion to his book Croft writes:

All languages conventionalize grammar to a certain extent; it is the conventions rather than the fluid aspects of language that are written into grammatical descriptions. But convention is a matter of degree and can change over time. The analyst must be able to tease apart the conventional and the functionally motivated; they do not occur neatly separated into modules. By recognizing that grammar is dynamic and evolving, one can perceive the consistency of the functional principles that govern language dynamics better than if one treats grammar as a static, abstract structure. (Croft 1991: 274)

2.4.7 *Other frameworks: Phrase Structure Grammar and Construction Grammar*

In phrase structure approaches, such as Head Driven Phrase Structure Grammar (HPSG), categories are regarded as feature complexes (Pollard and Sag 1994: 22). In HPSG features are not necessarily binary, but can be multivalued.

As noted above in Section 2.4.2, if syntactic categories are defined by making use of features, then the notion of syntactic category becomes epiphenomenal. In fact, as noted in Borsley (1996: 38), in Pollard and Sag's (1994) version of HPSG traditional categories do not exist any more, because HPSG categories provide not only syntactic information, but also semantic information in the SYNSEM attribute (see also Pollard and Sag 1994: 22, fn 8).

In Goldberg's (2006) Cognitive Construction Grammar framework conventional categories such as the word classes are regarded as constructions, and grammatical entities are not defined in an Aristotelian fashion: 'essentialist definitions for *non*-linguistic categories are the exception not the norm, particularly for inductive, empirical generalizations. To the extent that we wish to say that linguistic categories are like other categories, we would *not expect* them to be definable by necessary and sufficient conditions' (2006: 223; emphasis in original). Constructions play a role at every level of linguistic analysis from morphemes to more conventional patterns. In Croft's (2001) Radical Construction Grammar constructions are primitive and categories are epiphenomenal. Distributional analysis as a method for arriving at a taxonomy of word classes is rejected as constituting 'methodological opportunism' (2001: 41). See also Croft (2007), which is a critique of the methodology used in Aarts (2004*b*). I defend the proposed analysis in Aarts (2007).

In this chapter we have seen that grammatical categorization has always been a central concern of linguists from antiquity onwards. In the next chapter I will explore ways in which attempts have been made to deal with categorial fuzziness in grammar.

3

Grammatical Gradience

> [No] gradation or continuity *in either form or meaning*, has ever been found *in any language* on this planet.
>
> (Joos 1957: 351; emphasis in original)

> From the standpoint of what has become traditional in American linguistics, the question is not whether there are such things as continuous phenomena in parts of human behavior that lie close to linguistics—many would grant that there are—but whether such phenomena should be regarded as the object of linguistic study.... [W]hen one stops talking about switches and begins to talk about potentiometers, one does not necessarily cease talking about electrical systems.
>
> (Bolinger 1961a: 10, 11)

3.1 Introduction

The two views expressed above show the differences in opinion regarding linguistic categorization. The quotation from Bolinger recognizes the fact that the elements of language cannot artificially and rigidly be forced within certain predefined bounds. A certain degree of categorial flexibility—that is *gradience*—needs to be permitted, a point of view denied by Joos (see Section 2.4.1). We return to this opposition of views later in the chapter.

Gradience in grammar is usually characterized as the phenomenon of blurred boundaries between two categories of form classes α and β, such that certain elements can be said clearly to belong to α, others indisputably to β, with a third group of elements belonging to the middle ground between the two categories. This situation can be represented by ordering linguistic entities along a linear scale with α at one end and β at the other, and a blurred area in between (Quirk *et al.* 1985: 90; Leech *et al.* 1994: 57), as in Figure 3.1.

Alternatively, we might view gradience in set-theoretic terms, and posit that it obtains when categories overlap, and there thus exists an intersection $\alpha \cap \beta$, containing elements that possess α-like features as well as β-like features (Figure 3.2).

α / β

FIGURE 3.1 The linear representation of gradience

Note: The slashed lines indicate the blurred boundary between Categories α and β

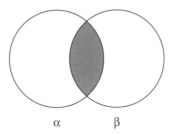

α   β

FIGURE 3.2 The set-theoretic representation of gradience

As will become clear in the course of this book, I will be arguing against this way of conceptualizing gradience between categories. Note, incidentally, that these representations do not allow for gradience *within* categories.

Before discussing linguistic gradience in more detail, it will be instructive briefly to trace the history of concepts such as 'vagueness' and 'imprecision' in the philosophical literature. This I will do in Section 3.2. Sections 3.3 and 3.4 will then discuss linguistic (mainly syntactic) approaches to gradience. The layout of this chapter broadly mirrors that of Chapter 2.

3.2 Notions of gradience in ancient and modern philosophy

Aristotle's system of categorization was rigidly all-or-none, as we saw in the last chapter, although he did seem to allow for the possibility of gradience, and even for the notion of prototype ('that which has more the nature of something'), as the following passage from his *Metaphysics* shows:

Again, however much all things may be so and not so, still there is a more and a less in the nature of things; for we should not say that two and three are equally even, nor is he who thinks four things are five equally wrong with him who thinks they are a thousand. If then they are not equally wrong, obviously one is less wrong and therefore more right. If then that which has more of any quality is nearer to it, there must be some truth to which the more true is nearer. And even if there is not, still there is already something more certain and true, and we shall have got rid of the unqualified doctrine which would prevent us from determining anything in our thought. (*Metaphysics*, IV, 4, 1592–1593)

It appears that Aristotle is talking about what I will be calling Subsective Gradience, that is, gradience within categories.

Early Greek philosophy approached the notion of vagueness with reference to the Sorites Paradox (see Chapter 1). Recall that this paradox concerns the fact that we cannot clearly say when a heap of sand ceases to be a heap if we take away grains of sand one at a time. Thus, it is not clear where a heap h becomes ¬h in a chain of entities α_{1-n}, where α_1 is clearly a heap and where α_n clearly is not, and where in each case α_x differs only minimally from α_{x+1}.

There was a resurgence of interest in imprecise predicates amongst philosophers of the nineteenth and twentieth centuries. The pre-modern writings on this topic are those of Gottlob Frege (see Section 2.2), which can be opposed to those of Ludwig Wittgenstein. As we have seen, Frege defended the classical view that concepts have sharp boundaries. Wittgenstein, who considered language to be inherently vague, was in many ways an early proponent of Prototype Theory (see Section 3.4.7). His treatment of the notion of a *Spiel* ('game') in terms of 'family resemblances' in his *Philosophical Investigations* is well known:

Consider for example the proceedings that we call 'games'. I mean board-games, card-games, ball-games, Olympic games, and so on. What is common to them all?—Don't say: 'There *must* be something common, or they would not be called "games"'—but *look and see* whether there is anything common to all.—For if you look at them you will not see something that is common to *all*, but similarities, relationships, and a whole series of them at that. To repeat: don't think, but look!—Look for example at board-games, with their multifarious relationships. Now pass to card-games; here you find many correspondences with the first group, but many common features drop out, and others appear. When we pass next to ball-games, much that is common is retained, but much is lost.—Are they all 'amusing'? Compare chess with noughts and crosses. Or is there always winning and losing, or competition between players? Think of patience. In ball-games there is winning and losing; but when a child throws his ball at the wall and catches it again, this feature has disappeared. Look at the parts played by skill and luck; and at the difference between skill in chess and skill in tennis. Think now of games like ring-a-ring-a-roses; here is the element of amusement, but how many other characteristic features have disappeared! And we can go through the many, many other groups of games in the same way; can see how similarities crop up and disappear.

And the result of this examination is: we see a complicated network of similarities overlapping and criss-crossing: sometimes overall similarities, sometimes similarities of detail.

I can think of no better expression to characterize these similarities than 'family resemblances'; for the various resemblances between members of a family: build, features, colour of eyes, gait, temperament, etc. etc. overlap and criss-cross in the same way.—And I shall say: 'games' form a family. (Wittgenstein 1953/1958: 31–2)

Wittgenstein's argument was that all games share a number of similarities, and that the notion of game is impossible to characterize in Aristotelian terms. Wierzbicka (1990: 358) challenges Wittgenstein by isolating a number of criterial properties common to all games. According to Wierzbicka, the word 'game' means something different in different languages, but the concept does have boundaries, and speakers of languages know subconsciously where they should be drawn.

Philosophers of science have also shown an interest in the notion of 'imprecision'. Thus, Popper has argued that precision in and of itself is not always desirable, and singles out language as a special case (cf. Schilpp 1974: 17; Chatterjee 1994: 23). A similar view was put forward by Quine (1960: 127), who held that '[g]ood purposes are often served by not tampering with vagueness', and that vagueness and precision are not incompatible with each other:

As Richards[1] has remarked, a painter with a limited palette can achieve more precise representations by thinning and combining his colors than a mosaic worker can achieve with his limited variety of tiles, and the skillful superimposing of vagueness has similar advantages over the fitting together of precise technical terms. (Quine 1960: 127)

Vagueness can also be useful in dealing with the linear properties of discourse. As an example Quine posits two concepts A and B, which can only be understood in relation to each other. It can then be useful to explain A first in vague terms, before proceeding to explicate B, after which A can be returned to.

Vagueness, especially in the guise of the Sorites Paradox, which so succinctly encapsulates the problem of indeterminacy, has remained a central focus of interest in modern philosophical thought, witness for example Burns (1991), Chatterjee (1994), Williamson (1994), as well as the papers in Ballmer and Pinkal (1983), and Keefe and Smith (1996a). Keefe (2000) offers a useful overview of the main theories of vagueness. The stoics, and especially Chrysippus (ca. 280–207 BC), held what has become known as the *epistemic view of vagueness*, an approach also defended recently by Williamson (1994). (See also Keefe and Smith 1996b: 17f., 59–60; Keefe 2000: 62f.). The epistemic view subscribes to classical logic and claims that vague predicates undoubtedly have sharp boundaries, but we are simply ignorant of where exactly those boundaries should be located. Another approach is to argue that a classical two-valued logic cannot handle vagueness, and that there is a need for a *many-valued logic* which, in addition to 'true' and 'false', allows for such values as 'indefinite' or 'degrees of truth'. The *pragmatic view* of vagueness

---

[1] Richards (1936: 48ff., 57ff., 69).

holds, like the epistemic view, that we should retain a classical logic, and that vagueness is the result of the way we use language. (See below for a similar view held by a linguist.) Finally, Keefe's book is a defence of a view of vagueness known as *supervaluationalism*. She describes this as follows:

The basic idea is that a proposition involving the vague predicate 'tall', for example, is true (false) if it comes out true (false) on all the ways in which we can make 'tall' precise (ways, that is, which preserve the truth-values of uncontentionally true or false cases of '*a* is tall'). A borderline case, 'Tek is tall', will be neither true nor false, for it is true on some ways of making 'tall' precise and false on others. But a classical tautology like 'either Tek is tall or he is not tall' *will* still come out true because wherever a sharp boundary for 'tall' is drawn, that compound sentence will come out true. In this way, the supervaluationalist adopts a non-classical *semantics* while aiming to minimise divergence from classical *logic*. (Keefe 2000: 17)

3.3 The linguistic tradition: early grammarians

Ever since classical times grammarians have been inveterate categorizers. But this does not mean that the pitfalls of categorization were not recognized. As we have seen, the Greeks debated whether in addition to nouns and verbs a third class of particles should be recognized. Later scholars also expressed doubts about the categories, or rejected them altogether. The Renaissance Spanish grammarian Sanctius (Francisco Sanchez) had little faith in the parts of speech 'in quibus tanta est inconstantia Grammaticorum, ut nihil certi nobis adhuc potuerint constituere' ('wherein such is the inconstancy of grammarians that they could provide us with nothing certain up to now'; quoted in Michael 1970: 52, my translation). As we saw in the previous chapter, by 1800 at least 56 systems of word classes had evolved among English grammarians. Although clearly still heavily influenced by the classical tradition, writers by that time had already begun to question the applicability of the Graeco-Roman classifications, and devised systems of their own (see Michael 1970, ch. 17). In the process some grammarians were clearly aware that the word classes are not mutually exclusive, as the passage below shows.

In parsing English it is not to be expected that every word should upon all occasions preserve its proper title; there is a certain blending of the parts of speech by which each sort of words is connected with the rest . . . yet the young Grammarians had better be taught to call these equivocal words by the name of that part of speech to which they are most nearly allied by natural resemblance. (Bullen 1797: 133; quoted in Michael 1970: 224–5)

Interestingly, this passage is also an early insight regarding the idea of a central exemplar, or prototype, in the linguistic writings of the period.

3.4 Twentieth-century approaches to gradience

3.4.1 *The post-Bloomfieldians and Bolinger*

As we saw in the previous chapters and from the quotations at the beginning of the present chapter, structuralist linguists such as Sapir and Bloomfield allowed for fluidity and indeterminacy in category boundaries. For post-Bloomfieldian structuralists such as Joos and Hockett, by contrast, the idea of continuity was anathema and 'discreteness' was held to be part of the 'design of language', along with, for example, arbitrariness, duality, and productivity (Joos 1950; Hockett 1959; Lyons 1977: 70; Asher 1994*b*: 876; Landsberg 1994: 2888). Thus for Hockett 'if we find continuous-scale contrasts in the vicinity of what we are sure is language, we exclude them from language' (1955: 17). Similarly, for Joos continuity and gradience must be 'shoved outside of linguistics in one direction or the other' (1950: 702). Joos forcefully denied that:

gradation or continuity *in either form or meaning*, has ever been found *in any language* on this planet. True, the sounds (and thus all the forms) occurring in the use of the language are variable by continuous gradation, and so are not only temperatures but all things and phenomena spoken of. But *in the design* of the language we never find a trace of those facts! (Joos 1957: 351, cited in Jacobsson 1977; emphasis in original)

There is a distinction here, which Joos does not make explicit, between two different uses of the term 'language'. The first sense is 'language as a system', which does not allow for continuity. The second use of 'language' refers to the *use* that is made of the system of language, that is, language in the narrow sense, much like the everyday sense of the term. It is essentially the same as performance, and *does* allow for continuity.

From the late 1950s onwards, structuralist certainties regarding the non-existence of continuity in linguistic categorization were questioned. In 1958 Rulon Wells presented a report at the Eighth International Congress of Linguists and exhorted delegates to be more open-minded about gradient phenomena:

In our attempts to discover structure we should pay more attention to continuities than we have done in the past. Where we have thought in terms of dichotomies—of a property being either definitely present or definitely absent, with no borderline cases, let us be more willing to look for and to recognize differences of degree, where the same property is present in lower or in higher degree. (Wells 1958: 655)

Roman Jakobson, a Prague School structuralist, while on the one hand saying that '[g]rammar, a real *ars obligatoria*, imposes upon the speaker its yes-or-no decisions' (Jakobson 1959; quoted in Bolinger 1961*a*: 8), also stressed the 'dynamic synchrony of language' which 'must replace the traditional pattern of arbitrarily restricted *static* descriptions' (Jakobson 1961: 248; quoted in Quirk 1965).

In 1961 Dwight Bolinger published his well-known *Generality, Gradience, and the All-or-none* (1961*a*). This short, but seminal, book deals predominantly with gradience in phonology, and is in many ways a reaction to the prevailing attitude of linguists such as Joos, whose views have been cited above. For Bolinger

[f]rom the standpoint of what has become traditional in American linguistics, the question is not whether there are such things as continuous phenomena in parts of human behavior that lie close to linguistics—many would grant that there are—but whether such phenomena should be regarded as the object of linguistic study.... [W]hen one stops talking about switches and begins to talk about potentiometers, one does not necessarily cease talking about electrical systems. (Bolinger 1961*a*: 10, 11)

If this quotation is compared with the passage from Joos shown above, we find that both linguists are talking about continuity at two distinct levels. As we have seen, Joos disallows continuity at the level of the design of the language, but readily admits to it at the level of language *use*. Bolinger argues for a recognition of the phenomenon of continuity both at the level of 'human behaviour', and at the level of the system of language.

In order to counterbalance the 'tyranny of linguistic categories' (Joos 1950: 703), Bolinger distinguishes between two types of continua, undifferentiated and differentiated. An example of the latter type of continuum is the earth's atmosphere, where there may be degrees of, say, air pressure. Another example is a graded increase in loudness. Linguistic examples, discussed in detail, are length and intonation. An undifferentiated continuum involves 'some indefinite point between two or more other points' (Joos 1950: 13). The example Bolinger gives is of a gas confined in a particular space, where at each spatial coordinate the gas has the same consistency. As for linguistic examples, Bolinger takes as his starting point the following sentence of Joos's: *They put their glasses on their noses.* When we hear this, we have to make a choice between a past and present tense interpretation of the word *put.* This is strictly an all-or-none choice, Joos had argued, and Bolinger concurs. However, Bolinger then investigates whether there might exist examples where the choice is *not* all-or-none, but possibly something in between. His answer is that there *are* such cases, and he cites the sentence *Put them away yet?* A hearer confronted with this question need not make an either-or choice, because the meaning of the utterance is somewhere between the present perfect and past tense reading. Here we have what Bolinger refers to as a *generality*, a situation where a particular linguistic item or locution can have more than one interpretation, but these interpretations need not necessarily be distinguished sharply for communication to go through when the item or locution is used.

As evidence for the generality in *Put them away yet?* Bolinger devised a test in which he asked respondents to fill in the gap in the following sequence (1961*a*: 18):

'Well, my assignment's almost done. You finish yours?'—'No, I ... n't.'

He found that an equal number of people filled in *have* and *did*, despite the fact that *have* is not a grammatically appropriate slot-filler, given the form of the verb *finish*. 'All the more reason, then,' Bolinger surmises, 'to suppose that the same randomness can apply to *put*, where whichever is chosen, *have* or *did*, is in apparent concord.' (Bolinger 1961*a*: 18)

In early editions of his textbook *Aspects of Language* Bolinger argues in favour of a representation of the boundaries between categories as a worn staircase, rather than as a new staircase (Figure 3.3). Bolinger does not make explicit why verbs should be positioned higher up on the staircase than adjectives and nouns, nor is it made clear why adjectives should be viewed as being intermediate between verbs and nouns. The representation as it stands suggests that gradience is not possible between verbs and nouns (unless it is viewed as a transitive concept, such that if there is gradience between A and C in a sequence A–B–C, there is also gradience between A and B and between B and C.)[2]

Bolinger has also written on *blending* (1961*a*, 1961*b*), a concept that is closely related to gradience. It will be discussed in Chapter 4.

Bolinger's work was cautiously welcomed by linguists advocating a discrete linguistics. Robert Stockwell concluded a review in *Language* by saying that

FIGURE 3.3 Bolinger's 'worn staircase'
Source: Bolinger (1975: 244)

---

[2] The discussion of gradience disappeared from the third edition of Bolinger's book, but the reason for this was economy and streamlining, not a loss of interest in the topic on Bolinger's part.

Bolinger's book can be seen as 'a useful corrective to the dogmatism that some of us too easily fall into' (1963: 91). In many ways Bolinger's book was pioneering, but very inchoate. He posed some interesting questions and gave some interesting examples, but these questions were never taken up systematically, and the examples remain anecdotal.

There is no mention of Bolinger's work in García (1967), but the data she discusses (auxiliaries in English) lead her to conclusions that are similar to Bolinger's:

[T]he best that linguists can (and perhaps ought to) do is to recognize a linguistic continuum when they see one, and not try to dichotomize an area of transition. Grammarians, however, have traditionally refused to recognize this continuum between grammatical and lexical items, and have steadfastly persevered in drawing what are probably very arbitrary boundaries about their domain. The reason is no doubt twofold: on the one hand, they wished to avoid getting involved in a thorough analysis of the lexicon, while on the other they were concerned with 'grammatical' phenomena. (García 1967: 866)

3.4.2 *Firth and Halliday*

In Britain J. R. Firth was an early advocate of recognizing boundary fluidity in language. Thus, for him, speech 'is a pattern without clearly defined boundaries' (1930/1964: 173). As for indeterminacy:

The empirical data of such sciences as linguistics are usually stated in technical restricted languages which must, nevertheless, involve indeterminacy, since technical terms are collocated with words of common usage in general language. Linguistics which does not fully recognize this element of indeterminacy cannot very well be applied to the study of language in society. There is need to recognize indeterminacy, not only in the restricted technical language of description, but also in the language under description. (Firth 1955: 97–8)[3]

Michael Halliday, who built on Firth's ideas, presented his notion of a 'cline' as a 'continuum of infinite gradation' (1961: 248–9). An example of a cline is the 'scale of delicacy' (1961: 272), a way of being more precise about describing the different degrees of similarity that obtain between particular form elements. Another example is the 'lexico-grammar cline', schematized as follows (Halliday and Matthiessen 2004: 43):

---

[3] My thanks to Rob Munro for discussing Firth's views, and for pointing out the quotations.

Lexico-grammar
(stratum of wording)

Grammar ←————————————→ Lexis
(closed systems, general in   (open sets, specific in meaning;
meaning; structure)   collocation)

Halliday's early work appeared at around the same time as the work of Bolinger in the United States and that of the Prague linguists.

3.4.3 *Transformational Grammar*

One of the earliest disagreements between Chomskyan and empirical linguists centred on the question of the use that can be made of primary linguistic data. In a review of Bolinger's (1957) book on interrogative structures, Lees (1960: 123) chides the former for providing a 'maze of unanalyzed, and perhaps in most cases useless, distinctions', and remarked that 'although it may ultimately be of far greater interest, characterizing the way utterances are *used* is very much more difficult, and correspondingly much less productive of new insights, than is characterizing the formal, or syntactic, features of sentences. I take the latter task to be the central concern of linguistic science at the present' (Lees 1960: 123). In Bolinger's reply Lees is likened to a 'clinician [who] has in his office a favorite rug under which he sweeps the scraps of data that will not fit in the drawers along the wall' (Bolinger 1960: 378). Despite overtures, mostly from the 'taxonomists', that both approaches should be taken to be complementary, up to this day the methodological bickering has never really stopped. See Aarts (2000) for further discussion. As with data, so with gradient phenomena. Generative linguists have always been averse to the notion of fuzziness in grammar. Whether or not to recognize gradience, and allow it to be part of one's grammatical framework, is again a methodological decision. It has always been felt that continuous phenomena, like language use, belong to the realm of performance, and do not concern theorists. Lees (1959), quoted in Bolinger (1961a: 9–10) talks of 'the increasingly more popular though delusive notion that linguistics must surrender its traditional "all-or-none" view of occurrence for a "probabilistic view in which we are concerned with the likelihood that one class will occur rather than another"'.[4] More recently Denis Bouchard has expressed the view that 'fuzziness is not present in Grammar in any way,...Rather, fuzziness is in the web, the background knowledge on which language is woven, and therefore it has no effect on the form and function of language' (1995: 33). Also:

---

[4] The quote within this quote is from *Logique, langage et théorie de l'information*, by L. Apostel, B. Mandelbrot, and A. Morf, which Lees was reviewing.

[T]he overwhelming evidence is that fuzzy categorization is involved only in the processes dealing with perception or beliefs about the 'external world' and that it is not intrinsically involved in the functioning of Grammar. Externalizing processes such as perception and belief must 'reach out,' whereas grammatical processes are strictly internal. If fuzziness is a property of externalizing processes only, grammatical processes could very well be strictly classical. It is very important to bear in mind the distinction between the form of the sentence, that is, *how* it expresses something, and *what* it expresses. Only the former is relevant to Grammar. (Bouchard 1995: 36–7; footnote omitted)

See also Bever and Caroll (1981), whose views are discussed in Section 3.4.4. An exceptional figure amongst interpretive linguists in this connection is Ray Jackendoff, who argues (1983: 155ff) that fuzziness and family resemblances should play a role in linguistic studies.

As the views of Joos, cited in Sections 2.4.1 and 3.4.1, and the quotations from Lees above indicate, the generativists agreed with the structuralists that the existence of E-linguistic and gradient phenomena should not so much be denied, but their study should be relegated to a time when we have a better understanding of the language system (structuralists) or of Universal Grammar (generativists). In other words, the strategy in these two paradigms was—*is*, in the case of the generativists—to abstract away from the wood in order to see the trees. The necessity for idealization has always consistently been stressed by generativists. In talking about the discreteness of grammar and grammaticality judgements, Bever notes:

To give up the notion that a grammar defines a set of well-formed utterances is to give up a great deal. This is not to say that it is impossible in principle that grammars are squishy [see Section 3.4.4 below on the notion of squishiness, BA]. Rather the possibility of studying precise properties of grammar and exact rules becomes much more difficult.... Thus, if we can maintain the concept of discrete grammaticality, we will be in a better position to pursue an understanding of grammatical universals. (Bever 1975: 601)

Chomsky has stressed the importance of idealization throughout his career. Ever since his (in)famous use of the phrase *homogeneous speech community* in the 1960s (Chomsky 1965: 3), he has regarded idealization as a first step towards approaching a plausible description of reality (see Chomsky 1965: 3 and 1980: 24f.; the latter includes a discussion of how the term homogeneous speech community was misunderstood). Some thirty years later, Chomsky is still stressing the importance of idealization as 'the only reasonable way to approach a grasp of reality' (1995: 7; also 1998: 115). One cannot fail to have sympathy for this view. Imagine one is asked to sort out—that is, bring order to—a box full of coloured ping-pong balls. Some are red, some are green, some are white, and some are a combination of two or more of these colours: red and green, red and white, green and white, red, green and white, and so on. The best way to go about the task at hand is surely first to sort the balls with only one colour and then deal with the multi-coloured ones. In grammar, too, it may be best to deal with the obvious clear-cut categories first, before tackling the gradient cases. Of course, the taxonomists will claim that the theorists will never get round to the multi-coloured balls, and there is some truth to this point.

Another aspect of idealization is the methodological decision to adopt what is sometimes referred to as the *Galilean style*. Chomsky explains this as follows:

> The phrase was used by nuclear physicist Steven Weinberg, borrowed from Husserl, but not just with regard to the attempt to improve theories. He was referring to the fact that physicists 'give a higher degree of reality' to the mathematical models of the universe that they construct than to 'the ordinary world of sensation'. What was striking about Galileo, and was considered very offensive at the time, was that he dismissed a lot of data; he was willing to say 'Look, if the data refute the theory, the data are probably wrong.'... But the Galilean style, what Steve Weinberg was referring to, is the recognition that it is the abstract systems that you are constructing that are really the truth; the array of phenomena is some distortion of the truth because of too many factors, all sorts of things. And so, it often makes good sense to disregard phenomena and search for principles that really seem to give some deep insight into why some of them are that way, recognizing that there are others that you can't pay attention to. (Chomsky 2002: 98–9, footnote omitted. See also Chomsky 1980: 8f.)

The idea of a Galilean style can perhaps be traced back further than Husserl. It was allegedly Hegel who opined that '*Wenn die Tatsachen mit der Theorie nicht übereinstimmen, umso schlimmer für die Tatsachen!* ('When the facts do not conform to the theory, too bad for the facts!'). See Boeckx (2006) for an extensive discussion of the Galilean style. For many the idea that the model is more important than the data will be startling, and some will feel that Chomsky shows disdain for empirical data. Chomsky's rejection of data-oriented methodologies is well known. See for example his comments in an interview I conducted with him (Aarts 1996).

Despite the dismissal of performance phenomena as being outside language in the narrow sense, a particular manifestation of gradience (different from the notion of gradience as 'categorial indeterminacy' which is the focus of this book) *has* played a role in Chomskyan linguistics, specifically in early discussions of the notion of 'degrees of grammaticalness' (Chomsky 1961: 233f.; 1965:

11, 77; 1955/1975: 129f.; Chomsky and Miller 1963: 291). Chomsky's teacher Zellig Harris had already discussed the notion of degree of acceptability, and noted that an adjective like *grandfatherish* will be judged more acceptable than *deepish*, which in turn will be more acceptable than *countryside-ish* or *uncle-ish*; see Harris (1957: 293).[5] In *Aspects* Chomsky carefully discriminates between acceptability and grammaticalness, now a widely accepted, if still controversial, distinction. Acceptability belongs to the domain of performance (or the related concept of (E)xternalized language), grammaticalness belongs to competence (or I(nternalized)-language). In Chomsky (1955/1975: 129), which predates *Aspects*, Chomsky asserts that 'a partition of utterances into just two classes, grammatical and nongrammatical, will not be sufficient to permit the construction of adequate grammars in terms of what we have broadly described as distributional analysis.' The following set of examples is given, where the first is deemed fully grammatical, the second partially grammatical and the third ungrammatical:

(1)   look at the cross-eyed elephant
      look at the cross-eyed kindness
      look at the cross-eyed from

In this early work Chomsky judged his well-known example *colorless green ideas sleep furiously* to be grammatical (1955/1975: 131). What is not clear is why this is grammatical but the second example in (1) only *partially* grammatical. By the early 1960s, Chomsky's discussion of the notion of 'degree of grammaticalness' is still confusing. He states that '[g]iven a grammatically deviant utterance, we attempt to impose an interpretation on it, exploiting whatever features of grammatical structure it preserves and whatever analogies we can construct with perfectly well-formed utterances. We do not, in this way, impose an interpretation on a perfectly grammatical utterance' (1961: 234). But surely, trying to find an interpretation is exactly what we do in the case of *colorless green ideas sleep furiously*. It appears then, that this sentence too is partially deviant, and this is the line Chomsky takes subsequently in the same paper. The *colorless* sentence is included in group (a) below, the elements of which 'are not as extreme in their violation of grammatical rules as [(b)], though they do not conform to the rules of the language as strictly as [(c)]' (1961: 235)

[5] On Harris's influence on the study of gradience, see also Ross (1973b: 231) who notes that his interest in nouniness 'arose from my fascination with offhand remarks of Zellig Harris in classes at the University of Pennsylvania in 1962 to the effect that some nominalized versions of a sentence were more noun-like than others'.

(a)   A grief ago; perform leisure; golf plays John; colorless green ideas
       sleep furiously; misery loves company; John frightens sincerity; what
       did you do to the book, understand it?
(b)   a the ago; perform compel; golf plays aggressive; furiously sleep ideas
       green colorless; abundant loves company; John sincerity frightens;
       what did you do to the book, justice it?
(c)   a year ago; perform the task; John plays golf; revolutionary new ideas
       appear infrequently; John loves company; sincerity frightens John;
       what did you do to the book, frighten it?

In short, the *colorless* sentence is deemed first 'clearly a well-formed sentence
(or, at least, more like one than [*furiously sleep ideas green colorless*])' (1961: 231),
but is then classed as semi-grammatical. In the same paper Chomsky makes an
attempt to formalize the notion of degree of grammaticalness by assigning to
each string of words 'a structural description that indicates degree of grammaticalness, the degree of its deviation from grammatical regularities, and the
manner of its deviation' (1961: 236). The way he aims to achieve this is by
assigning the words in a particular string to progressively more refined levels of
description. The string in question is then more or less grammatical at the
different levels. In Chomsky's words: 'The degree of grammaticalness is a
measure of the remoteness of an utterance from the generated set of perfectly
well-formed sentences, and the common representing category sequence will
indicate in what respects the utterance in question is deviant.' As a concrete
example consider the three example sentences in (2) given by Chomsky:

(2)   John loves company
       Misery loves company
       Abundant loves company

On one level, all these strings are grammatical, in that they all contain English
words. On the next level 'up' only the first two sentences are grammatical,
because they conform to the structural requirements of the grammar, such as,
for example, the fact that subjects should be realized by an appropriate category.
At the highest level of generality only the first sentence is fully grammatical,
because, unlike the second sentence, it does not violate the selectional restriction
that stipulates that the subject of the verb *love* must refer to an animate entity.
Naturally, we can go on adding levels and thus achieve even finer degrees of
grammaticalness. As to where to stop refining, Chomsky admits this is not clear.
See also Chomsky (1965: 152). Two further early approaches to sentences that are
deviant to some degree can be found in Katz (1964) and Ziff (1964). In the
Aspects model, sentences of the *colorless* ilk are regarded as 'borderline' (1965: 77),

that is to say clearly not indisputably grammatical, nor indisputably ungrammatical. As to how to deal with such sentences, Chomsky remarks that 'purely
semantic or purely syntactic considerations may not provide the answer in some
particular case. In fact, it should not be taken for granted, necessarily, that
syntactic and semantic considerations can be sharply distinguished' (1965: 77).
In *Aspects* Chomsky tentatively concludes that the syntactic component should
deal with deviance of *colorless*-type sentences. They are assigned a phrase
structure but only by a 'relaxation of certain syntactic conditions' (1965: 79).
Later on in the book it is proposed that these syntactic conditions are in fact
selectional restrictions formulated in terms of binary syntactic features (1965:
82). Under this approach, the *colorless* sentence can be ruled out because of a
mismatch between the syntactic feature carried by the verb, namely that it
requires a [+animate] subject, and the subject NP *colorless green ideas* which
is [−animate]. Returning to groups (a) and (c) above, in present-day terms they
would be deemed grammatical, but the elements of (a) would be pragmatically
deviant. Some three decades later in Barsky (1997: 96) Chomsky re-asserts his
belief that 'there is no two-way split' between grammatical and ungrammatical
sentences.

The early generative notion of *kernel sentence*, later abandoned (and then
re-introduced in the Minimalist Program), defined as basic those sentences to
which only obligatory transformations have applied (Chomsky 1957: 45, 1965:
17–18). This poses the interesting question of whether there are 'degrees of
kernelness' depending on how many transformations have been performed on
a particular sentence. The question was raised by psycholinguists, leading to
the *Derivational Theory of Complexity* (see e.g. Prideaux 1984), which asserted
that a sentence is progressively more difficult to process if progressively more
transformations have applied to it.

The notion of gradient grammaticality rears its head at various stages in the
later history of generative linguistics. Erteschik-Shir and Lappin (1979: 72)
discuss the following extractions from *picture noun phrases*:[6]

(3)   Who$_i$ did you see [pictures of t$_i$]?
(4)   Who$_i$ did you see [*a* picture of t$_i$]?
(5)   ?Who$_i$ did you see [*the* picture of t$_i$]?
(6)   *Who$_i$ did you see [*John's* picture of t$_i$]?

The claim is that these data progressively decrease in their degree of grammaticality. Kluender (1992: 238) also discusses these data—he adds *who did
you see* his *picture of* between (5) and (6)—and claims that the conditioning

---

[6] Traces and indices added.

factors are the 'referential specificity' and the 'degree of open-class member-ship in the head/specifier of the embedded DPs' from which the *wh*-element is extracted: extraction is easier from less specific NPs/DPs.

In Government and Binding Theory/Principles and Parameters Theory gradience in grammaticality judgements continues to play a role. Thus Belletti and Rizzi's (1988) paper on psych verbs recognizes several levels of grammat-icality, while Andrews (1990: 203) lists the following stigmata for his judge-ments: √, ?, ??, ?*, *, and **, ranging from 'completely acceptable and natural' to 'horrible'.

It is especially extraction phenomena that lead to gradience. Haegeman (1994: 565) discusses extractions from relative clauses (syntactic markup omitted):

(7)   *Whom do you know the date when Mary invited?
(8)   **When do you know the man whom Mary invited?

Without going into the technical details, the first example is less bad than the second, because in the case of (7) movement crosses fewer barriers than in (8). See also Ouhalla (1999: 282–3). What is notable is that no need is felt in generative theory to incorporate a formal notion of 'degree of deviance' into the theory. See Schütze (1996: 70ff.) for a description of experimental research that was conducted on degrees of grammaticality.

Transformational theory has also allowed for various types of hybridity and other types of indeterminacy, which is clearly in conflict with its avowed respect for classically conceived categories. Thus 'gerundives' such as *Mary's loving her sister (is touching)* were analysed in Chomsky (1970) as involving an S-node dominated by an NP-node. Jackendoff (1977: 51f.) proposes adding the phrase structure rule in (9) to generate the tree in (10):

(9) N″→ing – V″

(10)

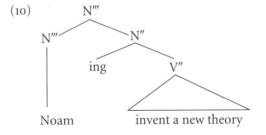

In this context the notion of degree again rears its head, but in a different guise. Positing (9) is not, Jackendoff notes, 'an unprincipled exception', but such rules can be seen as being 'part of a class of "deverbalizing" phrase structure rules' (Jackendoff 1977:51). Later in his book he remarks that '[g]erundive nominals are *the most NP-like* of the three complement types studied by Rosenbaum (1967)' (1977: 222; emphasis added). There are other examples of hybridity. Thus in GB-theory in a sentence like the following:

(11)   I would prefer for you to leave as soon as possible.

the element *for* is analysed as a hybrid *prepositional complementizer*, because on the one hand it performs the function of subordinator, on the other it functions as an objective Case assigner *vis-à-vis* the subject of the subordinate clause. Clearly *for* is not treated in an either/or fashion, as far as its categorial classification is concerned. The same is true for the element 'PRO', classed for the purposes of the Binding Theory (BT) as a *pronominal anaphor*: by virtue of being an anaphor it is subject to Principle A of the BT, while it is subject to Principle B by virtue of being a pronominal element. This leads to the *PRO Theorem*, which says that PRO has no governing category, and hence must not be governed. Consider also GB's Exceptional Case Marking constructions such as *I believe these issues to be problematic*, where the postverbal NP is object-like from the point of view of Case-marking (it gets its Case from the matrix verb), but subject-like from the point of view of theta theory (it gets its thematic role from the subordinate clause predicate). Finally, in GB-theory we also encounter *quasi-arguments*, for example weather-*it* (Chomsky 1981: 325), which have some of the characteristics of *true arguments*. These terms remind one of prototype members and marginal members of categories (see below), because quasi-arguments share some of the properties of true arguments.

Work in GB has also taken an interest in the Prague notion of markedness, which allows for some members of a particular category to be more equal than others, by allowing for default exemplars. As markedness is not exclusively a generative notion I will discuss it separately, and especially how it relates to gradience, in Chapter 4.

Let us return briefly to features. Recall that in P&P theory and earlier models the principal parts of speech are defined using the binary features $[\pm N, \pm V]$, such that nouns are $[+N, -V]$, verbs are $[-N, +V]$, adjectives are $[+N, +V]$, and prepositions are $[-N, -V]$. Notice that the plus-or-minus applicability of a particular feature is clearly an either/or choice, and the resulting categories show a mix of nominal and verbal properties. As Berg (2000: 269–70) observes, this set-up allows us to arrange the word classes in question in such a way that adjectives are positioned between verbs and nouns on a scale. This has the implication that adjectives are as similar to verbs as they are to nouns, a position he challenges (see also Section 3.4.4). While the system as described above does not allow for the features to apply to a certain degree (i.e. there are no degrees of N-ness or V-ness), in Chomsky's Minimalist Program features *do* allow for that dimension: they can be [±strong], that is, strong or weak (Chomsky 1995: 232). Chomsky suggests that the strength of features plays a role in language variation. The concept of feature strength is notable, because 'strong' and 'weak' are not absolute, but scalable, attributes, and hence imply a gradient. Perversely though, in the Minimalist framework even these features are interpreted as binary ([±strong]). Movement phenomena are sometimes also taken to be strong or weak, as this passage from Bernstein (2001: 547) shows:

An observation that can be made is that adjectives have a relatively greater tendency to precede the noun in a language like French than in languages like Spanish and Italian. Under the assumption that [DP-internal] noun movement is the mechanism that derives the postnominal surface position of the adjective, the crosslinguistic data suggest that nouns in French do not raise as high as nouns in Spanish and Italian do. Consideration of several less-studied Romance varieties further supports the idea of a continuum between relatively robust and relatively weak noun movement.[7]

In other recent theoretical work there is also a renewed interest in gradient phenomena. In some cases the strongly held anti-gradience views are reiterated. Thus Newmeyer (1998) insists that categories are classically bounded, and that prototype effects follow from 'the interaction of independently needed principles from syntax, semantics, and pragmatics' (1998: 208), a view that is not very novel (see above and below). He offers no account of what these principles might look like. Other recent studies are more open to the possibility of grammatical continuity, see for example Pinker (1999) on irregular verbs, Borsley and Kornfilt (2000) on 'mixed extended projections', and van Riemsdijk (1998, 2001) and Corver and van Riemsdijk (2001*a*, 2001*b*) on 'semi-lexical heads' (heads which are intermediate between functional heads and lexical heads). Corver and van Riemsdijk concede that 'as with all types of

---

[7] Reading the passage from Bernstein, one is reminded of Pullum's tongue-in-cheek comments many years ago on a possible future rapprochement between Chomskyan linguists and the 'Fuzzies' (i.e. Berkeley linguists):

What no one seems to have fully appreciated is that *current MIT syntax will blend very nicely with the work of the Fuzzies*. And the resultant amalgam will be unstoppable. Students of the early 1990s, I predict, will write dissertations on such topics as how point of view of participants affects relative strength of barriers, and their mixed GB/Fuzzy thesis committees will be delighted. An invincible coalition will have emerged: the anti-formalists in pursuit of the unformalizable. (Pullum 1991*a*: 54–5; emphasis in original)

categorization, there are elements, which cannot be put straightforwardly under one of the two classes. Certain lexical items display ambiguous behavior: they share properties with lexical categories and at the same time they display functional characteristics' (2001*b*: 3). The word class of preposition is given as an example: '[a]lthough they seem less functional in a sense than determiners, they are more "grammatical" than N, V and A' (2001*b*: 3). It is somewhat surprising to read such views in the work of two generativists *pur sang*, but it is an interesting indication of a shifting of perspectives regarding categorization in theoretical work.

Finally, in recent work on gerunds in the minimalist framework Ackema and Neeleman (2004: 172ff.) return to the English gerund and a number of other constructions under the heading of 'mixed categories'. They argue that a zero nominalizing affix is attached at different levels in the structure of the gerund, depending on the syntactic make-up of a particular string. Thus in their example *John's constantly singing the Marseillaise* the affix is attached at a higher level than in *John's constant singing of the Marseillaise*. See Chapters 7 and 8 for further discussion of gerunds.

3.4.4 *Generative Semantics*

During the 1970s the generative semanticists took up a midway position between descriptivists such as Bolinger and the generativists in their use of, and regard for, data (cf. Harris 1993: 209f. for discussion): like the descriptivists, they felt that data are of paramount importance; like the generativists, they felt that these data ought to be dealt with in a formal theory. This included gradient phenomena. The most well-known generative semantic defender of fuzziness was John Robert (Haj) Ross, who complained that 'the law of the Excluded Middle has, within the broad framework of generative grammar, always been assumed to hold for most of the predicates used in this theory' (Ross 1974: 111). Ross's work on gradient phenomena followed a period in which, along with other generative semanticists, he argued for category conflation, hence his papers 'Adjectives as noun phrases' (1969*a*) and 'Auxiliaries as main verbs' (1969*b*). In the early 1970s Ross developed the notion of a *squish* (1972: 316, 1973*a*: 98, 1973*b*, 1974: 113).

In his 1972 paper Ross discusses the perceived squish between verbs, adjectives, and nouns, and represents the relationship between them as follows:

(12)   Verb>Present   participle>Perfect   participle>Passive   participle>
         Adjective>Preposition (?)>'adjectival noun'>Noun (Ross 1972: 316)

He refers to this representation as a 'category space', and compares it to the distribution of the cardinal vowels in the 'vowel space' of a vowel chart. The idea is that there obtains a subtle shading between the categories verb, adjective, and noun, such that adjectives are in between verbs and nouns in terms of their syntactic versatility with respect to a number of syntactic phenomena. Ross cites a number of these phenomena, for example raising, which he claims applies virtually never to nouns, somewhat more often to adjectives, and quite commonly to verbs. As a further example, consider the data below (from Ross 1972: 320):

(13) a. I hate/(dis)like/love/?regret it that he talked so much.
      b. I am aware (?of it) that we may have to pay more.
      c. My regret (*of it) that he talked so much is well-known.

Ross remarks that 'the anaphoric (?) *it*...appears before *that* and *for-to* complements after a small class of verbs, and after only the adjective *aware of*, (in my speech), but after no nouns' (Ross 1972).

   Some pieces of evidence rely on now discredited analyses. For example, it is claimed that verbs are subject to the highest degree to a process of 'Fact Deletion', adjectives less so, while nouns are never subject to this rule:

(14) a. I regret (the fact) that you burned the warranty.
      b. I am aware (of the fact) that you told more than you knew.
      d. Tom was surprised (at the fact) that I know Greek.
      e. Tom's surprise *(at the fact) that I knew Greek could not be
          concealed.

Ross claims that his examples 'all manifest the same "funnel direction": nouns are more inert, syntactically, than adjectives and adjectives than verbs' (1972: 325). He also suggests that instead of the representation in (12) a 'circular' arrangement, as shown in Figure 3.4, might be preferable:

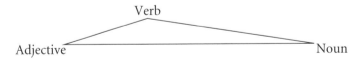

FIGURE 3.4 Ross's category space

He notes:

This would be the correct view of things if one could find not only phenomena with the structure suggested in (2b) [=V > A > N], where properties of A are 'between' those of V and N, but also phenomena like (2c) [= A > N > V], where N is 'between' V and A, and (2d) [= N > V > A], where V is 'between' N and A. I would not have any objections to such a system, but the only evidence I have been able to find so far all has the structure of (2b). (Ross 1972: 316–17)

I will return to Ross's conceptualization of how form classes relate to each other in Chapter 8.

Berg (2000) briefly surveys some of the different types of evidence for a Verb–Adjective–Noun continuum. In addition to the syntactic evidence there is semantic, pragmatic, and psycholinguistic proof. He also discusses (morpho)phonological evidence for positioning adjectives between verbs and nouns on a gradient, and he claims that adjectives are closer to nouns than they are to verbs, and hence that what he terms the 'equidistance hypothesis' is invalid.

While Ross's (1972) squish was rather sketchy, he provided a much more elaborate example of what he called a 'fake NP squish' in a paper the following year. The basic idea of this paper was to show that some noun phrases are more noun-phrasy than others. These are the 'copperclad, brass-bottomed NP's' (1973*a*). In his 1995 paper, also on degrees of NP-hood, they are called 'decent NP's', 'our best and brightest NP's', 'purebred NP's' and 'goody-goody-two-shoes NP's'. The less good examples are 'defective NP's' or 'noun phrasoids'. 'Noun-phrasiness' can be ranked along a scale, as shown in Figure 3.5 (Ross 1973*a*: 97):

(15)

←───────── More noun-phrasy ─────────

Harpo > Headway > there > tabs

FIGURE 3.5 Ross's NP-squish

Ross applies a number of tests which he claims apply to different degrees to nominal elements, such as, for example, Tag Formation, *Tough*-Movement, Left Dislocation, etc. In his 1973*b* paper Ross proposes the squish shown in Figure 3.6, again based on a battery of tests:

(16)   More nouny ─────────────→

that > for to > Q > Acc Ing > Poss Ing > Action Nominal > Derived Nominal > Noun

FIGURE 3.6 Ross's nouniness squish

Source: Ross (1973*b*: 141)

Examples of the cline are given in the following:

(17)   a.   *that* = *that*-clauses (*that Max gave the letters to Frieda*)
      b.   *for to* = *for* NP *to* V X (*for Max to have given the letters to Frieda*)
      c.   Q = embedded questions (*how willingly Max gave the letters to Frieda*)
      d.   *Acc Ing* = [[NP], [+Acc]] V + *ing* X (*Max giving the letters to Frieda*)
      e.   *Poss Ing* = NP's V+ *ing* X (*Max's giving the letters to Frieda*)
      f.   Action Nominal (*Max's/the giving of the letters to Frieda*)
      g.   Derived Nominal (*Max's/the gift of the letters to Frieda*)
      h.   Noun (*spatula*)

There are a number of differences between the 1972, 1973*a*, and 1973*b* papers. First of all the later papers are much more tightly argued, and there is an attempt to formalize the notion of squish, for example by introducing the concept of a 'well-behaved' squish, that is, a squish with very few exceptions in the cells of the matrix, and the notion of 'degree of class membership'. Secondly, the 1973*a* paper is concerned with what I will be calling Subsective Gradience (SG)—that is, gradience within a category—while the 1972 and 1973*b* papers deal with Intersective Gradience (IG)—gradience between categories—see Chapters 5 and 6. Ross makes no distinctions between these different types of continuities.[8]

Ross's (1973*a*) paper appeared in Bailey and Shuy (1973), which contains a number of further papers on perceived squishes in English. Of these Sag's is the most interesting. He proposes a 'progressive squish', which shows how a verb is more or less able to occur in the progressive form, depending on the degree of stativity the verb in question carries, as well as on a number of further syntactic contextual factors. The article is self-confessedly a 'progress report', and Sag concludes by saying that 'it would not be at all surprising if the criteria proposed for ascertaining stativity turned out to be "each a squish unto itself" ' (1973: 95).

Some years later Radford (1976) proposes a squish with auxiliary verbs at one end of the matrix, and full verbs at the other. Using six criteria, he plots out the auxiliaries and full verbs in a matrix. The criteria are the following:

1. Ability to take negative clitics (an auxiliary-like property)
  (*Jim can't leave/*Jim leaven't*)
2. Ability to take *do*-support (a verb-like property)
  (*Jim did leave/*Jim did will leave*)

---

[8] Thus despite its title—'Nouniness'—the 1973*b* paper argues for a cline between nouns and clauses, not for a cline of elements that are more or less nominal.

3. Ability to nominalize (a verbal property)
   (***John's canning/John's leaving*)
4. Ability to occur in untensed clauses (a verbal property)[9]
   (***I expect John to can leave/I expect John to leave*)
5. Ability to take *to* before a following infinitive (a verbal property)
   (***John can to leave/John wants to leave*)
6. Ability to display concord (a verbal property)
   (***John cans leave/John leaves*)

Radford arrives at the well-behaved squish shown in Table 3.1.

TABLE 3.1 Radford's squish

	Negative cliticization	*Do-* support	Nominals	Untensed clauses	*To* with inifinitive	Concord
will, would, can, could, shall, should, may, might, must, need (auxil.) *dare* (auxil.)	A (?? *may*)	A	A	A	A	A (not applicable to *past* forms)
do	A	n.a.	A	A	A	V
be (modal)	A	A	A	A	V	V
ought	A	A/%V	A	A	V	n.a.
used	??A	A/V	A	A %V	V	n.a.
be (auxil.) *be* (verb) *have* (auxil.)	A	A	V	V	n.a.	V
have (verb)	A	A	V	V	n.a.	V
have (modal)		V			V	
get *need* (verb) *dare* (verb)	V	V	V	V	V	V

Notes: 'A' = 'patterns like an auxiliary in this respect'; 'V' = 'patterns like a verb in this respect'; n.a. = 'not applicable'. It is not clear from Radford's article what '%' means. The line plots the lower limit of auxiliary-like behaviour.

[9] Radford's squish, shown on this page, does not allow for e.g. the following *I expect John to have left*, with *have* occurring in its infinitive form.

See also Bolinger (1980) on degrees of auxiliariness.

Ross's work has been severely taken to task. Geoffrey Pullum notes that:

> [Ross] has never been able to exhibit any phenomenon describable in terms of a truly well-behaved squish, one in which there really is a smooth gradient from A to B, with unblemished A-ness at the top left, unsullied B-ness at the bottom right, and no 'ill-behaved' cells of B-like qualities smack in the middle of the A's or vice versa. (Pullum 1976: 20)

Radford's (1976) proposal of an auxiliary–main verb squish is also dismissed. Pullum feels that 'none of [Radford's] material makes the "squishy categories" notion even remotely plausible, and that here, as probably in all other areas of syntax, squishes are a complete red herring, without descriptive or theoretical value of any kind' (Pullum 1976: 20). Instead of recognizing a squish, Pullum proposes a single category of verbs comprising both auxiliaries and main verbs. The peculiar properties of some of the verbs in this category are then handled in the lexicon.[10]

Additional criticism of Ross is expressed in Bever and Caroll (1981: 232–3). They reject grammatical gradience because they consider as misguided Ross's assumption that squishy data reflect a squishy grammatical architecture. Adopting a non-discrete grammar does not explain why squishy data obtain in the first place, they argue. Schütze (1996: 65) jumps to Ross's defence by retorting 'I do not see how one could ask for more of an account of "why the continua are the way they are" than Ross *et al.* provide, unless one already presupposes that the continua do not come from the grammar—language just *is* the way it is.' Bever and Caroll propose strict Aristotelian categories for grammar and explain squishiness effects by appealing to an 'interactionist framework' with behavioural explanations for the observed phenomena. As an example, they adduce the data below to add to Ross's nouniness squish:

(18)   *It bothers Herbie the whistling.

(19)   ??It bothers Herbie the whistling by Max.

Coupled with the observation that 'one of the fundamental goals in sentence perception is to isolate logically complete and coherent propositional sequences (e.g., subject–verb–object)' (Bever and Caroll 1981: 228), it follows that (19) is more acceptable than (18) because it is easier to process, since the string *the whistling by Max* is more clause-like than the string *the whistling*.

---

[10] Ironically, the 'auxiliaries as main verbs'-thesis was first put forward in Ross (1969*b*); see above. Pullum's position was further elaborated in Pullum and Wilson (1977). For further discussion of the auxiliary–main verb squish, see Chapter 5.

On the whole it is fair to say that in the history of linguistics 'squishiness was not a hit', as Harris (1993: 220) puts it, because Ross often did not succeed in much more than listing observations. His insights were often very valuable, though, and we will have cause to return to them later in this book.

In the early 1970s Lakoff took his cue predominantly from Ross and from Zadeh (1965) (see also Section 3.4.5) in developing his *fuzzy grammar*; cf. Lakoff (1973*a*, 1973*b*). In the second of these papers Lakoff aims to systematize Ross's observations, and looks at the factors that may influence the possible occurrence of adverb preposing. He then attempts to formalize some of the notions of fuzziness. At the end of his paper Lakoff is keen to counter a criticism that could be made of fuzzy grammar, namely that it is a performance phenomenon, not a competence phenomenon, and hence not really part of linguistics. He argues that the study of fuzzy phenomena is in the domain of rationalism and what he calls 'good-guy-empiricism', which is defined as follows:

The use of the empirical method, with 'observation' and 'experiment' broadly and sensibly construed to include native speakers' intuitions as the primary data of linguistics, to include what cannot occur as well as what can occur as primary data, and to restrict the use of texts, tape recordings, questionnaires, etc. to the place of secondary data at best, since such data is rife with mistakes, may or may not accord with speakers' intuitions, and does not show what is impossible. (Lakoff 1973*b*: 270)

For Lakoff '[i]n both fuzzy logic and fuzzy grammar, abstract linguistic rules have been formulated which require appeal to abstract fuzzy categories which do not themselves show up directly in the data but which are accorded the status of mental reality' (1973*b*: 290). Fuzzy grammar culminated in Lakoff (1987*a*). As we saw in Section 2.4.3, for McCawley logical categories have fuzzy syntactic counterparts which have semantic, 'internal syntactic' and 'external syntactic' dimensions. I will return to McCawley's work in Chapter 5.

3.4.5 *Logical approaches to linguistic vagueness: the Prague school, Zadeh, and Ross*

In Central Europe there was enormous interest in gradient phenomena in the 1960s. A number of very valuable papers were published by the Prague circle of linguists on cores and peripheries (Daneš 1966; Vachek 1966) and linguistic vagueness (Neustupný 1966). I have already mentioned Roman Jakobson in Section 3.4.1. Now often neglected, these papers were early attempts to be more precise about fuzziness in language, or, in the words of Daneš, 'to interpret the vagueness...in a non-vague manner' (1966: 14).

Daneš (1966: 12) proposes that linguistic elements be grouped in such a way that they are related to each other along a spectrum which shades from a Centre to a Periphery, and that there exists an area of overlap with a contiguous class called the Transition:

(20) Centre–Periphery–Transition

He gives a morphological example to demonstrate his point. English compounds can be identified using the criteria of stress, spelling, morphology, and meaning. Applying these criteria, we find that *blackboard* is centrally a compound because it has a peculiar stress pattern, it is spelt as one word, it morphologically behaves as a single word and it has a specialized meaning (such that e.g. there is no contradiction in talking about a *green blackboard*). The string *motor car* is less centrally a compound because of its 'regular' stress properties. (On compounds, see also Bauer 1998 and Giegerich 2004.)

More ambitious from a methodological point of view, Neustupný felt that

the main task of today's linguistics is to determine the full extent of vagueness, to analyse and explain it and to make possible the combination of its thorough consideration with the stream of the world linguistic tradition. (Neustupný 1966: 39; footnote omitted)

The term 'vagueness' is intended to cover a constellation of terms used by different linguists, some of which we have come across already, for example 'core', 'periphery', 'generality', and 'gradience'. Neustupný makes a distinction between what he calls *discourse vagueness* and *systemic vagueness*. The first term refers to vagueness amongst real-world objects (see Section 3.4.7 below), while the second term refers to vagueness within a system, such as language. In addition, Neustupný recognizes *approximation vagueness*, which obtains when a linguistic element starts to resemble another element (the example he gives is of marginal glottal stops resembling /h/), and *annihilation vagueness*. The latter obtains when a particular element approximates zero (for example, a glottal stop becoming almost unarticulated).

Neustupný's paper is an attempt to apply a 'logical theory of vagueness' to linguistic data (1966: 40f.), specifically that of Kubiński, from whose work Neustupný adopted the operators listed below:

ε   'is undoubtedly'; example: ε(xy) would mean 'x is undoubtedly y'
η   'is rather'; example: η(xyz) would mean 'x is rather y, than z'
ζ   'is rather something, than not-something'; example: ζ(xy) would mean 'x is rather y, than not-y'
ω   'to the same degree'; example: ω(xyz) would mean 'x is y and z to the same degree'

Neustupný exemplifies these operators linguistically by giving examples of how they might be used in a situation where there is an element whose wordhood is in doubt. For example, to express the fact that some element E is not clearly one word, nor clearly two words, but closer to being one word than being two, we can use the η-operator. The system illustrated in Figure 3.7 is offered (1966: 42):

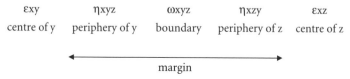

FIGURE 3.7 Neustupný's categorical system
Source: Neustupný (1966: 42)

Neustupný asserts that he is

convinced that by using the terms *vagueness, margin, boundary, periphery* and *centre* we come much closer in linguistics to the requirements of a dialectical way of thinking. 'Hard and fast lines', 'forcibly fixed boundary lines and differences in classes' are no longer prescribed to us as logical necessities.

Neustupný's model is attractive and promising, and my formalization of gradience in Chapter 8 will be seen to have affinities with it.

Another 'logical' approach to linguistic vagueness is found in the work of Lofti Zadeh (1965, 1987), who developed the notion of *fuzzy set theory*, which, as we have seen, influenced Lakoff (see e.g. Lakoff 1973a). Zadeh argued that membership of a set is not an either/or affair, but a matter of degree, and a fuzzy set is 'a class in which the transition from membership to non-membership is gradual rather than abrupt' (Zadeh 1972: 4).

Without mentioning Zadeh, Ross works out the idea of degrees of membership for the class of nouns. His 1973b nouniness squish, which was discussed in Section 3.4.4, is repeated here for convenience (Figure 3.8):

(21)

FIGURE 3.8 Ross's nouniness squish
Source: Ross (1973b: 141)

I also repeat examples of the cline:

(22) a. *that* = *that*-clauses (*that Max gave the letters to Frieda*)
   b. *for to* = *for* NP *to* V X (*for Max to have given the letters to Frieda*)
   c. Q = embedded questions (*how willingly Max gave the letters to Frieda*)
   d. *Acc Ing* = [[NP], [+ Acc]] V + *ing* X (*Max giving the letters to Frieda*)
   e. *Poss Ing* = NP's V+*ing* X (*Max's giving the letters to Frieda*)
   f. Action Nominal (*Max's/the giving of the letters to Frieda*)
   g. Derived Nominal (*Max's/the gift of the letters to Frieda*)
   h. Noun (*spatula*)

Ross proposes that

what is necessary is a relaxation of the claim that sequences of elements either are or are not members of some constituent class, like NP, V, S, etc. Rather I suggest, we must allow *membership to a degree*. Thus in particular, I propose that the previously used node S, sentence, be replaced by a feature [αS], where α ranges over the real numbers in [0,1]. Each of the complement types in [(22)] would be given a basic value of α, and rules, filters, and other types of semantic processes, would be given upper and lower threshold values of α between which they operate. (Ross 1973*b*: 188; footnote omitted)

He arrives at (23), which shows a 'degree of membership'-squish:

(23) *that* S   [1.0S]
      for to   [0.95S]
      Q   [0.86S]
      Acc Ing   [0.66S]
      Poss Ing   [0.43S]
      Action nominal   [0.15S]
      Derived nominal   [0.02S]
      N   [0.0S]

In Ross (1987, 2000) a mechanism for dealing with 'viability' is proposed:

The idea here is that it is possible for a sentence to deviate from a prototype, and yet not manifest any drop in acceptability. Losses in viability are cumulative, and only when there have been enough of them for a certain threshold value to be exceeded will the speakers of the language perceive that the sentence is less than perfect. (Ross 1987: 310)

Degrees of viability can be indicated using a 'viability prefix, P', such that on a scale '0 ≤ P ≤ 100, where if P is 50 or less, the sentence it prefixes will be heard as ungrammatical to various degrees (say, '?' ≤ 40, '??' ≤ 30, '?*' ≤ 20, '*' ≤ 10, '**' = 0), and if P is between 51 and 100, it will be given various degrees of syntactic well-being' (Ross 2000: 415).

Jackendoff (1983: 115f.) argues against the notion of 'degree of class membership'. In talking about birds he notes:

For instance, one might think of a typical bird such as a robin as 100% bird, but a penguin as perhaps only 71% bird and a bat as 45% bird. According to this view, the gradation of judgments is a consequence of the gradation of degree of membership, with values in the neighborhood of 50% resulting in the most difficult judgments. (The mathematics of fuzzy sets is developed in Zadeh (1965); the notion was popularized in linguistics by Lakoff (197[3*b*]).)

One difficulty with this view (pointed out to me by John Macnamara) is that a penguin is not 71% bird and 29% something else, it just *is* a bird. It may not be a typical bird, but it is still no less a bird than a robin or a sparrow is. One might respond by trying to interpret the percentages in terms of degree of confidence of judgment. But this makes the second objection only more patent: the theory provides no account of where the percentages might have come from. To derive the one-dimensional degree of membership, one needs a theory of the internal structure of the concepts in question—which is what we are trying to develop in the first place. Fuzzy set theory at best gives only a crude way to describe observations about category judgments; it does not even purport to address the mechanism behind them.

I will also argue in this book that linguistic formatives, while showing degrees of form class prototypicality, do not display degrees of class membership.

3.4.6 *Descriptive grammar*

As we saw in the last chapter, Otto Jespersen favoured an Aristotelian approach to categorization. Other grammarians did not. The American descriptive linguist George Curme, although he does not use the term 'gradience', described the phenomenon of overlap between categories. As an example, consider his discussion of the element *stone* in the noun phrase *a stone bridge* or *boy* in *a boy actor* (1935: 43f.). Curme argued that *stone* is a noun used as an adjective. In the NP *the above remark* the element *above* is said to be an adverb used as an adjective. Curme's description could be said to be a way of dealing with the perceived dual categorial nature of the prenominal elements in question: positionally and functionally they behave like adjectives, while formally they look like a noun and an adverb, respectively. Curme also discusses what he calls *adjective elements*, for example *John's* in *John's book*. These are said to have the force of adjectives, although cannot formally be classed as such. Although Curme does not use the term, it appears that we have a cline here from indisputable adjectives (like *happy, beautiful,* etc.) to nouns used as adjectives (e.g. *stone* in *stone bridge*). Somewhere in between are elements like *John's* in *John's book*:

happy (man) > *John's* (book) > *stone* (bridge)

Adjective >>>>>>>>>>>>>>>>>> Noun

We saw above that in the early 1960s in the United States there appeared to be two strands of thinking, one which regarded linguistics as more and more mathematical (hence 'mathematical linguistics', cf. Plath 1961), and one which stressed a less rigorous approach to linguistic categories and their boundaries. This methodological rift[11] is paralleled by the opposing concerns of linguists such as Chomsky who are interested in I-language, and those who are concerned with E-language, such as the earliest corpus constructors Nelson Francis at Brown University in the USA, and Randolph Quirk at University College London. Quirk (1965) bemoans the 'rigid discreteness' of the post-Bloomfieldians and takes the notion of gradience seriously. Like Halliday, he attempted to be more precise about relationships between elements. The principal topic of the paper is the existence of *serial relationships* between elements. The concept of a serial relationship is akin to the concept of gradience, but not quite the same. For that reason it will be discussed in more detail in Chapter 4.

David Crystal in a well-known article from 1967 used matrices to describe the optimal way to define the word classes in English. He argues that the best way to define a word class is by listing the phonological, morphological, lexical, semantic, and syntactic criteria that pertain to it. The syntactic criteria are paramount. A mere list of criteria, however, is not enough. They need to be graded. Crystal proposes a statistical approach, whereby the criterion that applies to most instances of a particular word class, and least to others, should rank highest. As an example of gradience between adverbs and adjectives he lists a number of criteria for adjectivehood and adverbhood and shows that items like *clear, interesting, regular*, etc. are central adjectives, and elements like *gradually, usually, clearly*, etc. are central adverbs, while other items can only be labelled as peripheral adjectives or adverbs. There will always be items which form part of what Crystal calls *bridge classes* (1967: 50). Such items are not assignable straightforwardly to one class or another, but display characteristics of more than one class. Crystal also gives an example of what I have termed Subsective Gradience in this book, within the class of nouns. I will discuss it in Chapter 5.

Three British linguists for whom the notion of dependency is central take the notion of grammatical indeterminacy in one guise or another seriously. Matthews (1981: 221f.), in describing the notion of dependency, distinguishes

---

[11] See also Section 3.4.3

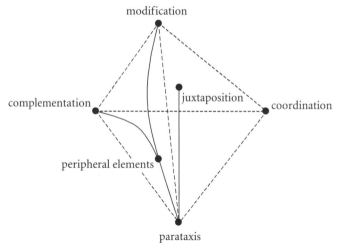

FIGURE 3.9 Matthews's tetrahedron
Source: Matthews (1981: 223)

between two types: modification and complementation. Neutral between the two are what he terms *peripheral elements*. Modification, complementation, and peripheral elements on the one hand are distinguished from coordination and simple juxtaposition on the other. This situation is graphically represented in the shape of a tetrahedron (Figure 3.9):

Parataxis in this representation is understood in the Bloomfieldian sense as two or more elements that are not related syntactically, but only intonationally (Matthews 1981: 32, 220). Matthews's model allows us to position the PP *for three hours* in *The race lasted for three hours* somewhere on the line between modification and peripheral elements, and *please* in *Could you please keep quiet?* somewhere in between parataxis and peripheral elements. The notion of gradience is used by Matthews to discuss the set of sentences below, where the functional status of the sentence-final PP is at issue (1981: 236–7):

(24)   I told it to my brother.
(25)   I dispatched it to my brother.
(26)   I carted it to Manchester.
(27)   I pedalled it to Manchester.
(28)   I wore it to Manchester.

In (24) *to my brother* is regarded as a complement, because the individual referred to by the NP is a participant of the process of telling. In (28) the PP is clearly a peripheral element. (26) is in between: you have to cart something somewhere, and the PP could be said to be a participant and a locative at the same time. The PP in (25) also resembles a complement and an adjunct. It differs from the PP in (26) by virtue of the fact that *my brother* is more participant-like than *Manchester.* (27) is positioned between (26) and (28) on Matthews's gradient because, although you can pedal something somewhere, it is not clear that the presence of a directional PP is required.

Dick Hudson's Word Grammar framework accommodates the notion of prototypes by making use of the *Best Fit Principle,* which is formulated as follows:

An experience E is interpreted as an instance of some concept C if more information can be inherited about E from C than from any alternative to C. (Hudson 1990: 47)

This approach allows for a particular element X to be assigned to a class Y, even if it does not display all the characteristics of that class. Thus 'a three-legged cat is still a cat, though not a prototypical one. The Best Fit Principle means that we condone a shortage of legs because of the lack of any better match' (Hudson 1990: 47).

More recently Anderson (1997) has worked on categorization and gradience. He sets up a 'minimal categorial system' of word classes as follows:

{P}   {N}   {N,P}   { }
verb   name   noun   functor

This classification is based not only on the fact that verbs are 'event specific', while nouns are 'entity-specific', but also on the 'predicativity/predicability' of verbs (indicated by the feature 'P') and the 'referentiality/referentiability' of nouns (indicated by the feature 'N'). For English and some other languages the system is modified (Anderson 1997: 59–60) as follows:

{P}   {P;N}   {P:N}   {N;P }   {N}   { }
aux   verb   adjective   noun   name   functor

Names are typical arguments which refer, but are never predicative. Nouns are considered intermediate between verbs and names: they are also typical arguments, but, unlike names, they can be predicative, hence the conjunction of the features 'N' and 'P'. Nouns and verbs are universal categories which can have central and peripheral members. Anderson notes that 'the notional characterization of further categories involves the interaction of just these two features'. The notation '{A;B}' signifies that a category is characterized by the features A and B, with A being the more dominant, that is, B is dependent on A. In '{A:B}' the features combine and are mutually dependent. As for gradience, for Anderson:

Categorial properties 'leak', but arguably in an orderly, hierarchical fashion. Not only is it possible in principle to distinguish non-central members of the word classes, but also, among these, there can be some which show properties more centrally associated with another minimally distinct class; moreover, these properties may even spread to more remote classes, but less so. (Anderson 1997: 73)

This echoes the Sapirean 'All grammars leak'. Anderson distinguishes what he calls 'strong gradience' from 'relative gradience'. The former is the type of gradience proposed by Bolinger where there is an indefinite number of intermediate points between two points on a cline. The latter is exemplified in Anderson's gradient shown below (1997: 72), which displays 'cardinal points':

4P::oN	3P::1N	2P::2N	1P::3N	oP::4N	oP,oN
aux	verb	adjective	noun	name	functor

As we have seen, 'P' and 'N' stand for the features 'Predicativity' and 'Nominal/referential'. In the representation above, each word class is defined in terms of the 'preponderance' (Anderson 1997: 72) of the features 'Predicativity' and 'Nominal/referential', expressed by the integers, determined as follows:

X alone = 4   X; = 3   X: = 2   ;X = 1   absence of X = 0

Gradience plays an important role in the grammars of the Quirk school, although it principally makes its way into the later of the two co-authored large grammars, Quirk *et al.* (1972) and Quirk *et al.* (1985). Here a gradient is defined as 'a scale which relates two categories of description (for example two word classes) in terms of degrees of similarity and contrast' (Quirk *et al.* 1985: 90). For Quirk *et al.* gradience is everywhere in grammar, not only amongst form and function categories such as main and auxiliary verbs, prepositions and conjunctions, active and passive sentences, subjuncts and adjuncts, subject complements and restrictive adjuncts, but also between semantic categories like extrinsic and intrinsic modality, stative and dynamic meaning, etc. Very often the existence of gradience between categories is only hinted at, or suggested by grammatical terminology prefixed by such elements as *semi-*, *quasi-*, *pseudo-*, etc.[12] A concrete example of gradience in Quirk *et al.* (1985) concerns the purported shading into each other of coordinative and subordinative structures. It will be discussed in detail in Chapter 7.

There are also a number of descriptive grammars in the functional tradition that make use of notions like prototype in their treatment of the structure of English; see for example Givón (1993).

---

[12] See also Biber *et al.*, e.g. on semi-determiners (1999: 280f.).

With the exception of Matthews (1981) and Quirk *et al.* (1985), many descriptive grammarians do not always *implement* the notion of grammatical indeterminacy in their work, at least not the intercategorial variety. Some note its existence, but in the end opt to approach the categories in an Aristotelian fashion. As an example, consider Rodney Huddleston's (1984: 93f.) discussion of the element *boy* in the phrase *boy actor* from George Curme's 1935 *Grammar of the English Language* (see Section 3.4.6). While Huddleston recognizes the existence of indeterminacy in grammar (at least in his 1984 grammar, as we saw in the previous chapter), for him *boy* in *boy actor* is a noun, and its modifying function does not turn it into an adjective, or even a 'noun used as an adjective', as Curme would have it. In Huddleston's account there is a clear desire to make an unambiguous choice to resolve the perceived dual character of *boy* in *boy actor*: it must be either a noun *or* an adjective. It cannot be allowed to be something in between. A further example occurs in a discussion of the distinction between verbs and nouns in Huddleston and Pullum *et al.* (2002: 81–2):

(29)   Destroying the files was a serious mistake.

Here *destroying*, traditionally called a gerund, is 'functionally comparable to a noun' (Huddleston and Pullum *et al.* 2002: 81) in resembling the word *destruction* in the phrase *the destruction of the file*. However,

the functional resemblance between *destroying* in [(29)] and the noun *destruction* is not at the level of words but at the level of the larger constituents that they head— between the clause *destroying the files* and the NP *the destruction of the files* rather than between the verb *destroying* and the noun *destruction*. At the level of the word, verb and noun are *quite sharply distinct* by virtue of the different dependents they take. (Huddleston and Pullum *et al.* 2002: 82; my emphasis, BA)

Thus, Huddleston (1984) and Huddleston and Pullum *et al.* (2002), in discussing borderline cases between grammatical categories, each time sever the categorial Gordian knot in an Aristotelian fashion by deciding that the elements in question must belong to one or another category. Huddleston does seem to allow for gradience within categories (i.e. what I call Subsective Gradience, SG) in setting up criterial properties for the various word classes which a particular element can satisfy to a greater or lesser extent. Thus he models a gradient for past participles (1984: 324) which 'illustrate well the tendency for the parts of speech to be very clearly different at their centres but much less easily distinguishable at their margins. We can range them on a scale from most verbal to most adjectival with at least three intermediate positions.' Huddleston and Pullum *et al.* (2002) also allow for SG (see e.g. footnote 2 in Chapter 5).

3.4.7 *Cognitive approaches*

Aristotle, apart from theorizing about categories, also thought about how they might be represented in the mind:

[s]peech is not the same for all men, any more than writing is, but the mental feelings for which words are signs, *are* the same for all, and likewise the things (*pragmata*) of which those feelings are symbols. (*De Interpretatione*, quoted in Householder 1995: 95)

According to Vivian Salmon, this thinking influenced seventeenth-century scholars such as John Wilkins in his *An Essay towards a real character, and a philosophical language* (1668). Consider the passage below:

As men do generally agree in the same Principle of Reason, so do they likewise agree in the same *Internal Notion* or *Apprehension of things....* That *conceit* which men have in their minds concerning a Horse or Tree, is the Notion or *mental Image* of the Beast, or natural thing. (Quoted in Salmon 1979: 107)

These sentiments quite remarkably prefigure current thinking in certain strands of psychology and linguistics, which is fuelled by a dissatisfaction with the classical model of categorization that has led psychologists and linguists to re-evaluate it. Within cognitive linguistics *Prototype Theory* (PT) holds that categories cannot be defined along Aristotelian principles, but that instead we should recognize that membership of a particular category may be a matter of more-or-less, rather than all-or-none. The seeds for the concept of a prototype in linguistic categorization are ancient, as the quotations above show, and various linguists have alluded to the idea. Thus, Jespersen (1924: 63) remarked that '[r]eality never presents us with an average object, but language does, for instead of denoting one actually given thing[,] a word like *apple* represents the average of a great many objects that have something, but of course not everything, in common.' Other precursors are Wittgenstein (see Section 3.2) and Berlin and Kay, who worked on colour terms (Berlin and Kay 1969).

However, PT only became prominent through the work of the psychologist Eleanor Rosch (1973*a*, 1973*b*, 1975, 1978). She showed that prototypes of real-world objects play a role in cognition, and are characterized by a number of perceived representative attributes, cf. Rosch (1978: 36). These attributes are not to be regarded as primitive components, but rather as 'dimensions along which different entities are regarded as similar' (Taylor 2003: 67). The experimental technique employed by Rosch and later researchers, to demonstrate prototype effects, involved the use of questionnaires in which subjects were asked to judge if a particular entity was a good or bad exemplar of a particular category (Rosch 1978: 36). Rosch is careful to stress that prototypes cannot be identified with specific members of particular categories, nor with a structure in the mind:

To speak of *a prototype* at all is simply a convenient grammatical fiction; what is really referred to are judgments of degree of prototypicality. Only in some artificial categories is there by definition a literal single prototype.... For natural-language categories, to speak of a single entity that is the prototype is either a gross misunderstanding of the empirical data or a covert theory of mental representation.... Prototypes do not constitute a theory of representation of categories. (Rosch 1978: 40)

Lakoff (1987*a*: 43ff.) discusses this point at some length and observes that 'prototypes act as *cognitive reference points* of various sorts and form the basis for inferences' (emphasis in original). Lakoff speaks of *prototype effects* which are superficial. He elaborates on the passage by Rosch by pointing out (1987*b*/1999: 391) that there are two common misconceptions regarding prototype effects: one is that the effects are given a structural interpretation (the 'Effects = Structure Interpretation'), such that goodness-of-example judgements are seen to directly reflect degrees of categorial membership. The other misconception is what he calls the 'Prototype = Representation Interpretation' (1987*b*/1999: 391), which states that categories are mentally represented making reference to prototypes. Much of the research in psychology subsequent to Rosch has been concerned with concepts (Murphy 2002).

Other well-known work in the 1970s on prototypes is Labov's (1973) psycho/sociolinguistic study, which was concerned with both categorization and the denotation of words. Labov studied terms used for drinking vessels such as those shown in Figure 3.10, and found in experiments that vessels with particular dimensions and shapes are more likely to be judged cups than objects with slightly different characteristics. Thus, a relatively shallow vessel with a handle and a small circumference (e.g. item 1 below) is likely to be called a cup, whereas a vessel with a wider circumference (e.g. item 4) is much more likely to be called a bowl. Labov also discovered that what is inside the containers influences the way in which subjects categorize them. Thus item 3 is more likely to be called a cup if it has coffee in it, a bowl if it contains mashed potato.

Recall that in Chapter 2 we discussed basic level categories. How does the notion of a basic level category relate to the notion of prototypes? The distinction is not all that clear. Rosch *et al.* (1976: 433) observe that prototypicality effects were observed at different levels of categorization, including superordinate and basic level categories in natural language, and that 'prototypes of categories appear to follow the same principles as basic categories'. Taylor (2003: 53) suggests that prototypes are the central members at the basic level.

Towards the end of the twentieth century the notion of prototype was applied more and more to linguistic categories and entities. An example of work done in the PT framework is Bybee and Moder's (1983) research on

FIGURE 3.10 Labov's vessels
Source: Labor (1973: 354)

prototypes amongst English strong verbs, which led them to claim that 'speakers of natural language form categorizations of linguistic objects in the same way that they form categorizations of natural and cultural objects' (1983: 267). Similarly Lakoff held that

[l]inguistic categories, like conceptual categories, show prototype effects. Such effects occur at every level of language, from phonology to morphology to syntax to the lexicon. I take the existence of such effects as prima facie evidence that linguistic categories have the same character as other conceptual categories. (Lakoff 1987a: 67)

Another application of PT to linguistic entities is Taylor's (2003: 202f.) discussion of the notions 'word', 'affix', and 'clitic' in linguistics. There are many others, which I will have cause to discuss in later chapters.

Wierzbicka criticizes linguists for using PT as an all-too-convenient concept in discussing the usage and meaning of particular words which are difficult to pin down precisely:

As Aristotle observed twenty-four centuries ago, it is very hard to construct a good definition of any concept. A great many scholars who had tried to construct definitions themselves, or who had critically considered other people's definitions, felt dissatisfied with them, and, as a result, lost faith in the very possibility of constructing adequate definitions of any concepts. When the notion of prototype became part of the semantic agenda and when it emerged that prototypes were apparently as easy to work with as definitions had been difficult, they gave a great sigh of relief and hailed the Prototype as the saviour of semantics. In fact, once the notion of prototype started to be used as a skeleton key which can open all semantic doors, it came to be used widely even in those cases where a definition would not really be difficult to construct at all. By resorting to prototypes, even the modest effort needed to construct a valid definition could be dispensed with, and a pseudodefinition based on the notion of prototype could be adopted instead. (Wierzbicka 1989: 736–7)

She criticizes Verschueren (1985) for suggesting that the definition of a *boat* as 'a man-made object that can be used for travelling on water' should be amended for boats with holes to 'a man-made object that can normally be used for travelling on water, but in which there can also be a hole', that is allowing for more or less prototypical boats. Wierzbicka argues instead that the definition of *boat* should read 'a kind of thing *made for* travelling on water'. See also Wierzbicka (1990) where, using the slogan 'prototypes save', she works out the idea that prototypes present meretricious solutions to definitional problems. For further criticisms of Prototype Theory, see Bouchard (1995) and Newmeyer (1998), to whose work I will return in later chapters.

3.4.8 *Functional-typological and discourse-typological linguistics*

For functional-typological scholars and discourse-typological linguists, prototypes and blurred categorial boundaries play an important role. Here I will look in some more detail at the role of gradience in these frameworks.

As we saw in the previous chapter, Givón (1984: 51f.) regards prototypical nouns as concrete, solid entities, whereas verbs denote rapid changes in the universe, that is, they are prototypically events and actions. He sets up a *time-stability scale* for nouns, adjectives, and verbs, with nouns being the most time stable, and verbs the least time stable. Adjectives take an intermediate position.

Hopper and Thompson (1980) claim that transitivity is a clausal property and that there exist 'degrees of transitivity'. They isolate the following nine (semantic) parameters of transitivity: PARTICIPANTS, ASPECT, PUNCTUALITY, VOLITIONALITY, AFFIRMATION, MODE, AGENCY, AFFECTEDNESS OF O[BJECT], INDIVIDUATION OF O[BJECT]. 'Taken together, they allow clauses to be characterized as more or less Transitive' (1980: 253). Thus, for example, a clause with two participants is more transitive than a clause with only one participant. Similarly, a clause which involves an agent which is 'high in potency' is more transitive than a clause whose agent is 'low in potency'. With these observations in mind, a clause like *Jerry likes beer* is less transitive than *Jerry knocked Sam down*. For a differently conceived transitive prototype, see Rice (1987).

Croft deals with blurred categories under the heading of 'boundary cases' (1991: 19). He remarks:

Our point here is simply that the clear-cut boundaries that the formalist method seeks to discover do not appear to exist in many places, and different linguists have 'let the grammar decide' in different ways. A legitimate question to ask is, Are the controversies that are generated by trying to draw a sharp distinction between, say, verb and auxiliary illuminating or obscuring the nature of language?

The functionalist answer is that they do obscure the nature of language. In the functionalist view, linguists should recognize the boundary status of the cases in question and try to understand why they are boundary cases. Boundary cases play an important role in the functionalist methodology. (Croft 1991: 23)

Croft discusses a number of examples of boundary cases, among them the passive or passive-like constructions in a number of languages.

3.4.9 *Optimality Theory*

Optimality Theory (OT) is a recent approach to the study of language, which allows the output representations of a given candidate set to be ranked against a set of violable criteria. The candidate which violates the least highly ranked criterion is 'optimal' and wins out. For recent overviews, see Barbosa *et al.* (1998), Kager (1999), Boersma *et al.* (2000), McCarthy (2001), Legendre *et al.* (2001), and Prince and Smolensky (2004).

Battistella (1996: 91) observes that OT may eventually be able to deal with certain markedness phenomena. As we will see in the next chapter, he has observed that there exists no theory of markedness, although Boersma *et al.* (2000: 2) claim that OT is just such a theory. Within the OT framework there have already been proposals to deal with gradience as manifested through the phenomenon of 'degrees of grammaticality'. Thus, in the extended OT framework proposed in Keller (1997, 1998, 2000) a ranking of candidates in terms of their degree of grammaticality is envisaged. He uses extraction phenomena from picture noun phrases (PNPS) as a case study. According to Keller, extraction from PNPS is constrained not only by the definiteness of the picture NP, as Kluender (1992) has argued (see Section 3.4.3), but also by the semantics of the matrix verb (extraction is easier if the matrix verb is a state verb) and the referentiality of the extracted NP (extraction is easier from non-referential NPs). Violations of these and a number of other constraints yield a ranking of candidates in terms of their degree of grammaticality which is claimed to confirm elicitation experiments conducted by Keller. See also Hayes's (2000) attempt to model gradient well-formedness in the OT framework and Boersma and Hayes (2001). Sorace and Keller (2005) provide a useful overview of theoretical and empirical work on degrees of grammaticality. In this book I will not deal further with gradience in acceptability/grammaticality. Instead, as noted in Chapter 1, the focus is on gradience conceived as 'categorial indeterminacy'.[13]

3.4.10 *Probability Theory*

Probability Theory is an emerging theory of language which argues that linguists must make use of the notion of probability to explain linguistic facts:

Language displays all the hallmarks of a probabilistic system. Categories and well-formedness are gradient, and frequency effects are everywhere. We believe all evidence points to a probabilistic language faculty. Knowledge of language should be understood not as a minimal set of categorical rules or constraints, but as a (possibly redundant) set of gradient rules, which may be characterized by a statistical distribution. (Bod, Hay, and Jannedy 2003: 10)

Manning (2003: 297) discusses stochastic syntax and criticizes 'categorical linguistics' both for insisting on hard boundaries for categories, as well as for explaining too little. As an example of the first problem he shows that the claims that most syntacticians make regarding subcategorization phenomena are in need of revision. He looks at the subcategorization frames for a number of verbs, including *consider* and *regard*, and the way they are presented in Pollard and Sag (1994). The subcategorization frames discussed in this book only cover the main patterns that are possible for these verbs, ignoring less common patterns.

The important question is how we should solve this problem: Within a categorical linguistics, there is no choice but to say that the previous model was overly restrictive and that these other subcategorization frames should also be admitted for the verbs in

---

[13] For a collection of articles on gradience conceived as indeterminacy in grammaticality/ acceptability judgements, see Fanselow *et al.* (2006).

question. But if we do that, we lose a lot. For we are totally failing to capture the fact that the subcategorization frames that Pollard and Sag do not recognize are extremely rare, whereas the ones they give encompass the common subcategorization frames of the verbs in question. We can get a much better picture of what is going on by estimating a probability mass function (pmf) over the subcategorization patterns for the verbs in question. (Manning 2003: 300–1)

Manning did this for the verb *regard*, and found that all of the patterns in (30) are attested in his corpus, but that the last four were quite infrequent, and that the first was by far the most frequently used pattern.

(30)   [—, NP as NP]
       [—, NP as AP]
       [—, NP as VP [ing]]
       [—, NP as PP]
       [—, NP NP]
       [—, NP VP [inf]]

Manning criticizes Pollard and Sag for taking arbitrary grammaticality decisions. For them only the first four subcategorization patterns of those shown above are grammatical. Facts such as those discovered by Manning demand a more flexible approach to complementation facts. Whereas stochastic models of syntax offer a mechanism for this, categorical models have no way of dealing with them.

As for Manning's second point that categorical models do not explain enough, his argument centres on constraints: some linguistic phenomena are subject to hard constraints in some languages, but are subject to soft constraints in others. Such facts can be explained in a model that can deal with constraints that vary in strength, but not in categorical frameworks.

Quantitative data can demonstrate that a language exhibits soft generalizations corresponding to what are categorical generalizations in other languages. A probabilistic model can then model the strength of these preferences, their interaction with each other, and their interaction with other principles of grammar. By giving variable outputs for the same input, it can predict the statistical patterning of the data. Beyond this, the model allows us to connect such soft constraints with the categorical restrictions that exist in other languages, naturally capturing that they are reflections of the same underlying principles. This serves to effectively link typological and quantitative evidence. (Manning 2003: 325)

Other interesting quantitative approaches to gradience can be found in Gries (2003), Forbes (2006), and Bresnan and Hay (2006).

3.4.11 *Other frameworks: Phrase Structure Grammar, Word Grammar,*
       Lexical-Functional Grammar, and Construction Grammar

Pullum (1991*b*) offers a Generalized Phrase Structure Grammar (GPSG) account of English gerunds, or *Nominal Gerund Phrases* (NGP), as he calls them, of the type *your breaking the record*. He discusses a large number of properties of the gerund, the most salient of which, as has often been observed, is that gerunds display both nominal and verbal characteristics. Specifically, their external distribution is nominal, while their internal syntax is verbal. Pullum offers a solution to the categorial and representational problems posed by NGPs which posits that they are NPs headed by a VP. The NGP *your breaking the record* is analysed thus:

(31)

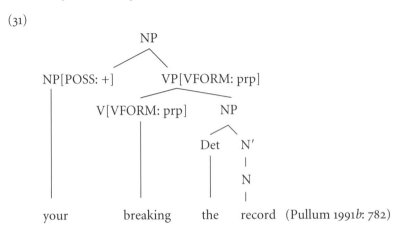

your   breaking   the   record   (Pullum 1991*b*: 782)

The fact that this structure violates the Head Feature Convention (HFC) of GPSG (which stipulates that the head features of a mother node must be the same as the head features on a daughter node functioning as head) is handled by the rule shown below (Pullum 1991*b*: 779):

(32)   N[BAR:2] → (N[BAR:2, POSS: +1]), H[VFORM:prp]
       where N[BAR: 2] is an NP, and H[VFORM:prp] is a present participle
       functioning as head

An absolute Feature Cooccurrence Restriction which says that VFORMs are verbs then overrides the HFC and ensures that the head is a verb, not a noun. GPSG thus allows for 'single-headed constructions with heterocategorial heads' (Pullum 1991*b*: 789). However, heterocategoriality is constrained, as Pullum explains:

[C]ontrary to what some have suggested concerning clines of properties from category to category (see for example Ross 1972, 1973[b]), we would not expect to find
arbitrary mixtures of syntactic characteristics from different categories in any constituent type. Instead, the phrasal head of some types of phrase may be sharply and
consistently of different type from the type we would expect from the usual effects of
the head-feature convention. In those cases where the grammar enforces a special
value for N or V on a head, we would get not an odd blend of syntactic properties but
rather a head with sharply and consistently different behavior from what would be
expected. (Pullum 1991b: 790)

In the same spirit as Pullum's account, Blevins (2005) proposes an analysis
that allows gerunds to be categorially underspecified in the lexicon. They
are then 'resolved' in the syntax, such that *signing* surfaces as a noun
in *Their signing of the treaty*, but as a verb in *Their signing the treaty*.
However, both structures overall are nominal. The latter is represented in
Figure 3.11.

A drawback of both Pullum's account and Blevins's account is that they
allow for exocentric phrases.[14]

Recent work in GPSG offshoot Head-driven Phrase Structure Grammar
(HPSG) recognizes mixed-category constructions, that is, constructions that
involve lexical items that belong to more than one category at the same time.
Malouf (2000a: 153) treats the English gerund as a mixed-category construction, and implements the insight that gerunds are nominal in their external
syntax and verbal in their internal syntax through a cross-classification of
head values (Figure 3.12) (see also Malouf 2000b):

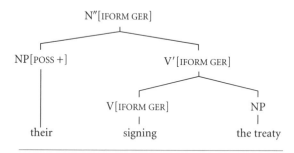

FIGURE 3.11 *Their signing the treaty*
Source: Blevins (2005: 34)

---

[14] Blevins (2005: 31f.) refers to this as 'principled exocentricity'.

(33)

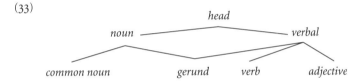

FIGURE 3.12 Malouf's mixed categories

In this representation gerunds are both a subtype of 'noun', and a subtype of the category 'verbal'. This ensures on the one hand that Verbal Gerund Phrases (VGerPs) behave syntactically like nominals. On the other hand this analysis will ensure that VGerPs are modified by adverbs (just like the other relational categories verbs and adjectives) and not by adjectives, which modify only common nouns. Also, the analysis brings out that VGerPs do not distribute like VPs, because the gerund is analysed as being a category in its own right, not as being verbal. In order further to account for the fact that verbal gerunds have the same complement-taking properties as the verbs from which they are derived, and to ensure that gerundial subjects are optional and can be in the genitive or accusative form, Malouf adds the following lexical rule (2000*a*: 153):

(34)

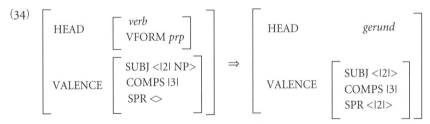

FIGURE 3.13 Malouf's lexical rule

This rule changes the -*ing* form of a verb into a gerund.[15]

Dick Hudson's (2003) Word Grammar (WG) account bears similarities to Malouf's analysis. In his example *We were talking about John having a sabbatical* the word *having* 'must be a verb, in fact an example of the ordinary verb HAVE, because it has a bare subject and a bare direct object and it can be modified by *not* or an adverb' (2003: 580). But 'it must also be a noun because the phrase that it heads is used as the object of a preposition (*about*), and

---

[15] Similar to mixed categories are Lapointe's (1993) *dual lexical categories* of the form $< X \mid Y >^0$ where both X and Y are lexical categories, and where X determines the external syntax of the phrase headed by X | Y, while Y determines its internal syntax (see Malouf 2000*b*: 59–60 for discussion).

could be used in any other position where plain noun phrases are possible'
(2003: 580). He goes on to say:

As nouns, gerunds contrast with common nouns, proper nouns and pronouns, all of
which are word-classes—i.e., classes of lexemes. The same is not true of their relationship to verbs, where gerunds differ from other verbs in their inflections. Any verb
which can be non-finite (i.e., any verb other than a modal and a handful of full verbs
such as BEWARE) can be a gerund, but gerunds are distinguished by their inflectional
suffix *-ing*. In WG, 'Inflection' and 'Lexeme' are sub-categories of 'Word', so an
inflected lexeme inherits from both an inflection and a lexeme (Creider and Hudson
1999). (Hudson 2003: 599)

This is illustrated by the following diagram from Hudson's article:

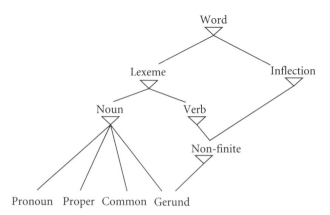

FIGURE 3.14 Hudson's model

For a critical discussion of this account, see Aarts (forthcoming). I will return
to gerunds in Chapters 6 and 8.

In Lexical Functional Grammar (LFG) Bresnan (1997) deals with mixed
categories by allowing for head sharing between categories, such that at the
level of LFG's c-structure (constituent/categorical structure) the categories in
question have different heads, while they share heads at f-structure (functional structure). See also Bresnan and Mugane (2006).

As we saw in Chapter 2, in Goldberg's (2006) Cognitive Construction
Grammar framework the scholastic conception of the categories is rejected.
Instead, prototype theory plays a prominent role. As an example, Goldberg
proposes an account of subject–auxiliary inversion (SAI) in terms of a
functional prototype (2006: 166–82). Regarding the function of SAI she
notes that

there are attributes that hold of the prototypical case, and conventional extensions of the prototype systematically differ from the prototype in displaying only a subset of the relevant attributes. On the basis of the distribution of SAI constructions, it is further suggested that the dominant attribute of SAI is NON-POSITIVE; this attribute of SAI constructions serves to motivate the form of the construction. (Goldberg 2006: 170)

3.5 Two types of gradience

In this book I will argue that a distinction should be made between two types of gradience, which I will call *Subsective Gradience* (SG) and *Intersective Gradience* (IG), respectively. SG involves a single particular class of linguistic elements, or a particular construction-type, whereas IG involves two classes of elements or construction-types. SG allows for a particular element x from category α to be closer to the prototype of α than some other element y from the same category, and recognizes a core and periphery within the form classes of language. By contrast, IG involves two categories α and β, and obtains where there exists a set γ of elements characterized by a subset of α-like properties and a subset of β-like properties. Classes α and β are said to 'converge' by virtue of the fact that there exist elements which display properties of both categories. Importantly, though, I will argue that α and β themselves are strictly bounded, and do not overlap. We do not therefore have elements that can be said to belong to both α and β at the same time. The intersection is between γ and the full set of α-like properties, and between γ and the full set of β-like properties.

The position I will defend in this book is that both Subsective Gradience and Intersective Gradience are widespread phenomena in grammar. In Chapters 5–7 I will discuss a number of case studies of SG and IG conceived as 'categorial indeterminacy', and I will propose a simple and elegant formalization of SG and IG that will take a mid-way position between proponents of the 'gradience-is-everywhere'-thesis and the categorizationalists. The issues discussed in this book have wider implications for the study of language, in that they pertain to the exploration of the tension between generally rigid linguistic concepts and the continuous phenomena they describe.

The next chapter will contrast the notion of gradience with a number of related notions.

4

Gradience and Related Notions

4.1 Introduction

The notion of gradience as defined in previous chapters bears a resemblance to a number of other phenomena in language. In this chapter I will discuss how gradience compares with related notions/ideas, some of which we have already come across fleetingly in earlier chapters.

4.2 Serial relationship

Quirk (1965) investigated a way of visually representing what he called a *serial relationship* (SR) between categories. In Quirk's words:

An item a_n in any set of structures whose similarity we are studying must be analysed in such a way as to demonstrate (1) all the features it shares with a_{n-1} in the set, (2) the features which make it unique, and (3) the features shared with the item a_{n+1}. The kind of overlapping gradience plotted for *x*, *y*, and *z* [in Table 4.1] constitutes what we have come to call 'serial relationship', and *z* would be said to be serially related to *x* on the one hand and to *y* on the other. (Quirk 1965: 210)

Table 4.1 visualizes the serial relationship between the elements x, y, and z, which is obscured in its notationally rearranged, but otherwise equivalent, counterpart Table 4.2.

Quirk's paper offers an example of an SR among verbs, shown in Table 4.3.

TABLE 4.1 An example of a serial relationship

	6	8	5	3	2	4	1	7
x	+	+	+	+	−	−	−	−
z	−	−	+	+	+	+	−	−
y	−	−	−	+	+	+	+	+

TABLE 4.2 Table 4.1 rearranged

	1	2	3	4	5	6	7	8
x	−	−	+	−	+	+	−	+
y	+	+	+	+	−	−	+	−
z	−	+	+	+	+	−	−	−

TABLE 4.3 A serial relationship in the verbal domain

	1	2	3	4	5	6	7	8
pretend	+	+	+	?	−	−	−	−
feel	?	+	+	+	+	?	−	−
say	+	+	+	−	+	−	−	−
know	−	+	+	+	+	−	−	−
find	−	+	+	?	+	+	?	+
think	+	+	+	+	+	+	+	+
declare	−	+	+	+	+	+	+	+
regard	−	−	?	?	?	+	?	?
like	−	−	+	+	−	?	−	−
persuade	−	−	−	+	+	−	−	−
make	−	−	−	−	+	+	+	+
call	−	−	−	−	−	+	+	+
elect	−	−	−	−	−	−	−	+

The verbs in Table 4.3 are classified with regard to the following frames:

1. They V so.
2. They V that he is Adj.
3. It is Ved that he is Adj.
4. They V him to be Adj.
5. He is Ved to be Adj.
6. They V him Adj.
7. He is Ved Adj.
8. They V him N.[1]

An interesting claim that the paper makes is that constructions containing certain verbs, such as *say* in *He is said to be very clever*, are possibly derived from similar constructions containing serially related verbs, in this case *feel* and *know* (cf. *He is felt/known to be very clever*), rather than from a non-existing

---

[1] Quirk notes that N and *him* in this frame are 'coreferential'. This is not really correct, as N is a property which is predicated of the person referred to by the pronoun *him*.

active construction (cf. *They say him to be very clever*). Quirk refers to this phenomenon as 'vertical derivation', as opposed to horizontal derivation, which would be a classical transformational relationship between properties 4 and 5. A further example of an SR is offered in Quirk (1995).

Coates (1971: 161f.) plots a serial relationship in Table 4.4 among adjective-head and noun-head combinations, using the criteria listed below:

1. The nominal head has single stress.
2. The modifier may act as head in a nominal group.
3. The modifier occurs in slot −1 (i.e. in terms of a slot-and-filler analysis of the nominal group, represented as . . . − 2 − 1 H + 1 + 2 . . . [H = Head]
4. The modifier is commutable.
5. The modifier has an adjectivalizing suffix.
6. The modifier may occur in predicative position.
7. The modifier may be separated from the Head by another modifier.
8. The modifier may be compared.

For Coates the phrase *criminal law* 'is the true denominal adjective plus head, shown to be serially related to central adjective plus head, to noun premodifier plus head, and to compound nouns' (Coates 1971: 162).

An SR in passive constructions is posited in Svartvik (1966). It will be discussed in detail in Chapter 7 on Constructional Gradience. Finally, a semantic application of the notion is proposed in Leech and Coates (1979: 87–8) to explain overlapping modal meanings, while SRs and blends (see Section 4.3 below) are invoked in the description of the patterning of Old English impersonals in Denison (1990).

TABLE 4.4 Coates's serial relationship

	1	2	3	4	5	6	7	8
a large building	−	−	−	+	−	+	+	+
a beautiful flower	−	−	−	+	+	+	+	+
a British passport	−	−	?−	+	+	+	?+	−
criminal law	−	−	+	+	+	−	−	−
the nervous system	+	−	+	+	+	−	−	−
a cotton dress	−	+	+	+	−	+	−	−
a garden gate	−	+	+	+	−	−	−	−
a cricket ground	+	+	+	+	−	−	−	−
an old maid	−	−	+	−	−	−	−	−
a green-house	+	−	+	−	−	−	−	−
a deck-chair	+	+	+	−	−	−	−	−

Despite Quirk's reference to gradience, serial relationships in my view only bear a superficial similarity to that notion. While grammatical gradience involves the elements of two or more classes or constructions overlapping or merging with each other in some way, SRs are the result of a dynamic shifting process within the system of a language which allows for an explanation of the existence of an otherwise unexpected patterning. Thus in the example above, by virtue of being 'sandwiched' between *feel* and *know* in the matrix we can explain the existence of *He is said to be Adj.*, despite the fact that an active counterpart does not exist. Nevertheless, SRs at least bear a family resemblance to IG. The notion of serial relationship was never fully developed by Quirk himself, and does not play a role in Quirk *et al.* (1972, 1985).[2]

4.3 Syntactic mixing: mergers

English allows various ways of mixing phrases, constructions, and clauses. Here is an—open-ended—list of possibilities:

(1) It's not the actual story, or even the people, that attract me to write about something. (ICE-GB S1b 048 109)[3]

(2) His letter is actually what decided me whether to apply for the job.[4]

(3) I don't know where his whereabouts are. (*Channel Four News, UK*, 19 July 1999)

(4) Are you prepared to track down who these people are? (*Channel Four News*, UK, 21 August 2000)

(5) In the federal government, it's never over until the fat lady rereads the fine print, and she moves her lips. (Barlow 2000: 333)

(6) If Tony Blair cannot make hay in such political sunshine, how will he fare when winter comes? (Barlow 2000: 338)

Sentence (1) seems to be a mixture of (7) and (8):

(7) It's not the actual story, or even the people, that attract me.

(8) It's not the actual story, or even the people, that persuade me to write about something.

Example (2) plausibly combines (9) and (10):

(9)   I decided whether to apply for the job.

---

[2] Interestingly, Ross (1973*a*, 1973*b*) regards his nouniness squish (see Section 3.4.4) as an instance of a serial relationship.

[3] Examples marked in this way are from the British component of the *International Corpus of English*.

[4] This is an attested example.

(10)   His letter is what decided me to apply for the job.

Sentence (3) looks like a hybrid of (11) and (12):

(11)   I don't know where he is.
(12)   I don't know (what) his whereabouts (are).

In (4) we seem to have a mixture of (13) and (14):

(13)   Are you prepared to find out who these people are?
(14)   Are you prepared to track down these people?

Finally, in (5) and (6) we have attested variations of the set expressions *it ain't over until the fat lady sings* and *make hay while the sun shines*.

In (1) it looks as if the verb *attract* is used both as an ordinary transitive verb, cf. (7), and as a causative verb, cf. (8). This attested example was uttered without an intonational break between *me* and *to write*, which means that the *to*-clause cannot be interpreted as a purposive adjunct. (In actual fact, even *with* a break a purposive interpretation for the *to*-clause would not be obvious.)[5] In (2), also, a verb that normally does not have a causative meaning seems to convey a causative intent on the speaker's part, as the paraphrases bring out. In (3) and (4) there is simply a mix-up of two semantically similar grammatical patterns. In Barlow's examples in (5) and (6) we have paradigmatic variations of set expressions in which particular 'slots' have been filled by unexpected words or phrases. The subconscious motivation for speakers to use mixed patterns may well be that they offer communicative advantages. Thus, as we have seen, in (1) and (2) using the verbs *attract* and *decide* in the pattern V + NP + *to*-infinitive has the contextual effect of evoking a number of causative verbs that occur in this pattern more regularly, such as *persuade*, *make*, *induce*, *entice*, etc.

Let's look at a few more examples from the literature. Lakoff (1974) discusses a series of constructions involving mixing, for example (15) and (16):

(15)   John invited *you'll never guess how many people* to his party.
(16)   John is going to *I think it's Chicago* on Saturday.

These cases are discussed under the heading of *amalgam*, defined as 'a sentence which has within it chunks of lexical material that do not correspond to anything in the logical structure of the sentence; rather they must be copied in from other derivations under specifiable semantic and pragmatic conditions' (Lakoff 1974: 321). Some of Lakoff's cases of amalgams are more pragmatic than

---

⁵ There's another example of the pattern in (1) in the ICE-GB corpus uttered by a different speaker:

(i)   If you're seeking to attract me to say anything about Douglas that is ungracious, you will fail.
        (S1b 043 085)

syntactic phenomena, instance his example *Take out the garbage, because I'm too lazy*, where the *because*-clause is said to modify an underlying performative verb *request*: 'Because I'm too lazy I request you to take out the garbage'.

A similar type of mixing occurs in what Massam (1999) has referred to as *thing is-constructions*. These are constructions of the type in (17):

(17)   The thing is is that everyone is going to the party.

Notice the gemination of the verb-form *is*. Massam claims that these constructions are fairly common, and offers a theoretical account of their syntactic properties. Although she does not discuss this construction in terms of mixing, it is not unreasonable to surmise that it is a hybrid of the constructions in (18) and (19):

(18)   The thing is that everyone is going to the party.
(19)   What it is is that everyone is going to the party.

Sentence (18) is what Collins (1991: 27) refers to as a *th*-cleft, while (19) contains a free relative clause.[6]

As a final example, consider (20) (from Haegeman 1994: 364):

(20)   John seems as if he does not like Mary.

In her textbook Haegeman uses this sentence in an exercise on the raising verb *seem*. Students are asked to determine why (20) is problematic for the assumption that *seem* is a one-place predicate. The answer is that because *seem* already has a clausal internal argument, namely *as if he does not like Mary*, the NP *John* will be an unlinked argument, because it cannot be an external argument of *seem*, nor can it have been raised out of the subordinate clause, which already has a subject argument, namely *he*. Haegeman does not appeal to the notion of mixing, but it is plausible that (20) is in fact a combination of (21) and (22):

(21)   John seems not to like Mary.
(22)   It seems as if John does not like Mary.

I will refer to structures such as (1)–(6), (15)–(17), and (20) as *syntactic mergers*.[7] Mergers involve a more or less spontaneous mixing of two different

---

[6] After writing this passage I came across the work of Tuggy (1996) who proposes an account of *thing is*-constructions in terms of blending. See also Barlow (2000), who briefly discusses them.

[7] The term 'merger' is also used in Leech and Coates (1979) and in Coates (1983) to describe the meanings of modal verbs. It is defined as follows:

This term applies where a token yields two interpretations, and where the meanings are mutually compatible in a reading of the passage; *ie* are in a both-and relationship. Merger may be regarded as a special case of ambiguity, in which the meanings are so closely related that, whichever we choose, the passage makes sense in roughly the same way. One may alternatively regard it as a 'contextual neutralization' of meanings which in other contexts would be clearly distinct. (Leech and Coates 1979: 81)

constructions. I will argue in Chapter 7 that they are not the same as blends and fusions, which involve conventionalized mixings. Here is an example of a blend:

(23)   He is all right to employ.   (Bolinger 1961*b*: 373)

As we will see in Chapter 7, this is arguably a blend of (24) and (25):

(24)   He is all right.
(25)   Employing him is all right.

4.4 Multiple analysis and reanalysis

It has been argued that there exist structures in English that can be analysed in more than one way. Quirk *et al.* (1985: 732f.) discuss a number of cases. As an example, consider the sentence below:

(26)   The board looked into the recent complaints.

According to Quirk *et al.,* we analyse this sentence either as in (27) or as in (28):

(27)   The board [v looked] [pp into the recent complaints]
(28)   The board [v looked into] [NP the recent complaints]

In (27) the main verb *look* is followed by a PP.[8] This analysis is motivated by the fact that something can intervene between the verb and the PP:

(29)   The board looked *closely* into the recent complaints.

In (28), by contrast, *look into* is regarded as a complex verb which takes an NP as its complement. The motivation for the complex verb analysis is the possibility of having (30) and (31) below:

(30)   The recent complaints were looked into — by the board.
(31)   What did the board look into —?

Because there are arguments for both analyses, Quirk *et al.* do not posit a single analysis for these structures, but opt for allowing *multiple analyses* in their grammar. In the theoretical literature the term *reanalysis* or *restructuring* is often used to deal with data like (27)–(31), see for example Radford (1988: 429f.). A recent example of a special type of reanalysis can be found in Kayne (2002) where he proposes movement of NP/DP-internal *many* from an AP

---

[8] According to Quirk *et al.* (1985), this PP functions as an adjunct, although it is more plausible to regarded it as a complement.

position to a determiner position to account for the dual categorial nature of the word. The term *reanalysis* is also used in diachronic linguistics: in Hopper and Traugott (1993: 32f.) it is discussed at length as the main mechanism inducing grammaticalization and change. See also Denison (1993: 74f.).[9]

It will be clear from the discussion above that multiple analysis and reanalysis are not the same as gradience. The first imposes two distinct structures for one and the same syntactic string, without implying that they shade into each other. However, the concepts of multiple analysis and reanalysis do at least bear a superficial resemblance to gradience, to the extent that all these notions can be said to constitute grammatical indeterminacies.

4.5 Gradience and Prototype Theory

The notion of gradience has obvious affinities with Prototype Theory, as discussed in Chapter 3. However, there are also important differences between the two approaches.

First, gradience is predominantly a grammatical phenomenon, which can be studied purely by considering linguistic elements and their configurations. Prototype Theory (PT), by contrast, has applications beyond linguistics. As Rosch observes in her later work:

[i]t should be noted that the issues in categorization with which we are primarily concerned have to do with explaining the categories found in a culture and coded by the language of that culture at a particular point in time. When we speak of the formation of categories, we mean their formation in the culture. (Rosch 1978: 28)

We should ask whether, and to what extent, PT has implications for *grammatical* categories and concepts. Does it make sense to talk about a 'prototype adjective' in the way we can talk about a 'prototype chair'? Is a 'prototype adjective' the same as a 'central adjective'? As we saw in the previous chapter, Rosch did not want to make the claim that we can identify a particular member of a category as the prototype. We also saw that Lakoff claimed that '[l]inguistic categories, like conceptual categories, show prototype effects' and 'I take the existence of such effects as prima facie evidence that linguistic categories have the same character as other conceptual categories' (1987a: 67). Recall also the quotation in Chapter 2 from Goldberg: 'To the extent that we wish to say that linguistic categories are like other categories, we would *not expect* them to be definable by necessary and sufficient conditions' (2006: 223; emphasis in original). These quotations raise

---

[9] Although see Haspelmath (1998) for a critical discussion of the need for reanalysis in grammaticalization theory.

the question of whether there are differences between what I have called gradience and prototypes. I will suggest that there are, and that perhaps Lakoff's assertion above 'that linguistic categories have the same character as other conceptual categories' may be too strong. There are differences between categories of real-world objects (like those researched by Rosch and her associates) and grammatical categories. First, in an obvious sense real-world objects are 'out there', whereas grammatical categories clearly are not. As a result, we are more conscious of the former. In experiments it makes sense to ask what the typical attributes of chairs are, and subjects will enumerate quite a few of their criterial attributes with facility, in line with a mental image they have of typical chairs. These attributes would include shape, height, colour, etc.[10] The mental representations of grammatical categories are not accessible in the same way as the representations of three-dimensional objects, as becomes clear from the fact that it does not make sense to ask subjects in an experiment to judge what the typical attributes of English adjectives are, or which of the items *happy, ill,* and *ultimate* is the most typical adjective. The reason is that most people do not know what an adjective is, let alone what a typical member of that class would look like, or how it would behave. Thus, whereas with real-world objects we can experimentally demonstrate that prototypes play a role, as Rosch has done, such techniques cannot be used to establish the existence of prototypical grammatical concepts. Unlike grammatical entities, real-world objects lead an existence independently of the prototype effects they bring about.

The second difference (related to the first) between real-world categories and linguistic categories concerns the nature of the criterial attributes used to characterize prototypes. For Taylor, the attributes of conceptual categories, 'far from being the abstract entities of autonomous linguistics, are properties of real-world entities which are readily accessible to competent users of a language in virtue of their acquaintance with the world around them' (2003: 44).[11] However, the attributes of grammatical categories *are* by their very nature abstract. Thus, in the case of grammatical form classes, we might say that a particular item belongs to some class or other by virtue of the nature of the abstract syntactic framework to which it belongs, and the attributes that make us classify a particular element as, say, an adjective (attributive/predicative position, gradability, etc.) are themselves part of that syntactic framework. The particular properties that make a chair a chair do not depend on

---

[10] On this matter, see also Neustupný (1966: 43, 49 fn. 13), who in a discussion of different types of vagueness refers to prototype effects with real-world objects as 'discourse vagueness'.

[11] Only a few lines underneath the passage quoted from Taylor, he remarks that '[u]ltimately, the attributes have to do, not with inherent properties of the object itself, but with the role of the object within a particular culture' (Taylor 2003: 44). Surely, the word *not* in this quotation should be followed by *only*?

any higher-level system that this object belongs to. Instead, they are part of the nature of the object itself. In other words, the features that characterize syntactic categories are *relational*, while the features that characterize chairs are *inherent*. Adjectives do not exist in and of themselves, whereas chairs do. The inherent nature of real-world concepts applies even to such notions as *mountain*, *knee*, and *fog*, sometimes called *vague entities* (cf. Ungerer and Schmid 1996: 15). These do not have sharply delimited boundaries, but are nevertheless real.

Thirdly, Labov's work (1973) has shown that experimental prototypicality judgements by subjects on three-dimensional containers such as cups and mugs can be influenced by the extra-linguistic environment. It seems to me that the extra-linguistic context plays no role in the assignment of elements to linguistic classes. However we define a form class linguistically, the real-world context in which it is used (as opposed to the intra-sentential context) has no bearing on that definition.

Nevertheless, despite the observed differences between conceptual and grammatical categories, it makes sense to speak of grammatical prototypes, and we can therefore accept Taylor's assertion, that at least

> there are some remarkable *parallels* between the structure of semantic categories and the structure of linguistic categories. Just as there are central and marginal members of the semantic category BIRD, so too a linguistic category like NOUN has representative and marginal members. (Taylor 2003: 202; my emphasis)[12]

To substantiate his point he discusses a number of examples of prototypes in grammar, such as prototypical words, affixes, and clitics, and prototypical grammatical categories. For example, nouns have typical phonological, morphological, and distributional characteristics which correlate with semantic criteria for 'nouniness' (Taylor 2003: 208f., 217). See also Taylor (1998), Section 3.4.4 and Chapter 7.

Returning to the differences between PT and gradience, it is noteworthy that linguists who advocate PT do so from two angles: a syntactic and a semantic angle. The emphasis is on the latter. In the words of Taylor '[s]ignificantly, the closeness of an item to the (semantically characterized) prototype tends to correlate, in many ways, with its closeness to the prototype defined on purely syntactic criteria' (2003: 217). In the gradience model I will be developing, the emphasis is on the purely syntactic characteristics of linguistic formatives. I take the position that there may well be a correlation between the syntax and semantics, but the syntax should be the primary point of departure.

---

[12] It is interesting that in the second edition of Taylor's book he speaks of conceptual categories, rather than semantic categories as in this quotation.

Finally, it is perhaps fair to say that PT deals mostly with what I have called subsective shadings in category membership, and has much less to say about intercategorial fuzziness.

Summarizing the differences between PT and gradience, PT is more concerned with the categorization of concepts and real-world objects, and to the extent that grammatical elements are discussed, the emphasis is on subsective fuzziness seen from a predominantly semantic angle. Adherents of the gradience model, by contrast, are exclusively interested in linguistic elements. They are concerned with both intracategorial and intercategorial fuzziness, seen from a syntactic angle. Gradience covers a wider area of grammar than does Prototype Theory.

It is worth reiterating that we should be aware of the fact that while there may well be 'parallels', to use Taylor's term, between real-world objects and linguistic categories, the prototype effects that have been observed for linguistic phenomena are descriptive observations that have been superimposed on the data, much like the very categories themselves. That is to say, one does well to remember that linguistic categories and the perceived prototype effects within and between them are the descriptive artefacts of linguistic theorizing. Prototype effects have to my knowledge not been demonstrated for grammatical categories by means of experiments such as those Rosch conducted in the case of real-world categories. We must therefore be careful not simply to transfer the notion of prototype from the domain of cognitive categories to the domain of grammar without qualification. This point seems often to be overlooked in work on linguistic categorization. This is one of the prime motivations for using the term gradience when talking about grammatical fuzziness.

4.6 Gradience and Markedness Theory

In the present section I will look at how markedness has been understood principally in the Chomskyan paradigm, and I will discuss how it relates to gradience.

Markedness can be regarded as a 'categorial asymmetry' (Battistella 1996: 19) in which certain members of a class are in some sense expected or default exemplars, because they display some expected property, while other members are special in some sense (e.g. as regards (structural) complexity, or through what Lyons (1977: 305f.) calls formal marking). As an example, nouns in many languages carry overt case. In a language like German this is the unmarked situation, whereas in English only a subset of nouns, namely pronouns, carry case. So case in English is a marked phenomenon.

Battistella (1996) traces some of the uses of the terms 'marked', 'unmarked', and 'markedness'. The first two of these have their roots in the work of the East European structuralists, particularly Roman Jakobson and Nikolai Trubetzkoy. For the latter certain correlations '[acquire] in linguistic consciousness the form of an opposition between the presence of some feature and its absence' (Trubetskoy, cited in Battistella 1996: 19). As this quotation makes clear, markedness assumes that either/or choices are made in language. In other words, the notion of markedness is characterized by *binariness*: a particular construction either possesses a feature (and is then marked '+'), or it does not possess that feature (and is then marked '−'). Work was done in the domains of phonology, semantics, morphology, and syntax and had a great influence on the field of linguistics.[13] The term 'markedness' was first used—in quotation marks—in Chomsky and Halle (1968: 137, fn 2). As noted in Battistella (1996: 73), the Theory of Markedness in generative grammar was influenced by the East European tradition as far as phonology is concerned. For syntactic research, however, a different framework evolved, especially in the 1980s. This I will concentrate on in the remainder of this section. (See Andersen 1989 for a historiography of the first 150 years of the study of markedness.)

In the framework which developed in the early 1980s (cf. Chomsky 1981: 8f.) the notions of *core* and *periphery* are central.

We will assume that UG [Universal Grammar] is not an 'undifferentiated' system, but rather incorporates something analogous to a 'theory of markedness'. Specifically, there is a theory of core grammar with highly restricted options, limited expressive power, and a few parameters. Systems that fall within core grammar constitute 'the unmarked case'; we may think of them as optimal in terms of the evaluation metric. An actual language is determined by fixing the parameters of core grammar and then adding rules or rule conditions, using much richer resources, perhaps resources as rich as those contemplated in the earlier theories of TG noted above. These added properties of grammars we may think of as the syntactic analogue of irregular verbs. We believe, however, that the theory of core grammar covers quite an extensive range, including many of the well-studied constructions of recent linguistic work. (Chomsky and Lasnik 1977: 430, footnote omitted)

The idea, then, is that for any language Universal Grammar specifies a core grammar, which can be envisaged as the grammar that is encoded in everybody's mind, in which a certain number of parameters are fixed. Parameters can be conceived of as mental 'switches' which are either set to 'on' or 'off', depending on the particular language. Probably the most well-known parameter is the

---

[13] For further extensive discussion of the East European contribution, see Battistella 1996, especially chs 2 and 3.

Head Parameter, which stipulates that languages are either 'head first' or 'head last', that is, heads either precede their complements, or follow them. English is a head-first language, Japanese is a head-last language. Parameters have been invoked as a way of explaining language change (cf. Lightfoot 1991), and came to play a central role in Chomsky's theory, so much so that he professed dissatisfaction with the name Government and Binding Theory and preferred Principles and Parameters Theory instead (cf. Chomsky 1995: 29–30).

What about the *periphery*? This, Chomsky argued, consists of

borrowings, historical residues, inventions, and so on.... [The] marked structures have to be learned on the basis of slender evidence..., so there should be further structure to the system outside of core grammar. We might expect that the structure of these further systems relates to the theory of core grammar by such devices as relaxing certain conditions of core grammar, processes of analogy in some sense to be made precise, and so on, though there will presumably be independent structure as well: hierarchies of accessibility, etc. (Chomsky 1981: 8)

Another important question is how the core is distinguished from the periphery. This is not at all clear. According to Chomsky

In principle, one would hope that evidence from language acquisition would be useful with regard to determining the nature of the boundary or the propriety of the distinction in the first place, since it is predicted that the systems develop in quite different ways. (Chomsky 1981: 9)

Returning to markedness, Battistella sums up the 1980s situation as follows:

For many generative grammarians working in the 1980s Principles and Parameters framework, markedness ends up referring to three related things: (1) a distinction between unmarked core and marked periphery; (2) a preference structure imputed to the parameters and parameter values of core grammar; and (3) a preference structure among the rules of the periphery. (Battistella 1996: 85)

Generativists thus envisaged a radical split between core and periphery, but allowed for some kind of gradience *within* both the core and the periphery. In other words, the possibility of having *degrees of markedness* seemed to exist; cf. also Chomsky (1986a: 147). Let us refer to this model as the *gradient markedness model*. In this framework a particular phenomenon radically belongs *either* to the core *or* to the periphery, but it may be a marked core phenomenon, or a marked peripheral phenomenon. As an example of markedness within the core, Chomsky (1981: 66f.) discusses the rule of S'-deletion (S-bar deletion), which allows verbs like *believe* to delete the S-bar node of a following clausal complement, allowing the matrix verb to assign objective

Case to the subject of the complement. Battistella (1996: 87) additionally cites Chomsky's (1981: 19, 69) discussion of *for* in infinitival constructions. Compare the patterns we find below:

(32)   a.   I'd like — to do something. (unmarked)
       b.   I'd like for you to do something. (marked)
       c.   I'd like you to do something. (marked) (from Battistella 1996: 88)

Battistella remarks that 'both possibilities with an overt subject are marked, with (presumably) the last as the more marked' (Battistella 1996: 88). (32b) and (32c) belong to the marked core, the unmarked option taking a null subject in its clausal complement, as in (32a).

As for Chomsky's later views, Battistella (1996: 91) interprets a footnote in one of Chomsky's early minimalist papers, where he says that '[m]arkedness of parameters, if real, could be seen as a last residue of the evaluation metric' (Chomsky 1992: 63, 1995: 213), as dispensing with the idea of having a graded core.

The concept of markedness in generative grammar seems to have offered theoretical linguists a tool for dealing with variation: parameters on their own are not enough; they need to be supplemented by the notion of markedness. Notice that the idea of a parameter is very much an either/or concept: switches, after all, do not allow for mid-way positions. As we have seen, the notions of core and periphery too are essentially distinct, and the theory does not appear to allow for a shading between the two. The gradient markedness model can be seen as a compromise between the gradient and all-or-none conceptions of the nature of grammatical architecture (although, of course, it was never intended to be like that).

A question we might ask is whether markedness, conceived of as a categorial asymmetry, is the same as subsective gradience. The answer is 'no'. Markedness divides categories into two, a core and a periphery, whereas subsective gradience recognizes a gradient amongst elements within categories. Markedness can be seen as a half-hearted way of recognizing that categories are not homogeneous, while at the same time retaining the either/or distinction of a core and periphery. In a markedness-theoretical approach it is often assumed— or perhaps we should say *pretended*—that the distinction between 'marked' and 'unmarked' is an obvious one.

How does Markedness Theory relate to Prototype Theory? Above I argued that MT is essentially an Aristotelian notion in advocating sharp boundaries between cores and peripheries, and between marked and unmarked terms. This view clashes with a suggestion by Newmeyer (1998: 199), who asserts that 'markedness is a relative concept, while prototypicality is an absolute concept'. To my mind, it is exactly the other way round.[14] Battistella (1996: 10) misrepresents Ross in saying that the latter equates markedness with the notion of prototype. What Ross actually said was that '[t]he notion of prototype...is essentially an outgrowth of the fundamental notion of *markedness*' (1987: 309; emphasis in original). Cf. also Lakoff (1987a: 60). Under this view prototypes subsume markedness phenomena. This seems much more on the right track than Newmeyer's claim that we simply do not need the notion of prototype at all, given that we have markedness. Again, it would seem that the exact opposite is the case.

Recent studies show that markedness is still a very fuzzy concept, that many questions remain unanswered, and that 'we ultimately must conclude that there is no theory of markedness per se' (Battistella 1996: 133). Those who utilize the concept of markedness do not seem to be prepared to bite the bullet and admit full categorial flexibility. From this perspective perhaps the study of markedness is a dead end, in that there appears to exist a self-imposed glass ceiling which does not allow variability to extend beyond certain parameters of binary variation.

---

[14] Newmeyer bases this observation on the existence of so-called 'relative markedness hierarchies', like the one where the term 'singular' is the least marked: singular < plural < dual < trial/paucal. Although it is true that we seem to have degrees of markedness here, it is nevertheless the case that each term in this hierarchy is less marked *absolutely* with respect to the next term further to the right on the hierarchy. Markedness is an opposition between pairs.

Part II

Gradience in English: Case Studies

5

Subsective Gradience

> A Good Apple tree or a Bad, is an Apple tree still: a Horse is not more a Lion for being a Bad Horse.
>
> (William Blake, 'On Homers poetry')

Subsective Gradience (SG) is the phenomenon whereby a particular set of elements displays a categorial shading in prototypicality from a central core to a more peripheral boundary. We can contrast Subsective Gradience with Intersective Gradience (IG): whereas with SG elements from only one category are involved, with IG there are two categories on a cline. IG will be discussed in detail in the next chapter. In what follows I will discuss a number of case studies of SG within the principal word classes (V, N, A, and P), as well as phrases and clauses. These case studies are intended to be a representative sample of examples of SG in the grammar of English. It might be argued that to some extent distinguishing between SG at the levels of the word classes and phrases is artefactual, and that, because word class elements never occur on their own but always in phrasal projections, we should only recognize phrasal SG. This would be true, were it not the case that there are examples where gradience is not projected from the lexical head upwards. These are cases where the phrasal projection of a non-prototypical head nevertheless behaves like a prototypical phrase. I have therefore maintained the distinction between word class SG and phrasal SG. Subsective Gradience that obtains within grammatical constructions ('Subsective Constructional Gradience') will be dealt with in Chapter 7.

5.1 SG within word classes

It is a contentious issue whether or not we can speak of prototypical elements of grammatical form classes in the way that we can speak of prototypical chairs or birds. In Chapter 4 I agreed with Taylor's assertion that we can at least speak of a parallelism between the prototype effects that obtain in real-world categories and grammatical ones. Ross has argued in a number of papers that within form classes there are better and worse exemplars, and furthermore that there are ways in which the existence of gradience can be demonstrated, for example by using matrices. In this section we look at some further evidence for SG in word classes.

5.1.1 *Verbs*

Along with nouns, verbs are central elements in the syntax of English sentences, and as such have been subject to a great deal of research (Aarts and Meyer 1995). From the point of view of this book an important issue is the question of how to categorize verbs. While most linguists agree that verbs are easily identifiable, namely as elements that can take tense endings, there is much less agreement about how the class of verbs should be carved up. There are a number of possible approaches:

1. There exist at least two distinct classes of verbs, auxiliaries and main verbs, which behave quite differently syntactically.
2. There exist two distinct classes of verbs, auxiliaries and main verbs, which display Intersective Gradience, such that the two classes converge on each other.
3. There exists a single class of verbs which contains elements that do not behave syntactically in a uniform way, but are nevertheless all main verbs.
4. There exists a single class of verbs which contains elements that do not behave syntactically in a uniform way, but are nevertheless all main verbs. Moreover, these verbs display a subsective gradient, such that we can distinguish more or less prototypical verbs.

All of these positions have been defended in the literature. The first is the one most commonly found in descriptive studies and (pedagogical) grammars of English. Perhaps the staunchest defender of this view is Frank Palmer in his books on the English verb (Palmer 1987, 1990). The distinction between auxiliaries and main verbs is motivated on semantic and syntactic grounds. Semantically auxiliaries are generally different from main verbs in that they do not assign a thematic role to their subject; they can only do so in combination with a main verb. Thus, in a simple sentence like *I didn't eat the sandwich* the auxiliary *do* is semantically devoid of meaning and it is the main verb that assigns an agent role to the subject. The same is true for other types of auxiliaries, such as aspectual *have* and *be*, although it is not true for the 'dynamic' modals, that is, those with subject-orientation, for example volitional *will*. There are also considerations regarding passivization: in general the auxiliaries are 'voice neutral', that is, they do not affect meaning when an active sentence containing an auxiliary is passivized. Here again subject-oriented auxiliaries are an exception. Syntactically, the auxiliaries display the NICE properties, as first formulated in Huddleston (1976a).[1]

As for the second position, Palmer alludes to the existence of gradience between the categories of auxiliaries and main verbs (1990: 201), but he does not work out any details. Radford (1976) does, and he claims that 'the "ideal" verb and the "ideal" auxiliary represent two extremes of a continuum, between which lie a perplexing variety of *semi-auxiliaries*—i.e. predicates which pattern in some respects like auxiliaries, in others like verbs' (Radford 1976: 9). His auxiliary–main verb squish was shown in Chapter 3. Quirk *et al.* (1985) also seem to defend position 2. They posit the gradient shown in Table 5.1 (over) between modal auxiliaries and main verbs.

At the same time, despite positing this gradient, Quirk *et al.* also offer criteria for distinguishing (modal) auxiliaries from main verbs, so it is not entirely clear whether they would want to impose a categorial boundary on the gradient in Table 5.1 between auxiliaries and main verbs (e.g. between (d) and (e)). Given that they evidently do not espouse position 4, it is not unreasonable to conclude that position 2 comes closest to their views.

The third position was first suggested in Ross (1969b), and is defended by Huddleston in a number of publications (e.g. 1976a). Ironically, it was Huddleston who introduced the NICE acronym, which started to lead a life of its own in descriptive and pedagogical work on the English language. However, Huddleston actually set out to reject the thesis that these combined properties define a separate class of auxiliary verbs. In a series of papers and book sections published during the 1970s, Huddleston and Palmer debated whether grammars should recognize two classes of verbs or not; see Huddleston (1974, 1976a, 1976b) and Palmer (1979, 1987, 1990). The third position is also held in Pullum (1976), Pullum and Wilson (1977), Warner (1993), and most recently in Huddleston and Pullum *et al.* (2002).

The fourth position is the one that seems to me to be correct. The gradient looks like Quirk *et al.*'s, except that it instantiates SG, rather than IG. This difference between positions 2 and 4 is very subtle, but quite crucial.

---

[1] NICE is an acronym for *negation, inversion, code,* and *emphasis,* processes which are exemplified in the sentences below:

(i)   He has left/He hasn't left.
(ii) He has left/Has he left?
(iii) He has left, and so has John.
(iv) He HAS left!

TABLE 5.1 Quirk *et al.*'s auxiliary verb–main verb gradient

One verb phrase

↑	(a)	CENTRAL MODALS *can, could, may, might, shall, should, will/'ll, would/'d, must*
	(b)	MARGINAL MODALS *dare, need, ought to, used to*
	(c)	MODAL IDIOMS *had better, would rather/sooner,* BE *to,* HAVE *got to,* etc.
	(d)	SEMI-AUXILIARIES HAVE *to,* BE *about to,* BE *able to,* BE *bound to,* BE *going to,* BE *obliged to,* BE *supposed to,* BE *willing to,* etc.
	(e)	CATENATIVES APPEAR *to,* HAPPEN *to,* SEEM *to,* GET + -*ed* participle, KEEP + -*ing* participle, etc.
↓	(f)	MAIN VERB + non-finite clause HOPE + *to*-infinitive, BEGIN + -*ing* participle, etc.

Two verb phrases

Source: Quirk *et al.* (1985: 137)

Defenders of position 2 recognize a categorial distinction between auxiliaries and main verbs, while allowing for both categories to converge on each other; proponents of position 4 argue for the existence of a single category of verbs displaying SG, without allowing for any categorial boundaries within it. The arguments for a single class of verbs are quite compelling. I will not discuss them in detail here, but refer the reader to the references mentioned at the end of the preceding paragraph.

It is noteworthy that Geoffrey Pullum, who criticized Radford for his auxiliary–main verb squish (see Section 3.4.4), and argued instead for a single undifferentiated category of verbs, nevertheless concedes that intuitively some verbs are more 'verby' than others:

Let us take *must* as our example, for intuitively there is no less verby verb in English. (I agree entirely that this informal intuition exists: I am only claiming that it is like the feeling that the slow worm isn't a lizard or the whale isn't a mammal. Slow worms *are* lizards, albeit legless; whales *are* mammals; and modals *are* verbs.) (Pullum 1976: 20)

He goes on to say about *must* that

if it is a verb, it is a peculiarly irregular one, for it lacks the past tense altogether (**he must/musted leave yesterday*). It is therefore an irregular, in fact a defective, verb. ... The modals are those verbs which have blank spaces against the entries for infinitive, -*en* form, and -*ing* form in their lexically entered paradigm lists. (Pullum 1976: 20)

It is now only a small step to bite the bullet, and concede that this intuition is more than a 'feeling', and allow for the grammar to recognize more or less typical verbs.[2]

There are other ways of approaching SG in the verb class. Thus we might say that transitive verbs (two-place and three-place predicates) are more prototypical than intransitive verbs (one-place predicates), which in turn are more prototypical than 'weather verbs' such as *rain, snow* etc. (zero-place predicates). We could refer to this as 'valency gradience'. By extension, the clauses which these verbs head would then also be more or less prototypical. It seems that this approach is not viable. Valency is an inherent property of verbs, and there is no reason to suppose that a verb that takes more arguments than some other verb is more prototypical for that reason alone. If we followed this line of reasoning we would have to say that verbs that take one internal argument ('monotransitives'), as contrasted with verbs that take two internal arguments ('ditransitives'), are less typical verbs. This is counterintuitive. Notice that the idea put forward here is similar to the one discussed in Hopper and Thompson (1980) (see Chapter 3), where they claim that there exist degrees of transitivity, except that for them transitivity is a property of clauses and involves a host of other—arguably purely semantic—parameters. For further discussion, see Chapters 7 and 8.

5.1.2 *Nouns*

Jespersen (1924) makes an interesting case for a subsective gradient among nouns where proper nouns semantically shade into common nouns. He writes:

[N]o sharp line can be drawn between proper and common names, the difference being one of degree rather than of kind. A name always connotes the quality or qualities by which the bearer or bearers of the name are known, i.e. distinguished from other beings or things. The more special or specific the thing denoted is, the more probable is it that the name is chosen arbitrarily, and so much the more does it approach to, or become, a proper name. If a speaker wants to call up the idea of some person or thing, he has at his command in some cases a name specially applied to the individual concerned, that is, a name which in this particular situation will be understood as referring to it, or else he has to piece together by means of other words a composite denomination which is sufficiently precise for his purpose. (Jespersen 1924: 70–1)

Jespersen's gradient is of course primarily a semantic/pragmatic one. Strang (1968: 114) regards proper names as 'a class intermediate between nouns and

---

[2] And indeed, in Huddleston and Pullum (2005: 22) the bullet seems to have been bitten: 'Go, *know*, and *tell* (and thousands of others) are prototypical verbs, but *must* is non-prototypical...'.

pronouns, akin to pronouns in all but their case and number system'. In Anderson (2004) names are reclassified as determinatives.

It is not difficult to establish a cline of nounhood purely on distributional grounds. In Chapter 3 I discussed Crystal (1967) on the English word classes, which makes use of matrices (see Section 3.4.6). Let us here turn to a discussion of Crystal's example of Subsective Gradience within the class of nouns. Recall that Crystal argues that the best way to define a word class is by listing the phonological, morphological, lexical, semantic, and syntactic criteria that pertain to it. He provides four criteria for nounhood in order of statistical prominence:

1. ability to act as subject;[3]
2. ability to take number inflection;
3. ability to co-occur with an article;
4. ability to take a nominal suffix.

The class of nouns is then represented as a set of intersecting circles, shown in Figure 5.1, each of which represents a subset of nouns which conforms to one or more of the criteria listed above. The elements in the 'central class' conform to all four criteria.

Crystal's account is useful, although as it stands, it is in need of modification. Note that he gives examples of nouns for only five of the eight areas in Figure 5.1 opposite. No examples are given for the areas I have marked A, B, and C. Let us look at these in more detail. They have the following features:

A		B		C	
$+1$		$+1$		$+1$	
$+2$		$+2$		-2	
-3		-3		-3	
$+4$		-4		$+4$	

Area A specifies a group of nouns that can act as subject, inflect for number, and take a nominal suffix, but cannot take an article. I cannot think of examples of nouns that would belong to this group. This would not be surprising if, as I suspect, there is an implicational relationship between criteria 2 and 3: any noun that can inflect for number can also take an article. In other words:

$$+2 \Rightarrow +3$$

---

[3] Note that the syntactic criteria given here for nouns are often formulated in the literature as shown here. These formulations frequently do not distinguish between word classes and their phrasal projections. Thus, 'ability to act as subject', can strictly speaking only be regarded as a nominal property in dependency-based frameworks, whereas in constituency-based frameworks the locution 'ability to head a phrase which functions as subject' is to be preferred.

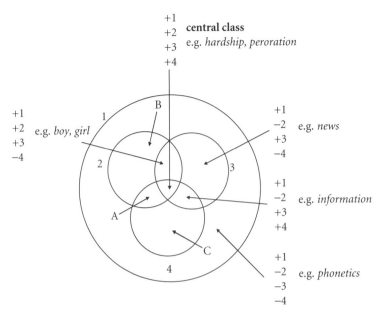

FIGURE 5.1 Crystal's representation of noun classes
Source: Crystal (1967: 46)

If this is correct, then there is no need to have both areas A and B in Figure 5.1. Note that the implication above does not work both ways: a noun that can take an article does not also necessarily inflect for number (as Crystal's example *news* attests). We can now re-draw Figure 5.1, such that the implication above is accommodated, and areas A and B are removed, by placing circle 2 inside circle 3 (Figure 5.2).

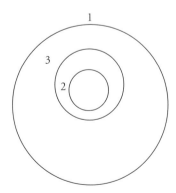

FIGURE 5.2 Figure 5.1 revised

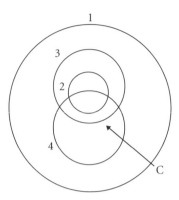

FIGURE 5.3 Figure 5.2 revised

But then this leaves area 4 unaccounted for. In order to deal with it, consider area C. This represents nouns that may act as subject and can take a nominal suffix, but cannot inflect for number, nor take an article. At least for a small number of nouns this seems to be a possibility, for example *fatherhood*. We can now add circle 4 (Figure 5.3).

However, is Crystal right in allowing nouns to be specified [−3] at all? In the case of a noun like *fatherhood*, at first sight characterizing this noun as [−3] seems to be correct, given that we cannot say **a fatherhood/*the fatherhood*. However, if we add premodifying or postmodifying elements, as in *the fatherhood of my friend Jim (is not in doubt)*, the result is perfectly fine. What about Crystal's example *phonetics*, marked [+1, −2, −3, −4]? Given the possibility of a phrase like *the phonetics of Bulgarian*, we should really reassign *phonetics* to the *news*-group of nouns; that is, it can be a subject and take an article, but cannot be inflected for number, nor does it take a nominal suffix. The conclusion is that we don't need to have an area C, as in Crystal's original Figure 5.1.

However, even if *phonetics* and *fatherhood* are perhaps not good examples of [−3] nouns, we still need to accommodate existential *there*, which is a noun, but only by criterion 1. We end up with Figure 5.4, which is much tidier than Figure 5.1, without redundant areas.

For Crystal word classes 'assume a grammar before one can begin to talk about them' (1967: 25), and: '[t]he problem of setting-up word classes is basically a question of discovery procedures, and the issues arising here are very different from the purely descriptive problem, where word class criteria are verified against an independently-verifiable grammar' (1967: 25). Instead of using an inductive methodology like discovery procedures, we might posit, as is now generally accepted, that all languages have nouns and verbs, and we

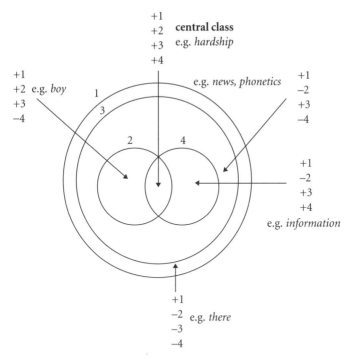

FIGURE 5.4 Figure 5.3 revised

might furthermore assume that these two classes are innate (see also Section 2.4.2). We can then derive the other word classes from them. Criteria like Crystal's can be regarded as the *defining criteria* for the class of nouns. Setting up such criteria inductively will constitute the (partial) setting-up of a grammar. The only type of criteria we should admit are morphosyntactic ones. With the adjustments suggested above, Crystal's system presents a useful way of accounting for gradience within word classes.

5.1.3 *Adjectives*

Consider the words *happy, thin, alive,* and *utter*. All these display one or more adjective properties. Yet *happy* is a more typical (alternatively, 'prototypical') exemplar of the class of adjectives than *thin*, which in turn is more centrally like an adjective than *alive* and *utter*. This can be said to be the case purely on grammatical grounds in that *happy, thin, alive,* and *utter* behave syntactically in an adjective-like way to different degrees, as the following examples make clear:

(1) a happy woman   (p_1: attributive position)
     she is happy   (p_2: predicative position)
     very happy   (p_3: intensification)
     happy/happier/happiest   (p_4: gradedness)
     unhappy   (p_5: *un-* prefixation)

(2) a thin man
     he is thin
     very thin
     thin/thinner/thinnest
     *unthin

(3) *an alive hamster
     the hamster is alive
     very (much) alive
     ?alive/more alive/most alive
     *unalive

(4) an utter disgrace
     *the problem is utter
     *very utter
     *utter/utterer/utterest
     *unutter

Using the matrix shown in Table 5.2 below, the higher degree of 'adjectivity' for *happy* and *thin* immediately becomes clear:

TABLE 5.2 Adjective criteria

	P_1	P_2	P_3	P_4	P_5
happy	+	+	+	+	+
thin	+	+	+	+	−
alive	−	+	+	?	−
utter	+	−	−	−	−

The criteria in this matrix do not exhaust the ways in which we can show that *thin* distributionally has more freedom than *utter*. *Happy*, *thin*, and *alive* are semantically and communicatively much more versatile in that they have clear lexical content. In addition, *thin* and *alive* can be used both literally (*This wall is so thin: we can hear everything the neighbours say*) and metaphorically (*His arguments were a bit thin*). By contrast, *utter* is semantically almost depleted of meaning, and close to having only an intensifying function, much like *very*. We can now establish the following gradient:

$$\xrightarrow{\text{less adjectival}}$$
$$happy > thin > alive > utter$$

In the matrices above the positive or negative specifications for the various criteria are only a snapshot of the language. Thus, I specified *alive* negatively for attributive position. But consider the following attested example:

(5)   Snow, who lives in Kentish Town, has *an alive presence*, an abiding awareness, a serious desire to seek the truth and make some sense of life amid the vortex of confusion in the modern world that daily manifests itself on screen, along with his charismatic ties. (*The Islington Tribune*, 19 November 2004; emphasis added)

It is not unlikely that in this example *alive* is coerced into attributive position by the phrases that follow it (*abiding awareness, serious desire*), so as to create a neat parallelism. One would expect that this is exactly the type of process that brings about changes in usage.

5.1.4 *Prepositions*

Huddleston and Pullum *et al.* (2002: 603) characterize prepositions as words that can take NPs as complements, can head PPs functioning as complements or non-predicative adjuncts, and can be modified by such words as *right* and *straight*. One possible, although by no means the only, way of dividing up the class of prepositions is as follows:

- **Simple:** *at, about, behind, between, by, down, from, in, inside, on, outside, through, to, towards, under, up, with*
- **Compound:** *into, onto, throughout, underneath, upon, within, without*
- **Complex:**
  - P + P: *as for, apart from, close to, next to, outside of, prior to, subsequent to, together with, up against, up to, upwards of*
  - Conjunction + P: *because of*
  - Adj + P: *exclusive of, previous to, subsequent to*
  - P + N + P: *as far as, by dint of, by means of, in accordance with, in aid of, in favour of, in spite of, on pain of*

Not all linguists would agree that a class of complex prepositions should be recognized, but let us adopt the taxonomy above as a starting point for discussion. Can a case be made for recognizing a gradient amongst the prepositions such that some are more centrally members of that class than others? It would seem that all these items have the same syntactic potential in being able to occur in a P+NP sequence. There are differences, however, in the degree to which they can be stranded. Huddleston (1984: 338) notes that short, frequent, and grammatically used prepositions allow stranding the most readily. Let us look at these factors in turn. Morphological complexity indeed appears to be relevant, as the data below illustrate:

(6)   He is standing on the grass > What is he standing on?
(7)   They live outside the country > ?What do they live outside?
(8)   She travelled together with her brother > ?*Who did she travel together with?
(9)   She left because of the rain > *What did she leave because of?
(10) He succeeded by dint of hard work > *What did he succeed by dint of?

In each case the preposition (sequence) is more complex, leading to a greater degree of unacceptability.[4]

What about frequency? A large-scale corpus-based study would be required to establish a correlation between frequency of occurrence and strandability. Were such a correlation to be found it would indicate that there are links between the syntactic versatility of linguistic entities (i.e. their prototypicality) and their frequency of occurrence. One would not, however, expect such links to obtain. For example, there is no reason to suppose that in the nominal domain the word *lake* is less prototypically nominal in terms of its syntactic behaviour than *table*, which is used more frequently. All that matters is the number of morphosyntactic tests a word passes; and both these items pass the tests for nouns.

As for grammatically used prepositions, these are items that have little meaning of their own, for example *of* in *What are you thinking of?*, as opposed to, say, *through* in the PP *through the window*, which instantiates a lexical use. While it is true that some lexical prepositions do not strand very easily, for example? *Which person did you walk beside?*/?* *Who were they sitting opposite?*, for others stranding is unproblematic, for example *Which door did you walk through?*/*Which table did you put the book on?* If it is indeed the case that grammatically used prepositions allow stranding more readily, and are therefore more prototypical, it is not clear why this should be so. In fact, the distinction between grammatical and lexical uses of prepositions is perhaps not very useful in determining whether a particular preposition is a more or

---

[4] Huddleston's generalization may be in need of some fine-tuning, though, because the following are perfectly fine:

(i)   What are we up against?
(ii) What is he up to?

However, perhaps the fact that (i) and (ii) are grammatical can be explained by noting that they have an idiomatic status.

less central member of its class. One indication of this is that there is a factor that goes against the strandability observation above, namely the fact that unlike central prepositions, as defined at the beginning of this section, grammaticalized prepositions are grammatically restricted in not allowing premodifiers, in the way that lexical prepositions like *before* in *three weeks before the war* do allow them, as Huddleston and Pullum *et al.* (2002: 601) note. This would make them less typical prepositions, thus 'cancelling out' the potential for strandability.

From what has been said so far we might conclude that all we need to say about SG in the class of prepositions, as traditionally conceived, is that items that can be stranded are more typical members of the preposition class than items that cannot. However, that conclusion would be premature. There have been proposals to re-assign a number of grammatical items from other word classes to the class of prepositions. One such class of items are often analysed as 'particles', which occur in a variety of syntactic environments, for example with so-called phrasal verbs:

(11)   She let me in.
(12)   He lashed out.

These sentences would be said to contain a transitive phrasal verb *let in* and an intransitive phrasal verb *lash out*, respectively. The elements *in* and *out* would then be seen as particles. However, we could also regard them as intransitive prepositions, a concept that is often attributed to Emonds (1976), but actually goes back much further, namely at least to Jespersen (1924: 88–9), as Kortmann (1997: 26f.) notes. For discussion, see Aarts (1989, 1992). Other items that can be admitted into the class of prepositions are discussed in Burton-Roberts (1991), Aarts (2001: 183f.), and Huddleston and Pullum *et al.* (2002: 599ff.). They include compound words like *hereby, therein, thereof, therewith*, etc., spatial terms like *ashore, downstairs, home, there*, etc., and temporal terms like *now, then, afterwards*, etc. Let us look at just two of these elements, *there* and *now*, as in the examples below:

(13)   The spider is right there.
(14)   I want to call him right now.
(15)   The students there are very industrious.
(16)   The question now is what the government will do.
(17)   She lives in Rome > She lives there.
(18)   They are doing it at the moment > They are doing it now.
(19)   *very/exceptionally there/*very/exceptionally now
(20)   *there bright/*now bright

These examples show that *there* and *now* can be preceded by the modifier *right* ((13) and (14)), they can postmodify nouns ((15) and (16)), and they can replace regular PPs ((17) and (18)), but they cannot be modified by intensifying words like *very* and *exceptionally* ((19)), nor can they themselves modify adjectives ((20)). In these respects they behave just like typical prepositions.

Huddleston and Pullum *et al.* (2002: 599–600) also include in the preposition class words that are traditionally called subordinating conjunctions, such as *although*, *because*, *since*, *when*, etc. (although not the class of complementizers).

If we admit all these words to the class of prepositions, and there are good reasons for doing so, as we have seen, then we have a much clearer cline of words being more or less prepositional: at one end we have items that strand easily and can be preceded by *right* and *straight*. Somewhere in the middle are the items that display only one of these properties. The least prepositional are the traditional subordinators, which do not strand and cannot be preceded by intensifiers. Arguably also at this end of the cline are a mixed bag of 'eccentric' items which have been called *marginal prepositions* (see Quirk *et al.* 1985: 667–8; Huddleston and Pullum *et al.* (2002: 631–2), which include the following:

- *notwithstanding*   This is an unusual item because it can be a preposition, as well as a postposition, as in the examples *his good manners notwithstanding/notwithstanding his good manners.*
- *ago*   This word is used as a postposition in constructions that express 'time when' as in *three years ago.* It also combines with adjectives, as in *long ago.*[5]

The gradient then looks as follows:

More typically prepositional > less typically prepositional

———►

Strandable prepositions > 'particles' > adverb-like *there, now,* etc. >
marginal prepositions > 'subordinators'

Notice that in setting up the gradient above I made no reference to the complement-taking potential of prepositions. This is quite deliberate. Unlike Huddleston and Pullum *et al.* (2002: 612), who say that '[p]rototypical prepositions have NP complements', I will not accept the view that intransitive prepositions are less prototypical members of their class than transitive prepositions. The reason for this is that intransitive prepositions and the expressions they are used in are not

---

[5] On *notwithstanding* and *ago*, see also Culicover (1999: 69–74). Quirk *et al.* also mention *less, minus, plus, times, over,* which often occur with numbers: *less six dollars, four minus/plus three, eight times, over fifty,* but, with the exception of *times,* these seem to behave like 'regular' prepositions in taking an NP complement.

in any way distributionally defective. Just as intransitive verbs are no less typical verbs than transitive verbs, and merely a subclass of the larger class of verbs, intransitive prepositions are a subcategory of the larger class of prepositions, but not less typical members of the category as a whole.

In this chapter I will not be discussing a number of items which resemble adjectives, such as *near* and *worth*, and items which have verbal characteristics, for example *bar/barring, following, excepting, excluding, granted*, etc. These will be dealt with in the next chapter, as instances of Intersective Gradience. I will also not deal here with the complex prepositions shown above. For these a case for a gradient has been made by Quirk and Mulholland (1964), who discuss $P^1N^1P^2N^2$ strings of the type *in spite of* N, and observe that they are fixed sequences (cf. **in the spite of, *in clear spite of*), in contrast to sequentially unrestricted strings like *on the table near* N (*cf. on a table near the door/on the big table near the door*, etc.). I will discuss the perceived gradience between complex prepositions and 'free' sequences in Chapter 7 on Constructional Gradience.

Summarizing our findings: there seems to be a convincing case for recognizing a syntactic gradient between central and peripheral members amongst the prepositions, based on differences in distributional potential amongst the items on the cline.

5.2 SG within phrases

SG within phrases has perhaps been most thoroughly studied in J. R. Ross's work in the early 1970s, which concentrated on the possibility of a string of elements being more or less NP-like. I discussed Ross (1973*b*) in Chapter 3, and repeat his 'nouniness' squish below, based on the examples in (21):

More nouny

→

that > *for to* > *Q* > *Acc Ing* > *Poss Ing* > Action Nominal > Derived Nominal > Noun

FIGURE 5.5 Ross's nouniness squish
Source: Ross (1973*b*: 141)

(21) a. *that* = *that*-clauses (*that Max gave the letters to Frieda*)
      b. *for to* = *for* NP *to* V X (*for Max to have given the letters to Frieda*)
      c. Q = embedded questions (*how willingly Max gave the letters to Frieda*)
      d. *Acc Ing* = [[NP], [+Acc]] V + *ing* X (*Max giving the letters to Frieda*)
      e. *Poss Ing* = NP's V + *ing* X (*Max's giving the letters to Frieda*)
      f. Action Nominal (*Max's/the giving of the letters to Frieda*)
      g. Derived Nominal (*Max's/the gift of the letters to Frieda*)
      h. Noun (*spatula*)

As we saw in Chapter 3, despite its title ('Nouniness'), Ross's (1973*b*) paper argues for a cline between noun phrases and clauses, not for a cline of elements that are more or less nominal.

Ross (1973*a*) deals with 'noun phrasiness', a theme he took up again in a lengthy 1995 article. He shows that the element *there* is an NP on the basis of sentences like *At no time were there believed to have been flies in this cake, were there?* where raising, passivization, number agreement, and tag formation apply. Nevertheless, *there* is less typically an NP than 'copperclad, brass-bottomed NP's like *Harpo*' (1973*a*: 96), as evidenced by the fact that its distributional possibilities are extremely limited. Newmeyer (1998: 235–40) discusses the following data selected from Ross's paper (some of the examples are his own):

(22) PROMOTION
    a. Harpo's being willing to return surprised me./Harpo surprised me by being willing to return.
    b. There being heat in the furnace surprised me./*There surprised me by being heat in the furnace.

(23) DOUBLE RAISING
    a. John is likely — to be shown — to have cheated.
    b. ?*There is likely — to be shown — to be no way out of this shoe.

(24) THINK OF . . . AS *NP*
    a. I thought of Freud as being wiggy.
    b. *I thought of there as being too much homework.

(25) WHAT′S . . . DOING *X*?
    a. What's he doing in jail?
    b. *What's there doing being no mistrial?

(26) BEING DELETION
    a. Hinswood (being) in the tub is a funny thought.
    b. There *(being) no more Schlitz is a funny thought.

(27) LEFT DISLOCATION
    a. Those guys, they're smuggling my armadillo to Helen.
    b. *There, there are three armadillos in the road.

(28) TOUGH MOVEMENT
    a. John will be difficult to prove to be likely to win.
    b. *There will be difficult to prove likely to be enough to eat.

(29) TOPICALIZATION
    a. John, I don't consider very intelligent.
    b. *There, I don't consider to be enough booze in the eggnog.

(30) SWOOPING
- a. I gave Sandra my zwieback, and she didn't want any./I gave Sandra, and she didn't want any, my zwieback.
- b. I find there to be no grounds for contempt proceedings, and there may have been previously./*I find there, which may have been previously, to be no grounds for contempt proceedings.

(31) EQUI
- a. After he laughed politely, Oliver wiped his mustache./After laughing politely, Oliver wiped his mustache.
- b. After there is a confrontation, there's always some good old-time head-busting./*After being a confrontation, there's always some good old-time head-busting.

(32) CONJUNCTION REDUCTION
- a. Manny wept and Sheila wept./Manny and Sheila wept.
- b. There were diplodocuses, there are platypuses, and there may well also be diplatocodypuses./*There were diplodocuses, are platypuses, and may well also be diplatocodypuses.

Let us now turn to some observations made by Ross in an unpublished 1981 paper, which are intended to show that idioms like (33)–(36) behave differently with respect to a number of rules, depending on the degree of nouniness of the nouns contained inside them.

(33) to stub one's toe
(34) to hold one's breath
(35) to lose one's way
(36) to take one's time

Ross noticed that there are restrictions on the distribution of these idiomatic phrases:

(37) *A stubbed toe* can be very painful.
(38) **Held breath* is usually fetid when released.
(39) **A lost way* has been the cause of many a missed appointment.
(40) **Taken time* might tend to irritate your boss.

(41) I stubbed my toe, and she hers.
(42) I held my breath, and she hers.
(43) *I lost my way, and she hers.
(44) *I took my time, and she hers.

(45) Betty and Sue stubbed their toes.
(46) *Betty and Sue stubbed their toe.

(47) Betty and Sue held their breaths.
(48) Betty and Sue held their breath.
(49) *Betty and Sue lost their ways.
(50) Betty and Sue lost their way.
(51) *Betty and Sue took their times.
(52) Betty and Sue took their time.

Lakoff (1987*b*: 64) added the data below:

(53) I stubbed my toe, but didn't hurt *it*.
(54) Sam held his breath for a few seconds, and then released *it*.
(55) Harry lost his way, but found *it* again.
(56) *Harry took his time, but wasted *it*.

The data in (37)–(40) show that only the verb *stub* can appear in its participle form in attributive position. (41)–(44) demonstrate that gapping is possible only in clauses coordinated with *stub one's toe* and *hold one's breath*. Sentences (45)–(52) show that *stub one's toe* and *hold one's breath* both allow pluralization, while only the latter allows a singular as well. By contrast, *lose one's way* and *take one's time* act alike in not allowing pluralization. Lakoff's data in (53)–(56) show that only *take one's time* resists pronominalization. The upshot of all these findings is that different idioms behave differently with respect to each of the rules, depending on their degree of nouniness. Ross set up the following nouniness scale:

> time < way < breath < toe
> (where *toe* is the nouniest noun)

McCawley (1998: 192f.) also considers the category of NP, which he regards not as a 'classical category' but as being fuzzy. Its semantic characteristic is that it is an argument of a predicate. Its internal syntactic dimension is that 'it has a form typical of items that express logical arguments', that is 'if it is a pronoun or proper name of the form Det N' (McCawley 1998: 192). From an external syntactic point of view an item is a noun phrase if it occurs in an argument position. In McCawley's framework, then, there exist 'dimensions of NP-hood'. He sets up Table 5.3, reminiscent of Ross's work (although without a reference to him), to demonstrate this phenomenon.[6]

---

[6] McCawley makes a distinction between two types of external syntactic dimensions for NPs: *external_s syntactic* and *external_d syntactic*. The distinction is not made very clear, but as far as I can see, the former refers to typical NP positions at the surface, while the latter refers to argument positions in 'deep structure', or items that have replaced deep structure NPs, e.g. clausal subjects.

TABLE 5.3 McCawley's dimensions of NP-hood

	Sem.	Int. Synt.	Ext.$_s$ Synt.	Ext.$_d$ Synt.
That town I can't stand	+	+	+	−
That John left shocked us	+	−	+	+
It shocked us that John left	+	−	−	−
Sophie is a lawyer	−	+	+	+
A brain surgeon he isn't	−	+	−	−
There was a man outside	−	−	+	+
He went home that day	+	+	(+)	+
He went home last Tuesday	+	(+)	(+)	+

Source: McCawley (1998: 193); see also McCawley (1977/1982: 197f.)

That day and *last Tuesday* are semantically NPs because of an understood predicate *on*.

Returning to Ross, his squishes have been severely criticized, as we briefly saw in Chapter 3. For Geoffrey Pullum 'squishes are a complete red herring, without descriptive or theoretical value of any kind' (1976: 20). For Newmeyer fuzziness is not part of the grammar, but merely a by-product of performance. In discussing Ross's work on *there* (see above) in his 1998 book, Newmeyer claims that all the distributional peculiarities of *there* 'follow from the lexical semantics of *there* and the pragmatics of its use' (1998: 189). The data in (22b) and (24b) are explained, so argues Newmeyer, because elements like *there*, whether they are construed as meaningless elements or otherwise, cannot occur in the positions shown because they 'are not able to intrude into one's consciousness' (1998: 189). (25b) is bad for a similar reason: 'abstract settings, etc., cannot themselves "act"; rather they are the setting for action' (1998: 189) (30b)–(31b) are out because elements like *there* are not able to be modified (it is not clear how this is relevant to (31), though), while (27b)–(29b) demonstrate that they cannot act as discourse topics. Finally, (26b) is ruled out because *there* is not followed by an existential verb, while (23b) and (32b) are deemed acceptable.

Both Bouchard (1995: 31f.) and Newmeyer (1998: 224–6) criticize Ross's NP-squish. Bouchard notes that all the tests depend on NP-referentiality, but stops short of couching this observation in a coherent alternative explanation of the facts. For example, all that he says about the facts in (45)–(52) is the following '[p]luralization in [(45)–(52)] raises the problem of distributive effects and of factors like the count/mass distinction; again aspects of referentiality' (1995: 32). What is the reader to make of this? To explain the unacceptability of (56) pragmatics is appealed to. It is only because this sentence describes an odd situation that it must be ruled out, according to Bouchard. (57) below is fine:

(57)   Instead of giving his time to a good cause, Harry wasted it.

Note, though, that this example involves a different idiom (*give his time* vs. *take his time*). For Bouchard, in the idioms *stub one's toe* and *take one's time* '*toe* is not a better example of a N than *time*; it is a better example of a THING' (1995: 33). Apparently, then, prototypes are recognized in the case of real-world objects, but not in the case of grammatical objects.

For Newmeyer the judgements given above also do not follow from the degree of NP-hood of the idiom chunks in question, but from independently needed principles. (38) and (40) are impossible because *held* and *taken* can never occur as premodifying elements, though Newmeyer concedes that he has no explanation for the badness of (39), given that we can say, for example, *a lost cause*. The facts in (43) and (44) are explained by Newmeyer by appealing to discourse factors. Consider the following data taken from his book (1998: 192; his (44)):

(58)   a.   I lost my way, and she her way.
       b.   I took my time, and she her time.
       c.   ?I ate my ice cream and she hers.
       d.   In the race to get to the airport, Mary and John lost their way, but we didn't lose ours (and so we won).

Newmeyer argues, contra Ross, that gapping *is* possible for *lose one's way* and *take one's time* (cf. (58a/b)), and surmises that it 'apparently requires a contrastive focus reading of the gapped constituent' (1998: 239). This explains why (58c) behaves like (43) and (44), and why (58d) is fine. The claim regarding gapping is unclear, and in general the reasoning is rather nebulous (notice the hedge 'apparently'). What is more, I do not see why (58c) should be queried. It is certainly not as bad as (43)/(44). Newmeyer is aware of this, because he puts only a question mark in front of (58c) despite claiming that it seems grammatically equally bad as (43)/(44). An additional problem for Newmeyer is that he argues for pragmatic explanations of the data, but it is not clear whether the 'contrastive focus' requirement for (58a/b) is in fact a grammatical rather than a pragmatic constraint.

Turning to the data in (45)–(52), Newmeyer, like Bouchard, puts forward the possibility that they fall out from the fact that toes and breaths can be individuated, but not ways and times. Finally, Newmeyer shows that *time* in the idiom *to take one's time* is pronominalizable:

(59) a. Harry took his time and wasted it.
   b. Harry took his time, which doesn't mean that he didn't find
      a way to waste it.

Criticism of Ross's work is justified in many cases because his data, and his judgements of the data, are not always clear. Ross was well aware of the drawbacks of his article, and that his findings were not couched in a theory (see 1973*a*: 128). While certainly not all of his data are convincing, and he offers the reader a mass of often not very transparent facts, he *does* convincingly demonstrate that members of form classes do not possess the same distributional potential. Appealing to pragmatic/discoursal explanations for these limited distributions, as Newmeyer and Bouchard do, is attractive in some cases. In other cases it is not. For example, it would be hard to think of a pragmatic/discoursal reason for the fact that we can say *a happy child* and *the child is happy/very happy/happier/happiest*, but not *the fool is utter/*very utter/*utterer/*utterest*. What is worse is that Newmeyer's and Bouchard's alternative pragmatic/discoursal explanations for the degrees of prototypicality of class members perceived by Ross are couched in the most general and ethereal terms, and sometimes make the wrong predictions. They do not (as yet) add up to a plausible alternative in the shape of a well-reasoned and coherent pragmatic theory of fuzziness.

5.3 SG within clauses

There are a number of different ways in which we can approach SG in clauses. One possible approach is to base the clausal prototype on complementation patterns. Traditional grammars, such as Quirk *et al.* (1985), make use of such patterns, for example SV (Subject–Verb; intransitive), SVO (Subject–Verb–Object; transitive), SVOO (Subject–Verb–Indirect Object–Direct Object; ditransitive), SVOC (Subject–Verb–Direct Object–Object Complement; complex transitive), SVOA (Subject–Verb–Direct Object–Adjunct), etc. It is the complementation properties of the verb that give each of these patterns their label. We might wonder whether there is any sense in saying that any one of these configurations has a privileged status and constitutes a more central type of clause than any of the other patterns. This question is similar to the issue raised with respect to 'valency gradience' in Section 5.1.1. The answer must surely be 'no', as each of these patterns model complete sentences, without there being a sense of defectiveness. However, it would be a different matter if one of the components were missing, as in, for example, (60):

(60)   I want [to give the elephant some chocolate]

Here a *to*-infinitival clause complements the verb *want*, but notice that its subject is missing (or non-overt[7]). I will return to the idea of incompleteness, which seems to play a role in identifying clausal prototypes, below.

A second approach is to establish a gradient within verb phrases (and hence also clauses) based on the notion of finiteness. Quirk *et al.* (1985: 149–50) propose a gradient between verb phrase types, using the following five criteria and resulting in Table 5.4:

1. Finite verb phrases can occur as the verb phrase of independent clauses.
2. Finite verb phrases have tense contrast.
3. There is person concord and number concord between the subject of a clause and the finite verb phrase.
4. Finite verb phrases contain, as their first or only word, a finite verb form which may be either an operator or a simple present or past form. *Do*-support is used in forming (for example) negative and interrogative constructions.
5. Finite verb phrases have mood, which indicates the factual, nonfactual, or counterfactual status of the predication.

TABLE 5.4 Quirk *et al.*'s scale of finiteness

	1	2	3	4	5	
Indicative	+	+	+	+	+	⎫
Subjunctive	+	?	−	−	+	⎬ Finite
Imperative	+	−	−	?	+	⎭
Infinitive	−	−	−	−	−	(Nonfinite)

Givón (1993: 288) establishes a cline of 'clausiness' based on a *finite clause prototype*, which he characterizes as follows:

In a typical simple clause in English, the subject and direct object roles are not marked morphologically, but rather are marked by their position relative to the verb—S–V–O. Indirect objects are marked by prepositions, and the verb is marked by tense–aspect–modality markers and various auxiliaries.

The notion of a finite clause prototype is appealing. The idea is that the most typical clause is a clause which carries tense, is independent, and complete (in a way to be made more precise below) at the same time. In view of this we must take account of the notion of subordination in characterizing

---

[7] The GB/P&P framework posits a phonetically null PRO subject here.

clausal prototypes, and one way of doing so is to say that a main clause is more typically a clause than a subordinate clause. It follows from this that nonfinite clauses are less prototypically clausal than finite clauses, because they are always dependent. In turn, verbless clauses would be even less centrally clausal. We can now establish a subsective clausal gradient as follows:

less clausal
→

main clause > finite subordinate clause > nonfinite subordinate clause >
verbless clause

However, this gradient does not take into account the distinction between embedded and non-embedded subordination. A number of linguists have proposed that there exists a cline of clause linking, such that we have parataxis at one end of the cline, embedding at the other end, and hypotaxis somewhere in between (cf. e.g. Huddleston 1984: 379f.; Lehmann 1988; Hopper and Traugott 1993). Under this view adjunct clauses, such as the concessive clause in (61), are less integrated in their matrix clause (i.e. more independent) than are complement clauses.

(61)   Although we saw an elephant, it wasn't an Indian one.

Adjunct clauses are hypotactically linked to their hosts, whereas complement clauses are embedded.[8] Neither type of clause can occur independently, but their degree of syntactic integration differs. We can incorporate the clause-linking gradient into the clausiness gradient as follows:

less clausal
→

main clause > hypotactic finite clause > embedded finite clause > hypotactic
nonfinite clause > embedded nonfinite clause > verbless clause

We are still not quite there yet. We need to take account of the fact that in many cases particular grammatical functions are left implicit. Examples are sentences such as (60) above, where the subject of the subordinate clause is unexpressed, although it is understood to be coreferential with the subject of the matrix clause. The clause can be said to be *desententialized* (Lehmann 1988: 193f.). The notion of *Complete Functional Complex (CFC)* introduced by Chomsky (1986a: 169) might be useful in this connection. This is understood as a unit in which 'all grammatical functions compatible with its head are realized'. Any clause that does not constitute a CFC (which I will here interpret as a clause that lacks one or more *overtly* expressed grammatical functions which the transitivity properties of the predicate of the clause in question require) is then by definition not a

---

[8] Some linguists have suggested that a high degree of morphosyntactic integration correlates with a high degree of connectedness between the states of affairs expressed in the sentence. See Hopper and Traugott (1993: 171) for discussion.

prototypical clause. We can extend the notion of completeness to include, for example, the presence/absence of complementizers. Taking this dimension into account, the gradient now looks like this:

less clausal

---

main clause > ('complete'>'incomplete') hypotactic finite clause > ('complete'>'incomplete') embedded finite clause > ('complete'> 'incomplete') hypotactic nonfinite clause > ('complete'>'incomplete') embedded nonfinite clause > ('complete'>'incomplete') verbless clause

Examples on the cline we have now established are shown below:

(62)   [We saw an elephant].   Main clause
(63)   [Although we saw an elephant], it wasn't
        an Indian one.
(64)   [You shout], we die.
(65)   We think [that we saw an elephant].
(66)   We think [we saw an elephant].
(67)   The elephant [that we saw] is angry with us.
(68)   The elephant [we saw] is angry with us.
(69)   [With John constantly shouting], the elephant
        became angry.
(70)   [While running], the elephant squirted water at us.
(71)   I don't want [the elephant to squirt water].
(72)   I want [to give the elephant some chocolate].
(73)   [The elephant angry with us], we ran away.
(74)   [Angry with us], the elephant squirted water.   Verbless clause

At the top end of the continuum we have a main clause which can stand on its own. At the other extreme we have a verbless clause, which clearly cannot be used independently. In between there are a number of finite and nonfinite clauses. As we have just seen, (63) contains a concessive subordinate clause which is hypotactically linked to the superordinate clause. (64) contains an incomplete conditional clause whose subordinator ('if') is suppressed.[9] Sentences (65) and (66) involve complement clauses. Both have all their grammatical functions realized, but notice that the subordinator is missing in (66). In (67) and (68) the subordinate clauses are finite relative clauses. Neither instantiates a CFC (the direct object is not expressed; though see below), and in addition (68) lacks a subordinator. Sentences (69) and (70), both of which contain non-embedded subordinate clauses, involve complete and

---

[9] The two components of this sentence could also be viewed as being paratactically linked, as Hopper and Traugott (1993: 173) suggest.

incomplete nonfinite adjunct clauses, respectively, whereas (71) and (72), with embedded subordinate clauses, contain examples of *to*-infinitival complement clauses, one of which lacks an overt subject. Finally, (73) and (74) are verbless clauses: (73) has an overt subject, while (74) does not.

Notice that (65)/(66) are higher on the gradient than (67)/(68). The reason is that another dimension affecting clausiness comes into play here, namely the level at which a clause is positioned in a tree. While the clauses in (65)/(66) are arguments of the main verb, the relative clauses in (67)/(68) are more deeply embedded, within an argument constituent. We could make our cline even more fine-grained by making a distinction between restrictive and nonrestrictive relative clauses. The latter are sometimes said not to be part of their host clause at all (see Fabb 1990; Haegeman 1988; Burton-Roberts 1999).

It is important to see that the positioning of these clauses on the gradient depends to some extent on one's grammatical framework. Thus, in (67) if you take the view that the relative pronoun functions as object, then the clause is more complete than if you adopt the view that this sentence involves an empty operator of some sort, as has been argued in the generative framework. In this particular case, whether we regard *that* as the object of the clause or not does not affect its position on the gradient.

Some of the dimensions affecting the degree of clausiness mentioned above are discussed from a cross-linguistic perspective in Lehmann (1988), who looks at a number of further dimensions, for example whether a clause has an illocutionary force of its own. Lehmann's paper takes a different angle, however, from the one adopted here: while I am concerned with SG within the category of clause—that is, with establishing a cline of clausiness—Lehmann is concerned with a typology of clause linking, specifically with the degree to which pairs of clauses can be said to be intertwined with each other. He establishes a number of gradients relevant to clause linking, for example the gradient that runs from 'clause' at one end to 'noun' at the other. This is referred to in the present book as Intersective Gradience. Lehmann, however, does not distinguish between SG and IG, which he might profitably have done to distinguish the cline he establishes between hypotaxis and embedding from his other clines. The former can be seen as instantiating Subsective Gradience along the parameter [more/less subordinate], as we have just seen.

5.4 SG in grammar

The notion of Subsective Gradience has close affinities with that of prototype. There are also differences, which I signalled in Chapter 4. SG can be defined along the following lines: in a category A, if for any two members α and β we can say that α is more A-like than β, then A displays SG. β is then decategorialized with respect to α. However, β, despite being less centrally A-like, does not become more like some other form class; it is merely a less prototypical member of A. An example of this involves the contrast between adjectives like *happy, thin,* and *utter.* As we have seen, *happy* and *thin* conform to a greater number of adjective criteria than *utter,* but we would nevertheless not want to say that *utter* has become more like some other form class. Similarly, the modal auxiliaries are less verb-like in several respects than full verbs; yet they do not become more like some other word class. The quotation at the beginning of this chapter from William Blake makes this point rather well: 'A Good Apple tree or a Bad, is an Apple tree still: a Horse is not more a Lion for being a Bad Horse'.[10] The point is also made by Putnam (1975/1992: 251) in discussing the notion of 'stereotype', which is close in meaning to 'prototype':

> The fact that a feature (e.g. stripes) is included in the stereotype associated with a word *X* does not mean that it is an analytic truth that all *X*s have that feature, nor that most *X*s have that feature, nor that all normal *X*s have that feature, nor that some *X*s have that feature. Three-legged tigers and albino tigers are not logically contradictory entities.

It is thus important not to confuse 'degree of typicality/representativity' within categories with 'degree of membership'.[11] Subsective Gradience involves members of grammatical categories conforming to a greater or lesser extent to the prototype. The distinction between Subsective and Intersective Gradience is not always recognized. In his early work Ross did not distinguish between SG and IG. His 1972 paper (which deals with a perceived squish between verbs, adjectives, and nouns) is concerned with intercategorial fuzziness, while his 1973 articles deal with subsective shadings.

To conclude this chapter, consider the following question: does gradience percolate upwards and/or downwards? If we establish SG for a particular word class by establishing that the class contains prototypical and less prototypical exemplars, does it then follow that we also have SG for the phrases or clauses that these elements head? Is a noun phrase headed by a peripheral noun a peripheral noun phrase? Taylor (1998: 185) claims that 'a construction schema that includes, as one of its parts, the category *adjective* (or *noun*), tends to inherit the fuzziness associated with the adjective (or noun) category. Prototype effects associated with word categories therefore propagate themselves throughout the grammar.' There is a hedge here, and Taylor is right to be

---

[10] From: 'On Homers [sic] Poetry', cited in Fodor (1998: 88).
[11] See also Section 3.4.6.

cautious. It appears that there is no straightforward answer to the questions posed at the beginning of this paragraph. There are clear cases of higher projection SG that are the result of word-level SG. For example, the fact that *there* (as discussed by Ross) is a non-prototypical NP is the result of *there* being a less typical noun (it cannot be preceded by a determiner, cannot take a plural ending, etc.). However, there are also cases where higher-level SG does not obtain where there is word-level SG. Thus *flour* is a non-count noun and for that reason a less prototypical noun. The phrases it heads can nevertheless occur in all NP positions (*Flour is an essential ingredient of bread/We need flour/The need for flour*), so its phrasal projection is not a less prototypical NP. So what we find is that lower-level SG sometimes leads to higher-level SG, but not always. However, the generalization that if we have higher-level SG it is always the result of lower-level SG does appear to be true. Thus we cannot have, say, a non-prototypical NP headed by a prototypical noun.

As one of the dimensions of gradience, Subsective Gradience is a property of grammar that can be demonstrated through a systematic investigation of the distributional properties of formatives. Attempts to give SG a bad press are without much force, because no viable alternative to explain the facts is offered. What is more, so long as we do not confuse the notion of 'shades of prototypicality within classes' with the idea of 'degrees of class membership', it is unclear why linguists would object to recognizing SG in grammar, given that it does not concern class membership as such. After all, if at any point in a particular grammatical process or derivation an element α is required, it does not matter whether α is a good or a bad example of the category it belongs to. SG should therefore be unproblematic for any framework that wishes to defend strict Aristotelian categorization. Thus, just as in the case of Blake's good and bad apple trees, we can say that a noun is a noun, a noun phrase is a noun phrase etc., even if there exist instances which are not prototypical exemplars.

In the next chapter I turn to Intersective Gradience, which obtains when elements display morphosyntactic characteristics of two categories simultaneously.

6

Intersective Gradience

O heavenly mingle!

(William Shakespeare, *Antony and Cleopatra*, I.5)

Recall that at the end of Chapter 3 I introduced the notion of IG as follows: IG involves two form class categories α and β, and obtains where there exists a set γ of elements characterized by of a subset of α-like properties and a subset of β-like properties. When there is gradience between two categories α and β we will say that these classes 'converge' by virtue of the fact that there exist elements which display properties of both categories. Given this definition, we can view IG as a kind of 'intercategorial resemblance'. I will maintain that grammatical categories are strictly bounded, and do not overlap. The intersection is between γ and the full set of α-like properties, and between γ and the full set of β-like properties. In what follows my aim is to critically discuss a number of case studies of IG which are intended to cover the borderline cases between the major word class categories of English grammar, as well as between phrases. We will see that many of the purported cases of IG are meretricious, and careful scrutiny reveals that they can be handled without an appeal to gradience, at least as traditionally conceived in terms of fuzzy categorial boundaries. As in the previous chapter, I maintain a distinction here between gradience at the word class level and at the phrasal level, principally because there are cases where the gradience seems not to be projected from the head upwards, but appears to obtain between phrases as wholes.

6.1 IG between word classes

6.1.1 *Gradience between pre-head elements within noun phrases*

In the pre-head zone within noun phrases traditionally two types of elements can occur: specifiers and modifiers. The former linearly precede the latter, which in turn precede the head noun. One would expect there to be categorial indeterminacies between the different types of pre-head element.

6.1.1.1 *Determinatives and pronouns*   Consider the sentences below:

(1)   *You people* should consider giving money to the needy.
(2)   *Us nurses* never get paid enough.

In these examples the italicized strings are NPs headed by *people* and *nurses*. Right at the beginning of the phrases we have the words *you* and *us*, respectively. Most linguists have analysed these words in an unambiguous way. Thus, Postal (1966: 193) regards *us* in (2) as an article: 'in such sequences we actually find the so-called pronouns *we/us* and *you* as *articles* in *surface structures*. And this is among the strongest evidence for our overall claim that so-called pronouns have essentially the same type of derivation and status as traditionally recognized definite articles' (emphasis in original). Jackendoff (1977: 106) adopts a variant of this proposal, as do Abney (1987) and Huddleston and Pullum *et al.* (2002: 422), the latter under the heading 'overlap between the determinative and pronoun categories'.[1] By contrast, Delorme and Dougherty (1972) have argued that in italicized sequences like the one in (2) *us* and *nurses* are pronouns in an appositive relationship. For Hudson (1990) and Spinillo (2003) these words are also pronouns, although they are not regarded as being in an appositive relationship.

It might not be unreasonable to posit a case of IG here. After all, elements like *you* and *us* are determinative-like by virtue of their phrase-initial position and because they cannot combine with undisputed determinatives (cf. *the you rich people/*the us nurses*). On the other hand, however, as (2) shows, the elements under discussion can show a case contrast, a typical pronominal property. It is this property that argues most strongly in favour of assigning words like *you* and *us* in the strings above to the class of pronouns by pointing out that otherwise they would be the only kind of determinative in English that can occur in the objective case. Similar issues arise for demonstrative elements like *this/that/those/these*, etc. in pre-head position within NPs. I will return to these in Chapter 8.

6.1.1.2 *Determinatives and adjectives*   In this section we will look at *many* and *such*. Starting with the former, consider the sentence below:

(3)   His many sins are legendary.

In this sentence *many* occurs between a determinative and a noun, and has been analysed as a (post)determiner (Quirk *et al.* 1985: 262). For Huddleston and

---

[1] Huddleston and Pullum *et al.* (2002) use the term *determinative* as a class label, and *determiner* as a function label. I follow this practice here.

Pullum *et al.* (2002: 539) *many* is a determinative, not an adjective, because it can occur as a 'fused determiner-head in a partitive construction' like (4), whereas adjectives cannot:

(4)   many of them

Compare:

(5)   *(the) good of them

Semantically, *many* is determinative-like in contributing a 'specifying' meaning to the NP. Huddleston and Pullum *et al.* concede that *many* also has adjectival properties. This is so given its possible prenominal position in noun phrases (e.g. *many books*). It would have to precede other 'contentful' adjectives, should they occur, as (6) and (7) show:

(6)   His many disgraceful sins are legendary.
(7)   *His disgraceful many sins are legendary.

As we saw in Chapter 4, Kayne (2002) deals with the seemingly hybrid nature of *many* by arguing that it moves from an adjective position inside NP/DP to a determinative position.

   The correct view would seem to be that *many* is more adjective-like than determinative-like, given that it can be modified by *very* and can occur in predicative position:

(8)   His very many sins are legendary.
(9)   His legendary sins are many.

Note also that *many* can take a comparative or superlative form:

(10)   *many* books/*more* books/*most* books

Seemingly running counter to an adjective analysis of *many* are data such as (11), where *many* precedes a determinative:

(11)   Many a film was watched by us over Christmas.

But examples like this are not really problematic because adjectives can also appear in this position, witness (12):

(12)   So *beautiful* a day it was, we all went on a picnic.

Turning now to *such*, this word is often analysed as a (pre)determinative when it occurs before nouns in NPs (*such a book*) but as a pronoun elsewhere (*his achievement was such that he was given a reward*). This dual categorization may well be correct, but it would be better if it could be avoided. Notice that like *many* the word *such* also has adjectival properties, a fact which prompts Biber *et al.* (1999: 280–1) to class this word as a *semi-determiner*. Such elements are 'determiner-like words which are often described as adjectives'. They 'have no descriptive meaning and primarily serve to specify the reference of the noun'. This amounts to positing a fuzzy boundary between determinatives and adjectives. However, Spinillo (2003, 2004) convincingly argues that *such* is in fact best analysed as an adjective. What is the evidence? Consider the following data:

(13) *Such people* never admit to being guilty.   (Siegel 1994: 482)
(14) The guilty person never admitted to being *such*.   (*ibid.*)

In (13) the element *such* appears immediately before the noun, while in (14) it appears in predicative position. Although (13) does not preclude an analysis of *such* as a determinative, the adjective analysis is much more plausible in the light of data like those shown below:

(15) two new *such* friends   (Siegel 1994: 482)
(16) more destructive *such* children   (*ibid.*: 485)
(17) future *such* events   (Carlson 1980: 247)
(18) a further *such* error   (Huddleston and Pullum *et al.* 2002: 435)

In these cases *such* occurs in what is clearly a sequence of adjectives close to the head. In short, while displaying properties of determinatives, *many* and *such* predominantly behave like adjectives.

6.1.1.3 *Determinatives and adverbs*   In the example below the element *that* is sometimes analysed as a determinative (Huddleston and Pullum *et al.* 2002: 547f.), sometimes as an adverb (Quirk *et al.* 1985: 447).

(19) I didn't think she was *that helpful*.

In (19) *that* shares properties of two categories, like the other cases of IG we looked at, in this case adverb and determinative. Its meaning is 'so' or 'very'. *That* is adverb-like in its position preceding an adjective, but determinative-like in its shape and expansional potential, as (20) shows:

(20) I didn't think she was *all that helpful*.

Ordinary determinatives also allow premodification by *all*, whereas adjectives do not (cf. *all that cake*, but *all helpful). We can also say *She wasn't as helpful as all that*. A drawback of analysing *that* as a determinative here is that there is no nominal head in this syntactic environment.

What about the cases where other determinative-like elements are used pre-adjectivally, for example *the, this, no, any, much, (a) little, enough,* and *all* (listed in Huddleston and Pullum *et al.* 2002: 549)? Some of these seem to be more determinative-like than *that* in (19) because they have meanings that are at least partially the same as the meanings they have as determinatives. For example, *that* in (21) has indexical meaning, just like its undisputed determinative counterpart, but it does not add definiteness in the way the determinative does, quite simply because adjective phrases are not marked for definiteness.

(21) The table is *that* long.

In (22) *the* modifies a compared adjective and adverb, and the same is true for (23), if we regard *more* as the comparative form of the adjective *many* (see Section 6.1.1.2).

(22) *The taller* he is, *the more easily* he will be able to reach the higher shelves.
(23) *The more* candidates we have, *the better.*

Consider also (24):

(24) *The bigger* the house is, *the better* your quality of life will be.

Jespersen (1909–1949, vol. VII, 14.6) notes that there are two different items *the* before comparatives, neither of which developed from the Old English determinative. One of these developed from the OE instrumental of *that,* namely *þy* with the meaning 'by how much' (as in (23)), the other developed from relative *þe.* In earlier stages of English there was often a *the* where it is now dropped, as in (25):

(25) What were thy lips *the worse* for one poor kiss? (Shakespeare, *The Merchant of Venice,* cited in Jespersen 1909–1949)

In some cases *the* is still obligatory:

(26) It changed critical habits in England for *the better.*
      (G. Saintsbury, *A Short History of English Literature,* 1919, cited in Jespersen 1909–1949)

In others it is optional:

(27) Not a soul will be any *the wiser.* (R. H. Benson, *The Dawn of All,* cited in Jespersen 1909-1949)

The analysis of *that* in (21) and *the* in (22)–(27) is particularly intractable in present-day English. In examples like (22) we can insert—just about—a noun after *taller:*

(28)   *The taller man* he is, *the more easily* he will be able to reach the
       higher shelves.

This would be an argument in favour of analysing *the* as a determinative,
but this is obviously not possible for the string *the more easily*. The strings
'Det.–Adj.^{comp}/Adv.^{comp}–(clause)' that we find in these examples seem to
involve a non-prototypical determinative, and are perhaps best analysed in
terms of a theory of constructions, given their formulaic nature.

6.1.1.4 *Adjectives and nouns*   Within noun phrases elements that can occur in
the slot Det—N are typically adjectives (adjective phrases, to be precise), but,
as Coates (1971) shows (see Chapter 4) some of these adjectives share
properties with nouns. Thus, elements like *racial, nasal, solar, electric, serial,
medical* are derived from nouns, and differ from prototypical adjectives like
interesting and *sad* in not allowing intensification by *very* or comparison
(although this is not true for all adjectives ending in -*al*, cf. e.g. *suicidal*).
They are nevertheless adjectives heading APs, if only peripheral ones, witness
the syntactic positions they can occupy and the presence of adjectival suffixes.
    In more compound-like phrases of the type *boy actor*, as discussed by
Curme (see Chapter 3), the element *boy* is more nominal than the adjectives
ending in -*al* discussed above. While it occurs in a typical adjective position,
we would not want to call it an adjective, because it does not behave like an
adjective in other respects (**the very boy actor*, **the boy young actor*, **the actor
is boy*). It could be argued, then, that we are dealing with a case of IG between
adjectives and nouns. For Curme the element *boy* in the phrase *boy actor* is a
noun 'used as an adjective'. Huddleston (1984: 93f.) objects to the locution 'an
X used as a Y' in connection with Curme's *boy actor*. He asks:

Is it being claimed that an X used as a Y actually is a Y or that it is merely functionally
like a Y? If it actually is a Y, then in what sense is it also an X?' If it is not a Y but just
functionally like one, how can this be reconciled with a definition of Y in terms of
function—if Y is defined as a word having a certain function, how can a word occur
with that function and yet fail to be a Y?

(See also Huddleston and Pullum *et al.* 2002: 537.) For Huddleston *boy* in *boy
actor* is indisputably a noun, and the fact that it modifies *actor* does not make
it an adjective, nor a 'noun used as an adjective'. I agree with Huddleston only
partially. Clearly, a 'noun used as an adjective' is not an adjective, but a noun,
and even Curme's answer to the question Huddleston poses at the beginning of
the quotation above would presumably be 'no'.[2] Huddleston's question 'if it is

---

[2] Having said this, Curme confuses the issue when he discusses the expressive power of nouns
(and other word classes) used as adjectives (*a cat-and-dog life, a dry-as-dust study*, etc.). Of these he

not a Y but just functionally like one, how can this be reconciled with a definition of Y in terms of function?' is a valid question to ask someone like Curme who defines adjectives in functional terms (1935: 42). If we then say that a particular element is a 'noun used as an adjective', then we may well ask in which sense that noun should not simply be classed as an adjective. However, Huddleston's question is valid only if adjectives are indeed defined by making reference *only* to their function. We can, however, also define adjectives distributionally, for example as elements which are able to occupy an attributive position in noun phrases, which are gradable, etc. If we do so, then there is no *inherent* objection to saying that a particular element is a noun used as an adjective, if we understand 'used' to mean 'distributed'. If we use this locution the nounhood of the element in question is undisputed; we are simply saying that the noun is distributed in a way that is more typical of adjectives. To make this clearer, consider an analogy: if we describe a particular instrument as 'a knife used as a letter-opener', there is no doubt that we regard the object in question as a knife. We are simply saying that it is employed in a way that is more typical of letter-openers. The knife on a particular occasion becomes 'like' a letter-opener. Where Curme goes wrong is his purely functional definition of adjectives. We must give him credit, however, for grappling with the discrepancy between on the one hand the modifying function that *boy* performs (typical of adjectives) and its form (nominal). Huddleston perhaps comes down a little too hard on Curme. It makes sense to say that in phrases like *boy actor* the element *boy* is a noun, not an adjective, nor something in between. Nevertheless, it seems reasonable to say that *boy* is decategorized, and hence *less* nominal than *boy* in the phrase *a tall boy*, simply by virtue of the fact that it is used attributively, not normally a nominal position (notice also that *boy* cannot be pluralized). Under this view, then, *boy* is a noun, which displays an adjectival property in this particular syntactic context. Ross's term *adjectival noun* is perhaps quite an appropriate one: it clearly signals that we are dealing with a noun, onto which some adjectival properties have rubbed.[3]

Croft (2001: 34–44) signals a problem for the account given here. If we say that a word like *utter* is an adjective by virtue of the fact that it can occur pre-nominally, although not in other adjective positions (as we have done in Section 5.1.3), then we also need to call *boy* in *boy actor* an adjective, as its distributional pattern is exactly the same as that of *utter* (*very boy actor/*very

says 'Sometimes the new adjective is used alongside of an older adjective but with a different meaning' (1935: 44). This *does* suggest that he regards 'nouns used as adjectives' as adjectives.

[3] McCawley (1998: 764) uses the term adjectival noun in a less felicitous way, namely as an element that is syntactically a noun, but whose semantics is typical of adjectives.

utter fool/*the actor is boy/*the fool is utter, etc.). We might then be tempted to posit multiple class membership for *boy*, which would then be either a noun or an adjective, depending on its syntactic environment. However, this solution is unattractive because many nouns can occur pre-nominally, and a great number of words would then end up in two categories, obscuring the fact that in most of its uses a word like *boy* is clearly a noun. The only cases where multiple class membership is warranted are examples like *maiden voyage*, discussed in Huddleston and Pullum *et al.* (2002: 537, fn. 4). Here *maiden* has a different meaning in attributive position than it has as the head of a phrase in typical NP positions (*a young maiden from Perth*).[4]

There are of course other possible analyses for phrases like *boy actor*. One approach, found in, for example, Zandvoort (1962: 266) is to speak of 'partial conversion' and say that in a phrase like 'the *boy king* (noun > adj.), *boy* is a noun and an adjective at the same time; it is used attributively, but it could not, for instance, take *-er* and *-est*, like most monosyllabic adjectives'. Of course, this violates Aristotelian principles of categorization. Another approach is to claim that all N–N sequences like *boy actor* are compounds, as in effect does Baker (2003: 193). The distinction between phrasal and compound status for N–N sequences is a hotly debated one. For discussion see for example Bauer (1998), Giegerich (2004), and Plag (2006). An advantage of treating all N–N sequences as compounds is that there would be no gradience between adjectives and nouns in these cases. However, the syntactic properties of *boy actor*, for example the possibility of the element *boy* coordinating with another element (*boy and girl actors*) or being modified ([*teenage boy*]*actor*) suggest this is a phrase, and so does the stress pattern. For a discussion of these criteria, see Huddleston and Pullum *et al.* (2002: 448f.).

Apparently similar to the case of *boy actor*, but in fact quite different, as we will see in a moment, is an example like (29), from Denison (2001):

(29)   I was remembering Marianne and *the fun times* we
        have had. (*OED*, 1968)

The word *fun* is interesting because, unlike *boy*, it can distribute more widely as an adjective. Denison observes a cline towards adjectivehood in the following examples:

---

[4] Croft would probably say that the methodological decision taken here not to lump the nominal modifiers of nouns with adjectives is a case of *language-internal methodological opportunism* (2001:41) which 'simply selects a subset of language-specific criteria to define a category when the criteria do not all match. That subset of criteria, or possibly just one criterion, defines the category in question. Mismatching distributions are ignored, or are used to define subclasses or multiple class membership'. For more discussion, see Croft (2007) and Aarts (2007).

(30)   She's so completely lovely and *fun* and joyful. (British component
       of the *International Corpus of English*, W1B-003 #73:1)
(31)   We have the Osborns, the Beals, the Hartungs, the Falmers, and
       us. Now let's think of *someone fun*. (*OED*, 1971)
(32)   ...perhaps send for that book you never bought earlier and have
       a really fun time with the wealth of designs from Iris Bishop or
       Wendy Phillips or whoever you like best. (*British National Corpus*,
       CA2 553)
(33)   It may not be *as fun* to watch it up close. (*Frown Corpus*, A17–113)
(34)   It was *so fun*. (1999, attested)
(35)   Valspeak is...the *funnest*, most totally radical language, I guess, like
       in the whole mega gnarly city of Los Angeles. (*OED Online*, 1982)

Fun in (30) looks like an adjective, because it is coordinated with other
adjectives. However, it is not unambiguously adjectival, because adjectives
can be coordinated with nouns. (Denison gives the example *it's lovely but
a mess*.) In (31) *fun* postmodifies a pronoun (cf. *someone happy*), while in (31)–
(34) other adjective properties manifest themselves clearly: modification by
really, *as*, and *so*, and, interestingly, the superlative ending in (35).

   For Denison *fun* is 'clearly a noun' in (36) and (37):

(36)   Painting is *more fun* and less soul-work than writing. (*OED*, 1927)
(37)   It was *such fun*.

To my mind, these should be positioned at the adjectival end of Denison's
cline, given that they involve a comparative form (i.e. 'funner') and intensification. Denison discusses a similar cline for the word *key*. Here are some
salient examples:

(38)   Occupants of *key offices* such as the Presidency or the
       Attorney-Generalship. (*OED*, 1926)
(39)   *The key verse* in this first section is verse 4; it is a crucial
       one (*Archer Corpus* 1959LLOY.H9)
(40)   More emotional weight is carried in the *key domestic* scenes
       in which...(*FLOB Corpus*, C01 103)
(41)   Noting that such incidents are not marginal but *key* to
       Edgeworth's plots...(Butler, 'Introduction', p. 41, Maria
       Edgeworth, *Castle Rackrent and Ennui*, Penguin)
(42)   There are a number of reasons why people lose their hair, stress
       is a *very key factor*. (*British National Corpus*, HVE 174)
(43)   Meiron Rowlands, one of the Ashley's *most key* appointments of this
       time...(*British National Corpus*, GU9 7)

For Denison in (38) and (39) *key* is a noun modifying another noun. In (40) what is interesting is that *key* is positioned in front of the adjective *domestic*. In premodifier sequences involving adjectives and nouns, adjectives are always ordered before nouns, which would suggest that *key* is an adjective in this example. In (41), as Denison notes, *key* is used without a determinative and is coordinated with another adjective. We might add to this that it has a complement here. In (42) it is intensified by *very*, one of the typical adjectival properties, and in (43) we have a superlative form. Denison concludes that 'there is no simple switch from N to A, rather a graded series of transitions' (2001: 11). But is this really so? As was not the case for *boy actor*, in which the element *boy* is syntactically unmalleable, as far as the adjectival properties that *boy* can assume are concerned (recall the impossibility of **the very boy actor*, **the boy young actor*, **the actor is boy*), the syntactic possibilities for words like *fun* and *key* are much greater. In fact we could argue that *all* Denison's examples of these words instantiate adjectives. This would be true even for examples like (38) and (39), given that examples like (42) and (43) are now attested in the language. In effect, we are applying Huddleston and Pullum *et al.*'s '*maiden voyage*-criterion' here (see above), to the extent that arguably *fun* and *key* have a different meaning in attributive position. Admittedly, this is clearer for *key* than for *fun*.

Adjectives and nouns resemble each other in further ways. Think of colour terms. These would appear to be adjectives when they occur attributively (*the red box*), but nominal when they appear in argument positions (*Red is my favourite colour*; *I like red*). But consider now the following intriguing problematic case noted in McCawley (1998: 768):

(44)   Ted wore a deep/*deeply blue necktie.

Here *blue* is nominal by virtue of the fact that it can be modified by an adjective, not by an adverb, but it behaves like an adjective because it itself premodifies a noun. McCawley argues for the possibility of allowing an element to belong to more than one syntactic category at the same time in a particular configuration. *Blue* would then be an 'A/N' in (44). According to McCawley, this dual analysis of *blue* is supported by the following data:

(45)   ?John is wearing a deeper blue shirt than he usually does.
(46)   *John is wearing a deep bluer shirt than he usually does.
(47)   ??John is wearing the deepest blue shirt that I've ever seen.

These sentences show that it is unacceptable to add comparative or superlative endings to either *deep* or to *blue* because they would conflict either with the A-part of the A/N or with the N-part of the A/N. Thus, the (adjectival) comparative and superlative endings in (45) and (47) demand that *blue* is a noun, but at the same time in modifying the noun *shirt*, the phrases *deeper/deepest blue* must be headed by an adjective. In (46) the comparative ending on *blue* demands that it is an adjective, while the adjective *deep* preceding it demands that it is a noun. However, there may be a way to avoid the undesirable dual categorization of colour terms in a particular syntactic configuration if we allow for the possibility that *deep blue* is an adjective–adjective compound when it occurs attributively or predicatively:

(48)   a [$_A$ deep blue] shirt
(49)   the shirt is [$_A$ deep blue][5]

In other uses the colour terms are either nouns (*this shirt is a deeper blue than that one*) or adjectives (*this yellow sofa is ugly*).

Consider next phrases like the following:

(50)   the rich, the fortunate, the ugly

These phrases are problematic because they appear to be NPs headed by adjectives. But if this were so, a generally accepted principle of grammar would be violated, namely endocentricity, which stipulates that all phrases must be properly headed.

One way to resolve the matter is to claim that *rich*, *fortunate*, and *ugly* are de-adjectival nouns, that is, nouns converted from adjectives. But this account is also not unproblematic, because we can insert for example *very* in front of *rich*, *fortunate*, and *ugly*, and in some cases we can add the prefix *un-*, as in (51):

(51)   The fortunate will go on holiday, the *unfortunate* will stay here.

In yet other cases we can have a comparative ending:

(52)   The *luckier* always mock those less fortunate. (Bauer 2005: 22)

Adams (2001: 20) notes that these expressions can be preceded by both adjectival and adverbial modifiers, cf. *the ostentatious rich*, *the completely innocent*, while Strang (1968: 113) suggests that '[l]ike all the others, this class is isolated on formal grounds; we might say that the forms look as if they have moved half-way

---

[5] Jean-Philippe Prost (p.c.) has suggested to me that *deep* in *deep blue necktie* could be regarded as an adverb. He cites the example *it cut deep into his flesh*. Here, *deep* modifies the verb *cut*, and is arguably an adverb (although a case could also be made for calling it an adjective). In *deep blue necktie* the word *deep* would then be an adverb modifying the adjective *blue*. If he is right, this would be another way out of McCawley's conundrum. However, *deep* is unlikely to be an adverb in *deep blue necktie* because the kinds of adverbs that modify adjectives are normally intensifiers or *-ly* adverbs.

along the road from being adjectives to being nouns, and strayed a bit as well as not going all the way.' She speaks of *partial conversion,* a term that was also used for these formations in Zandvoort (1962: 268f.). If this is correct, it would seem that different words have converted to different degrees. Thus, we can add a plural suffix to a word like *hopeful* (*These Olympic hopefuls are heroes in their countries.*), but not to many others (**These innocents were hounded by the police.*). Perhaps the optimal solution would be to posit an empty element that functions as a nominal head, and can often be interpreted as a semantically bleached noun like 'people' or 'thing'. This would then also explain why we can insert both adjectival and adverbial modifiers. The phrase *the completely innocent* would then be analysed as in (53):

(53)　[$_{NP}$ the completely innocent $\emptyset_N$]

Here *completely* is an appropriate adjectival modifier. As for *the ostentatious rich,* here we could say that *ostentatious* modifies the zero head. However, we cannot always infer a noun like 'people' or 'thing', as Huddleston and Pullum *et al.*'s (2002: 417) examples in (54) and (55) and the attested example in (56) testify:

(54)　(We are going to attempt) *the utterly impossible.*
(55)　(This is verging on) *the immoral.*
(56)　Back to you in *the dry.*[6]

Although it is less easy to think of a noun to supplement here, there is still a sense of a missing nominal. Huddleston and Pullum's solution is, to regard words like *rich, fortunate,* etc. as *fused modifier-heads,* that is, as adjectives that have fused with an unexpressed head. This is an interesting proposal, but it does beg the question exactly what is the nature of the head that the adjectives have fused with. If this is an abstract zero head, then how can this proposal be distinguished from an analysis in which a zero head is not fused with the modifier, as in (53)? We might also ask what is the categorial status of the fused modifier-head. Is it perhaps an 'A/N', as in McCawley's account of colour terms? What is more, Huddleston and Pullum *et al.* are forced to concede that because we can also say *the pure in heart* 'we must allow... for a head to fuse with a post-head modifier, as well as for the usual case where the fusion is with a pre-head modifier' (2002: 418). In other words, *the pure in heart* is an amalgam of *pure* + abstract head + *in heart.* The fusions are becoming a bit like amorphous lumps. The advantage of the solution shown in (53) is twofold: first, problems like those I have just raised for the

---

[6] Said by a weatherman standing in the rain to a colleague in the studio.

fused modifier-head analysis do not arise, and, secondly, an analysis like (53) obviates the need for positing gradience in the guise of partial conversion, or for assigning a word to two categories in a particular configuration.

As a final example of noun–adjective resemblance, McCawley (1998: 764f.) discusses cases of what he calls *syntactic mimicry*. Compare (57) and (58):

(57)   This sentence is difficult to translate.
(58)   This sentence is a bitch to translate.

In (58) the element *bitch* is said to mimic the adjective *difficult* in (57). Ross (1973*b*) has called such words *adjectival nouns*. Other examples include (59), discussed in detail in Aarts (1998).

(59)   This is a bitch of a problem. (cf. *a difficult problem*)

I will not discuss examples like these further here.

6.1.1.5 *Adjectives and adverbs*   The classes of adjective and adverb show so many similarities that some linguists have argued that they should not be distinguished, at least as far as certain subclasses are concerned. Thus Lyons (1968: 326f.) regards manner adverbs and adjectives as positional variants of the same word class.[7] Further close similarities between adjectives and adverbs have also been noted, for example modification by *very*, and the possibility of taking comparative and superlative forms. There are two respects in which they are usually said to differ. One is that adjectives are much more inclined to take complements. According to Jackendoff (1977: 78) '[o]n the whole, adverbs take no complements'.[8] Another respect in which they appear to differ is their potential to modify nouns. Indeed, Huddleston and Pullum *et al.* (2002: 563) exclude the possibility of adverbs modifying nouns: 'Adverbs characteristically modify verbs and other categories except nouns, especially adjectives and adverbs'.

However, despite this claim it appears to be possible for adverbs to occur in pre-nominal positions, as the following examples show:

(60)   the *then* head of the National Security Council, Henry Kissinger
        <W2C-010 064> ('HK who was *then* head of the National Security
        Council')
(61)   We would like an *upstairs* toilet. ('We would like a toilet which
        is located *upstairs*')
(62)   the *now* generation (Quirk *et al.* 1985: 453)

---

[7] See also Radford (1988: 138ff.), Baker (2003: 230f.).
[8] Although see Huddleston and Pullum *et al.* (2002: 571f.), who disagree.

The item *then* usually combines with nouns that express an office, or some other official role, while other adverbs in attributive position often express locative or temporal meanings, although notice that not all such items may occur attributively: *the shop is there/*the there shop*. As in the previous sections, the italicized items in (60)–(62) are adjective-like as far as their syntactic position is concerned, while retaining properties of another word class, in this case adverbs. This becomes evident for example from the fact that we can modify *then*, as in *the [(way) back then] Head of the National Security Council* (cf. *I met her (way) back then*).

However, the above only holds true if we regard words like *then, upstairs,* and *now* as adverbs. As we have seen, Huddleston and Pullum *et al.* do not allow adverbs to modify nouns. For them, *then, upstairs,* and *now* are prepositions (see Chapter 5). However, we might point to the fact that adverbs may modify pronouns, as in the examples that follow:

(63) *Almost everyone* left before midnight.
(64) *Nearly everybody* liked the film.

Huddleston and Pullum *et al.* (2002: 430) only allow adjectives to exceptionally modify pronouns as in *lucky you, silly me*. As for (63) and (64), although examples involving pronouns are not explicitly mentioned, phrases of this type involve degree adverbs, which would be treated as NP-external peripheral modifiers (2002: 436f.) in the same way as *almost* in *almost the end*. The phrases *only you* and *just them* (2002: 430) are similarly analysed as NP-external modifiers, cf. *[only [NPyou]]*. What about (65) where *almost* modifies *success* directly?

(65) *She congratulated him on his almost success. (Huddleston and Pullum *et al.* 2002: 563)

As the asterisk indicates, this is explicitly excluded as an example of an adverb modifying a noun. In short, for Huddleston and Pullum *et al.* (60)–(64) are only apparent counterexamples to the claim that adverbs may not modify nouns.

However, a search on the web reveals that the judgement for (65) is too severe, as the following selection shows:

(66) To pre-celebrate *their almost-success*, we entered their 30+ year old Dacia and headed for Kilini where we took the ferry to Zakinthos. (http://frank.itlab.us/zakinthos/index.html)
(67) A *noble almost-success*, Jessie is a musician who has not been able to make his dreams pay the rent. (http://www.filmjerk.com/nuke/article587.html)

Consider also:

(68)   And, so, Dubya got *his almost-victory* in 2000 by trading on our
         rightful distaste for Clinton's behavior—and by racking up more of
         those thinly disguised bribes than had ever been seen in any electoral
         campaign in the history of the world. (http://eatthestate.org/06-23/
         EatEconomy.htm)

(69)   Lurch and his boys and girl have declared—well, *an 'Almost Victory'* in
         both Afghanistan and Iraq. (http://www.reader-weekly.com/Reader/
         Reader_Weekly/Ed_Raymond/217ed.html)

(70)   Despite this there were still some high points in the season. Namely
         David Coulthard's victory at the Monaco Grand Prix, and *Kimi
         Raikkonen's almost victory in France.* (http://tisc.planet-f1.com/
         Features/Interviews/story_10182.shtml)

The writers of these examples display various degrees of confidence in their
use of the *almost N* combination, witness the fact that some of them use a
hyphen between *almost* and the noun. Another author uses inverted commas.
Nevertheless, these attested examples show—although perhaps only as an
incipient innovation in the language—that adverbs can mimic adjectives,
and are therefore in an intersective gradient relationship with them.

6.1.2 *Gradience between verbs and other word classes*

6.1.2.1 *Verbs and adjectives*   Lyons (1968: 324) notes that Plato and Aristotle
regarded adjectives as verbs because the function of both is predication.
However, in English a distinction between these categories can be drawn on
distributional grounds, which is not to say that indeterminacies do not arise.
Consider the sentences below:

(71)   She is a *working* mother.

(72)   He pointed towards the *setting* sun. (Huddleston 1984: 320)

(73)   But it is left to the *then still living* Robin Cook to enter the epitaph on
         the war on terror, of which Iraq is argued to be so necessary an
         ingredient. (*The Guardian*, 17 December 2005)

(74)   She understood that with *his approaching death*, she would lose
         him forever. (*The Guardian*, 4 March 2006)

(75)   He told me an *amazing* story.

(76)   *a rarely heard work by Purcell* (Huddleston and Pullum *et al.* 2002: 541)

(77)   *a failed businessman* (*ibid*: 542.)

In (71) *working* has verbal and adjectival properties: it is verbal because of its
-*ing* ending and because it can be premodified by an adverb (*a hard working*

mother), but adjectival because it occurs pre-nominally. Note, however, that this word cannot be preceded by *not* (**not working mother*), nor can we have aspectual markers (**(hard) having worked mother*) or dependents (**working for the government mother*). All of these properties are verbal in nature. Conversely, despite its attributive position, *working* cannot be intensified (**very working mother*), nor is it gradable (**more/most working mother*), and it cannot occur in predicative position (we do have *this mother is working,* but here *working* is part of a present progressive verb phrase). On balance it is reasonable to conclude that *working* is rather more verbal than adjectival. Huddleston makes the same point for (72), cf. *the slowly setting sun.*[9] In this connection (73) is particularly interesting, with *living* being preceded by modifiers that can modify both verbs and adjectives (cf. *the then still alive/popular Robin Cook*). However, if we add a manner adverb, *living* becomes indisputably verbal: *the then still happily living Robin Cook.* In (74) there is a syntactic ambiguity: we can regard *his* either as a possessive determinative in an NP which complements *with,* or as a subject determinative which is part of a clause (a 'gerund'). Either way, using the same arguments as we have done above, the word *approaching* is rather more verbal than adjectival on balance (**his quick approaching death/his quickly approaching death*). See also below and Section 8.4.2. In (75) the word *amazing* is an adjective, witness the fact that we can have *a quite amazing story* and *the story is (quite) amazing.* Brekke (1988) argues that there is a constraint at work that determines whether a particular verb can have a corresponding adjective ending in *-ing.* The *Experiencer Constraint* states that:

A given verb does not have a corresponding *-ing* adjective unless
a. its underlying root has an Experiencer argument, and
b. its surface subject represents an argument other than an Experiencer (Brekke 1988: 177)

This explains why **a very growing opposition* is not possible, while *a very amusing story (to me)* is fine: the latter has an Experiencer role (which may be overt or covert), while the former does not. Interestingly, Brekke's constraint can explain why (78) below is possible, where *concerning* is used in the sense 'worrying':

(78) [The housing crisis] is concerning. (*Camden New Journal,* 2004)

Here *concerning* has an underlying Experiencer role, and the subject is not an Experiencer. The use of this word as an adjective in this way has not gained general currency yet.

---

[9] Because I assume here that only phrasal expansions can act as modifiers, we will say that *working* and *setting* in these examples are in fact VPs. The same considerations apply to the examples that follow below.

For Brekke *working* and *setting* are verbs, not adjectives, because no Experiencer role is assigned. However, Borer (1990) signals a problem for the conclusion that these words are verbs:

[I]f they are verbs, we must account for the obvious ways in which their distribution and properties differ from those of other verbs: normal verbs, even in their participial form, do not (necessarily) have a 'property' reading..., they do not occur (prima facie) in prenominal positions, they can be accompanied by complements, and they do not (at least in some models) occur in non-sentential projections, or without a subject. (Borer 1990: 95–6)

Furthermore, she cites the data in (79)–(82) below as problems for the view that prenominal *V-ing* words are verbs (1990: 102):

(79)   a very/rather high-jumping cow
(80)   a very/rather soundly-sleeping beauty
(81)   a very/rather low-flying spacecraft
(82)   a very/rather self-explaining incident

She writes: 'If, indeed, modification by *very* is the litmus test for adjective-hood, we must assume that the compounded expressions in [(79)–(82)] are adjectives.' (1990:102) Borer then relates the sentences in (79)–(82) to (83)–(86):

(83)   The cow jumped very high.
(84)   The girl slept very soundly.
(85)   The spacecraft flew very low.
(86)   This incident explains itself very well/much.

She then notes that '[i]n [(83)–(85)] *very* modifies the adjectives *high*, *low*, *soundly*, and in [(86)] it modifies the entire predicate.' What Borer appears to be overlooking, surprisingly, is the fact that *very* can also modify adverbs. To my mind *high*, *soundly*, *low*, and *well/much* are adverbs modified by another adverb. If this is correct, then we can maintain the view that *jumping*, *sleeping*, *flying*, and *explaining* are verbs.

   Notice that the passage quoted above from Borer's work is heavily hedged ('necessarily', 'prima facie', 'at least in some models'). Notice also that underlying Borer's criticism is a desire to maintain strictly Aristotelian categories, such that for a word to belong to a category it must display all and only the properties associated with that category. Under this view *working* and *setting* cannot be verbs because they do not display all the properties of verbs. Borer's claim that pronominal *V-ing* words cannot be verbs only holds good if gradience is denied a role in grammar. We can, however, be less rigid by maintaining that *working* and *setting* are marginal members of the verb class, which is in an intersective relationship with the class of adjectives.[10]

In (76) and (77) *heard* and *failed* are likewise verbal, given their *-ed* ending and the preceding adverbial modifier. Notice also that these formatives cannot occur in predicative position. Borer (1990: 100) discusses some further examples:

(87) a. the *moved* car
      b. the *unmoved* car
(88) a. the *crushed* resistance
      b. the *uncrushed* resistance
(89) a. the *occupied* city
      b. the *unoccupied* city

If the reasoning in the preceding paragraphs is valid then the italicized words in (87a)–(89a) are also best regarded as verbs, given the *-ed* ending and the fact that verbal modifiers are possible, cf. *the quickly moved car, the violently crushed resistance*, and *the illegally occupied city*. Notice that the italicized words cannot be preceded by *very*, nor are they gradable. However, interestingly, they *can* be prefixed by *un-*, as (87b)–(89b) show, a typical adjectival property. So where does this leave us? It would seem that like *heard* and *failed*, the words *moved*, *crushed*, and *failed* are verbs, but they are slightly more towards the adjectival end of the cline, given the fact that they can take the *un-* prefix.

Consider next the following sentences:

(90) They were *arrested* by the police.
(91) He was *disgusted* by the whole thing.
(92) The mirror was *broken*.

We might want to say that these examples constitute another case of IG between verbs and adjectives. In (90) the element *arrested* is clearly verbal: we have an ordinary passive sentence containing a passive auxiliary *be* which is followed by a past participle (which cannot be premodified by *very*) and by an agentive *by*-phrase, and the sentence has an active counterpart. In (91) the word *disgusted* has both verbal and adjectival properties: it is verbal to the extent that it carries passive morphology, it is followed by a *by*-phrase, and the sentence has an active counterpart. It is adjectival in that it can have

---

[10] In a passing comment at the end of his 1991 paper Pullum (1991*b*) suggests that in the phrase *some quietly sleeping children* the string *quietly sleeping* might be an AP with a VP head. See Chapter 3 and below on Pullum's treatment of gerunds as NPs with VP heads.

a statal reading, and could be said to occur in predicative position. What is more, it can be intensified (*very disgusted*) and is gradable (*more disgusted/ most disgusted*). Notice also that we can have *he seemed disgusted by the whole thing* (Huddleston and Pullum *et al.* 2002: 1437), where *be* has been replaced by a verb that cannot be followed by past participle. In (92) *broken* has either an actional reading (=verb, cf. *the mirror was broken by hooligans*) or a statal reading (=adjective, cf. *the mirror was already broken/the mirror seemed broken/the mirror is unbroken*), cf. Huddleston (1984: 322–3) and Huddleston and Pullum *et al.* (2002: 1436f.). Words like *disgusted* and *broken* are referred to in Huddleston and Pullum *et al.* (2002: 78) as *participial adjectives*. Confusingly, in the case of sentences like *they were very worried* and *they were married* both *very worried* and *married* (not the sentences as a whole) are described as *adjectival passives* later in the book (2002: 1436f.). The label is infelicitous to my mind, most clearly for the string *very worried*, where *worried* is an adjective, as the authors themselves observe, because the term 'passive' is applied as a rule to constructions, not to phrases. For this reason I will treat examples like (90) and (91) as cases of *Subsective Constructional Gradience* in Chapter 7, because the criteria distinguishing them (e.g. passivization) involve the sentential construct as a whole.

Finally, consider (93):

(93)   This isn't a real phone, it's a *pretend* phone.

Unlike the oft-discussed *-ing/-ed* premodifiers, here we seem to have a verb in the base form appearing in attributive position. One way to analyse *pretend* in this example would be to regard it as instantiating verb-to-adjective conversion. However, while this type of derivation exists in English, it is marginal, and usually accompanied by a stress shift, as in *ab'stract>'abstract, fre'quent>'frequent*, and *per'fect>'perfect*, mentioned in Bauer (1983: 229) as examples. Note that apart from its attributive position *pretend* does not behave like an adjective in other ways: it cannot be modified by *very* and cannot occur in predicative position. However, it does not behave like a verb either as regards its distributional potential. Perhaps the best way to look at this example is to regard *pretend* as a *mention* of a verb, rather than as an item that is used to modify a noun. In other words, the meaning would then be as in (94):

(94)   a 'pretend' phone

This analysis would be supported by the way a phrase like (94) is pronounced, that is, with *pretend* prosodically set apart by short pauses before and after it.

I now turn to gradience between verbs and nouns.

6.1.2.2 *Verbs and nouns*   Perhaps the most often cited instance of categorial indeterminacy in English is the gradience that obtains between verbs and nouns. Many authors have noted that there exist elements that display nominal properties in their external distribution, and verbal properties in their internal syntactic make-up. The term 'gerund' (or one of its—not always equivalent— variants 'gerundive', 'gerundival', 'gerundive nominal', 'nominal gerund phrase', 'gerund participle', 'gerundial (noun)', 'verbal gerund', 'nominal gerund', etc.) is used for this phenomenon. It causes confusion because it is used in different ways by different authors. Just to get a taste of the different approaches to the gerund, here is a selection of recent quotations from the literature:

A traditional name for the *-ing* form of a verb in English when it serves as a **verbal noun**, as in *Swimming is good exercise, Lisa's going topless upset her father* and *I enjoy watching cricket*, or for a verbal noun in any language. (Trask 1993: 118; emphasis in original)

Verbs may also end in *-ing*; this form is referred to as the present participle or the gerund. (Haegeman and Guéron 1999: 56)

The gerund is of the category N and behaves syntactically as a noun. It is, however, a verbal noun (in traditional terms), that is, it has the internal composition of a VP. As such it is generally derived by zero-derivation or conversion. (Miller 2002: 286)

English gerunds are indeed just what the traditional grammarians said: single words which are both verbs and nouns. (Hudson 2003: 611)

Quirk *et al.* (1985: 1292, fn. a) reject the term gerund, and list the following sentences to demonstrate a gradient from purely nominal to purely verbal elements (1985: 1290–1):

(95) *some paintings of Brown's*
(96) *Brown's paintings of his daughters*
(97) *The painting of Brown* is as skilful as that of Gainsborough.
(98) *Brown's deft painting of his daughter* is a delight to watch.
(99) *Brown's deftly painting his daughter* is a delight to watch.
(100) I dislike *Brown's painting his daughter.*[11]
(101) I dislike *Brown painting his daughter.* (when she ought to be at school)
(102) I watched *Brown painting his daughter.* ('I watched Brown as he painted'/'I watched the process of Brown('s) painting his daughter')
(103) *Brown deftly painting his daughter* is a delight to watch.
(104) *Painting his daughter,* Brown noticed that his hand was shaking.

---

[11] Strictly speaking, (99) and (100) ought to be interchanged, as in (99) the adverb *deftly* modifies *painting*, thus making it more verbal than *painting* in (100), which lacks this modifier.

(105)   *Brown painting his daughter that day,* I decided to go for a walk.
(106)   *The man painting the girl* is Brown.
(107)   *The silently painting man* is Brown.
(108)   Brown *is painting* his daughter.

In (95)–(98) *painting* is clearly nominal for a number of reasons: in (95) and (96) the nominal properties are the presence of the determinative *some* and the genitival NP, the plural *-s* ending and the PP complement; in (97) the nominal properties are the presence of the determinative *the* and PP complement, while in (98) a genitival NP and a premodifying adjective phrase are present. Huddleston and Pullum *et al.* (2002: 81) use the, to my mind, rather infelicitous term *gerundial noun* for the *-ing* forms in (95)–(98). In (101)–(108) *painting* would appear to be verbal, by virtue of the fact that in most of these cases it takes a nominal complement. ((107) is an exception, but can be said to be verbal because of the preceding adverb.) The seemingly mixed, that is fuzzy, examples are (99)–(103), which are traditionally called gerunds. They combine nominal characteristics (e.g. argument position, the occurrence of a possessive element) with verbal characteristics (e.g. the occurrence of a complement).

There have been many discussions in the literature as to how to treat gerunds. In Chomsky (1970: 187) *painting* in structures like (99) is called a *gerundive nominal*, which is transformationally derived (unlike *derived nominals*, which, despite their name, are listed in the lexicon). They are regarded as Ss which are dominated by an NP. See Schachter (1976) for a non-transformational analysis of gerundive nominals. In Chapter 3 I discussed Pullum (1991*b*) and Blevins (2005), both of which treat gerunds as NPs with verbal heads. Malouf (2000*a*, 2000*b*) and Hudson (2003) deal with gerunds using the mechanism of *multiple default inheritance*. Most of these theoretical accounts are problematic in one way or another. A failing they all share is the fact that they have no way of accounting for the fact that in a structure like (99) the verbal properties greatly outweigh the nominal properties. Thus in (99) *painting* has only two nominal properties:

- it is the head of a phrase positioned in the subject slot, a typical NP position;
- it occurs with a genitival determinative.

But there are many more verbal properties:

- *painting* has a verbal inflection;
- it occurs with an NP complement;[12]

---

[12] And note that further complements are possible: *Brown's painting me a picture.*

- it is preceded by a manner adverb;[13]
- it can be preceded by *not*;
- passivization of the italicized string is possible: *His daughter's being deftly painted by Brown* is a delight to watch;
- a perfective auxiliary can be inserted: *Brown's having deftly painted his daughter* was a true feat.

These facts lead to a clausal analysis of the string *Brown's deftly painting his daughter* in (99). Analyses like those of Chomsky (1970), Pullum (1991*b*), and Blevins (2005) appear to be compromised because they take the fact that gerunds can occur in typical NP positions to be a necessary and sufficient reason for positing an outer nominal shell with a verbal core. It would seem to me that the ability to occur in NP positions is neither a necessary nor a sufficient reason for having an NP shell if we allow other constituent types to be positioned in canonical nominal positions. We need to allow for the possibility of elements or phrases occurring in non-canonical positions elsewhere in the grammar, as the discussion of the phrase *boy actor* in Section 6.1.1.4 has made clear.

I will return to a discussion of the so-called gerund in Chapter 8, where I will account for the imbalance of nominal and verbal properties in a principled way.

6.1.2.3 *Verbs and prepositions/conjunctions*   There exist a number of words that appear to straddle the borderline between verbs and prepositions on the one hand, and between verbs and conjunctions on the other.

Starting with the former, here is a list, taken from Quirk *et al.* (1985: 667), who discuss a class of *marginal prepositions*:

bar, barring, excepting, excluding, save, concerning, considering, regarding, respecting, touching, failing, wanting, following, pending, given, granted, including

Not all these items mix the components 'verbal' and 'prepositional' in equal measure. Take the rather old-fashioned item *save*: few people would judge it to be very verbal—despite the homophonous verb *save*—which is not surprising, because etymologically it is not verbal at all (it derives from Latin *salvus*, 'safe'). Notice also that the various different meanings of *save* (e.g. 'except' and 'rescue', etc.) are not related. Other items on the list could be regarded as verbal by virtue of their *-ing* ending. Olofsson (1990) discusses a case study of the word *following*. He notes that the prepositional use has

---

[13] Other types of adverbial modification are also possible, e.g. by *because*-clauses and result clauses, as Jackendoff (1977: 222) has observed.

increased over time, a finding which is confirmed in recent work by this author (Olofsson, p.c.). He sets up two paraphrase tests which allow us to decide whether a particular instance of *following* is verbal or prepositional. In (109) the stretch of words containing *following* can be replaced by a relative clause ((110)) which indicates a verbal status for *following*. Although Olofsson does not mention this, essentially this test brings out that *following* has a subject when it is verbal.

(109)   This continued most of the week following that ill-starred trip to church.

(110)   This continued most of the week which followed that ill-starred trip to church.

As for (111), he notes (1990: 27): 'where *following* cannot be interpreted as a postmodifier and paraphrased by means of a relative clause, it seems that the paraphrase best capable of rendering the basic meaning is one in which the subject is a clause and *follow* is used as the predicate verb', as in (112).

(111)   He bled profusely following circumcision.
(112)   [He bled profusely] followed circumcision.

As is to be expected, there are a number of cases that are indeterminate between a verbal and prepositional reading. Thus in (113) both paraphrases are possible.

(113)   There was a marked improvement in general condition following the exchange transfusion...

In this case Olofsson assigns *following* to the preposition class 'with some hesitation' (1990: 32).[14]

Notice that it is the case for many of the marginal prepositions that if they are put in context, it turns out that they only have a whiff of verbalness around them. Consider the following sample of items in a sentential context:

(114)   My call is *regarding* your mortgage.
(115)   *Pending* the results of the investigation, we will not prosecute you.
(116)   *Considering* his previous record, I will not offer him this position.
(117)   We'll send you a copy of the book, *including* a free gift.

For (114) there is no felicitous paraphrase making use of the verb *regard,* and it appears this word is fully prepositional. Notice also that *regarding* can be stranded: *What is your call regarding? It's regarding your mortgage.*

---

[14] On *following*, see also Manning (2003: 313f.).

In (115) we can paraphrase the first part of this sentence as *While the results of the investigation are pending,* but here the NP *the results of the investigation* has been promoted from prepositional object position to subject position. As it stands (115) has no recoverable subject. In (116) although we could say that *considering* is understood to have the same subject as *offer* in the matrix clause, notice that we cannot expand the sentence felicitously in such a way that *considering* gains full verbal status while retaining its *-ing* ending. Thus for example *?Although/ while/because I am considering his previous record, I will not offer him this position* sound odd, and in any case such a paraphrase is only possible if the main clause verb is in the present tense (cf. **Although I am considering his previous record, I didn't offer him the position*). In (117) a paraphrase involving a verb is possible, and the subject of *including* is recoverable. However, notice that we can substitute *with* for *including* here without a change of meaning. Perhaps because of the synchronically often weak link to the full verb which the items in question clearly derive from, it would be best to regard them as being (almost) fully converted prepositional forms, their only connection to the verb being their *-ing* ending. However, we can agree with Huddleston (1984: 346) that of the items in (114)–(117) the last two are perhaps most clearly verbal because they have a recoverable subject. Huddleston and Pullum *et al.* (2002: 611) claim that the boundary between prepositional constructions and verbal constructions in the following sentences is 'slightly blurred':

(118)   Turning now to sales, there are very optimistic signs.
(119)   Bearing in mind the competitive environment, this is a
          creditable result.
(120)   Having said that, it must be admitted that the new
          plan also has its advantages.

While it is true that subjects for these sentences are recoverable only from the context, unlike in (116) and (117) where they are sententially recoverable, this doesn't make the *-ing* forms in (118)–(120) more prepositional. To my mind they are fully verbal.

Kortmann and König (1992) set up a gradient of 'degree of reanalysis' of lexical items from participles to prepositions:

Lowest degree of reanalysis			Highest degree of reanalysis	
facing	*considering*	*according to*	*during*	*past*
lining	*failing*	*allowing (for)*	*pending*	*ago*
preceding	*barring*	*owing to*	*except*	*bar*
succeeding	*following*	*notwithstanding*	*concerning*	

The cline is based on the general properties of prepositions, as well as on a number of changes that applied to verbs in being reanalysed as prepositions. The latter include the following (Kortmann and König 1992: 674ff.):

- Changes in word order. For example, in Middle English *alle the moneth during* and *Durynge that persecucioun* were possible, but later only the latter order;
- Participles lost inflectional endings;
- Changes in grammatical relations and control. For example, in the sentence *Concerning your request, I would like to inform you...*, which contains a dangling participle, a direct object becomes the object of a preposition;
- Semantic bleaching. For example, English *barring* is no longer felt to mean 'keep out with a bar';
- Loss of selectional restrictions. For example, in *Regarding your recent inquiry...* the NP would be pragmatically odd as the direct object of the verb *regard*;
- Univerbation. English *notwithstanding* displays a welding together of morphemes with an opaque lexical item as a result;
- Morphological and phonological erosion. Examples are English *past* (derived from *passed*), *ago* (derived from *agone*);
- Loss of verb stem. For example, English *during* is not related to a verb that is in use;[15]
- Development into an affix. Examples are reanalysed verbs which can be used as affixes in derivation, as in English *tres-* (from Latin *trans*).

The five (vertically arranged) groups above have undergone these changes to varying degrees in such a way that the items in the groups on the left are more verbal than those in the groups on the right.

Consider next the following examples:

(121)　He took me for a fool.

(122)　I want them for my wives. (i.e. 'I want them *to be* my wives'.)[16]

(123)　He took me for dead.

(124)　What do you take me for (i.e. 'to be')?

---

[15] Kortmann and König also mention *pending* as having lost its verbal stem, but this isn't correct, witness the fact that we can say *While the results of the investigation are pending...*, as noted above.

[16] This sentence is uttered in a British TV commercial by a sheik who is offered a lift home to his palace by two women driving through the desert in a smart sporty car. To return the favour he offers them accommodation. Later in the story the women overhear the sheik saying 'I want them for my wives'. They are shocked because they think he is referring to them. However, they have misunderstood the sheik as in the next shot we see a line-up of cars of the type the women were driving.

(125)   He regards me as an idiot
(126)   He wants them as his wives.
(127)   He regards me as foolish.
(128)   ?What do you regard me as?

In examples (121)/(122)/(124) and (125)/(126)/(128) the elements *for* and *as* look like straightforward prepositions in that they are followed by NPs. However, this analysis is problematic for (123) and (127), where they are followed by adjective phrases. In Aarts (1992) I argued that *for* and *as* can be analysed as inflectional elements in the Government and Binding theory framework. One would then need to analyse the postverbal strings in the examples above as small clauses (i.e. [$_{SC}$ me for a fool], [$_{SC}$ them for my wives]). Perhaps more plausibly, we could regard *from* and *as* as 'prepositional copulas', an analysis which has been proposed in Emonds (1984), that is, as words that are essentially verbs but which possess some prepositional qualities.

Finally, consider the italicized strings in the following sentences:

(129)   *Supposing (that)* you left early in the morning, you would then get there on time.
(130)   *Seeing (that)* you are now an adult, we can expect more mature behaviour.

Quirk *et al.* (1985: 1001f.) refer to elements such as *supposing (that), seeing (that), provided (that),* and *assuming (that)* as *marginal subordinators*, while Kortmann and König (1992: 683) call them *deverbal conjunctions.* The latter is a more transparent term, given that we are talking about the verb–conjunction boundary. The items in question mix verbal and conjunctional properties differently. Thus, Quirk *et al.* (1985: 1003) note that, just as is the case for participles, *supposing* and *that* in (129) can be separated (cf. *Supposing for the sake of argument that...*), whereas this is not possible for *seeing* and *that* in (130) (cf. **Seeing for the sake of argument that...*). Notice also that a change in meaning has occurred for *seeing (that).* These facts show that *supposing* is more towards the verbal end of the verb–conjunction gradient than *seeing*.

6.1.2.4 *Verbs and adverbs*   Consider the following examples:

(131)   This oven is *scorching* hot.
(132)   The sea water is *freezing* cold.
(133)   My socks are *soaking* wet.

Further examples are *haunting-strange* (Marchand 1969: 88), *hopping mad, piping hot, wringing wet,* and *yawning dull* (Adams 2001: 97). We might argue that we have a case of IG here between verbs and adverbs because in these cases the italicized items are adverb-like by virtue of the position they occupy modifying adjectives, but verb-like in having an *-ing* ending. However, perhaps this is only seemingly the case. For one, as Huddleston and Pullum *et al.* (2002: 550, fn 7) suggest, such combinations are relatively fixed, and do not seem to be very productive:

(134)   *The morning was *blinding* bright. (cf. *blindingly bright*)
(135)   *That point is *glaring* obvious. (cf. *glaringly obvious*)

Indeed, Adams (2001) regards them as adjective–adjective compounds. This is not unreasonable in view of the fact that the *-ing* forms can also occur as noun modifiers:

(136)   the scorching heat
(137)   the freezing cold
(138)   ?the soaking towel

Furthermore, at least for the verb *scorch*, we also have a separate adverb, namely *scorchingly*. In conclusion, despite appearances we need not posit IG between verbs and adverbs on the basis of examples such as (131)–(133).

6.1.3 *Further cases*

6.1.3.1 *Adverbs, prepositions, and conjunctions*   Consider the following examples, taken from Bolinger (1971: 26–7):

(139)   He ran down the road.
(140)   She swept off the stage.
(141)   We backed up the stream.

If we replace the final NPs by pronouns we get:

(142)   He ran down it (did his running somewhere down the road).
(143)   She swept off it (did her sweeping somewhere not on the stage).
(144)   We backed up it (did our backing at some point upstream).

Bolinger argues that the set immediately above differs from the one below:

(145)   He ran down it (descended it).
(146)   He swept off it (departed from it majestically).
(147)   We backed up it (ascended it in reverse direction).

The elements *down*, *off*, and *up* are prepositions in the last two sets of sentences. However, Bolinger claims that in (145)–(147) these elements are in constituency with both the verb that precedes them and the NP that follows. He calls them *adpreps* (1971: 28),[17] that is, elements that are prepositions and adverbs simultaneously. As such, they can be said to be positioned in the intersection of the adverb and preposition classes.

Jacobsson (1977) expands on the distinction between adverbs and prepositions, and includes conjunctions in a discussion of *intergradation* between these word classes, as Jespersen (1894: 193) had done before him, noting that '[a] good deal of confusion arises from *some words being both prepositions and conjunctions*' (emphasis in original). We will look here at some of Jacobsson's examples. First, consider the gradience that is perceived to obtain between prepositions and conjunctions. Central prepositions are characterized by three criteria (Jacobsson 1977: 40–1):

- They cannot be followed by a *that*-clause (**We are aware of that he is ill.*)
- They cannot co-occur with an infinitive (**I am uncertain of to go or not.*)
- They cannot be followed by a personal pronoun in the subjective case.

Central conjunctions, by contrast, conform to two criteria:

- They coordinate sentences, clauses, or constituents of the same grammatical rank.
- They introduce subordinate clauses.

We may or may not agree with the accuracy of these definitions, but let us accept them as stipulated by Jacobsson.

Jacobsson discusses a number of elements which can be said to be more or less prepositional, and arrives at the following cline, ranking the elements from least prepositional (i.e. conjunctional) to most prepositional (1977: 49):

than, as, but, except, like, besides

The ordering of elements on a cline depends on 'which criteria are applied and how they are weighted' (1977: 49). This obviously leaves a lot of room for disagreements between linguists about the number and type of criteria applied, and how they are ranked in order of prominence. In fact, most of the time, no ranking is posited by linguists at all.

All the items above have conjunctional as well as prepositional features, and one would therefore expect Jacobsson to propose something like the set-theoretic representation shown in Figure 6.1 for the sequence of elements above.

---

[17] The term is borrowed from A. A. Hill. Bolinger also uses the term *prepositional adverb* for elements that are adverbs in phrasal verbs (*look **up** the number*), but prepositions elsewhere (*look **up** that tree*).

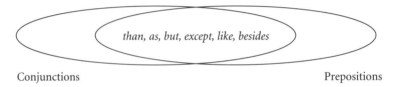

Conjunctions   Prepositions

FIGURE 6.1 A set-theoretic representation of Jacobsson's cline

In fact, in the end, what he proposes is to make an either/or choice when he says that '[w]hether prepositional or conjunctional in function, these particles are best regarded as subordinators' (1977: 49).

According to Jacobsson, even elements that can be regarded as belonging centrally to a particular class nevertheless sometimes exhibit gradience. Thus the following example of *and*, a central coordinator in almost everyone's book, can be argued to be subordinative, witness the fact that the matrix verb agrees in number with *Peter*:

(148)   Peter, and perhaps John, plays football.

In (149) *and* isn't linked to anything, and could therefore be regarded as some sort of adverb.

(149)   And how are you getting on at school?

Jacobsson's paper to some extent covers the same ground as Quirk *et al.'s* (1985) discussion of gradience between subordination and coordination (see Chapter 7). He concludes that 'coordination and subordination are notional, not formally identifiable, entities which means that they are not sharply separate and cannot always be discussed in terms of either/or' (1977: 53). And: '[c]oordination and subordination are ultimately related to the way the speaker organizes the information conveyed by the utterance' (1977: 53).

Consider also the data in (150)–(152), discussed in Huddleston and Pullum *et al.* (2002: 1312):

(150)   Everyone but Jill was told.
(151)   *But Jill everyone was told.
(152)   Everyone but $^{\%}$I/$^{\%}$me was told.[18]

They note that *but* in (150) can be a preposition or a coordinator, with the meaning 'except'. It is like a coordinator, and unlike a preposition, in that the string *but Jill* cannot be fronted, as (151) shows. However, if the word

---

[18] '%' means 'grammatical in some dialects'.

following *but* is a pronoun, as in (152), then it can carry either nominative or accusative case, although accusative case is more common. This shows that *but* is either construed as a preposition taking an accusative object, or as part of a coordinated subject NP (*everyone but I*).

In many of the cases we have looked at so far, positing gradience has been a reasonable approach to the problem of categorization posed by the data. However, we must be careful when we posit gradience. The strategy that is frequently employed by linguists who advocate the existence of gradience is the following: as their starting point they employ a number of (usually traditional) categories which they subsequently set out to undermine by claiming that the boundaries between them are vague. In other words, a grammatical description is assumed which posits a number of form classes α, β, and γ, which, although syntactically distinct, are argued to be on a cline, that is intersectively gradient. Jacobsson's description of adverbs, prepositions, and conjunctions is a concrete example. He *aprioristically* assumes that these three distinct grammatical categories exist. Close examination then reveals the perception that the three categories are in fact hard to keep apart, that is to say that there is gradience between them. What Jacobsson does not consider is the possibility that the taxonomy which he used as a starting point may in fact have been flawed. It is important to stress that the existence and extent of pervasiveness of IG are a function of the categories of the adopted taxonomic framework. Thus, for example, if it is claimed that there is boundary fluidity between two categories α and β, then it must first be established that α and β actually exist as form classes, that is, that they are 'grammatically real'. Langacker (1987: 19) seems to be making this point when he observes that

to posit a continuum is not to abandon the goal of rigorous description: we must still describe the individual structures in explicit detail, even as we articulate their parameters of gradation.

However, Langacker (1987: 18) also claims that most grammatical categories cannot be precisely delimited, as is clear from the passage below:

[Another] dimension of the discreteness issue concerns the propriety of positing sharp distinctions between certain broad classes of linguistic phenomena, thereby implying that the classes are fundamentally different in character and in large measure separately describable. The nondiscrete alternative regards these classes as grading into one another along various parameters. They form a continuous spectrum (or field) of possibilities, whose segregation into distinct blocks is necessarily artifactual.

Langacker's views lead to a conundrum, because these two points of view work in opposite directions. The problem is this: if you are able to 'rigorously describe' categories in such a way that they are characterized exhaustively and mutually exclusively, then logically gradience simply ceases to exist, because in categorization 'rigorous description' must mean setting up Aristotelian categories that do not allow multiple class membership or fuzzy boundaries. If Langacker were to deny this, and claim that this is not what 'rigorous description' means, then the burden is on him to make clear what he *does* mean by that phrase. It is perhaps paradoxical for adherents of gradience models that their starting point must always be rigid discreteness. Returning to Jacobsson, and bearing the observations above in mind, I would like to argue that Jacobsson's purported case of IG is in fact a bogus one. Ever since Emonds (1976: 172f.) it has been common to conflate the categories preposition and conjunction. In each of the cases below the italicized element is claimed to be a preposition.

(153) a. John arrived *before* the last speech.
       b. John arrived *before* the last speech ended.
       c. John arrived *before* (hand).

(154) a. I haven't seen him *since* the party.
       b. I haven't seen him *since* the party began.
       c. I haven't seen him *since*.

The only difference between the different instantiations of *before* and *since* is that in the a-sentences the preposition takes a nominal complement; in the b-sentences it takes a clausal complement; while in the c-sentences the preposition is intransitive. If this is correct, then simply by looking more closely at the data we eliminate the fuzziness perceived by Jacobsson, and we can do away with the boundary between prepositions and conjunctions, at least as far as elements such as *before* and *since* are concerned.[19]

---

[19] Bill Croft feels that my criticism of Jacobsson is unfair and asks 'Why is this *only* a difference that can be ignored? Why isn't it sufficient to distinguish between the categories? . . . [T]here is no a priori justification for either lumping or splitting'(p.c.). The reason why the different grammatical distribution of *before* and *since* should not lead to splitting is that it can be explained by making reference to the complement-taking properties of these elements. These properties create subcategories within form classes (e.g. *transitive verb, intransitive verb*), hence *subcategorization*, but not new form classes. The phenomenon is quite pervasive in grammar. We wouldn't want to say that *believe* in *I believed the story* and *believe* in *I believe that he is right* belong to different word classes. In general the strongest argument in favour of conflating categories is that wielding Occam's razor leads to a more streamlined (and hence more learnable) grammar. In the example under discussion the case for lumping is a persuasive one, as it results in particular elements (*before* and *since*) being assigned to only *one* form class, rather than to three. On the grounds of elegance and categorial parsimony this is surely preferable to splitting. See Croft (2001: 65ff.) for a critique of linguists' use of distributional evidence, specifically the lumping approach. For a detailed critique of my lumping analysis of words like *before* and *since*, and the distributional approach to categorization in general, see Croft (2007) and my response in Aarts (2007).

Let us also again look at Jacobsson's 'subordinator use' and 'adverb use' of *and*. In (148) above, repeated here as (155), *and* was argued to be subordinative, given the fact that the verb agrees in number with *Peter*. In (149), repeated as (156), *and* was regarded by Jacobsson as some sort of adverb, given that it 'dangles' at the beginning of a sentence.

(155)   Peter, and perhaps John, plays football.
(156)   And how are you getting on at school?

However, there are alternative ways of dealing with these sentences. Notice that rather than positing gradience between a coordinative and a subordinative use of *and* in (155), we could say that this sentence is a syntactic blend between the constructions in (157) and (158):

(157)   [Peter *and* perhaps John] play football.
(158)   [Peter plays football] *and* [perhaps John plays football].

In both (157) and (158) *and* is firmly a coordinating conjunction. We could also say that the string *and perhaps John* in (155) is merely parenthetical, and plays no role in its host clause. If either of these alternative approaches is correct, we can dispense with the notion that there is gradience between *and* as a coordinating conjunction and *and* as a subordinator. As regards (156), clearly *and* is a pragmatic discourse particle here, linking the sentence in question not so much to lexical material that is actually present, but to the preceding conversational context, which is about how the addressee is getting on.

Prepositions and conjunctions have also been regarded as closely related in other frameworks. Recall from Chapter 3 that although generativists in general dislike the idea of admitting gradience into their grammar, 'classical' GB did not seem able to avoid calling an element like *(for) to* a 'prepositional complementizer' in sentences such as (159) and (160):

(159)   We want (for) them to visit us this Christmas.
(160)   We are keen for Billy to do it.

The dual nature of *for* comes about as a result of its introducing a subordinate clause and acting as a Case assigner at the same time. According to Culicover (1999: 57), *for* is neither a preposition nor a complementizer. I will return to *for* and Culicover's views on this word in Chapter 8. Also worth mentioning at this point is Kayne's analysis of the word *of* as a complementizer in some varieties of English (as in *John should of left*). See Kayne (1997).

6.1.3.2 *Adverbs and nouns*   In English there are a number of lexical items that are sometimes analysed as adverbs, sometimes as nouns. These include words like *yesterday* and *today*. Students invariably label them as adverbs, until it is pointed out to them that they can occupy typical NP positions. Even some linguists find these words troublesome, leading to confusing analyses. Thus, for Strang (1968: 113–14) these 'partly noun-like words' are 'derived from **temporal adverbs**—*yesterday, to-day,* etc.' She considers them to be only *partly* nominal because they 'have only singular number and cannot collocate with determiners, adjectives or numerals (though there are "fully converted" nouns from them that do ["All our yesterdays..."])'. All the properties she enumerates for them (typical NP distribution, possibility of taking an -'s ending), however, are nominal; no adverb-like properties are mentioned. It looks as if Strang is confusing the *form* and *distribution* of these words with the *function* typically performed by adverbs, namely that of adjunct. There is no intersective categorial indeterminacy between adverbs and nouns in these cases. However, what we *can* say is that because these words do not have a fully noun-like distribution, this puts them on a subsective gradient within the class of nouns.

6.1.3.3 *Adjectives and prepositions*   There are a number of elements that have adjectival and prepositional properties. Among them are *like, unlike, due, near, far, worth,* and *close* (Huddleston and Pullum *et al.* 2002: 606f.). Here I will focus on *near*.

   One of the first linguists to discuss *near* was Ross (1972: 318–19) who posits a gradient between adjectives and prepositions, on which *near* is positioned. The squish shown in (161) is adjectival at its leftmost extreme, prepositional towards the right:

(161)   *proud* > *opposite* > ***near*** > *like* > *in*

Ross regarded this sequence as a 'subsquish' within the larger squish shown in (162):

(162)   **Verb** > Present participle > Perfect participle > Passive participle > **Adjective** > Preposition (?) > 'adjectival noun' > **Noun** (Ross 1972: 316)

He puts forward three types of evidence for his claim: Preposition Deletion, PP Postposing, and Pied Piping. I will discuss only the first of these here. Consider the data below:

(163)   proud *(of) you
(164)   opposite ?(from) the school
(165)   near (to) the wall
(166)   like (*to) a monster
(167)   in the house

These examples show that true adjectives do not allow Preposition Deletion, while the items further down the cline progressively do, and true prepositions cannot occur with another preposition. *Near* clearly occupies an intermediate position here, as regards its word class status, in that it optionally allows Preposition Deletion.

Maling (1983) classifies *near* as an adjective. Despite the fact that it can be followed by an NP (*near the house*), it is only superficially a preposition. She bases her conclusion on data such as the following (1983: 270):

(168)   Kim put the lamp *nearer* (to) the bed.
(169)   the *near* shore/a *near* miss/take the *nearest* one to you
(170)   Chris didn't go *enough near/near enough* (to) the water to get wet.

In (168) *near* has a comparative ending, while in (169) each time it modifies a noun. In (170) the element *enough* must follow *near*, it cannot precede it (compare the behaviour of the undoubted adjective *sensible*: *enough sensible/ sensible enough*). As for the fact that *near* can take an NP complement, the explanation is that it is 'perhaps the only surviving relic of the class of transitive adjectives' (1983: 266). Maling adopts an Aristotelian either/or categorial stance by classifying *near* as an adjective, and essentially ignores the fact that this element syntactically resembles a preposition, by explaining away its complement-taking properties through an appeal to the notion of syntactic relic.

Anderson (1997: 74f.) agrees with Maling's classification of *near* as a transitive adjective. As he puts it, '[a]pparently, a property associated with verbs [i.e. taking an NP complement] "leaks" down into the next most P-full class [i.e. adjectives], to be reflected in members which, as "relational", are more verb-like than the central membership of the class' (1997: 74).[20] However, unlike Maling he does not

---

[20] Recall from Chapter 3 that Anderson posits the following word class system (1997: 59–60):

{P}	{P;N}	{P:N}	{N;P }	{N}	{ }
aux	verb	adjective	noun	name	functor

Names are non-predicative referential arguments. Nouns are intermediate between verbs and names. They combine the features 'N' and 'P', because they are also arguments, and can be predicative, unlike names. The notation '{A;B}' signifies that a category is characterized by the features A and B, with B dependent on A. In '{A:B}' the features are mutually dependent. Prepositions are functors, indicated by '{ }'. Recall also that weightings can be assigned to these classes as follows:

4P::oN	3P::1N	2P::2N	1P::3N	oP::4N	oP,oN
aux	verb	adjective	noun	name	functor

if we assume that

X alone = 4   X; = 3   X: = 2   ;X = 1   absence of X = 0

disregard the fact that *near* has prepositional properties. He proposes the following cline of elements that mix adjectival and prepositional properties:

(171)   {P:N}   {(P:N);}   {(P:N):}   {;(P:N)}   { }
        close   near   like   worth   at
        due

The words *close* and *due* are prototypical adjectives which combine P and N features in mutual dependence: the weighting for the P and N components is {2P:2N}. (See footnote 20 for an explanation of the weightings.) For *near*, which involves a second-order categorization, we have a weighting of 3 for the (P:N)-component (=adjective), for *like* it is 2, while for *worth* the weighting is 1. This cline is based on the distributional behaviour of the elements in question. Thus, as Anderson notes (2001: 78–9), *like* and *worth* can be preceded by *enough*, but *near* cannot, just like regular adjectives:

(172)   a.   Chris looks enough like you to be your twin.
        b.   Sailing is great fun, but owning your own boat isn't enough
             worth the trouble for me to want to buy one.
        c.   *The book is enough near the fence.
        d.   *He is enough clever to be offered the job.

Near is therefore to the left of *like* and *worth*, but because *worth* cannot occur pre-nominally and cannot be preceded by *very*, it is to the right of *like* on the cline. Newmeyer (1998: 201f.) deals with the problem of *near* by arguing that this word simply belongs to two categories, a conclusion which Huddleston and Pullum *et al.* (2002: 609) also draw. I will return to *near* and *like* in Chapter 8.

6.2 IG between phrases

In most cases of IG between word classes we can say that the gradience projects upwards to the phrasal expansion of the items concerned. Thus, in the NP *a working mother* there is indeterminacy over the word class status of *working* (verb vs. adjective; see section 6.1.2.1), which projects upwards to the phrasal level (VP vs. AP). However, there are a few cases in the grammar of English where gradience can be said to obtain between phrases as wholes. As we will see, not all of these cases can be upheld as instances of IG.

6.2.1 *Adjective phrases and noun phrases*

Leech and Li (1995) discuss the 'grammatical indeterminacy' between noun phrases and adjective phrases functioning as subject attributes and object attributes. They note that NPs in these functions resemble APs in a number of respects. For example, in a sentence like (173) below the object attribute appears without an article, which 'gives the NP a more adjectival quality' (1995: 186):

(173)   A U.S. marine...says he was tortured and sentenced to death while he *was held hostage* at the U.S. Embassy in Tehran.

In (174) the nominal expression appears to be gradable, a typical adjectival property:

(174)   Mrs Tyler is finding it *a bit of a strain* looking after her on deck.

Finally, consider (175) and (176):

(175)   They have found the area *a desirable place*.
(176)   ...and the constant passage of heavy and rapidly increasing traffic *made them a danger* to the community.

In (175) the NP *a desirable place* contains what Leech and Li call a dummy noun, which is so devoid of meaning that the NP as a whole can easily be replaced by the AP *desirable* on its own. In (176) there is number discord between the postverbal NP *them* and the attribute *a danger*. This can be explained if we regard the noun *danger* as being adjectival, and if adjectives are singular by default, as Leech and Li argue.

As noted, Leech and Li state that their concern is with grammatical inde-terminacy between NPs and APs (i.e. Intersective Gradience), and they con-tend that in certain contexts NPs become adjectival. If we look at their data more closely, we find that not all of their examples convincingly demon-strate intercategorial indeterminacy. With the exception perhaps of (174), which could be seen as an example of IG between the N and A categories because the adjectival property of gradability has rubbed onto the noun *strain*, in (173), (175), and (176) the 'adjectival NPs' are categorially solidly nominal in being headed by what are incontrovertibly nouns. Thus, while it is true that in (173) *hostage* lacks a determinative, I do not see why that should make this noun syntactically more like an adjective, and Leech and Li do not make clear why they think this is the case. The position in which it occurs can be occupied by both APs and NPs. In (175), while it is true that the head noun is semantically empty, syntactically it is still clearly a noun head-ing an NP. In (176) it is contentious to say that adjectives are singular by default, as Leech and Li have done, because in English adjectives are not specified for number. Again, I would say that *a danger* is quite straightfor-wardly an NP.

What some of Leech and Li's data *do* support is the idea that there exist degrees of prototypical NPs *à la* Ross; that is to say, the authors' data instantiate Subsective Gradience. We could say that these nouns are decategorialized (Taylor 2003: 219), a fact also observed by Hopper and Thompson (1984, 1985), who show that nouns may lose morphological and other attributes, such as for example determinatives, when they do not refer. This is most clearly the case in (173): *hostage* is less typically an NP than had a determinative been present, but it is still an NP. In (175) we could say that the similarity between the NP *a desirable place* and the AP *desirable* is a case of what I will be calling *weak convergence* (see Chapter 8), which takes place when elements resemble each other semantically, but not syntactically. As to the number discord between *them* and *a danger* in (176), this has a perfectly straightforward semantic explanation: if *danger* were in the plural, then the sentence would mean something completely different, namely that each of the entities referred to by *them* would *individually* constitute a danger. What the sentence in fact means is that these entities are *collectively* a danger.

From the concluding remarks of their paper it is clear that Leech and Li confuse IG and SG, as the following passage shows:

> In 1973 John Robert Ross published an article with the intriguing title 'A fake NP squish' (Ross 1973*a*), in which he argued that not all constituents which have NP characteristics are 'copperclad, brass-bottomed NP's', but that to varying degrees, different kinds of NP may lack some NP characteristics. We consider that the data and observations presented in this chapter confirm this view, showing a somewhat similar 'NP squish' to that noted by Ross. However, we see 'our' squish as specifically relating NP complements in different ways and to different degrees to AP complements, and would argue that the squish is genuine rather than fake! (Leech and Li 1995: 199)

In short, their paper mostly fails in its professed aim of demonstrating intersective grammatical indeterminacy, but can profitably be salvaged if we reinterpret at least some of their data as being cases of SG.

6.2.2 *Adjective phrases and prepositional phrases*

The attributive position inside NPs is sometimes filled by PPs, as in the following examples:

(177)   And the suspension is designed for *off-road* use and it makes it a bit bouncy on the road <Survey of English Usage S2A-055 140>

(178)   She's wearing a *with-it* dress. (Quirk *et al.* 1985: 1336)

(179)   He doesn't seem to know what is meant by the notion of *with-profits* bonds.

(180)   By contrast, new homes near the *under-construction* Ashburton
Grove stadium are to be sold with a premium price tag. (*Islington Tribune*, 15 October 2004)

If we regard the elements *in*, *through*, *up*, and *above* in the following examples as intransitive prepositions (a now fairly widely accepted analysis), then they too involve PPs in attributive position:

(181)   She thinks she's part of the *in* crowd.
(182)   This is not a *through* road.
(183)   Where can I find the *up* escalator?
(184)   The *above* examples are instructive.

So it looks as if in these cases we have gradience between PPs and APs. However, while the P–NP strings in (177)–(180) occupy a typical adjectival position, this seems to be the only adjectival property that they possess. Notice that we cannot place intensifiers like *very* in front of them, though *very with-it dress* is probably not too bad. On the other hand typical PP modifiers such as *right* and *straight* are also disallowed. Interestingly, the writers of these examples seem to have regarded the P–NP strings as compound-like entities, given their use of hyphens. In fact, most of the examples here seem to be set combinations of some kind which display a certain degree of fossilization. This is especially the case for frequently occurring combinations like (177), but less so for newly coined examples like (180). In (177) fossilization manifests itself through the decategorization of the NP following the preposition, which lacks a determinative. Inserting one (*off-the-road*) does not lead to a bad result, but in automotive contexts this is mostly not done. Notice also that the string *off-road* is not very likely to occur elsewhere in sentence structure (cf. ?*He loves to drive his car off-road*). The degree of fossilization is so great for items like *off-road* and *with-it* that some dictionaries list them separately, labelling them as adjectives. It seems to me that on balance the italicized items above are best regarded as PPs, but less than prototypical ones, which, given the position they occupy, are in a relationship of IG with adjective phrases.

6.2.3 *Noun phrases and prepositional phrases*

Consider the sentences below:

(185)   Under fives go free.
(186)   The under fives go free.

In these examples we have a plural morpheme apparently appended to a numeral (*five+s*). However, observe that although numerals can be pluralized (*fives and sixes*), we cannot have a pluralized numeral in subject position:

(187)   *Fives go free.
(188)   *The fives go free.

The bracketing of the string *under fives* in (185) should therefore be as in (189), rather than as in (190):

(189)   [[$_{PP}$ under five]s]
(190)   [$_{PP}$ under [fives]]

It seems that an unusual process has taken place here, such that a PP is first converted into a noun and then pluralized:

(191)   [$_{PP}$ under five] > [$_N$ under-five] > [[$_N$ under-five]+s] > [$_N$ under-fives]

This analysis is confirmed by the fact that a 'noun' like *under fives* can occupy positions which regular nouns (NPs) can also occupy, as in the examples in (192)–(195), analysed as in (196)–(199):

(192)   *Under threes* can keep you up all night.
(193)   Care workers like *the under threes* best.
(194)   Going places with *cheerful under threes* is fun.
(195)   *The Islington Under Threes Group*

(196)   [$_{NP}$ [$_N$ under threes]] can keep you up all night.
(197)   Care workers like [$_{NP}$ the [$_N$ under threes]] best.
(198)   Going places [$_{PP}$ with [$_{NP}$ [$_{AP}$ cheerful][$_N$ under threes]]] is fun.
(199)   [$_{NP}$ The [$_{NP}$ Islington][$_{NP}$[$_N$ Under Threes]] [$_N$ Group]]

In view of these data, which argue in favour of PP>N conversion, there is no good reason to posit gradience between NPs and PPs.

6.3 IG in grammar

As we have seen from the case studies of IG between word classes and between phrases, the possibility of elements combining morphosyntactic features from more than one category is not very exceptional. It is in fact quite common. This type of gradience typically occurs in the syntax in locations where we can distinguish 'slots' that are normally filled by a particular class of elements. Thus in NP structure categorial uncertainty occurs between elements that can occupy the specifier and premodifier positions (i.e. determinatives and adjectives), as well as between different types of premodifiers (i.e. adjectives and other elements that can occur pre-nominally). I have argued that many of the cases of Intersective Gradience we have looked at in this chapter are much less persuasive if we look at them more closely. On more than one occasion we found that the boundaries between categories were really quite sharp, and that a particular formative could be assigned to class α rather than to class β because on balance it displayed more α-like properties than β-like properties. We also found that a number of perceived instances of IG can be subsumed under SG. Does this mean that Intersective Gradience should be eliminated from the grammar altogether? The answer is 'yes' if we define IG in terms of fuzzy boundaries, as has been done by many of the authors whose work was discussed in this chapter. The answer is 'no' if we conceive of IG as the occurrence of situations in which elements conform to an intersection of sets of *properties*, rather than an intersection of *categories*. In Chapter 8 I will develop a model of gradience which incorporates this conception of IG. But first we turn to a consideration of constructional gradience in the next chapter.

7

Constructional Gradience

> The notion of grammatical construction [can be] eliminated, and with it, construction-particular rules. Constructions such as verb phrase, relative clause, and passive remain only as taxonomic artifacts, collections of phenomena explained through the interaction of the principles of UG, with the values of parameters fixed.
>
> (Chomsky 1995: 170)

> What makes a theory that allows constructions to exist a 'construction-based theory' is the idea that the network of constructions captures our grammatical knowledge of language *in toto*, i.e. **it's constructions all the way down**.
>
> (Goldberg 2006: 18; emphasis in original)

7.1 Introduction

In this chapter I will discuss gradience obtaining either *within* a particular construction-type (Subsective Constructional Gradience) or *between* two different syntactic constructions (Intersective Constructional Gradience), including clauses. Before we can sensibly talk about constructional gradience we need to define what is meant by the term 'construction', since it is used prolifically in the linguistic literature with very different definitions. In the next section I will give a bird's-eye overview of the history of the notion. As we will see, in the Chomskyan paradigm constructions are regarded as epiphenomena, although more recently they have begun to attract attention again. In Section 7.3 I will attempt to define the notion, while in Section 7.4 I will look at some examples of constructional gradience. Section 7.5 presents some conclusions regarding the notion of constructional gradience.

7.2 A brief history of the notion 'construction'

7.2.1 *Structuralism and Transformational Grammar*

The structuralists were not always very clear about what they meant by the notion 'construction'. Thus for Bloomfield '*[s]yntactic* constructions...are constructions in which none of the immediate constituents is a bound form' (1933: 185; emphasis in original). For Harris 'all sequences which are similar in respect to stated features' belong to one construction (1951: 325), while Gleason (1955: 132) simply says that a construction is 'any significant group of words (or morphemes)'.

In early Transformational Grammar the term 'construction' is used quite freely (cf. e.g. Chomsky 1965). More recently, theoretical linguists have denied that the notion of 'construction' has a role to play at all in theoretical linguistics.[1] For Chomsky grammatical constructions are epiphenomenal. He recognizes their utility for language description, but says that 'they have something like the status of "terrestrial mammal" or "household pet"' (Chomsky 2000: 8). As a result, as the quotation at the beginning of the chapter makes clear, '[t]he notion of grammatical construction [can be] eliminated, and with it, construction-particular rules.' This view is worth discussing at some length. For Chomsky constructions are an accidental by-product of the system of grammar that generates the expressions of a language, much like looking at a cloud and recognizing a face in it: the semblance of the face is not a property of the cloud, but a coincidental side effect. Or it is like saying that a synthesis that results after combining certain chemicals (a chemical 'construction') is a coincidental substance. For many linguists this is counterintuitive. For Chomsky, constructions have no privileged status as primitives in the theory. The term 'epiphenomenon' is also used by Chomsky for the notion of language itself. In the narrow sense the term 'language' refers to the language capacity, the wired-in abstract module of the brain which he calls Universal Grammar. It has also been called I(nternalized)-language (Chomsky 1986a). In the wider sense, 'language' refers to the way this term is used colloquially, namely as denoting the external manifestations of UG, for example in locutions like 'mind your language', 'the Dutch language', or 'the primary use of language is communication'. It is then called E-language. But does it make sense to say that constructions are epiphenomenal? Aristotle held that 'language is [exists] by convention, since no names arise naturally' (quoted in Robins 1990: 22). Similarly, de Saussure notes that '[l]inguistics . . . works continuously with concepts forged by grammarians without knowing whether or not the concepts actually correspond to the constituents of the system of language.' He then asks: 'But how can we find out? And if they are phantoms, what realities can we place in opposition to them?' Furthermore, for de Saussure 'there are no linguistic facts apart from the phonic substance cut into significant elements' (1916/1974: 110). Surely this is

---

[1] Pace, e.g., Pullum and Zwicky (1991: 252) who 'regard the notion of a construction as the crucial basis of syntax'.

correct, and maybe it is best to argue that *all* linguistic categories are fictitious components of grammatical descriptions, and have no real-world existence of their own. If this is so, then the notion of a taxonomic artefact loses its force. In any case, the question must be asked, even if constructions *are* epiphenomenal, why are certain syntactic patternings observable in (E-)languages, often with consistent meanings? Even as mere spin-offs, constructions are worthy of study. In regarding certain linguistic constructs as epiphenomena, some of the important insights of twentieth-century linguistic study seem to get thrown out with the bathwater. Take X-bar Theory. Current thinking within Chomsky's Minimalist Program dispenses with X-bar Theory on the grounds that it falls out from minimalist assumptions. As Chomsky (1995: 241f.) puts it: 'minimal and maximal projections are not identified by any special marking, so they must be determined from the structure in which they appear; I follow Muysken (1982) in taking these to be relational properties of categories, not properties inherent to them'. Although far from perfect, and much criticized (cf. e.g Pullum 1985; Kornai and Pullum 1990), X-bar Theory does seem to provide a neat blueprint for observed E-linguistic phrase structure configurations, and hence a handy descriptive tool.

7.2.2 *Descriptive grammar*

Descriptive linguists generally opt for purely structural definitions. Thus, for Huddleston (1984: 3) a 'construction' designates

the sentence and any constituent, except the minimal ones, the words. Thus with 'constituent' we are as it were looking upwards: *x* is a constituent if it is part of some element higher in the hierarchy; and with 'construction' we are looking downwards: *x* is a construction if it is analysable into, i.e. constructed from, one or more elements lower in the hierarchy.

Huddleston also speaks of 'construction-types', for example the imperative construction (1984: 7).

For Crystal

a particular type of construction (a 'constructional type' or 'pattern') [is] defined as a sequence of units which has a functional identity in the grammar of a language, such as subject + verb + object (with reference to clauses), or determiner + noun (with reference to phrases). Most specifically, it refers to a token of a constructional type, in the sense of string, e.g. *the + man + is + walking*. (Crystal 2003: 102)

The definition given in Zwicky (1987: 389) comes close to that of Crystal: a syntactic construction is 'a (formal) syntactic pattern' or 'syntagmatic category, expressing a characteristic (functional) relationship among its parts'. What is interesting is that for Zwicky constructions are categories of some sort.

Huddleston's definition is more wide-ranging than those of Crystal and Zwicky, which actually seem to exclude Huddleston's initial characterization. To draw an analogy with real-world entities such as buildings: Huddleston focuses on buildings in general (*any* building) and their parts, whereas Crystal and Zwicky stress the functionality of particular types of buildings, for example schools, churches, museums. At different levels of abstraction, however, all these definitions are serviceable.

7.2.3 *Cognitive Linguistics*

A more recent approach to the notion of 'construction' can be found in Cognitive Linguistics. Lakoff stresses meaning in his characterization of constructions, in which a sequence of elements is paired with a specification of its meaning and/or use (1987*a*: 467). For Lakoff a cognitive grammar 'will be a radial category of *grammatical constructions*, where each construction pairs a cognitive model (which characterizes meaning) with corresponding aspects of linguistic form' (1987*a*: 463). Moreover, 'syntax is to a very significant extent (though by no means entirely) dependent on semantics, pragmatics, and communicative function' (1987*a*: 488). To demonstrate his use of the notion of construction he offers a lengthy case study of English *there* and the constructions in which it appears. In doing so he makes use of a cognitively based grammar that employs his cognitive model theory.

Taylor (1998, 2002, 2003: 222f.) also stresses the importance of pairing off form and meaning in defining the notion of a construction, where meaning is understood broadly as including for example stress, intonation, and discourse features. Thus, a construction is said to be 'roughly equivalent' to 'sentence pattern' or 'phrasal pattern' (Taylor 1998: 177), and it is 'a schema or template, which captures what is common to a range of expressions, and which, at the same time, sanctions the creation of new expressions of the respective type' (1998: 177). These schemas (e.g. NP–V–NP–NP for ditransitives) need to be complemented by a specification of the type of items that can occur in the patterns. 'This requires that we appeal to the semantics of the construction' (1998: 178). In addition, mention might in some cases need to be made of factors such as prosody, intonation, etc. In a chapter of his book on categorization (2003) entitled 'Syntactic Constructions as Prototype Categories', Taylor discusses the yes/no interrogative and transitive constructions. I will return to his work below.

7.2.4 *Constructionist frameworks*

Ideas similar to those found in Lakoff (1987*a*) regarding constructions also feature in a recent theory of language called *Construction Grammar* (CxG). In Goldberg (1995: 4) a construction 'C is a form-meaning pair $< F_i, S_i >$ such that some aspect of F_i or some aspect of S_i is not strictly predictable from C's component parts or from other previously established constructions'. More recently she has written that in her variant of CxG, which she calls *Cognitive Construction Grammar* (CCxG), '[a]ll levels of grammatical analysis involve constructions: learned pairings of form with semantic or discourse function, including morphemes or words, idioms, partially lexically filled and fully general phrasal patterns' (Goldberg 2006: 5). In slogan form 'it's constructions all the way down' (2006: 18).

Goldberg (2006: 213f.) notes that in fact there currently exist a number of constructionist approaches which differ from each other in various ways. Thus, for example, in 'Fillmorean' Construction Grammar, which Goldberg refers to as *Unification Construction Grammar* (UCxG), grammar and usage are strictly separated, unlike in other CxG frameworks, including Goldberg's own CCxG (2006: 215).

CxG in general bears some similarities to other recent linguistic theories, such as HPSG, in being monostratal and constraint-based. Syntactic and semantic information are combined (at least in UCxG) in Attribute Value Matrices (AVMs), familiar from HPSG. In an early paper Fillmore, Kay, and O'Connor (1988) looked at the *let alone*-construction, and Kay and Fillmore (1999) discuss the *What's X doing Y*-construction (WXDY), as in *What's this lolly doing in your pocket?* Syntactically and semantically the WXDY-construction displays a number of peculiarities which warrant regarding it as a unified constructional whole. Figure 7.1 illustrates the AVM for the WXDY construction.

The representation is designed to abstractly diagram the relations between five elements: BE, *doing*, *what*, and the elements X and Y. Constructions such as WXDY interact with other constructions in English, and in this way license the expressions of the language. Kay posits 'a cline of constructions, from the relatively productive to the relatively frozen' (1995: 174). Unlike in Generative Grammar, then, the construction has a central role in this theory of language.

A recent version of CxG is Bill Croft's (2001) Radical Construction Grammar (RCxG), which is 'a nonreductionist theory of syntactic representation. Constructions, not categories and relations, are the basic, primitive units of syntactic representation' (2001: 47–8). Constructions are primitive, not atomic entities in RCxG, which allows them to be complex.

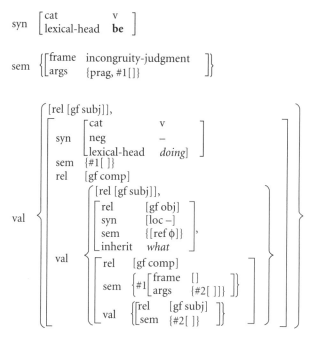

FIGURE 7.1 AVM for the WXDY construction
Source: Kay and Fillmore (1999: 20)

In Jackendoff's constructionist approach (2002: 172ff.) a number of 'constructional idioms' are discussed, each of which has one or more open positions which can be filled by variables (indicated by lower case categorial labels):

(1) [_{VP} V np PP]
     e.g. *take NP to task*

(2) The '*way*'-construction:
     [_{VP} v NP pp]: *V pro_e's way PP* ['pro_e' is coreferential with the subject]
     e.g. *Bill belched his way out of the restaurant.*

(3) Resultatives:
     [_{VP} v np ap]
     e.g. *Wilma watered the tulips flat.*

These three constructions are on a cline: in (1) there is one open slot (the NP-position), in (2) there are two (NP and PP), while in (3) all the positions are left open, a very 'free' construction. Jackendoff notes:

[I]n each of these cases . . . we have come to regard the construction not as a lexical rule that creates new verb argument structures 'in the lexicon,' but rather as a lexical item in its own right that undergoes free combination with verbs. What makes these cases unusual is that the verb does not determine the VP's syntactic argument structure. Rather, the construction itself determines the VP's syntactic argument structure, in violation of the Head Constraint, and the verb satisfies a free position in the construction. (Jackendoff 2002: 176)

Jackendoff rejects the Chomskyan doctrine that constructions are epiphenomenal. He instead proposes a generalized notion of constructions such that they are 'slightly unusual but perfectly respectable lexical items that combine with ordinary words according to ordinary procedures' (2002: 178). See also Culicover and Jackendoff (2005).

For further work in CxG see for example Shibatani and Thompson (1996), some of the papers in Kay (1997, 2002), Fried and Boas (2005), Goldberg and Casenhiser (2006), and Fillmore *et al.* (forthcoming).

7.3 The notion 'construction'

As a first approximation to come to grips with the notion of construction, we might say that a syntactic construction is a string of elements (words, phrases, etc.) that has a distinctive patterning which plays a role in different parts of the grammar. Put differently, in an everyday and pre-theoretical sense, the term 'construction' designates a particular configuration of elements that has an identifiable grammatical role to play. These characterizations give prominence to the linear ordering of elements, and exclude semantic considerations from the definition. Various types of concatenations qualify as syntactic constructions, for example strings such as those in (4)–(12) below:

(4)   noun+noun (e.g. *home entertainment, blackboard*)
(5)   determinative+noun (e.g. *the book*)
(6)   subject+verb+object (e.g. *I love you*)
(7)   P+NP+P (e.g. *in the care of, for the sake of*)
(8)   V+NP+*to*-infinitive (e.g. *(I) believed her to be in love; (I) want him to stay*)
(9)   verb+direct object (e.g. *(I) did it.*)
(10) verb+indirect object+direct object (e.g. *(I) sent her some flowers*)
(11) operator+subject+verb+direct object (e.g. *Have you lost your way?*)
(12) *It*+form of the verb *be*+focus+*who/that*-clause (e.g. *It was Alison who called me*)

These are all superficially different: (4) and (5) contain two word class elements; (6) contains functional elements and a word class element; (7) contains a word class element and a phrasal element; (8) displays a mixture of these two types of elements, together with the more general label 'to-infinitive'; in (9)–(11), as in (6), we have a mixture of word class categories and functional categories, and finally in (12) the pattern contains specific lexical items, such as *it* and *who*, as well as the pragmatic label 'Focus'.

For Huddleston (5)–(12) would qualify as constructions, while (9)–(12) would be specific construction-types. For Crystal and Zwicky presumably only (5), (6), (9), (10), (11), and (12) qualify as constructions, because they have a specific function in the grammar: (5) is a phrase, (6) is a clause, (9) and (10) are complementation patterns, the string in (11) is a clause type, while (12) is a focus construction. Notice that the strings in (7)–(12) have specific names: complex preposition construction, catenative construction, transitive construction, ditransitive construction, interrogative construction, and cleft construction.

Because Subsective Gradience and Intersective Gradience involving word classes and phrases have already been dealt with in Chapters 5 and 6, I will adopt a slightly narrower and more conventional conception of the notion of construction by taking (6)–(12) to be syntactic constructions.

In this book whether or not categories and/or constructions 'really' exist will not be an issue. The view I will take is that even if either or both are epiphenomenal, categories and constructions are convenient devices to describe the syntactic 'fallout' of whatever is produced by UG. Like cognitive linguists, then, I will grant them a lease of life, but unlike cognitivists, I will assume that they are characterized primarily syntactically.

7.4 Constructional Gradience

Having defined the notion 'construction', we are now in a position to characterize 'constructional gradience': constructional gradience can be either of the subsective kind, where a particular string of elements conforms to a greater or lesser extent to a prototype construction, or it can be intersective in nature; in the latter case it obtains if in a particular string of words we can identify properties of a construction α as well as properties of a construction β. We turn now to an overview of a number of examples of what could be seen as cases of Subsective Constructional Gradience (SCG) and Intersective Constructional Gradience (ICG) found in the literature. These will be critically assessed in Section 7.5, where I will also draw some conclusions about the nature of SCG and ICG.

7.4.1 *Subsective Constructional Gradience (SCG)*

As we have seen, with Subsective Constructional Gradience a particular string of elements conforms to a greater or lesser extent to a prototype construction.

Several authors have written on Subsective Constructional Gradience—although they do not use that term—among them Lakoff (1977), Ross (1987), Winters (1990), and Taylor (1998, 2003). Some of the illustrative case studies of SCG that follow are based on their work. At the outset, it is crucial to take note of an important point made by John Taylor: 'Marginality with respect to a construction is not to be equated with a decline in acceptability; marginal instantiations of a construction need not be any less grammatical than more central members' (1998: 192, 198).

7.4.1.1 *Pseudoclefts*   In Ross (1987), a plea is made for the notion of *prototype syntax*. The idea here is that particular elements or configurations of elements are more prototypical if their distribution is maximally unconstrained. Ross extends this idea to constructions, and in doing so introduces the notion of *viability* (see Chapter 3). While the difference between acceptability and viability in Ross's paper is not entirely clear, the data he discusses do convincingly show that prototypicality plays a role in constructional syntax. An example from Ross's paper concerns pseudocleft constructions. Consider the sentences below:

(13)   What Molly discovered was a Grand Unified Theory.
(14)   Where Molly lived was in London.
(15)   What Molly is is brilliant.

According to Ross, (13) with an NP in the focus position is more prototypically a pseudocleft construction than (14), which contains a focused PP. (14) in its turn is a more typical pseudocleft than (15), with its focused AP. Ross substantiates his intuitions by showing that (13) is distributionally more versatile than (14) or (15), as (16)–(18) show:

(16)   Was what Molly discovered a Grand Unified Theory?
(17)   ?Was where Molly lived in London?
(18)   ?*Is what Molly is brilliant?

The acceptability of the interrogative pseudoclefts is seen to be linked to the degree of prototypicality possessed by their non-interrogative counterparts. Similarly, adding an auxiliary verb in (19)–(21) below leads to a progressive loss in what Ross calls viability:

(19)   What Molly discovered might be a Grand Unified Theory.
(20)   ?Where Molly lived might be in London.
(21)   ?*What Molly is might be brilliant.

Ross (2000) returned to pseudoclefts.

7.4.1.2 *Constructions involving subject–auxiliary inversion (SAI)*   Taylor: (2003: 227) discusses yes/no interrogatives such as *Is that a fact?* and argues that, just like 'regular' grammatical categories, constructions such as these also display prototype effects. This particular example, according to Taylor, is syntactically clearly an interrogative, but the construction as a whole is only peripherally interrogative. The reason is that semantically it does not ask a question: its illocutionary force is one of surprise. He goes on to say that the expression can be seen as a construction in its own right, of which all the specific characteristics need to be detailed, for example the fact that it is unproductive (**Are those facts? *Were these facts?*). I will return to Taylor's claims in Section 7.6.

Goldberg (2006: 166ff.) discusses SAI constructions more widely. She challenges the claim that no functional generalizations can be made regarding this pattern. Instead, she claims that there is a prototypical case whose dominant characteristic is NON-POSITIVE. Extensions of the prototype lack one or more of its attributes. The prototype for SAI is 'non-prototypical sentence' which isn't actually instantiated. Apart from NON-POSITIVE, its attributes are 'non-predicate focus', 'non-assertive', 'dependent', and 'non-declarative'. Among the extensions of the prototype are yes/no questions (NON-POSITIVE, non-declarative), counterfactual conditionals (NON-POSITIVE, dependent, non-asserted), and initial negative adverb clauses (NON-POSITIVE). These extensions 'reconstrue the category of SAI as a halo of constructions that stand in *contrast* to prototypical sentences' (2006: 178; emphasis in original). The form of the construction (i.e. the inversion pattern) is motivated as follows: '[b]y positioning the auxiliary in a non-canonical position, the construction conveys that the polarity involved is not the canonical, positive polarity; i.e. no positive word-to-world fit is asserted' (2006: 180). A general conclusion of the study of SAI is that 'functional motivations often underlie seemingly idiosyncratic facts of grammar' (2006: 181).

7.4.1.3 *Verb + NP and Verb + NP + NP constructions*   In the sentences below the postverbal NP is in construction with the verb:

(22)   I kicked *the ball.*
(23)   That shirt suits *you.*
(24)   This book weighs *three kilograms.*

The first sentence contains a typical direct object, from a purely grammatical point of view: *the ball* is a syntactically required NP positioned immediately after the verb and is an argument of that verb. Furthermore, it can be fronted under passivization. The second and third sentences are distributionally less versatile in that neither can be passivized. The difference between (23) and (24) is that the postverbal NP in the latter has an adverbial feel to it ('how much does that book weigh?'), whereas the former does not. I will discuss (24) in Section 7.4.2.5 on Intersective Constructional Gradience between complements and adjuncts. As regards (22) and (23), it is not unreasonable to say that the postverbal NP in (22) is a prototypical direct object, while the NP after the verb in (23) is a peripheral DO. Allerton (1978: 72, 2006: 164) uses the label *objoid* for the postverbal NP in (23), while the postverbal NPs in (25) and (26) are termed *indirect objoids*:

(25)   The dog cost Oliver five pounds.
(26)   The journey took Oliver five hours.

These NPs are like indirect objects in terms of their distribution in the V+NP+NP construction, but unlike typical NPs in that they cannot be fronted under passivization. See also Allerton (1978) on what he calls 'indirect-objectiness'. Gries (2003) models ditransitive prototypes in English using authentic corpus data and multifactorial statistical techniques. In identifying the prototype he takes into account a large number of diverse factors, including animacy of the participants, length of the NP arguments, definiteness, information packaging considerations, etc.

7.4.1.4 *Transitive constructions*   Similar to the Verb–Object construction, but mainly semantic in nature, as we will see, is the transitive construction as discussed in Taylor (2003: 231f.). It contains a number of slots, which are easy to describe syntactically with the formula NP–V–NP. However, the semantic aspects of the construction are considerably more complex. Taking his cue from work by Lakoff (1977) and Hopper and Thompson (1980), Taylor lists twelve semantic characteristics of the construction. Among these are the fact that the construction involves exactly two participants, the subject NP is the agent, the event is punctual, and so on. All of the constructions below deviate from central cases of transitives for one or more reasons:

(27)   The lightning destroyed the tree.
(28)   We approached the city.
(29)   I dug the ground.
(30)   He brushed his teeth.
(31)   I carried the suitcase.
(32)   Mary helped John.
(33)   John obeyed Mary.
(34)   I watched the movie.
(35)   John saw Mary.

I will not discuss all of these, but will merely highlight a few cases. In (27) the subject is not a typical animate agent, but 'otherwise the event in [(27)] is highly transitive' (Taylor 2003: 208). In (29) the direct object is only partially affected, while in (30) the patient is part of the agent and not maximally individuated. In (33) the event is not under the control of a subject-agent, the typical situation, but it is controlled by the object-patient. Finally, (34) is more transitive than (35) because in the former sentence the event denoted by the verb is under the control of the subject.

7.4.1.5 *The possessive construction*   Amongst the most detailed discussions of prototype constructions, along with Lakoff's (1987*a*) discussion of *there* (see Section 7.2.3), is Taylor's (1996) book on possessives. For Taylor a prototypical possessive relation semantically involves the following features (1996: 340):

(36)   THE POSSESSION GESTALT
   a.   The possessor is a specific human being.
   b.   The possessed is an inanimate entity, usually a concrete physical object.
   c.   The relation is exclusive, in the sense that for any possessed entity, there is usually only one possessor. On the other hand, for any possessor, there is typically a large number of entities which may count as his possessions.
   d.   The possessor has exclusive rights of access to the possessed. Other persons may have access to the possessed only with the permission of the possessor.
   e.   The possessed is typically an object of value, whether commercial or sentimental.
   f.   The possessor's rights of access to the possessed are invested in him through a special transaction, such as purchase, inheritance, or gift, and remain with him until the possessor effects their transfer to another person by means of a further transaction, such as sale or donation.
   g.   Typically, the possession relation is long term, measured in months and years, not in minutes or seconds.
   h.   In order that the possessor can have easy access to the possessed, the possessed is typically located in the proximity of the possessor. In some cases, the possessed may be a permanent, or at least regular accompaniment of the possessor.

Possession can be articulated by a great variety of linguistic expressions. Among them are possessive constructions (*my dog, the dog is mine*, etc.) and verbs such as *possess, own, have,* etc. As Taylor observes, each of these different ways of expressing possession conforms to the gestalt in a different way. Taylor sets up the cline of expressions in (37)–(43), each of which involves the verb *have.* In the examples we can detect a gradual distancing from the prototype:

(37)   Do you have a bank account?
(38)   The house has three bedrooms.
(39)   You have a lot of patience.
(40)   We have a lot of crime in this city.
(41)   I have some work to do.
(42)   I have to go to town this afternoon.
(43)   The guests have arrived.

Here I will only mention what Taylor says about the extremes of the cline. The example in (37) deviates from the prototype in a number of ways. Among them is the fact that a bank account is not a physical object ((36b)); it is not of itself of value ((36e)), and cannot be transferred ((36f)). In (43) we have perfective *have,* which barely has any possessive meaning at all, except perhaps, as Taylor notes, as an extension of the notion of 'accessibility' (cf. (36h)): the current relevance expressed by the perfective form indicates that the guests are here now, that is to say 'accessible'.

7.4.1.6 *Complex prepositions*   As we saw briefly in Chapter 5, Quirk and Mulholland (1964) discuss $P^1N^1P^2N^2$ constructions of the type *in spite of (his success),* and observe that they are fixed sequences (cf. **in the spite of (his success), *in clear spite of (his success)*), in contrast with sequentially unrestricted strings like *on the table near* (*cf. on a table near the door/on the big table near the door* etc.). They observe:

[W]hile the polarity of the highly interdependent (*in spite of*) and the freely dissociable (*on the table near*) is clear-cut, we are not here dealing with a simple binary classification. However convenient sharp distinctions may be between grammar and lexis, closed system and open class, it is important to realise here as elsewhere that, between the poles realisable in $P^1N^1P^2N^2$ sequences, there is a continuum or gradient, and that in fact it is largely through the productive power of these sequences that we keep the form-class 'preposition' open-ended in English. (Quirk and Mulholland 1964: 65)

On the basis of nine criteria (listed below) they represent $P^1N^1P^2N^2$ sequences as a gradient involving five classes, as shown in Table 7.1. The criteria are:

1. invariability of P^2;
2. N^1 has no number contrast;
3. N^1 is invariable as to article or zero article selection;

4. P¹ is invariable;
5. P² N² cannot be replaced by a genitive;
6. P² N² cannot be deleted;
7. P² N² cannot be replaced by a demonstrative;
8. the lexical isolation of N¹;
9. N¹ does not admit free premodification by an adjective.

Each of these five classes is in fact subdivided into subclasses which form subgradients, and Table 7.1 'is generalized from the numerical preponderances in the subclass matrices on which it is based, and these in turn are a numerically biased abstraction from the total matrix recording the restrictions observed with each PNPN sequence individually.' A typical example of each of the classes in Table 7.1 is shown below:

Class I: *in spite of*
Class II: *in search of*
Class III: *in praise of*
Class IV: *in need of*
Class V: *at the request of*

The gradient in Table 7.1 is certainly not a perfect one (not 'well behaved', to use Ross's term), which may indicate that the items in question are not in a gradient relationship. A number of linguists are sceptical about the notion 'complex preposition', among them Huddleston (1984), Seppänen *et al.* (1994), and Huddleston and Pullum *et al.* (2002: 620f.). Huddleston (1984: 343f.) lumps P+P (*because of*) and P+N+P (*by dint of*) together. The main problem he signals for the complex preposition analysis is the fact that a sequence like *on behalf of* in a phrase like *on behalf of my father* is as fixed as *by dint of* in *by dint of hard work*, and yet we can have *on my father's behalf* but not **by hard work's dint*, which suggests that the string *behalf of my father* is a regular NP. The fixedness peculiarities of *on behalf of*, Huddleston suggests, are best treated in the lexicon.

TABLE 7.1 The complex preposition gradient

Classes	Parameters								
	1	2	3	4	5	6	7	8	9
I	+	+	+	+	+	+	+	+	+
II	+	+	+	+	+	−	+	−	+
III	+	+	+	+	+	+	−	−	−
IV	+	+	+	−	+	+	−	−	−
V	+	+	+	−	−	+	−	−	−

But if we accept this, he goes on to say, then there is no reason for *by dint of* not to be dealt with in the lexicon as well. Huddleston proposes analysing 'complex prepositions' as prepositional idioms, but concedes that this is 'a tricky area [of grammar] where it ill becomes us to be dogmatic' (1984: 344). Whichever way we look at the matter, it seems to be reasonable to posit a gradient between more or less fixed $P^1N^1P^2N^2$ constructions.

7.4.1.7 *The passive gradient*   In the previous chapter I briefly discussed the sentences in (44)–(46) in terms of intersective gradience between verbs and adjectives.

(44)   They were *arrested* by the police.
(45)   He was *disgusted* by the whole thing.
(46)   The mirror was *broken*.

In (44) the element *arrested* is clearly verbal: it carries a verbal ending, the sentence in which it occurs has an active counterpart, and *arrested* has a dynamic meaning which cannot be premodified by *very*. In (45) the word *disgusted* has both verbal and adjectival properties: it is verbal because it has the -*ed* ending that is found on passive participles, it has an active counterpart, and is followed by a *by*-phrase. However, it could also be regarded as adjectival for several reasons: it can be said to be positioned in predicative position, it can be intensified (*very disgusted*), it is gradable (*more disgusted/most disgusted*), and we can replace *was* by *seemed* (Huddleston and Pullum *et al.* 2002: 1437). In (46) *broken* can have two readings: a dynamic one (=verb, cf. *the mirror was broken by hooligans*) and a statal one (=adjective, cf. *the mirror was already broken/the mirror seemed broken/ the mirror is unbroken*), cf. Huddleston (1984: 322–3) and Huddleston and Pullum *et al.* (2002: 1436f.). I noted in Chapter 6 that it is preferable to look at these data in another way, namely in terms of Subsective Constructional Gradience, because one of the main criteria that distinguishes them is passivization, which is a process that applies to constructions as wholes. The idea of a *passive gradient* was worked out in detail in Svartvik (1966), and was adopted by Quirk *et al.* (1985: 167f.). For them (44) is a central passive, (45) is a semi-passive, while (46) is a pseudo-passive (a statal passive in Huddleston's (1984: 322) terminology). Svartvik's gradient is more fine-grained. He sets up the following classes:

α   'Animate agent passives' (e.g. *He was given this puppy by a farmer in the Welsh hills.*)

β   'Inanimate agent passives' (e.g. *We've been well rewarded by our visit to Bognor Regis.*)

β/γ   'Janus-agent passives' (e.g. *These sex differences ... can also be initiated by injection of anterior pituitary extracts.*)

γ   'Agentless passives' (e.g. *Many varieties of laterals are heard in English.*)

δ   Comprises 'Attitudinal passives' (e.g. *We are encouraged, therefore, to use the radar data to obtain drop-size distributions*) and 'Emotional passives' (e.g. *Gerald was suddenly very annoyed.*)

ε   'Nonagentive passives' (e.g. *The die is cast.*)

ζ   'Compound passives' (e.g. *But Cavill was unimpressed by this sally.*)

The criteria for deciding to which class a particular passive belongs are the following: in the first instance the possibility of having an unproblematic active transform (e.g. *A farmer in the Welsh hills gave him this puppy*) determines whether a construction belongs to classes α–γ or δ–ζ. Classes α and β have an actual *by*-agent (animate or inanimate) whereas γ has no actual *by*-agent, but could potentially have one. Members of class β/γ are called Janus-agent passives because the PPs that occur with them can be interpreted as agent-like or adjunct-like. Class δ is in an intermediate position on the gradient in that it has verbal properties in allowing an active transform (e.g. *[Somebody] encouraged us . . . /[Somebody] annoyed Gerald*) and is adjectival in allowing an 'intensive active transform' (e.g. *[Somebody] made us feel encouraged . . . /[Somebody] made Gerald annoyed*). It also allows actual/potential qualification (*very encouraged/annoyed*) and coordination with adjectives (*encouraged/annoyed and tired*). The attitudinal and emotive passives are distinguished by the fact that the former do not take potential or actual quasi-agents,[2] whereas the latter do. Members of class ε (which includes statal passives) do not take an actual or potential agent, and the relation to an active form is weak. The compound passives are not really passives at all, given the fact that the *un-* prefix turns the word it is attached to into an adjective.

Svartvik notes that these classes cannot be rigidly kept apart, and can contain subgradients, like class δ. What is most noticeable about this passive gradient is the fact that it is purely syntactically motivated, especially through the role of the passive transformation: the higher up the scale a particular string is positioned, the more prototypically passive it is. In fact, he suggests that '[a]s we proceed down the passive scale, it becomes increasingly difficult to consider the passive in terms of a transformational voice relation, since this is being gradually replaced by a different relation which we call "serial"' (1966: 159). (See Chapter 4 for an explanation of this term.)

As we have seen, the passive data discussed in this section can be seen as exemplifying either Intersective Gradience if we view the facts from the point of view of the pivotal element (i.e. the word ending in *-ed*), much like the gerund

---

[2] These are '[l]exically determined agents [which] are introduced by a variety of prepositions' (Svartvik 1966: 102). Example: I was interested *in her.*

(see Section 6.1.2.2), or as Subsective Constructional Gradience if we view the data more holistically. The latter is preferable because the passive involves a classical transformational relationship between well-defined regular patterns.

7.4.2 *Intersective Constructional Gradience (ICG)*

As noted above, Intersective Constructional Gradience obtains if in a particular string of words we can identify properties of two constructions. In the following sections are some (alleged) instances.

7.4.2.1 *Genitival constructions*   Leech, Francis, and Xu (1994) discuss two genitival constructions of English, the Saxon genitive (*X's Y*, e.g. *Jim's book*) and its counterpart with *of* (*the X of Y*, e.g. *the wheels of the bicycle*). In an effort to find out what determines the choice of one construction over the other, they isolate a number of criteria, of which they choose three for the purposes of their analysis: the semantic category of X, the semantic relationship between X and Y, and the kind of texts in which the constructions occur. Using the statistical technique of logistical modelling, they then set out to demonstrate the existence of gradience between the two constructions. Their findings are that all three criteria are significant, and that furthermore the most important factor is the semantic class of X, followed by the text type and the relationship of X to Y. Logistic modelling allows for a further refinement of these findings: it turns out that with regard to semantics the degree of humanness of X is criterial, such that the higher the degree of humanness of X, the more likely it is that it will take the Saxon genitive. The overall ranking of the other semantic 'levels' is as follows (Leech *et al.* 1994: 71):

1. X is human
2. X is a place
3. X is a human organization
4. X is animal (but not human)
5. X is abstract (apart from time)
6. X is concrete and inanimate (apart from place)

They note the following:

The existence of a gradient between the two constructions is particularly clear from the characteristics of this factor. Level 1 (human X) makes a very strong contribution to the choice of the genitive—and thus confirms the stereotypic explanation of the genitive given in many grammar books. On the other hand, the fact that levels 2, 3 and 4 identify classes associated with quasi-human characteristics is evidence for the genitive's being in this respect a 'fuzzy edged' category.... Oversimplifying, we might see level 1 as the 'hard core' of the genitive category, level 6 as being the 'hard core' of the *of*-construction category, and levels 2–5 as being intermediate. (Leech *et al.* 1994: 72; footnote omitted)

Leech *et al.*'s paper purports to be about categorial gradience, as its title ('The use of computer corpora in the textual demonstrability of gradience in linguistic categories') and the quotation above indicate, but in fact its subject matter is how users of English *choose* between the two constructions. The authors succeed in demonstrating that the criteria for choosing one or the other construction can be ranked, such that the applicability of a certain criterion unquestionably leads to the choice of the Saxon genitive, while the applicability of a criterion at the opposite end of the list leads to language users opting for the *of*-genitive. However, demonstrating that there exists a ranking of the criteria that determine the choice of one rather than the other construction does *not* demonstrate gradience between the grammatical constructions themselves. In other words, in showing that certain factors are at work when speakers of English choose one construction rather than the other, we are not showing that the Saxon genitive resembles the *of*-genitive grammatically. From the point of view of their syntax these constructions are as distinct as can be.

7.4.2.2 *Taylor's possessive constructions gradient*   Taylor (1996, 1998) argues for a cline between three types of construction: prenominal possessives (*[the boy]'s shirt*; the shirt belongs to a specific boy), possessive compounds (*[the boy's] shirt*; it is a shirt of the type worn by boys), and non-possessive compounds (*[the boy band]*). There are many cases where it is difficult to classify a particular string of elements. Thus, in (47) with regard to *a man's skull* it is difficult to decide whether we are dealing with a prenominal possessive reading (*[[a man]'s skull]*: 'the skull of an unspecified man'), or with a compound reading (*[a [man's skull]]*: 'the skull of a (male) human').

(47)   The archaeologists discovered fragments of a man's skull.

Taylor goes on to show that the boundary between possessive compounds and non-possessive compounds is also not a sharp one. He gives the example of *students' union/students union*:

Uncertainty as to whether the expression merits a possessive apostrophe goes hand in hand with uncertainty as to whether the expression should be construed as a possessive (on the lines of *children's playground*) or as a compound with a plural noun modifier (on the pattern of *accounts clerk, greetings card*). (Taylor 1998: 197)

He notes that '[t]he evidence of possessives ... validates the notion of syntactic construction itself, whose prototype is characterized in terms of a cluster of properties, pertaining to syntactic, semantic, and phonological (as well as

TABLE 7.2 Characteristics of prenominal possessives, possessive compounds, and non-possessive compounds

Prenominal possessives	Possessive compounds	Non-possessive compounds
Referential (usually definite), i.e. 'instance specification'	Non-referential, i.e. 'type specification'	Non-referential i.e. 'type specification'
Possessor nominal referential (topical, and usually definite)	Possessor nominal non-referential, or weakly referential	Modifier nominal non-referential
Possessor nominal often human or animate	Possessor nominal almost always human or animate	Modifier nominal typically non-human
Possessor and possessee may be pre- and postmodified	Little possibility of modification of head noun or modifier	Little possibility of modification of head noun or modifier
Variable interpretation	Conventionalized interpretation	Conventionalized interpretation
Final stress	Initial stress	Initial stress
Written with word space and apostrophe	Written with word space and apostrophe	With lexicalization apostrophe and word space may be omitted

Source: Taylor (1996: 313)

pragmatic, and perhaps even orthographic) aspects' (1996: 314). The similarities between the three constructions emerge from Table 7.2 above.

Notice that, despite talking about 'syntactic constructions' and mentioning syntactic properties, the characteristics given by Taylor in Table 7.2 hardly refer to syntax at all. In fact, only the characteristic about modification refers to syntax.

For a semantically driven account of constructional gradience between determiner genitives (*John's book*) and descriptive genitives (e.g. *women's magazine*), as well as between s-genitives and NN sequences, see Rosenbach (2006).

7.4.2.3 *Coordination and subordination*   Constructional gradience has been argued to exist between coordination and subordination by Kruisinga (1932: 501), who noted that '[i]t is perhaps hardly necessary to observe that the distinction between coordination and subordination is a relative one, allowing of intermediate cases' (cited in Matthiessen and Thompson 1988: 318, fn 5). He talks of 'Apparent Coordination' (Kruisinga 1932: 510) and 'Apparent Sub-Clauses' (1932: 514), indicating the fuzzy status of these notions. Van Valin

(1984) discusses a number of interesting cases of constructions in non-English languages that can be said to be in between coordination and subordination. Consider the example below from Jacaltec (Craig 1977):

(48) Ch-in   xubli   an x-Ø-(h)in-tx'ah-ni   xil kape   an
     NPST-1sgABS whistle 1p PST-3ABS-1sgERG-wash-SUFF CL clothes 1p
     'I washed the clothes whistling'

     (N)PST = (non-)past; 1 sg = 1st person singular; ABS = absolutive;
     ERG = ergative; SUFF = suffix; CL = classifier

Van Valin observes that 'the verb in the first clause must be in the neutral non-past tense form, and the two clauses must have the same subject. The tense interpretation for the whole sentence is a function of the tense inflection of the verb in the second clause; there is therefore G[rammatical] C[ategory] dependence between the clauses' (1984: 546). Grammatical category dependence can be defined as dependence between clauses from the point of view of voice, mood, tense, pronoun reference, etc. The example instantiates a structure that can be located on a cline between coordination and subordination, because it instantiates non-embedding and dependency, the latter by virtue of grammatical category linking. Following Olson (1981), Van Valin calls the combination of features [+dependent, −embedded] *cosubordination* (1984: 546). By contrast, subordination can be characterized by the features [+dependent, +embedded] while coordination instantiates the features [−dependent, −embedded].

In Chapter 5 we discussed work by Lehmann (1988) on clause integration. Recall that this author is concerned with a typology of clause linking, specifically with the degree to which pairs of clauses are integrated with each other. As we have seen, Lehmann does not distinguish between Subsective and Intersective Gradience, which would have been useful to distinguish the cline he establishes between hypotaxis and embedding—arguably a case of SG—from his other clines, which are best regarded as instances of IG, for example the gradient that runs from 'clause' to 'noun'.

In modern descriptive grammar gradience between coordination and subordination is also hinted at in Huddleston (1984: 380, 382–3), while Quirk *et al.* (1985: 927–8) work out the idea in the most detailed way.[3] They argue that one would expect gradience to occur between these two grammatical construction-types given the fact that both are grammatical linking devices. Quirk *et al.* establish six syntactic criteria to characterize coordinating conjunctions. These are then used to construct the matrix shown in Table 7.3 (most of the example sentences are from Quirk *et al.* 1985: 921f.). The more criteria the item conforms

---

[3] See also Cristofaro (2003: 22–5).

to, the more it is like a coordinating conjunction, and the less it is like a subordinating conjunction. The criteria are not ranked in order of importance.

    a. The item can only occur at the beginning of a clause. Example:
      John plays the guitar, and *his sister plays the piano.*
      *John plays the guitar; his sister and *plays the piano.*

    b. In a sequence of coordinated clauses A and B, where B contains the item, B cannot precede A. Example:
      They are living in England, or *they are spending a vacation there.*
      *Or they are spending a vacation there, they are living in England.

    c. A sequence of coordinating conjunctions is impossible, whereas subordinating conjunctions and conjuncts *can* combine with other linkers. Examples:
      *He was unhappy about it, and but *he did as he was told.*
      He was unhappy about it, and yet *he did as he was told.*
      He asked to be transferred, because *he was unhappy* and because *he saw no prospect of promotion.*

    d. The item can link clauses, but also predicates and other types of constituents. Example:
      I [may see you tomorrow] or *[may phone later in the day].*
      *He [did not spend very much], so that *[could afford a trip abroad].*

    e. The item can link subordinate clauses. Example:
      I wonder [whether you should go and see her] or *[whether it is better to write to her].*
      *They didn't stay [although they were happy], but *[although they were bored].*

    f. The item can link more than two clauses. Example:
      The battery may be disconnected, the connection may be loose, or *the bulb may be faulty.*
      *Kate watched television, but *Gerry was reading,* but *Pete was singing.*

TABLE 7.3 Quirk *et al.*'s coordination–subordination gradient

Criteria		a	b	c	d	e	f
Coordinators	*and, or*	+	+	+	+	+	+
	but	+	+	+	+	±	−
Conjuncts	*yet, so, nor*	+	+	×	+	−	−
	however, therefore	−	+	−	−	−	−
Subordinators	*for, so that*	+	+	+	−	−	−
	if, because	+	±	−	−	−	−

Source: Quirk *et al.* (1985: 927)

Although we might quibble with some of the finer analytical points regarding this matrix,[4] this does not detract from the insight that coordination and subordination are in a relationship of ICG with each other.

7.4.2.4 *Verb complementation: monotransitive, ditransitive, and complex transitive constructions*   Quirk *et al.* (1985: 1218f.) posit a gradient between their monotransitive, ditransitive, and complex transitive constructions, illustrated below:

(49)   We like *all parents* to visit the school.
(50)   They expected *James* to win the race.
(51)   We asked *the students* to attend a lecture.

All three sentences conform to the pattern V+NP+*to*-infinitive. The claim is that in (49) the postverbal NP is not an argument of the verb, in (51) it clearly is, while in (50) the NP is subject-like *vis-à-vis* the verb that follows it, but object-like *vis-à-vis expect*. Syntactically and semantically the grammatical status of the NP *James* in (50) does appear to be indeterminate: it is object-like to the extent that it can be fronted under passivization, just like the NP in (51), and it can be replaced by a pronoun in the objective case. However, the NP is also subject-like because *expect* can be followed by *there* (*They expected there to be a fire at the hospital*), and when the NP + *to*-infinitive string is passivized, the meaning stays the same. Thus, *they expected the race to be won by James* means the same as (50). Notice also that the NP + *to*-infinitive string can be replaced by *it*. In older versions of Transformational Grammar the problem of the dual nature of the postverbal NP in constructions like (50) was solved by proposing that *James* is a subject at deep structure which is raised to object position at the surface level ('Raising-to-Object'; Postal 1974). Discussions of structures like (50) caused rifts in the generative camp, with Chomsky himself arguing against a raising analysis (1973), and analysing (49) and (50) in the same way. Descriptively oriented worked has tended to make the opposite choice in analysing *James* as a direct object. See Huddleston and Pullum *et al.* (2002: 101f.) for a recent treatment. In each analytical tradition, therefore, an either/or choice has been made (see Aarts 2004*c* for further discussion). I will return to the structures in (49)–(51) in Chapter 8.

A further example of gradience between the dependents of verbs is discussed in Hudson (1991). In this paper he claims that the indirect object

---

[4] For example, there is some disagreement in the literature as to whether (i) or (ii) is the correct representation for coordinative structures:

(i)   [Clause] [coord. conj. Clause]
(ii)   [Clause] coord. conj. [Clause]

is an argument 'which has some characteristics in common with both the agent and the patient, but not enough of either to qualify as subject or OO/O2 [=direct object]. This leads to the development of a compromise grammatical relation which is half-way between a subject and an object' (1991: 352). Ozón (2007), using a number of criteria, observes that recipient indirect objects (*I gave Mary a present*) in ditransitive constructions are more complement-like than beneficiary NPs (*I bought Mary a present*), which in turn are more like complements than ethical datives (*He grimaced her a dirty look*). This represents a kind of gradience between complements and adjuncts, which I turn to next.

7.4.2.5 Complements and adjuncts   Consider the sentences below:

(52)   This book weighs *three kilograms.*
(53)   She lives *in London.*
(54)   She treated him *badly.*

The first sentence was discussed in Section 7.4.1.3. I noted there that the postverbal NP has an adverbial feel to it ('how much does that book weigh?'). Sentence (53) contains the verb *live*, whose meaning changes if the PP is left out. The prepositional phrase is thus clearly a complement in that it follows the main verb of the clause, and because it is obligatory. However, the PP also feels adverbial in that it specifies a location, which is very much an adverbial function. Quirk *et al.* (1985: 505) use the hybrid functional label *obligatory predication adjunct* for the PP in (53), which would be a terminological contradiction for many linguists. Compare (53) with (55):

(55)   I live my life in London.

Here a cognate object has been inserted after the main verb, and this has demoted the PP from its status as a complement to an undisputed adjunct. Sentence (54) contains the well-known problem verb *treat*, which is followed by *badly*, which looks like both a complement and an adjunct. Notice, though, that *badly* feels slightly more adjunct-like than *three kilograms* and *in London* in that in other contexts it can function as a manner adjunct. We can thus establish a constructional gradient among sentences involving what by definition must be complements due to their obligatoriness, but nevertheless have adjunct-like qualities.

As a further example of Intersective Constructional Gradience between complements and adjuncts, but this time within phrases, see Keizer (2004). She discusses post-head PPs in noun phrases whose status as complements or modifiers is not always easy to determine.

7.4.2.6 *Syntactic blends and fusions*   Blending is a phenomenon in grammar where particular properties of two lexical items or constructions are fused into novel lexical items or constructions. Other terms that are used for this are *apo koinou*, *amalgam*, *contamination* or, in the lexical domain, *portmanteau word*. Jespersen (1894: 188) suggested that blends are the result of speakers 'wavering' between the use of two constructions, which amounts to regarding blends as performance errors, a view also espoused in Biber *et al.* (1999: 1064–6). This may well be so, although of course this does not mean that they are not worthy of study. Indeed, if anything, they have been severely understudied, and probably play an extremely important role in language change. New coinages are usually produced in an *ad hoc* fashion, although they may become permanent, especially the lexical types. Examples of the latter include *brunch* (*breakfast* and *lunch*), *smog* (*smoke* and *fog*), and, more recently, *ginormous* (*gigantic* and *enormous*) and *chunnel* (*channel* and *tunnel*). See Adams (1973: 139–40, 2001: 138–41) for further examples.

For our purposes the most interesting types of blends are the syntactic ones. In Aarts (1992: 90f.) I suggested that blending may be a process that lies at the root of certain changes in language.[5] With regard to verbs of negative causation (V^{nc}; e.g. *prevent (from)*, *keep (from)*, etc.), I surmised that the pattern $V^{nc}+NP+to$-infinitive was pushed out of the English language by the pattern $V^{nc}+NP+$-*ing*. Thus, while Middle English and Early Modern English allowed the equivalents of (56) and (57), present-day English allows only (56):

(56)   I prevented him from leaving.
(57)   I prevented him to leave.

The evidence for the demise of $V^{nc}+NP+to$-infinitive, through the agency of $V^{nc}+NP+$-*ing*, comes from such data as (58) and (59) (from Visser 1963–1973: 2370):

(58)   keep them fra giftes to gif
        'keep (prevent) them from giving gifts'
        (ca. 1391, in *How Good Wijf Taught D*, Skeat 111)

(59)   Or who shall let me now, On this vile bodie from to wreake my wrong
        'Or who shall prevent me now from avenging my wrong on this vile body' (1590–1596, in Spenser, *The Faerie Queene*, II.8.28)

In these sentences *from* and *to* both occur in what are arguably syntactic blends. Because both *from* and *to* can be regarded as functionally identical (namely as inflectional elements; see Aarts 1992 for arguments supporting this view), one of the two had to win out in constructions like (56) and (57) above, and this was the construction with *from*.

---

[5] See also Denison (1990), mentioned in Section 4.2.

Here's a further example of a blend, mentioned in Denison (1993: 183):

(60) this goodman... preyde his wyf ful   tendirlye | that a Norse to
      this man...   begged his wife very tenderly | that a nurse to
      geten hire in hye
      get   her   in haste
      (ca. 1410. Lovel. *Merlin* 6344; cited in Visser 1963–1973: §2060)

This can be seen as a mix between a V+NP+*to*-infinitive pattern and a *that*-clause.

As for Modern English, Jespersen (1909–1949, III.2, 7.1f.) discusses what he calls *contact clauses*, examples of which are given below:

(61) This is *the house* they bought.
(62) There is *a person in the street* claims he's Jesus.

In both (61) and (62) the relative pronoun is missing, which leads to a closer contact between the two juxtaposed clauses, such that they appear to share the italicized strings. The clauses can thus be seen as being blended.

Bolinger (1961*a*) only briefly discusses blends, but returns to the topic in a paper in *Language* (1961*b*). The main point of the latter was to demonstrate the inadequacies of the transformational derivation of certain constructions, and to demonstrate *current* change: 'A grammar that hopes to reflect the creativity in language should not overlook the genuinely active zones where the coordinates themselves are yielding—not in a diachronic sense, but dynamically, here and now. These are syntactic blends' (Bolinger 1961*b*: 381). As an example of a blend from Bolinger's work consider (63)–(65):

(63) He is all right.
(64) Employing him is all right.
(65) He is all right to employ.   (Bolinger 1961*b*: 373)

Here (65) is a blend of (63) and (64). Notice that in (63) and (64) *all right* is predicated of *he* and *employing him*, respectively. By using (65) the language user can imply both (63) and (64) at the same time. Consider now the next set of sentences from Bolinger's paper:

(66) The man is necessary.
(67) Convincing the man is necessary.
(68) *The man is necessary to convince.

The ungrammaticality of (68) is explained by observing that there is no logical connection between the man being necessary and the necessity of convincing him, whereas in the case of (63)–(65) we can say that if 'employing him' is all right, then 'he' must also be all right. On these constructions, see also Jespersen (1909–1949: III.2, 11.6 f.).

In Chapter 4 I discussed mergers, and characterized them as on-the-hoof coinages involving two constructions. How do mergers differ from blends? A first observation to make is that the two components of syntactic mergers are much less tightly integrated than syntactic blends: when two elements or chunks of elements are merged they are still independently recognizable. This is not so in a blend. Secondly, often mergers constitute constructional *hapax legomena*, in that you are much less likely to come across them often, or find them to be used by many speakers. They may or may not be idiosyncratic to a particular speaker or occasion, but the important point is that they have not gained general currency. Thirdly, they are much more likely to be regarded as performance errors—justifiably or not—than true syntactic blends. Nobody would find anything odd about (65), whereas the examples of mergers we looked at are somehow noteworthy. I will treat blends as instances of constructional gradience, while regarding mergers as a separate, more peripheral, phenomenon. (This is the reason they were discussed in Chapter 4.) Anacolutha—gobbledegook utterances that can be viewed as the result of online speech production failure—are even more marginal, and are perhaps best regarded as ungrammatical expressions. Spoken language is replete with such utterances.

Often also regarded as blends, but perhaps best treated separately, are *syntactic fusions*. Matthews (1981: 185f.) defines *fused constructions* as involving an element which is the complement of a controlling and dependent predicator. Thus in (69) there is a fusion of *they made him* and *he do it*:

(69)   They made him do it.

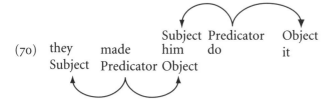

(70)   they   made   him   do   it
        Subject   Predicator   Object

The fusion is between the two predications. In (71) we get the dependencies shown in (72):

(71)   It tastes nice.

(72)

This is said to be a fusion of a copulative with an intransitive construction. While the fusion analysis makes sense for (69) from a syntactic, if not from a semantic, point of view—after all, the people referred to as 'they' did not 'make him'; rather, they 'made him do it'—for (71) it makes much less sense. What exactly is (71) a fusion of? According to Matthews there is a yoking of 'the copulative (as in *It is nice*) with the intransitive (as, perhaps, in *It tastes*)'. But notice the 'perhaps', which points to some doubt on Matthews's behalf. Rightly so, it seems to me, as *it tastes* is not a possible sentence in English. If anything, we have a raising construction here, such that *it* is raised out of the complement clause *[it nice]* to the matrix clause subject position.

Consider next the sentences in (73) and (74):

(73)   *Whatever you say* will be recorded.
(74)   *Whoever drove past* will know about the accident.

The italicized strings in these structures, which involve sequences which have clause-like properties as well as nominal properties, are called *nominal relative clauses* in Quirk *et al.* (1985) and *fused relatives* in Huddleston (1984) and Huddleston and Pullum *et al.* (2002: 1068f.). What is fused in a single *wh*-element are the functions of head and 'prenucleus'. In Huddleston and Pullum *et al.* (2002: 1073) the structure of the NP *what she wrote* in *I really liked what she wrote* is as follows:

(75)

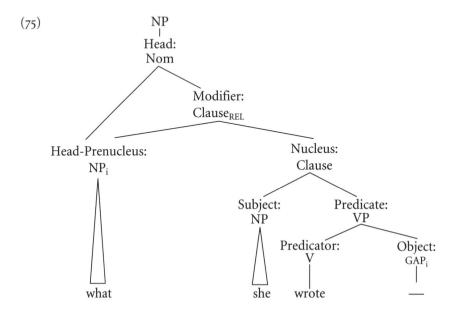

The italicized strings in (73) and (74) are NPs by virtue of the fact that they can occur in typical NP-positions. Furthermore, as Huddleston (1984: 402–3) notes, they induce subject–verb concord (cf. *what errors remained* were/*was *of a minor nature*) and, like regular subject NPs, cannot be moved rightwards (cf. **It must be insane whoever wrote this letter* and **It must be insane the boss*). They are clausal because of their Object–Subject–Verb structure. Van Riemsdijk (2001) analyses sentences like this by making use of the notion of a *graft*. The example in (76) below is analysed as in (77) (2001: 10):

(76)   He carried what the crew took to be gasoline.

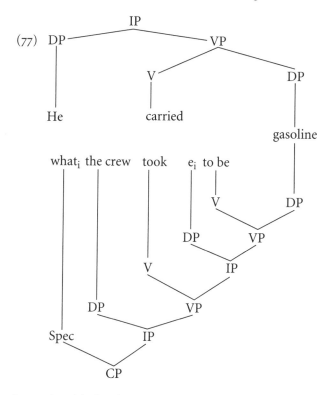

(77)

In an intuitively obvious sense, the lower (upside down) portion of this representation is grafted onto the upper portion.

A further example of a fusion are what are called *fused-head constructions* in the *Cambridge Grammar of the English Language*, exemplified in (78) and (79) (from Huddleston and Pullum *et al.* 2002: 410):

(78)   Where are the sausages? Did you buy *some* yesterday?
(79)   The first candidate performed well, but the *second* did not.

Here *some* and *second* are said to instantiate a fused determiner-head and modifier-head, respectively.

The picture that is emerging is that amongst the expressions that involve a 'mixing' of structures there exists a cline of degrees of syntactic integration, with fusions positioned at the highly integrated end of the gradient (i.e. in these constructions the component parts are welded together intimately), and anacolutha at the least integrated end (i.e. here the components are merely loosely glued together). Blends and mergers are positioned roughly half-way along the gradient:

'Mixed' structures

←——————————————————————————→
fusions   blends   mergers   anacolutha

Of course, this is to some extent an arbitrary dissection, because fusions, blends, mergers, and anacolutha can probably not be sharply distinguished. Consider, for example, the sentence below:

(80)   The new design of the shop will attract people in.

Is this a blend or a merger? What is clear is that it is a mix of a simple transitive construction (*attract people*) and a phrasal verb construction (*bring people in*). To the extent that *attract NP in* does not sound all that unusual, it is probably a blend.

Despite the fact that it is not always easy to discriminate between fusions, blends, and mergers, the examples we looked at in Chapter 4 and in this chapter are fairly clearly distinguishable in terms of the extent to which they are separable into different constructions. Another way of putting this is to say that fusions and blends are grammaticalized to a much greater extent than mergers. Although they are mostly incidental configurations, mergers do have the potential to become 'recognized constructions' of the language, but here we will regard them as being a distinct phenomenon from gradience.

7.5 Constructional Gradience in grammar

Two different approaches to constructions and Constructional Gradience (CG) emerge from the case studies we have looked at in this chapter. On the one hand there is the view held by cognitive linguists and construction grammarians that constructions and the gradience that obtains between them must be characterized both in terms of meaning/usage and syntax. For the cognitivists semantic considerations are usually paramount, whereas among construction grammarians views differ as to how much emphasis is placed on syntax and semantics (see Section 7.2.4). The other approach is to study constructions and CG from a purely syntactic angle, as we have seen in the work of Ross, Svartvik, and Quirk *et al.* I will argue that the semantics attributed to constructions is often too vague (Section 7.5.1), too elaborate (Section 7.5.2), or too skeletal (Section 7.5.3). For this reason I will adopt a syntactic approach to constructions in Section 7.6.

7.5.1 *Vague meaning*

Winters (1990), working in a cognitive grammar framework which stresses the idea that syntax mirrors meaning, identifies a number of features that play a role in making a construction prototypical, namely frequency, productivity, salience, transparency, autonomy, and naturalness. To take one of these, frequency, Winters says that prototypical constructions are more frequent.

In English, to use the basic sentence and word order again as examples, SVO is dominant in declarative sentences, and simple, active, affirmative declarative sentences are in turn the most frequent and, accordingly, the most prototypical. (Winters 1990: 290–1)

The problem with this is that it leads to circularity: why are simple, active, affirmative, and declarative sentences the most prototypical? Because they are the most frequent. Why are they the most frequent? Because they are the most prototypical. The same problem obtains with the other features. To be fair to Winters, she recognizes the circularity problem towards the end of her paper, but does not propose a solution to deal with it. Circularity is not the only problem for Winters. Take the feature transparency. For Winters prototypical constructions communicate their meaning maximally efficiently, with the speaker and hearer agreeing about what has been said to the greatest degree. She compares the two sentences below:

(81) He picked up his daughter, and he packed his suitcase, and he found his keys and he drove away.
(82) When he had picked up his daughter and packed his suitcase, he found his keys and drove away.

Both sentences express the same sequence of events: 'pick up', 'pack', 'find', and 'drive'. However, (82) is deemed to be more transparent because the subordinator 'gives the hearer a clue as to the kind of processing that will be necessary' (Winters 1990: 293). Quite apart from the circularity problem that also obtains here, transparency is rather a vague notion, and it is not clear how one would go about determining which factors influence it, and how to measure it.

For Taylor meaning also plays an important role, as we have seen. As far as Subsective Constructional Gradience is concerned, he identifies two factors that are important: the conjoined factors of 'centrality and productivity' and the factor of 'coercion'. Taylor makes no mention of Winters's work, but his 'centrality and productivity' are similar to her 'productivity'. Central constructions are subject to fewer constraints than peripheral constructions. His example involves clauses with NPs and PPs as subject (*The cat sat on the mat/Under the bed is a good place to hide it.*). The former are syntactically more versatile and also more productive. Marginal constructions are not, however, deemed any less acceptable than central ones. As for coercion, he notes that what can happen is that a 'construction's semantics "coerces" the semantic value of one of its parts, such that the part becomes compatible with the construction's overall meaning' (Taylor 1998: 194). Thus, in the non-prototypical *Joe sneezed the napkin off the table* the verb *sneeze* has been coerced into what is otherwise a regular pattern in English (cf. *Fred drove the car into the ditch*). Similarly, in the PP-as-subject example above, the PP is coerced into a nominal location reading. While attractive, the idea of coercion relies on a precise specification of the meaning of constructions, which is often not available.

7.5.2 'Too much' meaning

Consider again the examples from Sections 7.4.1.4 and 7.4.1.5. While, as always in Taylor's work, the examples he discusses are carefully considered and argued, they nevertheless also instantiate a number of problems with the cognitive linguistic way of viewing constructions in general. In each case it becomes apparent that the syntactic parts of constructions seem to be relatively easy to describe, while the semantic parts are very complex and intricate. The way Taylor gets around the complexity problem is to invoke the notion of a gestalt (Lakoff 1977). In the case of the transitive construction, he suggests that language users conceive of the transitive construction as a unified whole, which is simpler than its constituent parts taken together. The properties of the construction 'it would probably be true to say' are 'understood relative to a prior understanding of the gestalt' (Taylor 2003: 232). But what is the exact nature of the gestalt, and what is its relationship with the list of properties? How and why are the properties understood only after the gestalt is understood? And how do we know that the twelve semantic properties claimed to apply to the transitive construction (see Section 7.4.1.4) and the eight properties of the possessive construction (see Section 7.4.1.5) are *all and only* the relevant ones? How do we decide that a particular property is part of a particular construction? A final problem regarding the cognitivist view of constructions is learnability. How can children learn complex constructions with such a plethora of meanings? And how do we know that they will learn all and only the properties of a particular construction, and not a subset of them? With regard to possessives, Taylor (1996: 345) notes that '[p]rototype accounts presuppose the reliable identification of the prototype. To propose a prototype account of possessive relations requires that one of the many relations invoked by the possessive morpheme is singled out as basic, from which all other senses can be related, in some way or other'. The problem here, to my mind, is that Taylor's characterization of his possession prototype is perhaps too involved, and it is difficult to see how it can be acquired. This problem is compounded in Taylor's discussion of his prenominal possessive prototype (1996: 344), which is perceived to be not extensive enough, and is replaced by a model of Durieux's with *three* gestalts. All these problems are avoided if constructions are defined purely syntactically.

7.5.3 *'Too little' meaning*

In Construction Grammar (CxG) approaches, the meanings carried by constructions are explicitly specified (in Attribute Value Matrices or otherwise). While it may be true that constructions have special meanings, as in the *What's X doing Y*-construction (see Section 7.2.4), we do not need to spell these meanings out in detail to understand the structural properties. In fact, in true interpretivist fashion one could say that the meaning of, say, the WXDY-construction is triggered by the syntax, not vice versa. The following passage from Kay and Fillmore (1999) seems to confirm this:

We now turn to the external sem value of Fig. 1 [see Section 7.2.4 above, BA]. The AVM constituting the unique element of this set contains a frame attribute whose value is a scene or state of affairs involving a judgment of incongruity. A frame introduced by a predicator may be thought of as a conceptual unit which is evoked (or denoted) by the predicator and which gives the overall structure to the conceptual object expressed by a clause headed by that predicator. . . . The value of the arg attribute is a set whose members are the participants of the frame, often called slots in the AI literature and for most practical purposes equivalent to the arguments of a predicate. (Kay and Fillmore 1999: 21)

As noted in Section 7.2.4, in Unification Construction Grammar (UCxG), grammar and usage are separated. This is not the case in usage-based versions of Construction Grammar, for example Goldberg's Cognitive Construction Grammar (CCxG). In usage-based models facts about how constructions are actually used are incorporated into the model. However, these meaning/usage specifications are often rather skeletal.

7.6 A purely syntactic approach to constructions

Having rejected semantic considerations in determining constructional prototypes, the question now arises how we can profitably characterize Subsective Constructional Gradience and Intersective Constructional Gradience without appealing to semantics. As noted above, in my view the only way of doing so is by making reference to the distributional potential of particular constructions. The most typical exemplar of a construction will be the one that is distributionally the most versatile. I will elaborate this point by taking a detailed look at two examples of constructional gradience discussed above.

First, consider transitive constructions. Recall that Hopper and Thompson and Taylor stipulated a number of criteria to do with, for example, the animacy of the agent, the degree to which the direct object is affected by the action denoted by the verb, etc. (see Section 7.4.1.4). For these linguists, the sentence *John kissed Mary* is more transitive than *John saw Mary*. We might wonder if this approach to constructions, which makes reference to semantics, is a viable one. If we look at the matter from a purely syntactic angle, then all one would want to say about transitive constructions is that they involve a predicate which must be satisfied by two arguments. Under this view, both sentences above are equally transitive. We can still concede that a particular NP is a less typical agent than another one in any given pair of sentences, but 'degree of agenthood' is an issue that should be dealt with in the quite separate semantic component of the grammar.

Consider next the case of interrogative constructions. To my mind it makes no sense, as Taylor has suggested, that the string *Is that a fact?* is peripherally interrogative (see Section 7.4.1.2). From a purely syntactic point of view we have a very simple copular structure which displays subject–auxiliary inversion. There is nothing marked or in any way structurally out of the ordinary here. This makes this sentence a central interrogative syntactically. Taylor (2003: 183) proposes that a central yes–no interrogative is a structure 'which requests no more than a specification of polarity', and argues (2003: 227) that meaningwise 'the sentence is a rather marginal exemplar, in that it does not ask for polarity specification. It could even be argued that it is not even a question at all, instead, it serves purely as an expression of speaker surprise'. But this cannot be right. Taken in isolation, the expression *Is that a fact?* cannot be assigned an illocutionary force at all. It could be an expression of surprise, to be sure, but it is equally possible that it is a question, depending on the context. As a matter of fact, just about *any* interrogative can be assigned an array of illocutionary forces, given the right context, a point which Taylor himself also makes. The undesirable corollary of Taylor's characterization of *Is that a fact?* as being a non-prototypical interrogative is that we will only be able to determine whether a particular interrogative is a prototypical exemplar in a specified context. Thus in the context of (83) the expression *Is that a fact?* would not be a central interrogative (because in the most likely discourse scenario—that is, when surprise is expressed—it does not elicit a yes–no answer). However, in (84) *Is that a fact?* can be either an utterance of surprise or a simple question:

(83) A You can often see foxes in suburban London.
      B Is that a fact?

(84) A Troublesome interpersonal relationships are often caused by
         an unhappy childhood.
      B Is that a fact? (Or is it a Freudian interpretation?)

In Taylor's framework it is not possible to look at a sentence in isolation and determine whether it is a prototypical structure or not, precisely because of the need to make reference to the context. This means that an independent notion of a syntactic prototype cannot exist, because the syntax of a construction cannot be prised apart from its semantics. I find this undesirable, because what we want to be able to do is decide on the basis of structural and distributional properties whether a given construction is prototypical or not. Here's an analogy: just as we would want to be able to say that a particular kind of building is a prototypical church (it has a spire, windows with a special shape, etc.), while other buildings are not, the fact that a church can be used as a concert hall has no bearing on the issue of whether the church is a typical one or not. For Taylor a church used as a concert hall would be a less typical church.

The problem, then, with Taylor's approach is that in characterizing constructions he takes into account not only the *structure* of the interrogatives, but also the *use* that can be made of such structures. (As we have seen, this is also typical of various versions of Construction Grammar, e.g. Goldberg's Cognitive Construction Grammar.) This leads to complications of the type I have signalled above. In work on syntax, it has long been recognized that we should strictly keep structure and use apart when considering clause types and the illocutionary force we can assign to them. Huddleston (1994) makes this point forcefully for the opposition 'interrogative' vs. 'question', the former being a purely syntactic notion, while the latter is pragmatic. In fact, Taylor does not disagree with this point of view when he rejects the Searlean view that the clause types have a fixed syntax and semantics,[6] and we need to appeal to

---

[6] This is often referred to as the Literal Force Hypothesis. See Levinson (1983: 263).

pragmatics to explain that interrogatives can have different illocutionary forces. He proposes instead that the yes–no interrogative has a range of different senses. I can go along with this, provided that we substitute the word 'uses' for 'senses'. The crucial point is that when we are engaged in characterizing a *syntactic* prototype, the fact that the illocutionary force of *Is that a fact?* in a particular context can be an expression of surprise or the act of asking a question, or whatever, is neither here nor there.

In the next chapter I will tie together my deliberations regarding the different types of gradience discussed in the last three chapters.

Part III
Formalization

8

Modelling Syntactic Gradience

A great many English words may, if considered isolatedly (as parts of 'language'), belong to more classes than one; but in each particular application (in 'speech') they can only belong to one, and it is generally easy to determine which one.

(Jespersen 1909–1949, VII: 41, 1924: 62)

Adjectives you can do anything with.

(Humpty Dumpty in *Through the Looking-Glass* by Lewis Carroll)

8.1 Introduction

In previous chapters we have looked at two ways in which grammar can be said to display gradience. Form classes can be subsectively gradient in displaying intra-categorial prototype effects, such that we can speak of typical nouns, adjectives, and verbs, or they can be intersectively gradient in exhibiting convergence between categories. It is important to reiterate the point I made in Chapter 6 that the existence and extent of pervasiveness of Intersective Gradience are a function of the categories of the adopted framework: if it is claimed that there is gradience between two categories α and β, then it must first be established that α and β actually exist as word classes. In other words, the well-motivated setting-up of discrete categories of form classes is logically prior to claiming that gradience obtains between them. Paradoxically, adherents of gradience models must face the fact that their analytical point of departure should always be rigid discreteness. As we have seen, in discussions of continuous phenomena grammarians who advocate the pervasiveness of gradience often assume the existence of a number of categories which they then undermine by claiming that the boundaries between them cannot be sharply delineated. A concrete example of this was Jacobsson's description of adverbs, prepositions, and conjunctions, discussed in Chapter 6. Jacobsson takes the existence of these categories as given, and then subjects them to close scrutiny. He concludes that the three categories have fluid boundaries. What he fails to do is question the taxonomy of categories he started out with. In this chapter we will look at Subsective Gradience and Intersective Gradience in the light of Bertrand Russell's work on vagueness. I will argue that while grammars need to recognize SG and IG, we should constrain the proliferation of gradience whenever possible. I will attempt to be more precise about the phenomenon of gradience. To this end I will devise a formalization of SG and IG which makes use of morphosyntactic properties to establish whether an item belongs to a particular class or to a 'bordering' one by weighing up the form class features that apply to the item in question. I will argue that it can be maintained that the boundaries between categories are sharp. I reiterate here that I focus on gradience conceived of as 'categorial indeterminacy', and do not deal with gradience in acceptability/grammaticality judgements.

8.2 Vagueness, representations, and gradience

As we saw in Chapter 2, Russell (1923/1996) held that vagueness can only exist in the eye of the beholder; the real world is discrete and not vague at all, merely its representation. One of his examples involves looking at two people from a distance: what we perceive is an image of two individuals that look similar in outline, but not in detail. We can see their silhouettes, but not their faces. Because of the distance, the image is blurred. However, if we move closer, we see that these two individuals look quite different. Seen from close by, their faces are distinguishable: one has a big nose, the other has beady eyes. Thus the initially perceived vagueness is a result of our inadequate perception. Another of Russell's examples, already mentioned in Chapter 2, involves two glasses of water: recall that one of these contains pure water, while the other is infected with typhoid bacilli. Observed with the naked eye, even from close by, the glasses of water are indistinguishable, but if one moves closer, very much closer in fact, by using a microscope, the difference between them becomes apparent. Thus, even from close proximity, two entities may look very similar, but the vagueness is eliminated by approximation. Russell's point, then, is clear: there is never any reason for appealing to the notion of vagueness. It simply does not exist, so long as you observe closely enough.

Now, what about language? Could it be the case that vagueness in grammar, here conceived of as grammatical vagueness, is also simply not part of the architecture of the system of language, but merely a property of the way that we perceive and describe it, that is, merely a property of our *representation* of the mental system of grammar? I would like to suggest that the answer to this question should be affirmative in many cases. As we have seen, some of the examples of IG that we find in the literature can be disproved merely by 'looking more closely', in a Russellian fashion, much in the way that Wierz-bicka has argued that in defining the meanings of words like *game* and *boat* we should not uncritically use prototypes, but apply more precision in our efforts to assign lexical meanings. (See Section 3.4.7.)

In actual fact, what happens in grammar is a little more complex, in that 'looking more closely' can lead not only to the perception of difference, but also to the perception of sameness. As we have seen, for Russell, looking more closely leads to the discernment of *difference*. In the next section I will discuss some examples where this situation obtains in grammar. However, in grammar we also come across situations which are the *reverse* of the Russellian situation: as we will see in Section 8.2.2, there are cases where looking more closely results in the discernment of *sameness*. However, as will become clear presently, the important point is that whatever the result, difference or sameness, in both cases we achieve a desirable goal, namely the elimination of vagueness.

8.2.1 *Eliminating vagueness by looking more closely: apparent sameness*

There are many examples in grammar where close scrutiny of two seemingly identical elements, form classes, or constructions leads to the discernment of difference. As an example, consider the sentences below:

(1)   She seemed to be happy.
(2)   She wanted to be happy.

These sentences appear to be structurally identical in involving the pattern NP + V+*to*-infinitive +AP. In fact, however, as all linguists would agree, and as any introductory textbook to grammar will relate, the similarities are only very superficial. In (1) we have a raising construction in which the matrix verb's subject position is dethematized, and the subject is raised from the lower clause; in (2) *want* is a control verb, whose subject controls the interpretation of the non-overt subject of the subordinate clause. By describing the two sentences in these terms, their vaguely being the same in fact turns out to be spurious. It is important to be aware that what are obvious and commonplace facts of grammar to us now have not been common knowledge for all that long.

8.2.2 *Eliminating vagueness by looking more closely: apparent differences*

What about the converse situation? Are there cases in the grammar of English where looking more closely leads to the perception of sameness? Such cases do indeed exist, although they are much more controversial. Descriptive gram-mars make a distinction between conjunctions and prepositions, as in the following examples, previously discussed in Chapter 6:

(3)   John arrived *before* the last speech.
(4)   John arrived *before* the last speech ended.
(5)   John arrived *before* (hand).

In (3) *before* is held to be a preposition, in (4) it is said to be a conjunction, while in (5) it would be an adverb. We saw in Chapter 6 that Jacobsson has argued on the basis of such data that there is boundary vagueness between prepositions, conjunctions, and adverbs. In other words, although syntactically distinct, these form classes are argued to be on a cline, that is, intersectively gradient. However, we might argue that the 'gradient descriptivist' is not looking closely enough in assigning the element *before* in each of the sentences above to a different word class. In (3)–(5) *before* can be assigned to the same word class, namely that of preposition. The difference between the different elements *before* is then one of subcategorization.

8.2.3 *Determinatives: a further case of apparent sameness?*

Here is a more controversial example. Consider the strings below:

(6)   *That* house
(7)   What is *that*?

Here *prima facie* the two words *that* appear to be identical: they are pronounced the same and semantically they are both deictic. However, this example is an instance where descriptive grammars have argued that, despite their superficial similarity, if we inspect the syntactic behaviour of the two italicized elements above more closely we could say that the two *that*s are grammatically quite different, so that in fact we should apply two different labels to them: determinative in (6), and pronoun in (7).[1] After all, in (6) *that* occurs inside a noun phrase, where it specifies the head noun *house*, whereas in (7) *that* is a head in its own right, that is, it is not dependent on some other nearby element. This, then, is a straightforward Russellian glasses-of-water-situation, as in the case of the raising and control constructions in Section 8.2.1. But is this really so? We could also say that in this particular case the grammar is not trying to delude us, and that the two *that*s in (6) and (7) not only look the same, they *are* in fact grammatically the same, much in the same way that the three *before*s in Section 8.2.2 are the same. As we saw in Chapter 6, Postal (1966) argued that the italicized elements in (6) and (7) are both determinatives. More recently, Dick Hudson has argued that they are both pronouns (Hudson 2000*a*), though with different subcategorization

---

[1] Strang (1968: 124f.) labels *that* in (6) a determiner, while *that* in (7) is called a *determiner pronoun*.

properties: in both cases *that* is the head of the phrase in which it occurs which may, or may not, take a complement. (6) contains a transitive pronoun, whereas in (7) the pronoun is intransitive. Elements like *the*, *a*, and *every* obligatorily take a nominal complement. Under such a view the class of determinatives ceases to exist. (See also Spinillo 2004.) It is perhaps ironic that the descriptive grammarians who advocate pervasive gradience in their work seem to be totally unconcerned by the fact that in the case of such homophonic elements as *that*, *those*, etc. they posit two categories. What they are in fact doing is making a clear all-or-none choice in assigning such elements to two distinct and mutually exclusive classes. The fact that homophony obtains, however, must be some indication that the forms are the same, or at least related. A similar situation obtains with elements like *in*, *on*, *at*, etc. which are analysed as adverbs by many linguists when they are part of so-called phrasal verbs, but as prepositions when they head P + NP sequences. Again, surely the most attractive position to take is to say that an element like *in* is either always an adverb, or always a preposition. See Aarts (1989) for discussion.

I hope that the point I have been trying to make here is a persuasive one: Intersective Gradience is quite often—although not always—the fall-out of the way grammarians have set up their grammatical descriptions, and not a property of the grammatical system itself. In the next section, I will try to be more precise about gradience by proposing a formalization of the notion.

8.3 A formalization of Subsective Gradience and Intersective Gradience

Is it possible to be more precise about gradience? In this section I will make an attempt at formalizing what I perceive to be the characteristic properties of SG and IG. The formalizations offered here should be regarded as prolegomena to a principled theoretical account of grammatical gradience.

8.3.1 *Subsective Gradience*

The following formalization of SG allows for degrees of prototypicality within grammatical categories.

SUBSECTIVE GRADIENCE

If $\alpha, \beta \in \gamma$, where γ is a form class characterized by morphosyntactic properties $\{p_1 \ldots p_n\}$;

and α is characterized by $\{p_1 \ldots p_x\}$, such that $0 < x \leq n$;

and β is characterized by $\{p_1 \ldots p_y\}$, such that $0 < y < x$;

then   α and β are in a subsective gradient relationship, such that α is a
more prototypical member of γ than β.

I will take the morphosyntactic properties of a formative to be the potential
and actual distributional characteristics it displays *in a particular configuration*. Thus, the syntactic properties of the element *design* in the string *the
design of the house* include the fact that it is preceded by a determinative; that
it is followed by a PP; that it *can be* preceded by one or more modifiers such as
new, beautiful, etc. By contrast, in the string *they intend to design new houses*
the lexical item *design* displays quite distinct distributional properties: it is
preceded by the infinitival marker *to*; it can be preceded by a manner adverb
such as *swiftly*; it is followed by a direct object NP, etc. Crucially, it cannot be
preceded by *the* or by an adjective. Following Croft (1991: 6), we can make use
of the notion of *morphosyntactic test* to determine which are the syntactic
properties that characterize a particular element. For Croft a morphosyntactic
test involves 'a grammatical construction, one or more features of which
define or require a specific type of linguistic unit to satisfy it or fill it. The
unit can be a lexical class, a higher level constituent, a dependency relation—
in sum, any element of linguistic structure.'

Under the characterization of SG above, an adjective like *thin* is a more
prototypical adjective than *utter*, because the former conforms to more
adjectival properties than the latter (cf. Chapter 5 and below). It is important
to stress that I am not claiming that there are degrees of class membership, as
Zadeh has done: *utter* is as much an adjective as *thin* is; it is merely less
prototypically a member of that class. In this context recall the Blakean
dictum, cited in Chapter 5, 'A Good Apple tree or a bad, is an Apple tree
still: a Horse is not more a Lion for being a Bad Horse'.

Having said this, there *are* instances of SG—and *utter* is a case in point—
where an element may bear a *semantic* resemblance to another word class. Thus,
utter resembles adverbs in having an intensifying meaning. Similarly, phrases
may resemble other phrases semantically, as in the examples from Leech and Li
(1995) discussed in Chapter 6. In Section 8.3.2 below I will refer to this property
as *weak convergence*. Crucially, though, there are no *syntactic* points of overlap.
The presence of the latter leads to what I will call *strong convergence*, a case of IG.
Weak convergence does not always obtain with cases of SG: there are many
peripheral adjectives that do not semantically resemble other word classes (*mere*
is an example).

SG can be demonstrated, then, on syntactic grounds, leading to a graded
distinction between more or less prototypical members of form classes, while
allowing for particular members of a form class to converge weakly on other
form classes.

8.3.2 *Intersective Gradience*

Turning now to IG, I will attempt to model the intuition that Intersective Gradience obtains if a particular element syntactically partakes of two categories to some degree.

INTERSECTIVE GRADIENCE

If α, β are form classes characterized by morphosyntactic properties $\{a_1 \ldots a_m\}$ and $\{b_1 \ldots b_n\}$, respectively;

and $\exists$ Ж, Ж a grammatical formative which conforms to a set of syntactic properties $\{c_1 \ldots c_p\}$, such that $\{c_1 \ldots c_x\} \subset \{a_1 \ldots a_m\}$ and $\{c_{x+1} \ldots c_p\} \subset \{b_1 \ldots b_n\}$;

then α and β are in an intersective gradient relationship with respect to Ж, and its projection ЖP.[2]

Here the element Ж partakes of the categories α and β by displaying characteristics of both classes. The notion of intersection in the term 'Intersective Gradience' thus refers to the intersection of sets of properties, and not, crucially, to an intersection of the categories themselves. I thus exclude the possibility of a formative in a particular configuration belonging to two form classes at the same time.[3]

As mentioned in the preceding section, the model makes use of the notion of convergence: just as in the case of real-world objects it is possible for the characteristics of some object A to be transferred onto an object B, such that it becomes more A-like, the same applies to the abstract entities that populate grammars. Thus, we have seen that *utter* can be said to *weakly converge* on the adverb class in *semantically* resembling adverbs. Distributionally, it indisputably belongs to the adjective class (cf. *utterly*, clearly an adverb). Where we have *strong convergence* (i.e. all the cases where $x \neq (p - x)$ in the formalization above), an element also displays one or more *syntactic* properties of another class. IG manifests itself through strong convergence.

---

[2] It has been pointed out to me that the formalism in the text does not allow for an element to possess all the properties $(a_1 \ldots a_m)$, or all the properties $(b_1 \ldots b_n)$. It seems unlikely that this actually occurs in languages, although this is a matter for empirical verification. If such cases can be found, the *such that*-clause should read:

$\{c_1 \ldots c_x\} \subset \{a_1 \ldots a_m\}$ and $\{c_{x+1} \ldots c_p\} \subset \{b_1 \ldots b^n\}$ or
$\{c_1 \ldots c_x\} \subseteq \{a_1 \ldots a_m\}$ and $\{c_{x+1} \ldots c_p\} \subset \{b_1 \ldots b_n\}$ or
$\{c_1 \ldots c_x\} \subset \{a_1 \ldots a_m\}$ and $\{c_{x+1} \ldots c_p) \subseteq \{b_1 \ldots b_n\}$

The following situation is excluded, for obvious reasons:

$\{c_1 \ldots c_x\} \subseteq \{a_1 \ldots a_m\}$ and $\{c_{x+1} \ldots c_p\} \subseteq \{b_1 \ldots b_n\}$

[3] The qualification 'in a particular configuration' is important here. As we will see below, the word *painting* can be analysed either as a verb or as a noun, depending on the syntactic company it keeps, although there is nothing to stop us from saying that the word in isolation belongs to two classes.

As formulated above, the model above makes a number of claims. First, notice that there is an implicational relationship between SG and IG: with the exception of cases of 'true hybridity' (where $x = (p - x)$; see below and Section 8.7), all cases of IG are *ipso facto* also cases of SG. This is so because all the cases of elements from a category α that are intersectively gradient with category β by definition 'abverge', to coin a new word, from the core of α, and are therefore not prototypical members of α. This does *not* mean that SG and IG need not be distinguished, because there are cases of SG where there is no convergence on another category. Put formulaically, IG = SG + strong convergence. Secondly, the model predicts that the syntactic properties that a form class conforms to are unique to that class. And finally, the definition allows an element in a particular syntactic context to display characteristics of at most two classes. I will return to the last two points below.

Let us now look at some abstract applications of the formalism above. Consider first an element Ж which is characterized by seven properties ($p = 7$): properties 1–3 are associated with form class α (so $\{c_1 \ldots c_x\} = 3$), while properties 4–7 are associated with class β ($\{c_{x+1} \ldots c_p\} = 4$). In this case $x \neq (p - x)$ obtains, because $3 \neq (7 - 3)$. So here Ж belongs to class β and we are dealing with a case of strong convergence (β converges on α).

In the next example, assume again that Ж is characterized by seven properties ($p = 7$): but this time properties 1–4 are associated with form class α (so $\{c_1 \ldots c_x\} = 4$), while properties 5–7 are associated with class β ($\{c_{x+1} \ldots c_p\} = 3$). In this case again $x \neq (p - x)$, because $4 \neq (7 - 4)$. This time Ж belongs to class α, and again we have a case of strong convergence (α converges on β).

In both these cases a particular element is *coerced* into a class on the basis of the distributional properties it displays.

Finally, suppose we have a grammatical formative Ж that can be characterized by eight syntactic properties (thus $p = 8$): properties 1–4 are associated with form class α (so $\{c_1 \ldots c_x\} = 4$), while properties 5–8 are associated with class β ($\{c_{x+1} \ldots c_p\} = 4$). In this case $x = (p - x)$ holds because $4 = (8 - 4)$, and we have a case of true hybridity. See Section 8.7 for further discussion of this notion.

8.4 Some applications

In the following sections I will look at some applications of the formalizations of SG and IG, by returning to a selection of the case studies discussed in Chapters 5, 6, and 7.

8.4.1 *SG in the adjective class*

In Chapter 5 I compared the syntactic behaviour of a number of adjectives, namely *happy, thin, alive,* and *utter.* I argued that *happy* is a more prototypical exemplar of the class of adjectives than *thin,* which in turn conforms to more adjectival properties than *alive* or *utter.* Examples like the following make this clear:

(8)   a happy woman   (p_1: attributive position)
       she is happy   (p_2: predicative position)
       very happy   (p_3: intensification)
       happy/happier/happiest   (p_4: gradedness)
       unhappy   (p_5: *un-* prefixation)

(9)   a thin man
       he is thin
       very thin
       thin/thinner/thinnest
       *unthin

(10)   *an alive hamster
       the hamster is alive
       very (much) alive
       ?alive/more alive/most alive
       *unalive

(11)   an utter disgrace
       *the problem is utter
       *very utter
       *utter/utterer/utterest
       *unutter

Using the matrix shown in Table 8.1, we can tabulate the properties shown in (8)–(11):

Here *happy, thin, alive,* and *utter* can be assigned the label 'adjective', which as a class is characterized by syntactic properties $\{p_1 \ldots p_5\}$. *Happy* is

TABLE 8.1 Adjective criteria

	P_1	P_2	P_3	P_4	P_5
happy	+	+	+	+	+
thin	+	+	+	+	−
alive	−	+	+	?	−
utter	+	−	−	−	−

characterized by p_1-p_5, *thin* is characterized by p_1-p_4, *alive* conforms to criteria p_2, p_3, and perhaps p_4, while *utter* is characterized by p_1 only. This makes *happy* a more prototypical adjective than *thin*, which in turn is more centrally adjectival than *alive* and *utter*. In Aarts (2004b) I listed only the words *happy*, *thin*, and *utter* in Table 8.1. It was pointed out to me by a reader that with regard to the adjectival properties shown here, I must be taking the possibility of an element occurring in attributive position as a sufficient (i.e. criterial) property of adjectivehood, and that, therefore, the listed properties do not have equal status. I was asked whether a word that cannot occur attributively, but can have one or more of the other properties, can be more adjectival than *utter*, and the suspicion was voiced that this is not the case. The answer is that such words *do* exist, examples being adjectives that can only occur predicatively, which include many of those beginning in *a-* in English, e.g. *alive*. The word *afraid* is another example, cf. *the man is afraid/*the afraid man*. If we add *afraid* to the matrix it looks like Table 8.2.

TABLE 8.2 Adjective criteria

	P_1	P_2	P_3	P_4	P_5
happy	+	+	+	+	+
thin	+	+	+	+	−
afraid	−	+	+	+	+
alive	−	+	+	?	−
utter	+	−	−	−	−

Afraid can thus be seen to be more adjectival than *alive* and *utter*, but less adjectival than *happy*. However, notice that it conforms to the same number of adjectival properties as *thin*, although not the same ones.

8.4.2 *IG between verbs and nouns: the English gerund*

Consider sentences (12)–(14), repeated from Chapter 6:

(12) *Brown's deft painting of his daughter* is a delight to watch.
(13) *Brown's deftly painting his daughter* is a delight to watch.
(14) I dislike *Brown painting his daughter*.

In (12) *painting* has five nominal properties: (1) the presence of a genitival determinative; (2) modification by an adjective; (3) the string which *painting* heads is in a typical nominal position; (4) *painting* takes a PP complement; and (5) *painting* can be followed by a restrictive relative clause (Pullum 1991b: 769): *Brown's deft painting of his daughter that I bought is a delight to watch.* There is also one verbal property for *painting*, namely the *-ing* ending. The five nominal properties far outweigh the verbal ones—$p = 6$, $x = 1$, and $x \neq (p - x)$ holds, because $1 \neq (6 - 1)$—and we can consequently say that (12) represents a case of strong convergence such that *painting* is a noun converging on the verb class.

In (13) the number of nominal properties of *painting* is two: (1) there is a genitival determinative, and (2) the word *painting* heads a phrase which is positioned in the subject slot, a typical NP position. Its verbal properties total six: (1) it takes a verbal ending and (2) an NP object.[4] Furthermore, (3) it is preceded by an element which can modify a verbal unit, in this case a manner adverb,[5] and (4) it can be preceded by the negative particle *not*. Finally, voice and aspect are also relevant, as a number of linguists have noted (cf. e.g. Chomsky 1970; Jackendoff 1977: 7f.; Huddleston 1984: 314; Miller 2002: 283f.), witness that (5) we can passivize the italicized string: *His daughter's being deftly painted by Brown* is a delight to watch, and (6) we can add a perfective auxiliary: *Brown's having deftly painted his daughter* was a true feat. Therefore: $p = 8$, $x = 2$, and $x \neq (p - x)$, because $2 \neq (8 - 2)$. Again we have a case of strong convergence, but this time we classify *painting* in (13) as a verb approximating the noun class, and the italicized string in (13) as a clause.

What about (14)? Here the number of nominal properties of *painting* is only one: it heads a phrase that is positioned in a typical nominal position. It has the following verbal properties: (1) *painting* has a (non-genitival) subject (if we replace *Brown* by a pronoun, it must carry objective case); (2) it takes a verbal ending; and (3) there is an NP object. In addition, notice that (4) *painting* in (14) can be preceded by *deftly* (a manner adverb) and (5) by *not*. It cannot be preceded by *deft* (cf. **Brown deft painting his daughter*), nor be followed by a PP-complement (cf. **Brown painting of his daughter*). Also, (6) passivization is possible: *I dislike his daughter being painted by Brown*, as is (7) the addition of auxiliaries: cf. *I dislike Brown having painted his daughter* or *I dislike Brown having been painting his daughter*. Therefore, this is another case of strong convergence, as $p = 8$, $x = 1$, and $x \neq (p - x)$, because $1 \neq (8 - 1)$. We again classify *painting* in (14) as a verb, and the italicized string in (14) as a clause. Clearly, *painting* in (14) is more to the verbal end of the scale than (13), by virtue of having fewer nominal and more verbal properties.[6]

---

[4] And note that further complements are possible: *Brown's painting me a picture.*

[5] Other types of adverbial modification are also possible, e.g. by *because*-clauses and result clauses, as Jackendoff (1977: 222) has observed.

[6] The gradient in (12)–(14) can be refined for verbs that allow predicative attributes. Thus, *the ruthless shooting dead of the youths* is an NP, like (12), but involves one more verbal property than (12), namely the presence of the attribute *dead*, which, interestingly, in this sentence *precedes* its subject (*the youths*). A similar situation obtains in binominal NPs of the type *an idiot of a surveyor* ('the surveyor is an idiot'; cf. Aarts 1998, den Dikken 2006).

It is important to stress that there appear to be constraints on the mixing of categorial properties. For example, a preponderance of categorial features of one type or another does not guarantee a grammatical result, as the following sentences make clear:

(15)　*He is always thinking about *Brown's deft painting his daughter*.
(16)　*He is always thinking about *Brown's deftly painting of his daughter*.
(17)　*He is always thinking about *Brown deft painting his daughter*.
(18)　*He is always thinking about *Brown deftly painting of his daughter*.

In (15) we have three nominal properties (*painting* takes genitival and adjectival premodifiers and the string occurs as the object of a preposition) and two verbal properties (the -*ing* ending and the NP object), and yet the construction as a whole is ungrammatical. The italicized portion of (16) also has three nominal and two verbal properties, although they differ from the properties in (15), as the reader can easily verify. In (17) and (18) the verbal properties outweigh the nominal ones, again in different ways. So why are these structures ruled out? One possible explanation could be to say that their ungrammaticality is due to general constraints. Thus in (15) an AP modifier of *painting* and NP object are incompatible, while in (16) a manner adverb premodifier and PP complement don't mix. Similarly in (17) and (18) nominal and verbal properties are incongruously mixed within a VP projection: in (17) an AP premodifier and an NP complement; in (18) a manner adverb premodifier and a PP complement. These mixtures seem to violate a general constraint that also applies to non-gerundial clauses: *He deft paints his daughter/*This deftly painting of his daughter*, etc. But then what does 'incongruously mixed' mean? After all, genitival -'s (a nominal property) *can* mix freely with both verbal and nominal properties, as (12) and (13) demonstrate. Why is genitival -'s an exception? Another way to approach (15)–(18) would be in terms of mental processing: after hearing/reading the word *Brown('s)* in these examples the first word that follows 'flips over' the construction in one way or the other. Thus in (15) upon hearing/reading *deft* we classify the head *painting* as a noun, but we then encounter an NP object immediately after the head, which leads to a categorial clash. We can give a similar account for (16)–(18). However, while this explanation is promising, it cannot explain why such clashes do not lead to ungrammaticality in structures such as (19) and (20)—admittedly slightly archaic—which also mix nominal and verbal properties:

(19)　*The shutting of the gates regularly at ten o'clock*...had rendered our residence...very irksome to me. (Mary Shelley, *Frankenstein*, 1818)

(20)   Then, with a more comical expression of face than before and *a settling of himself comfortably*...he launched into some new wonder. (Charles Dickens, *Master Humphrey's Clock*, 1840–41)[7]

Here in processing the italicized strings from left to right we encounter only nominal properties, until we reach the adverbs, which do not render the structures ungrammatical. Denison (1998: 271) notes that Visser (1963–1973, section 1120) observes that structures like this were only in use until the end of the nineteenth century. This suggests a constraint came into force at some point in time which ruled them out, or perhaps we should say 'is in the process of ruling them out' because (19) and (20) do not sound too bad even now. I will not undertake here to unravel the constraints that are operative in constructions such as (15)–(20), but will only say that there evidently must be historical factors at play in pinning them down, such that over time the notion of 'incongruously mixed' must be characterized differently.

One advantage of dealing with structures like those above in terms of a balancing of morphosyntactic properties is that we do not need to recognize a category of 'gerund' in addition to nouns and verbs. This is a real benefit, as the label 'gerund' has been used in confusing ways by different authors, as we saw in Chapter 6. However, the traditional label 'verbal noun' *is* useful, despite the bad press it has had, provided that it is used solely for those elements that are predominantly nominal, like (12), while we can use the term 'nominal verb' for elements that are mostly verbal, such as (13) and (14). These labels have the additional advantage that they do not add to the inventory of existing categories.[8]

The present account of IG has affinities with the work of a number of linguists. Thus, Matthews (1981: 179) refers to a construction like *(I dislike) Brown's painting his daughter* as 'residually like an ordinary noun phrase', while Huddleston (1984: 313) speaks of a 'sharp distinction' between verbs and nouns and of verbal properties 'outweighing' nominal ones in some cases, and vice versa in others. Hudson (1990: 45ff.) explains prototype effects in terms of the *Best Fit Principle* which states that 'An experience E is interpreted as an

---

[7] Both (19) and (20) are from Denison (1998: 271), who in turn cites other authors.

[8] Note that 'verbal noun' is used by most authors to designate structures like (13) and (14), which I consider to be predominantly verbal. Huddleston (1984: 313) objects to the term 'verbal noun' as a label for all gerunds, because it gives greater weight to the nominal properties of a particular element than to the verbal properties. I agree, but given Huddleston's own views (see below) he could have adopted the same strategy as proposed here: i.e. use 'verbal noun' for (12) and 'nominal verb' for (13) and (14). The terminological confusion is not dispelled by the use in Huddleston and Pullum *et al.* (2002: 1187f.) of the terms 'gerundial noun' for what I call a 'verbal noun', and 'gerund-participle form of the verb' for what I call 'nominal verb', as well as for the traditional present participle.

instance of some concept C if more information can be inherited about E from C than from any alternative to C'. This approach allows for a particular element X to be assigned to a class Y, even if it does not display all the characteristics of that class. Thus 'a three-legged cat is still a cat, though not a prototypical one. The Best Fit Principle means that we condone a shortage of legs because of the lack of any better match' (Ibid.). My approach is also compatible with Anderson's (1997) treatment. He assigns the categorization {P;(N;P)} to structures like *(I dislike) Brown's painting his daughter.* As in the present account, Anderson quantifies the contributions made by the verbal and nominal components of the gerund, making use of the gradient shown in (21), and the weightings in (22), both repeated from Chapter 3:

(21)   {P}   {P;N}   {P:N}   {N;P}   {N}   { }
       aux   verb   adjective   noun   name   functor

(22)   4P::0N   3P::1N   2P::2N   1P::3N   0P::4N   0P,0N
       aux   verb   adjective   noun   name   functor

Recall that 'P' and 'N' stand for the features 'Predicativity' and 'Nominal/referential'. In (22) each word class is defined in terms of the 'preponderance' (Anderson 1997: 72) of the features 'Predicativity' and 'Nominal/referential', expressed by the numbers, which are determined as follows:

(23)   X alone = 4   X; = 3   X: = 2   ;X = 1   absence of X = 0

Using this schema, {P;(N;P)} is a mixed category with both verbal (P = verb) and nominal properties ((N;P) = noun), where the former ('P;' = 'X;' in (23)) is assigned the weighting '3', while the latter ('; (N;P)' = ';X' in (23)) is weighted '1' (Anderson 1997: 85; see also Section 3.4.6).[9]

Finally, Miller's (2002: 287f.) conclusion that POSS-ING strings (as in (13)) are clausal, contrary to the claims of many other linguists, is in harmony with the account presented above.

8.4.3 *IG between verbs and adjectives*

In Chapter 6 we looked at a string like (24):

(24)   She is a *working* mother.

Here *working* has verbal as well as adjectival properties. It is verbal because (1) it has an *-ing* ending and because (2) it can be premodified by an adverb (*a hard working mother/a still working mother*). It also has one adjectival property

---

[9] Given (21), strictly speaking the gerund ought presumably to be characterized as {(P;N);(N;P)}, but Anderson generally uses just {P} for 'verb'.

in occurring attributively. As we saw in Chapter 6, though, *working* is not fully verbal in that we cannot have negation (**not working mother*) or aspectual markers (**a having worked mother*), and elements occurring in this position cannot take internal complements. *Working* is also not fully adjectival: we cannot have intensification (**very working mother*), or comparison (**more/ most working mother*), and *working* cannot appear in predicative position (*this mother is working* does not count because here *working* heads a present progressive verb phrase). The word *working* is therefore rather more verbal than adjectival ($p = 3$, $x = 2$, and $2 \neq (3 - 2)$).

8.4.4 *IG between adjectives and prepositions:* near *and* like

In this section I return to the element *near*, which we looked at in Chapter 6. We saw that for Maling (1983) *near* is classed as a transitive adjective, and is only superficially a preposition. Huddleston (1984: 348) remarks that the classification of *near* 'remains somewhat indeterminate, and however it is analysed we need to include some ad hoc account of its peculiarities'. For Newmeyer (1998: 201f.) and for Huddleston and Pullum *et al.* (2002: 609) *near* belongs to both word classes, although for the latter its prepositional uses are more widespread. They note that *near* is 'highly exceptional in its syntax, combining a number of adjectival properties with those of the preposition' (2002: 609). I will also conclude that *near* as a lexeme belongs either to the class of adjectives or to the class of prepositions in any one configuration, although not to both classes at the same time.

Recall that Maling based her conclusion that *near* is an adjective on data like those shown below (1983: 270):

(25)   Kim put the lamp *nearer* (to) the bed.
(26)   the *near* shore/a *near* miss/take the *nearest* one to you
(27)   Chris didn't go **enough near/near enough* (to) the water to get wet.

She observes that in (25) *near* takes a comparative ending, while in (26) it modifies a noun. In (27) *enough* must follow *near*—it cannot precede it—just as is the case with undoubted adjectives, cf. *happy enough/*enough happy*. The fact that *near* can also take NP complements, as in (28), is explained by surmising that *near* is perhaps a surviving transitive adjective (Maling 1983: 266).

(28)   I saw him *near* the bar.

We can approach Maling's data in a different way, using the formalism introduced above, and making use of a number of tests introduced in Huddleston and Pullum *et al.* (2002: 606):

- Prepositions but not adjectives can occur as head of a non-predicative adjunct in clause structure.[10]
- AdjPs, other than those restricted to attributive or postpositive function, can mostly occur as complement to *become*; in general, PPs cannot.
- Central adjectives accept *very* and *too* as degree modifiers; in general prepositions do not.
- Central adjectives have inflectional or analytic comparatives and superlatives; in general, prepositions do not.[11]
- Central prepositions license NP complements; in general adjectives do not.
- Central prepositions accept *right* and *straight* as modifiers; adjectives do not.
- Prepositions taking NP complements can normally be fronted along with their complement in relative and interrogative constructions, as in *the knife [with which she cut it]* or *I don't know [to whom you are referring]*; in general, adjectives cannot.

We can add to this:

- Central adjectives can be followed by *enough*: *She is old enough to be your sister.* (Maling 1983)
- PPs can be preceded by *enough*, as Maling (1983) has noted: *She is enough at ease to do the interview*; APs generally cannot.

Let us start with (28). Applying the criteria above (see also Huddleston and Pullum *et al.* 2002: 609), we find that:

- The phrase *near the bar* is predicative, because it can take *him* (or even *I*) as its subject expression. Huddleston and Pullum *et al.*'s first criterion is therefore of no help in deciding the issue, because it makes reference to non-predicative adjuncts.[12]
- *Near the bar* cannot be a complement of *become*. This makes the string PP-like.

---

[10] Adjectives must pass the *predicand requirement*, which stipulates that they must be licensed by an overt or implied subject expression: 'Adjectives cannot head clause-initial phrases unless they are related to a predicand, whereas prepositions can' (Huddleston and Pullum *et al.* 2002: 530).

[11] Huddleston and Pullum *et al.* (2002) list the previous criterion and the present one under one bullet point.

[12] Huddleston and Pullum *et al.* (2002: 609) cheat a little in choosing their examples judiciously when they generalize in saying that 'examples like (i) show that *near* fails the predicand test [see footnote 10] for adjectives':

(i) *This place is a dead end, but [near/nearer the city] there's plenty going on.*

In most cases locative expressions will have an identifiable subject expression, allowing a classification of words like *near* as adjectives.

- Modification by intensifiers is possible: *very near the bar*. This is an adjectival property.
- Comparative and superlative forms are also possible: *nearer/nearest the bar*. This is also an adjectival property.
- *Near* takes a bare NP complement, a prepositional property.
- Modification by *right* (but not *straight* or *enough*) is possible, again a prepositional property.
- A relativized version is possible: *the bar near which I saw him*. This makes *near the bar* PP-like.
- Some speakers would accept postmodification by *enough* resulting in *near enough the bar*, which argues for analysing *near* as an adjective.

We find that *near* is preposition-like with respect to most criteria in a simple sentence like (28). Disregarding the first, inconclusive, criterion, we can say that p = 7, x = 4, and because x ≠ (p − x), that is, 4 ≠ (7 − 4), this is a case of strong convergence: *near* is a preposition converging on the class of adjectives. Notice that even if we regard postmodification by *enough* as inconclusive (Anderson 1997: 78 has a '?' before *near enough the fence*), this conclusion still stands.

Turning now to (25), we can say that *nearer* in *nearer the bed* is prepositional by virtue of the fact that: (1) it cannot be a complement of *become*; (2) it takes an NP complement; and (3) because we can relativize the string in question: *the bed nearer (to) which the lamp is positioned*. At the same time *nearer* is adjectival by virtue of the fact that (1) it can be intensified: *(very) much nearer the bed*, and because (2) it has a comparative ending. The fact that *nearer the bed* can take *the lamp* as its subject, and is therefore a predicative expression is inconclusive with regard to the first criterion. Note that *nearer (to) the bed* cannot be preceded by *enough*, nor can *nearer* be followed by *enough* (*nearer enough the bed*), but then this does not tell us much, because prototypical comparative adjectives can also not be followed by *enough*: *he was cleverer enough to be appointed*. Modification by *right* or *straight* is also not possible in (25). Again, however, we cannot conclude that *near* is not a preposition, because not all prepositions allow modification by these words. In sum, p = 5, x = 3, and because x ≠ (p − x), that is, 3 ≠ (5 − 3), we again have a case of strong convergence, such that *nearer* is a preposition converging on the class of adjectives. As for the comparative form *nearer*, Pullum (2002) has suggested that this is an inflected preposition. In this connection Newmeyer (2000: 243) notes that there is nothing exceptional about prepositions occurring in comparative constructions, witness the fact that we can also have (29):

(29)   The seaplane right now is more over the lake than over the mountain.

This would mean 'the seaplane is *over-er* (i.e. *more over*) the lake than over the mountain'. An element like *over* takes an analytic comparative, unlike *near*, which takes a synthetic comparative. We should add here that from a subsective point of view *over* is more prepositional than *near* in not allowing premodification by *very*: **very over the lake*. Even further towards the prepositional end of the cline are words like *at*, which do not occur in any type of comparative construction, nor allow *very*: **more at the bus stop/*very at the bus stop*.

Returning to Maling's data, sentence (26) involves a clear case of *near* occurring as an adjective: here the italicized items are without doubt adjectival by virtue of (1) their attributive position; (2) the possibility of modification by an intensifier like *very*; (3) the (possibility of a) comparative ending (*the nearer shop*); and (4) postmodification by *enough*: *a near enough guess*. Notice that *near* cannot be preceded by typical prepositional modifiers such as *straight* or *right*.

In (27), in the phrase *near enough the water*, the word *near* has two prepositional properties, namely (1) the fact that it takes an NP complement and (2) the fact that we can say *the water near enough which he stood*. There is just one adjectival property, namely (1) postmodification by *enough*, which adjectives allow but prepositions do not. Notice that we cannot add *enough* before *near*, nor an intensifying element like *very* or *right*. We also cannot add a comparative ending. All this means that in *Chris didn't go near enough the water to get wet* the element *near* is a preposition, converging on the class of adjectives. Thus $p = 3$ and $x = 2$, and $x \neq (p - x)$ holds.[13]

In conclusion, the data suggest that Maling was wrong in analysing *near* exclusively as a transitive adjective. In some syntactic contexts (most, in fact) it is a preposition, in others an adjective. Pace Maling, in the cases where it is followed by an NP, *near* is a preposition.

Consider next (30), from Anderson (1997: 77), and (31)–(32), slightly amended from Huddleston and Pullum *et al.* (2002: 608):

(30)   Jocelyn offered a like suggestion.
(31)   Like his father, John had been called to give evidence.
(32)   John is becoming like his father.

In (30) *like* is an adjective occurring in attributive position, which can (possibly) be postmodified by *enough* (*?a like enough suggestion*). Notice, however, that it cannot be premodified by *very* or take a comparative form.

---

[13] For some speakers (27) is only marginally acceptable (cf. e.g. Newmeyer 2000: 243, fn 12, for whom the string *near enough the water* is impossible).

In (31) *like* would seem to be a preposition: it heads a non-predicative adjunct, it takes an NP complement, and it cannot be preceded by intensifiers or take a comparative form. If we apply the tests to (32), we find that again they point to a predominantly prepositional analysis of *like*, pace Huddleston and Pullum *et al.* (2002: 608), who regard *like* as an adjective here. The adjectival properties of this word are the following: in addition to *like his father* being positioned after *become*, it can be preceded by *very* (*very like his father*) and it can take a comparative form (*more like his father*). However, the prepositional properties of *like* seem to outnumber the adjectival ones. Thus, *like* takes an NP complement, it can be premodified by an adverb (*just like his father*) or by *enough* (*We can use a photograph of his dad instead, because he looks enough like his father to fool the authorities*, but not **He looks like enough his father*), and fronting is just about possible (*his father like whom he is becoming more and more*). Recall from Chapter 6 that Anderson (1997) proposes the following adjective–preposition cline:

(33) {P:N} {(P:N);} {(P:N):} {;(P:N)} { }
     close near like worth at
     due

Assigning weightings to the adjectival component ('(P:N)') (see the end of Section 8.4.2 above), we derive the sequence in (34) where *near* has more adjectival content than *like*, that is, it is positioned closer to the adjectival end of the cline than *like*:

(34) {P:N} {(P:N);} {(P:N):} {;(P:N)} { }
     4 3 2 1 0
     close near like worth at
     due

Like Maling (1983), Anderson analyses *near* as an adjective. To my mind, *near* and *like* can be adjectives or prepositions, depending on the syntactic configuration in which they occur. In this respect my account agrees with Huddleston and Pullum's. However, given the discussion above, my findings are in harmony with Anderson's regarding the relative positions of *near* and *like* on the cline above, because *near* in its adjectival use displays more adjective-like properties than *like*.

8.4.5 *Complementizers and prepositions*

The element *for* can occur in at least three different syntactic environments. In (35) below it is clearly an ordinary preposition:

(35)   I bought it for her.

Another use, discussed in Chapter 6, occurs when *for* is used as some sort of copular element:

(36)   I want them for my wives. (i.e. 'I want them *to be* my wives'.)

Here I will concentrate on the use of *for* as illustrated in the sentences below (repeated from Chapter 6):

(37)   We want (for) them to visit us this Christmas.
(38)   We are keen for Billy to do it.

We saw that *for* has a dual nature here: it introduces a clause that functions as a complement of the matrix verb, and acts as a Case assigner at the same time, witness the accusative Case on the pronoun *them* in (37). In GB theory, *for* is analysed in these cases as a 'prepositional complementizer' (see Section 3.4.3). Recently, Culicover (1999: 59f.) has argued that '[t]here is a single element *for* that is neither a preposition nor a complementizer, but a *sui generis* category that shares properties with both prepositions and complementizers' (1999: 57). His argumentation runs as follows. First, he discusses the following data (1999: 59):

(39)   a.   For Terry, I bought this book.
       b.   For Terry to learn French, I bought this book.
(40)   a.   I bought for Terry the book that I had seen.
       b.   I bought for Terry to read [the book that I had seen].
(41)   a.   I bought this book yesterday for Terry.
       b.   I bought this book yesterday for Terry to read.
(42)   a.   This book is for Terry.
       b.   This book is for Terry to read.
(43)   a.   What this book is for is for Terry.
       b.   What this book is for is for Terry to read.
(44)   a.   *For Terry is the purpose of this book.
       b.   *For Terry to read is the purpose of this book.
(45)   a.   *I bought this book for — yesterday [a person that I wanted to impress].
       b.   *I bought this book for — to read [a person that I wanted to impress].

After presenting these data Culicover remarks that '[w]hile some of these properties are also shared with *that*-clauses, the identical distribution of *for*-NP and *for*-NP-*to*-VP appears non-accidental and easily explained if we take *for* to be a preposition in both cases'. But then he goes on to discuss further data which involve non-purposive *for*-strings and for which a prepositional analysis of *for* is not warranted:

(46) a. *For you to call me at 1 a.m.* would irritate my parents.
b. It was a great thrill for us *for Rodney to discover himself standing in front of such a huge crowd.*
c. It is important *for there to be some consistency here.*

A prepositional analysis in these cases is problematic because the positions in which the italicized strings above occur are not PP-positions, as (47a) and (47b) indicate:

(47) a. *For you would irritate my parents.
b. *It was a great thrill for us *for Rodney*.

But *for* also cannot be a complementizer, given the facts in (48) which demonstrate that an adjunct can follow an undisputed complementizer like *that*, but not *for*.

(48) a. It was a great thrill for us that at 1 a.m. Elvis suddenly called.
b. It was a great thrill for us for Elvis to suddenly call at 1 a.m.
c. *It was a great thrill for us for at 1 a.m. Elvis to suddenly call.

The overall conclusion is as follows:

> The characterization of the relationship between the two *for*s [*for* in (39)–(45) and *for* in (46)] and the complementizer *that*, then, appears to be the following. First, the constituents initiated by *for* are of the same syntactic type, call it *for* P. Such a constituent must have overt *for* if there is an overt subject, and no *for* or empty *for* if there is no overt subject. Second, the clause is adverbial if the interpretation of *for* is purposive, and an argument expressing a proposition otherwise. Third, the clauses initiated by *that* are arguments, in general, but are of a different syntactic category, which we may call CP, following the usual convention. (Culicover 1999: 60–1)

No label is assigned to syncategorematic *for* by Culicover.

There are reasons for thinking that *for* is a complementizer with preposition-like properties. One is that in some cases we can leave *for* out (cf. (37)), which would not be possible if this element were a 'true' preposition, as (49) shows:

(49) *I want it my child

In this respect *for* behaves like *that*, the complementizer *par excellence* (although with the proviso that *for* must introduce a nonfinite clause). However, the version of (37) that contains *for* is fairly unusual, at least in British English.

Another reason for not analysing *for* as a preposition, as Huddleston and Pullum *et al.* (2002: 1182–3) note (like Culicover), is that the *for*-string occurs in a position where 'regular PPs' cannot occur. What's more, *for* can be followed by *there* (cf. (50)) or by subject idiom chunks (cf. (51)), which prepositions do not allow. Finally, the string following *for* can be passivized, which shows that this element is not in construction with the NP that immediately follows it (cf. (52a) and (52b)).

(50)   I'm eager for *there* to be an inquest.
(51)   I'm keen for *the coast* to be clear by early evening at the latest.
(52)   a.   I'm happy *for* Jon to take the photograph.
         b.   I'm happy *for* the photograph to be taken by Jon.

On the basis of these observations one might want to say that the generative label 'prepositional complementizer' is quite apt, as it recognizes that *for* is a complementizer *au fond* with prepositional qualities. In terms of the present chapter, *for* would be a complementizer converging on the preposition class. However, another way to approach these data would be to incorporate complementizers within the class of prepositions, thus allowing prepositions to take NPs or clauses as complements, as in (39b)–(43b). Prepositions are not barred from subject position in principle, as Jaworska (1986) has shown. The fact that a P+clause can appear in subject position in (46a), but not a P+NP in (47a), can be explained by appealing to semantics: there is no way of construing a meaning for the latter. The same can be said for (44a) and (44b). (47b) is simply pragmatically odd. In the case of (50)–(52) we would then say that the preposition *for* takes a clause as its complement. For further discussion of the possibility of conflating the classes of preposition and complementizer, see Section 8.9 below.

8.4.6   *Constructions:* V + NP + *[to-infinitive]* vs. V + *[NP + to-infinitive]*

Constructional gradience can also be handled using the formalism proposed in this chapter. Consider the V+NP+*to*-infinitive string below, discussed in Section 7.4.2.4:

(53)   They expected *James* to win the race.

Here we might posit Intersective Constructional Gradience between two constructions, namely (54) and (55):

(54)   V NP [*to*-infinitive]
(55)   V [NP + *to*-infinitive]

The morphosyntactic properties in support of the analysis in (54) are the following: (1) the NP receives objective case if it is a pronoun (*they expected him to win the race*) and (2) the NP can become the subject of the matrix clause under passivization (*James was expected to win the race*). By contrast, the morphosyntactic properties that speak in favour of (55) are as follows: (1) the postverbal string can be replaced by *it* (*They expected it*); (2) when the postverbal string is passivized the overall meaning of the sentence does not change (*they expected James to win the race = they expected the race to be won by James*). In this connection, note that *James* receives its thematic role from the VP headed by *win*, not from *expect*; (3) the postverbal position can be occupied by the semantically empty element *there*, which can only occur in subject positions; (4) the postverbal position can be filled by idiom chunks that can only occur in subject positions (e.g. *I expect the bird to have flown by noon*). Therefore, p = 6, x = 4, and x ≠ (p − x), that is, 4 ≠ (6 − 4). On the whole, then, we can assign (53) to construction pattern (55), rather than (54), and we can say that pattern (55) converges on pattern (54). As noted in Chapter 7, the analysis of constructions such as (53) is highly contentious, and different grammarians will draw different conclusions as to how best to analyse them (see Aarts 1992, 2004c). However, what seems to be uncontentious is that (53) displays a mixture of morphosyntactic properties that can be associated with two different construction-types.

8.5 The present account vs. the Aristotelian and 'Sorites' models

How does the model of IG presented here differ from Quirk *et al.*'s gradient from Chapter 6, repeated here in full?

(56)   *some paintings of Brown's*
(57)   *Brown's paintings of his daughters*
(58)   *The painting of Brown* is as skilful as that of Gainsborough.
(59)   *Brown's deft painting of his daughter* is a delight to watch.
(60)   I dislike *Brown's painting his daughter.*
(61)   *Brown's deftly painting his daughter* is a delight to watch.[14]
(62)   I dislike *Brown painting his daughter.*
(63)   I watched *Brown painting his daughter.*
(64)   *Brown deftly painting his daughter* is a delight to watch.
(65)   *Painting his daughter*, Brown noticed that his hand was shaking.
(66)   *Brown painting his daughter that day*, I decided to go for a walk.

---

[14] I have interchanged (60) and (61) as compared with Quirk *et al.*'s order in Section 6.1.2.2, because the former lacks an adverbial modifier.

(67)   *The man painting the girl* is Brown.
(68)   *The silently painting man* is Brown.
(69)   Brown *is painting* his daughter.

The crucial difference is that the present model imposes strict categorial cut-off points within the gradient, as shown in Figure 8.1.

(70)

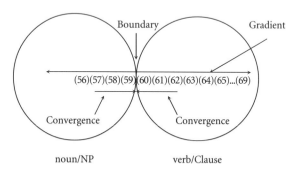

FIGURE 8.1 The noun/NP–verb/clause gradient

The gradient is modelled here as two categories converging on each other, but with a clear boundary. The model predicts that IG obtains not only with respect to particular elements such as *painting*, but also with respect to the *projections* of those elements. Thus, in the case of, for example, (60) *I dislike Brown's painting his daughter*, the lexical item *painting* is a verb which is convergent on the class of nouns. Its projection, the string *Brown's painting his daughter*, is a clause, which is convergent on a noun phrase.

Why insist on sharp boundaries between categories, and why deny the possibility of multiple class membership, as in the Aristotelian model? The principal reason is that a certain degree of idealization is necessary in order for a description of a language to be possible at all, so as to make sense of the wealth of linguistic facts that we face within particular languages and cross-linguistically. With regard to linguistic categorization, it methodologically makes sense to adopt an Aristotelian model of the categories as a starting point, which can then progressively be relaxed through falsification, rather than proceeding the other way round. In this connection, note that it is impossible to prove a negative, namely that strict boundaries do not exist. There is also a learnability issue: a grammar that allows all the examples of IG discussed here to be handled as dually assigned elements will be hard to acquire.

The model I have presented here denies the existence of fluid boundaries and multiple class membership, but concedes that gradience exists: it is built into the model by making use of the notion of convergence. By adopting sharp boundaries, as well as a convergence-driven concept of gradience, the model is a compromise between the discrete Aristotelian view of categorization, as adopted in most formal approaches to language, and the traditional approach to gradience which adopts an unconstricted Sorites-style smooth cline with no clear transition-point between the categories.

8.6 The syntactic properties of the categories

A number of questions arise concerning the syntactic properties that the formalism presented in Section 8.3 makes use of. Some of these are not without problems, and I will not pretend that I have the final answer to all of them. The following points need to be addressed:

- How can we be sure to identify all the relevant properties, and are all the properties equally important?
- How can we know that a particular property is an independent one and not merely a variant of an already identified property?
- Is it indeed the case that the syntactic properties that characterize a particular form class are unique to that class, as was claimed above?
- Is it true that an element belonging to a particular class can converge on at most one other word class in any one syntactic configuration?

8.6.1 *How can we be sure to identify all the relevant properties, and are all the properties equally important?*

It would be quite impossible to establish exactly which are *all* and *only* the properties that characterize particular observed elements, so as to be able to assign them to one form class or another, not least because languages are not static entities. However, I would contend that this is not necessary, because in line with a Popperian heuristic we can only ever *approximate* a model of reality. In most cases we can be sufficiently confident—as confident as we can be, given the accumulated knowledge of centuries' worth of work on grammar—that we can identify a sufficient number of criterial properties pertaining to a particular element or construction. Having said this, what does seem to be necessary is that we need to impose some kind of bound on the properties that are to be used. What I propose is to restrict the number of these properties in the following ways. First, they are all strictly morphosyntactic in nature. Secondly, as will be clear from the discussion of examples such as (12)–(14) in Section 8.4.2, the only properties referred to are those that pertain to the projection(s) in which the elements under investigation occur. More specifically, each of the properties concern a number of well-defined positions which may include: the subject position of the element, determiners, adjuncts, complements, the element's morphosyntactic make-up, and the position the phrase in question occupies in the larger containing structure.[15] Limiting the number of properties in this way is an improvement on Neustupný's (1966) impressionistic system in which there is no mechanism that can determine that 'x is rather y than z' or 'x is rather y than not-y' (see Section 3.4.5). Also, Neustupný cannot account in a precise way for convergence between categories (which he calls approximation vagueness). The present proposal straightforwardly and accurately assigns (61) to a position on the gradient in which it converges more closely on the noun class than does (62). Regarding the proposed balancing of properties, Martin Haspelmath (p.c.) asks 'Suppose there are two categories with 50 properties each. If an observed item has 23 or 24 properties of one of them, does that make it so different from another item that has exactly 25?' I would answer 'yes' to this question. One property can make all the difference, as a comparison between *Brown's painting of his daughter* and *Brown's painting his daughter* makes clear: the former is nominal, while the latter is clausal. It is merely the presence of the preposition that tips the balance and makes the first string nominal. Incidentally, the hypothetical situation Haspelmath sketches is unlikely to occur in language, if we limit the number of properties for a given category in the way suggested above.

As to the question of the relative importance of the various properties, it has been suggested to me that the morphosyntactic properties that I make use of ought perhaps to be weighted. Further research may show that this is indeed the right way to proceed. At present, however, it is not obvious how such a weighting might be implemented. While there are computational procedures for modelling the weighting of properties, these are not uncontroversial, for a number of reasons: first, there are different ways of assigning weightings, and there is disagreement as to which procedure is the optimal one. Secondly, weightings are based on large-scale corpora, but there is no agreement about the precise compositional make-up of such corpora. In this connection Newmeyer (2003: 695) has noted that:

[c]orpora reveal broad typological features of language that any theory of language variation, use, and change has to address. Two examples are the prevalence of

---

[15] Following a useful suggestion made in Haspelmath (1996), we can distinguish an element's *internal syntax*, e.g. the possibility of it taking certain dependents (which would include its morphosyntactic shape), from its *external syntax*, e.g. the possibility of it occurring in a particular (argument) position.

preferred argument structure and the predominance of third person reflexives. And it goes without saying that facts drawn from corpora are essential for engineering applications of linguistics. But it is a long way from there to the conclusion that corpus-derived statistical information is relevant to the nature of the grammar of any individual speaker, and in particular to the conclusion that grammars should be constructed with probabilities tied to constructions, constraints, rules, or whatever.

Because the use of corpora described above is controversial I have opted to work with the reasonable null hypothesis that all the properties are equal. On this issue, see also Hudson (1990: 45f., 1996: 76), who defends this view.

8.6.2 *How can we know that a particular property is an independent one and not merely a variant of an already identified property?*

As an example of this situation, let us return to the verbal properties that characterized the gerund. Readers will have noticed that I treated the possibility of an element being premodified by an adverb or by the negative particle *not* as separate verbal properties of that element. Is this correct? It has been put to me that arguably modification by a manner adverb or negative particle can be regarded as one and the same property, because any element that can be modified by an adverb can also be negated. However, because adverbial modification and negation can be instantiated on their own as well as conjointly, I have opted to regard them as separate properties. Empirical decisions of this type will need to be taken in each and every case for individual formatives if we are to have any hope of being able to assign class membership in a principled way.

8.6.3 *Is it indeed the case that the syntactic properties that characterize a particular form class are unique to that class?*

I think it would be relatively uncontroversial to say that the most well-established classes, such as nouns and verbs, do not share any distributional properties. Thus, for example, only a noun can occur in the position of 'X' in the frame 'Det Adj X', and only a verb can take a tense ending.[16] There do exist some potential counterexamples. Thus, it is well-known that both adjectives and adverbs can be preceded by a small group of intensifying adverbs, so that we can have for example *very good* and *very quickly*. Such facts show that the degree of convergence between any two classes may vary, and indeed could

---

[16] Notice that I am not saying that these classes cannot converge upon each other. I am merely saying that the property of taking morphological tense markers, for example, is a uniquely verbal property that does not apply to nouns.

also be taken to indicate that the classes in question should be conflated. In fact, this has been argued for adjectives and adverbs by a number of linguists (see e.g. Lyons 1966: 219f. and Radford 1988: 138f.). Similarly, adverbs are often said to modify adjectives and verbs, but not all adverbs are the same, and it is for this reason that I have been referring to 'manner adverbs' in the discussion above where modification by a manner adverb was used as a criterial property. These cannot modify adjectives.

8.6.4 *Is it true that an element belonging to a particular class can converge on at most one other word class in any one syntactic configuration?*

The model proposed here assumes that gradients are constituted of contiguous categories, very much à la Ross's 'circular' arrangement (1972: 316–17; see also Section 3.4.4) and that convergence can only involve two categories. This is a strong claim to make, but such an arrangement is warranted by the facts discussed in this chapter. I cannot think of any cases where an element converges on more than one class in a particular syntactic configuration by showing characteristics of more than two classes. Were such cases to be found, the model presented here would require modification. I will discuss categorial contiguity in more detail in Section 8.9.

8.7 'True hybridity'

The view of gradience that I have put forward above—that is, one where we have SG within categories and IG between categories through convergence, but with sharp categorial boundaries—would be considerably strengthened if there were no cases of true hybridity, because such cases would show that the boundaries between categories are fuzzy. Recall that I have so far characterized a true hybrid as an element that heads a structure where there is a perfect balance between the syntactic properties of two classes displayed by that structure. As we saw in Section 8.3, this happens when $x = (p - x)$. Now, it is of course not possible to prove a negative by showing that certain constructions do not exist, but it *is* possible to look at the behaviour of some (near) ungrammatical examples, which might be argued to be true hybrids.

Consider (71):

(71)   **The writing this book* was a difficult job. (van der Wurff 1993: 363)

Here we have two nominal properties (the italicized string occurs in a nominal position and the head is preceded by *the*) and two verbal properties (the *-ing* ending and the NP object). Van der Wurff notes that this structure was possible at one time in English. Interestingly, observe that it is not possible to 'save' (71) by adding pre-head modifiers:

(72)   *The stylish writing this book* was a difficult job.
(73)   *The stylishly writing this book* was a difficult job.

Neither adding an AP modifier nor an AdvP modifier nudges the italicized string in (71) into the nominal or verbal domains. The reason why (71) is bad may well be the true hybrid status of the italicized string. The hypothesis that English (and perhaps languages in general) does not tolerate truly hybrid structures would be in line with van der Wurff's 1993 and 1997 studies in which he argued that there have been forces in English which have pushed the English gerund either to the nominal end of the spectrum or to the verbal end from 1900 onwards.[17]

Consider next the following set of examples, analogous to (71):

(74)   I'm tired of *all that feeding the animals every day.* (Quirk *et al.* 1985: 1064)
(75)   *This smoking your pipe on every possible occasion* will ruin your health. (*ibid.*)
(76)   Let's have no more of *this bringing food into the computer room.* (Huddleston and Pullum *et al.* 2002: 1189)
(77)   So although I could imagine that we could, uhm, on our joint salary, get perhaps quite a high mortgage, it's *the paying it back at the beginning* that's going to be difficult. (Survey of English Usage, DL-C030625)
(78)   The days had been very full: the psychiatrist, the obstacle courses, *the throwing herself from the hold of a slowly chugging train.* (Sebastian Faulks, *Charlotte Gray* [1998; Vintage, 1999] x.111; cited in Denison 2001)

These examples suggest that perhaps constructions of this type have not completely disappeared from the language. In all these cases there are two nominal properties (the italicized strings occur in NP positions, and they take determinatives) and two verbal properties (the *-ing* ending and the NP object). Again, it is not possible to tip the balance in these cases by adding pre-head AP or AdvP modifiers. If we do so the results are marginal, if not ungrammatical:

(79)   I'm tired of *all that* *slow/??slowly feeding the animals every day.*
(80)   *This* *quick/??quickly smoking your pipe on every possible occasion* will ruin your health.

---

[17] See also Denison (1998: 268ff.). Fanego (1998) discusses the 'verbalization' of the early Modern English gerund, and notes that eModE gerunds 'exhibit a much greater degree of hybridization and structural instability than their Present-day English counterparts' (1998: 109). See also Fanego (2004).

(81)   Let's have no more of *this *surreptitious/??surreptitiously bringing food into the computer room.*

(82)   ...it's the **quick/??quickly paying it back at the beginning* that's going to be difficult.

(83)   ...the **helpless/??helplessly throwing herself from the hold of a slowly chugging train*

It is also not possible to add negative, voice, or aspect markers. Notice, however, that although (74)–(78) are a little odd-sounding, they are somehow slightly less unacceptable than (71). What could be the reason for this? Probably it has nothing to do with the post-head adjuncts that appear within the italicized strings, namely *every day, on every possible occasion, into the computer room, at the beginning,* and *from the hold of a slowly chugging train,* because these can occur as VP adjuncts (cf. *I drink milk every day/on every possible occasion/I brought food into the computer room/He paid me back at the beginning/She fell from the hold of a slowly chugging train*), or as NP adjuncts (cf. *Meat every day/on every possible occasion is not good for you/??Food into the computer room will be forbidden/Her fall from the hold of a slowly chugging train*), and are hence compatible with an analysis of the *-ing* form as a noun or as a verb. Maybe the fact that pre-head manner adjuncts are slightly more acceptable than pre-head APs in (79)–(83) nudges the construction as a whole into the verbal domain, at least for some speakers.

At first blush similar to (74)–(78) is the sentence in (84) from Schachter (1976), cited in Pullum (1991*b*: 771):

(84)   *This burning the midnight oil of yours* has got to stop.

Here there are two verbal properties, namely the *-ing* ending and the NP complement, but three nominal properties, namely the NP position in which the phrase *this burning the midnight oil of yours* occurs, the presence of the determinative *this*, and the presence of the PP *of yours*. This makes the subject string in this sentence predominantly nominal. Interestingly, though, we again do not seem to be able to add prenominal dependents to *burning*:

(85)   *This reckless burning the midnight oil of yours has got to stop.

(86)   *This recklessly burning the midnight oil of yours has got to stop.

Pullum dismisses the construction in (84) under the rhetorically laden heading 'Facts not relevant to the synchronic status of the N[ominal]-G[erund]P[hrase]' (1991*b*: 771f.). This is so because it needs 'special mention' in the grammar of English and is 'a nonproductive construction in which a gerund verb phrase is used AS IF it were an N^1 denoting an activity (especially a characteristic or repeated one)' (Pullum 1991*b*: 773; emphasis in original).

He goes on to say that 'I cannot say that I understand it fully, but perhaps it should be compared to the hyphenated-compound-adjective construction seen in phrases like *the easy-to-please image has been adopted*' (1991b: 773). What makes (84) so troublesome, of course, is the unwelcome fact for Pullum that there is a construction-internal PP, which is unexpected if his analysis of NGPs as NPs with VP-heads is correct (see Section 3.4.11). But surely we cannot simply reject data like (84) if they do not suit our theory. The construction in question undermines Pullum's analysis. It also undermines two further approaches to the gerund, namely Hudson's, also discussed in Section 3.4.11, and Ackema and Neeleman's (2004) treatment, briefly mentioned in Section 3.4.3. Recall that Ackema and Neeleman regard English gerunds as mixed categories, and argue that a zero nominalizing affix is attached at different levels in their tree structure representations. In their example, *John's constantly singing the Marseillaise*, the affix is attached at a higher level than in *John's constant singing of the Marseillaise*:[18]

(87)

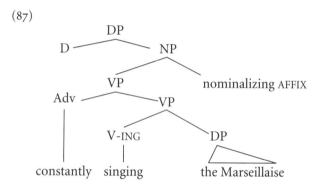

(88)

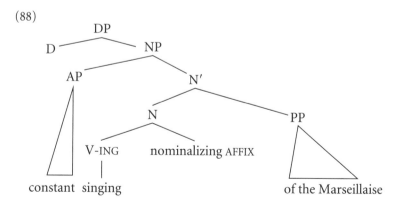

---

[18] The trees that follow do not actually appear in Ackema and Neeleman's book, but are adapted from the trees they supply for examples of the Dutch 'nominal infinitive' (2004: 176).

If these structures are correct, the question arises how we can explain the presence of the PP *of yours* in (84), which can only modify a noun, but which would have to be attached in a tree *below* the nominalizing affix:

(89)

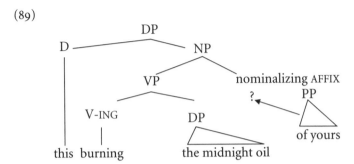

Despite the similarities shared with constructions like (74)–(78), I will regard the italicized string in (84) as nominal, not as a true hybrid, given that it displays a preponderance of noun-like properties.[19]

Let us turn now to *apparent* cases of true hybridity, that is cases where, although x = (p − x) holds, the structures can be coerced categorially. (90) is an example:

(90)   I dislike *Brown's painting his daughter.* (= (60))

Here the italicized string is apparently verbal and nominal in equal measure: the two nominal properties are that (1) *painting* is preceded by a genitival determinative, and (2) it heads a projection in a typical NP position, namely the direct object position of the verb *dislike*. Its two verbal properties are (1) that it has a verbal ending, and (2) that it takes an NP complement. We thus seem to be dealing with a true hybrid here: x = (p − x) holds, because the total number of properties is four (p = 4), while x = 2 and 2 = (4 − 2). Notice, however, that as was not the case with the examples discussed above, we can position a manner adverb or *not* before *painting* (*Brown's deftly/not painting his daughter*; cf. (61)). Also, voice and aspect markers can be added. It is not, however, possible to insert an adjective before *painting* (**Brown's deft painting his daughter*). This tips the balance in favour of categorizing *painting* as a verb, despite its being preceded by a genitival specifier.

---

[19] It has been suggested to me that the PP could be adjoined to the NP in (87), as in (i):

(i)   [$_{DP}$ Det [$_{NP}$[$_{NP}$[$_{VP}$ V-ing DP] AFFIX] [$_{PP}$ of yours]]]

But this poses rather more questions than it answers, mostly with respect to the nature of the nominalizing affix.

In some cases, a construction can be nudged in two directions. Thus (91) can be changed into the verbal construction in (92) or the nominal construction in (93):

(91)   *Dancing* is one of my favourite activities.
(92)   *Dancing the tango* is one of my favourite activities.
(93)   *Manic dancing* is one of my favourite activities.

In a particular situation the speaker/writer of a structure like (91) is likely to have either an activity (verb) in mind or a concept (noun).

Consider next (94), discussed in Chapters 6 and 7:

(94)   The mirror was broken.

Is *broken* a verb or an adjective? The answer is that it could be either. But again, crucially, it is possible to coerce the construction in two directions by adding lexical material:

(95)   The mirror was *broken* by hooligans. (verb)
(96)   The mirror was already *broken*. (adjective)

Again, in writing/uttering a structure like (94) a writer/speaker will have either an eventive or statal meaning in mind. See also Huddleston (1984: 322–3) and Huddleston and Pullum *et al.* (2002: 78,1436f.).

In the course of the discussion the definition of 'true hybrid' has changed slightly: true hybrids are headed by elements which are characterized by an equal number of properties from two categories and *cannot be nudged into one or the other category by adding modifiers*. The conception of SG and IG defended in this book (convergence + sharp boundaries) is supported by the fact that most examples of true hybrids are ungrammatical or near-ungrammatical in English. If true hybrids *were* acceptable, this would mean that elements can belong to two categories at the same time and that the borderline between these categories is indeterminate. Given that true hybrids are not acceptable, it follows that the borderline between categories is a sharp one and that an element must be coerced in one direction or the other. If I am on the right track in thinking that languages have a tendency to avoid true hybridity, it is not hard to see why this might be so: cases where the categorial scales are perfectly balanced are presumably hard to process mentally, and hence disfavoured by language users.[20]

---

[20] A mystery remains: *why* is it that if we add either a nominal or verbal modifier to the truly hybrid strings in (71) and (74)–(76) the result is bad? If the italicized portions in these sentences are truly balanced categorially, one would expect the addition of an AP or AdvP to tip the balance. Thus we would expect the highlighted portion to be nominal in (72) and verbal in (73), but the results are equally bad.

8.8 The nature of grammatical categories

The behaviour of grammatical categories is interesting in the light of the distinction between natural kind categories (*fish, bird*) and nominal kind categories (*vessel, tool*). Recall from Chapter 2 that the former have fixed boundaries, while the latter have potentially fuzzy boundaries. Membership of natural kind categories is determined by the internal make-up of the entities to be classified (e.g. a fish is a fish by virtue of its biological features), and elements can be more or less 'fishy' or 'birdy' without being less of a fish or less of a bird, while membership of nominal kind categories is determined by criterial attributes. McCawley, cited in Taylor (2003: 215), observes that:

Parts of speech are much more like biological species than has generally been recognised. Within any part of speech, or any biological species, there is considerable diversity. Parts of speech can be distinguished from one another, just as biological species can be distinguished from one another, in terms of characteristics that are typical for the members of that part of speech (or species), even though none of those properties need be instantiated by all members of the parts of speech (or species). (McCawley 1986: 12)

However, perhaps it would make more sense to say that grammatical categories like the word classes are somewhere between natural kind and nominal kind categories. On the one hand they are clearly not like the natural kind categories, because they do not involve three-dimensional concrete real-world natural entities, but they do have affinities with such categories: first, grammatical categories have clear boundaries, as I have argued above. Furthermore, a grammatical element can be a more or less typical member of a category without *necessarily* becoming more or less like another word class (recall Blake's apple tree), although in cases of IG grammatical categories *do* resemble other word classes by converging on them. In this latter respect grammatical categories resemble both natural kind categories (e.g. a whale looking like a fish) and nominal kind categories (recall Labov's cups and mugs, discussed in Chapter 3). However, this should not lead us to suppose that grammatical categories are nominal kind categories, because whereas we can have a mental representation of a prototype vessel (a nominal kind term), we can have no such mental image of a prototype adjective. Grammatical categories should perhaps be regarded as a category of categories in their own right, what we might call *grammatical kind categories.* This would make grammatical categories unique, in line with thinking in the Chomskyan paradigm, where language is said to make use of a specialized, rather than a general, cognitive apparatus, and presumably therefore also of specialized categories.

8.9 The contiguity of grammatical categories

The model proposed above assumes that gradients are constituted of contiguous categories. This is reminiscent of Ross (1972: 316), who proposed the linear arrangement in (97a), briefly discussed in Chapter 3 and above, where adjectives are in between verbs and nouns, while he leaves open the possibility that the 'circular' arrangement in (97b) for the focal categories in (97a) is perhaps more appropriate:

(97) a.   **Verb**>Present participle>Perfect participle>Passive participle >
     Adjective>Preposition (?)>'adjectival noun'>**Noun**

    b.

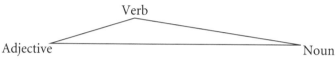

Recall from Chapter 3 that Ross arrived at this squish by citing data like the following:

(98) a. I hate/(dis)like/love/?regret it that he talked so much.
     b. I am aware (?of it) that we may have to pay more.
     c. My regret (*of it) that he talked so much is well-known.

He observes that the *it* we have in (98) occurs after a number of verbs, as well as after *aware of*, but not after nouns. A general conclusion of his paper is that nouns are the most inert category from a distributional point of view, followed by adjectives and then verbs:

To wax metaphorical, proceeding along the hierarchy is like descending into lower and lower temperatures, where the cold freezes up the productivity of syntactic rules, until at last nouns, the absolute zero of this space, are reached. (Ross 1972: 317)

The present model is similar to that of Ross, but differs from Ross's ideas by not assuming that a particular category can be 'in between' two others, as in (97a). I propose instead that nouns, verbs, and adjectives relate to each other as illustrated in Figure 8.2.

   The circles in the representation in Figure 8.2 represent categorial spaces. The arrows indicate that IG may obtain between these form classes such that particular elements can be positioned at various distances from the core, while converging on another class. As we have seen, any one element under scrutiny can converge on only one other category, so that in the image in Figure

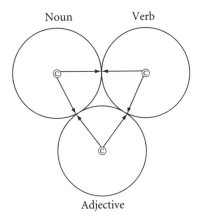

Noun   Verb

Adjective

FIGURE 8.2 Gradience within and between the categories of noun, verb, and adjective

Note: © represents the core of the categories.

8.2 only one arrow at a time can 'apply'. Recall that with SG there is no convergence, and elements are positioned more or less closely to the core of the category they belong to.

Figure 8.2 leaves a number of word classes unaccounted for, for example determinatives and prepositions. The former are intersectively gradient with (pro)nouns in constructions like *us politicians* (see Section 6.1.1.1) and with adjectives, as we saw in the discussion of *such* and *many* in Section 6.1.1.2. As for prepositions, in his 1972 squish, shown above in (97), Ross tentatively (hence the '?') positions them between adjectives and nouns. Given our discussion of prepositions ending in -*ing* in Chapter 6, prepositions have affinities with verbs, but also with adjectives, as we saw above when we looked at the element *near*. The revised picture that emerges is shown in Figure 8.3.

What about adverbs? As we saw in Chapter 6, they (or a subset of them) are often regarded as positional variants of adjectives. I will not adopt this view here, and regard them as a separate class. However, by virtue of the convergence between these two classes (see Section 6.1.1.5), they must be represented as being contiguous. Moreover, adverbs can also share properties with determinatives, as we saw in Section 6.1.1.3. The representation of categorial spaces now looks like Figure 8.4.

Notice that in Figure 8.4 adverbs are not contiguous with prepositions. This follows if we regard a whole host of elements that *look* like prepositions as prepositions (e.g. *before*, *after*, so-called particles, etc.), which is not the case in many accounts of gradience (e.g. Jacobsson 1977). See also Sections 6.1.3.1 and 8.2.2 above.

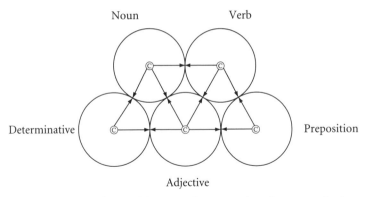

FIGURE 8.3 Gradience within and between the categories of noun, verb, determinative, adjective, and preposition

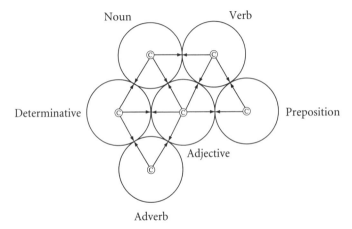

FIGURE 8.4 Gradience within and between the categories of noun, verb, determinative, adjective, preposition, and adverb

There are two remaining classes, namely the complementizers and the coordinators. Both of these contain functional items. Turning to complementizers first, in line with recent thinking I will assume that there are only four complementizers: *that, whether, if,* and *for.* A large group of elements that are traditionally analysed as subordinating conjunctions (*since, after,* etc.) can be accommodated in the class of prepositions, as we saw in Chapter 6, and in Section 8.2.2 above. Although I did not discuss them, this group includes items such as *(al)though, because, when, whereas, while,* etc. (See Huddleston

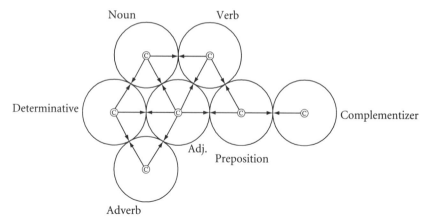

FIGURE 8.5 Gradience within and between the categories of noun, verb, determinative, adjective, preposition, complementizer, and adverb

and Pullum *et al.* 2002: 971, 1011f. for discussion.) Of the four complementizers there is only one that converges on another word class, namely *for*, as we saw in Section 8.4.5. On the basis of this fact we can expand our image of the word class space as shown in Figure 8.5.

Finally, we come to the coordinators. As we saw in Section 6.1.3.1, there are words that have coordinator-like properties and preposition-like properties. The word *but* is a case in point. Huddleston and Pullum *et al.* (2002: 1312) discuss the following set of sentences (repeated from Chapter 6):

(99)   Everyone but Jill was told.
(100)   *But Jill everyone was told.
(101)   Everyone but %I/%me was told.[21]

In (99) *but* can be a preposition or a coordinator (meaning 'except'). It is like a coordinator, but unlike a preposition, because the string *but Jill* cannot be fronted, cf. (100). However, when *but* is followed by a pronoun, cf. (101), it carries nominative or accusative case. Huddleston and Pullum suggest that this demonstrates that *but* is construed either as a preposition taking an accusative object, or is regarded as part of a coordinated subject NP (*everyone but I*). Data such as this suggest that the coordinator class should be contiguous with the preposition class. But coordinators also bear similarities to adverbs, as we saw in Section 7.4.2.3. This is especially clear with words like *yet* and *so.*

---

[21] '%' means 'grammatical in some dialects'.

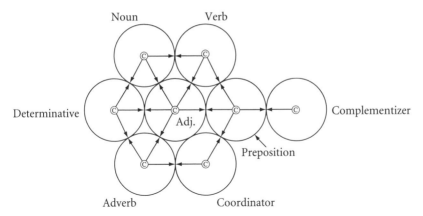

FIGURE 8.6 Gradience within and between the categories of noun, verb, determinative, adjective, preposition, complementizer, adverb, and coordinator

The coordinator class should therefore also be contiguous with the adverb class. The revised picture now looks like Figure 8.6.

Notice that in Figure 8.6 one set of arrows is missing, namely those between the adjective and coordinator classes. This indicates an absence of convergence between these categories. I can think of no formatives that display properties of these two classes, unless we take into account phrases like *the* AND *gate* and *the* OR *gate* used in electronics (Rob Munro, p.c.), where the coordinators occupy typical adjective positions. Here's an example from the web:

(102) The output of the AND gate goes HIGH briefly, but the monostable output goes HIGH and stays HIGH for a definite interval known as the **period** of the monostable.
(www.doctronics.co.uk/Subsystems/AND_gate.htm)

Interestingly, adjectives emerge from the representation in Figure 8.6 as the most versatile in being capable of resembling the syntactic behaviour of the other categories. The position of adjectives in Figure 8.6 above is in harmony with the observations of Baker (2003: 190) for whom verbs are predicates that license subjects, nouns are referring entities, while 'there is nothing special about adjectives', that is, it is enough to say that they are not nouns or verbs.[22] It looks like Humpty Dumpty was right when he said to Alice in *Through the Looking-Glass* that you can do anything with adjectives.

---

[22] For Baker the other word classes are functional, not lexical, categories.

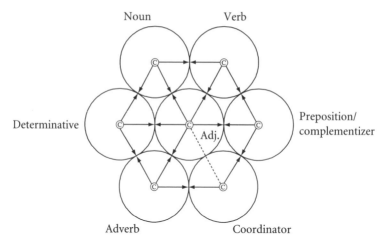

FIGURE 8.7 Gradience within and between the categories of noun, verb, determinative, adjective, preposition/complementizer, adverb, and coordinator

From Figure 8.6 it also emerges that complementizers are the least versatile, and this could be explained by pointing to the well-defined role these elements play in grammar. Having said that, the picture presented in Figure 8.6 could be 'tidied up' by assuming that complementizers belong to the class of prepositions, as has been proposed in the literature; see for example Emonds (1985: 281ff.). Figure 8.7 would then be the result.

Arguments against this view, which amounts to saying that complementizers are heads, are presented in Huddleston (1984: 341) and Huddleston and Pullum *et al.* (2002: 955–6). The latter give three reasons for claiming that complementizers are not heads. The first is that *that* 'is frequently omissible', which leads to the observation that '*that* is simply a syntactic marker of subordination, and in contexts where the subordinate status of the clause is predictable from features of the matrix structure the marker may be omissible' (2002: 955–6). Secondly, if we assume that complementizers are heads, then we would have to assume that in some cases the main clause predicate determines the form of the complement of that head, as happens in (103), where the subordinate clause contains a subjunctive verb form.

(103)   We insist [that the work *be* finished this week].

Thirdly, it is observed that adjuncts that belong in the subordinate clause can precede *that*:

(104)   The boat was such an attraction that I was afraid, [*if he came near it again*, that I should never see the last of him].

This is taken to show that *that* is part of the subordinate clause, not a head taking a bare clause complement. Let us look at each of these arguments in turn. As for the claim about omissibility, note that it does not apply to other complementizers. These do not allow omission (cf. e.g. *I asked *(whether) he was happy*). Regarding the second point, while it is true that in (103) a subjunctive verb form is selected by the main clause predicate, we might turn this argument round and say that in (105) it is the complementizer that is selected by the main clause predicate:

(105)   They asked me *whether/if/*that* I needed help.

In addition, the complementizer determines whether the clause that follows is finite or nonfinite. These facts would point to the complementizer being a head. Finally, with regard to (104) notice that the *if*-clause has the status of what we might call a 'proleptic parenthetical' whose interpretation is prosodically determined by the lower pitch level at which it would be uttered. In this particular case we could regard the *if*-clause as purely an utterance phenomenon, in the way this has been argued for non-restrictive relative clauses (see Haegeman 1988; Fabb 1990; Burton-Roberts 1999; Dehé and Kavalova (2006)), and therefore outside the scope of grammar altogether. In short, the arguments against regarding complementizers as heads are not entirely convincing, and I will therefore adopt Figure 8.7 as the final representation of word class space. It is motivated by the case studies discussed in this chapter, and elsewhere in this book, which support a view of grammar where categories converge. It makes the claim that a particular element at any one time converges on at most one other class. This is a strong claim, which I have attempted to falsify by looking for counterexamples. So far I have not come across any. Were they to be found then the model would require modification.

8.10 Conclusion

This book grew out of a feeling of discomfort both with uncompromising, strictly Aristotelian, approaches to categorization, and with frameworks that put few or no bounds on fuzziness in grammar. I have argued that there are two types of gradience: Subsective Gradience and Intersective Gradience. SG is intra-categorial in nature, and allows for prototypes, that is, for members of a class to display the properties of that class to varying degrees. IG is an inter-categorial phenomenon which is characterized by two form classes converging on each other. I have attempted to be more precise about the exact character of SG and IG, as well as the notion of convergence, by proposing intuitively simple and precise formalizations which make use of sets of morphosyntactic criteria. The intuition behind my proposals is that a particular formative may possess properties of one or two categories to different degrees, resulting in gradience, but that the categories in question can nevertheless be clearly delimited. IG is arguably far less widespread than is often claimed because many perceived cases are the fall-out of the less than optimal way grammarians have set up their categorial taxonomies.

References

Aarsleff, H. (1982) *From Locke to Saussure: Essays on the Study of Language and Intellectual History.* London: Athlone.

Aarts, B. (1989) 'Verb-preposition constructions and small clauses in English', *Journal of Linguistics* 25(2): 277–90.

—— (1992) *Small Clauses in English: The Nonverbal Types.* Topics in English Linguistics 8. Berlin and New York: Mouton de Gruyter.

—— (1996) Unpublished interview with Noam Chomsky, MIT. Partially published in Aarts (2000).

—— (1998) 'Binominal noun phrases in English', *Transactions of the Philological Society* 96(1): 117–58.

—— (2000) 'Corpus linguistics, Chomsky and Fuzzy Tree Fragments', in C. Mair and M. Hundt (eds), *Corpus Linguistics and Linguistic Theory.* Amsterdam: Rodopi, pp. 5–13.

—— (2001) *English Syntax and Argumentation*, 2nd edn. Basingstoke: Palgrave Macmillan.

—— (2004*a*) 'Conceptions of gradience in the history of linguistics', *Language Sciences* 26(4): 343–89.

—— (2004*b*) 'Modelling linguistic gradience', *Studies in Language* 28(1): 1–49.

—— (2004*c*) 'Grammatici certant.' Review article of Huddleston and Pullum *et al.* (2002). *Journal of Linguistics* 40(2): 365–82.

—— (2006) 'Conceptions of categorization in the history of linguistics', *Language Sciences* 28(4): 361–85.

—— (2007) 'In defence of distributional analysis, *pace* Croft', *Studies in Language* 31(2): 431–43.

—— (forthcoming) 'Approaches to the English gerund', in G. Trousdale and N. Gisborne (eds), *Constructional Explanations in English Grammar.* Topics in English Linguistics. Berlin and New York: Mouton de Gruyter.

—— and McMahon, A. (eds) (2006) *The Handbook of English Linguistics.* Malden MA: Blackwell.

—— and Meyer, C. F. (1995) (eds) *The Verb in Contemporary English: Theory and Description.* Cambridge: Cambridge University Press.

—— Denison. D., Keizer, E., and Popova, G. (eds) (2004) *Fuzzy Grammar: A Reader.* Oxford: Oxford University Press.

Abney, S. (1987) The English noun phrase in its sentential aspect. Doctoral dissertation, MIT.

Ackema, P. and Neeleman, A. (2004) *Beyond Morphology: Interface Conditions on Word Formation.* Oxford: Oxford University Press.

Adams, V. (1973) *An Introduction to Modern English Word-formation*. London: Longman.

—— (2001) *Complex Words in English*. Harlow: Pearson Education/Longman.

Adamson, S., Law, V., Vincent, N., and Wright, S. (eds) (1990) *Papers from the 5th International Conference on English Historical Linguistics*. Amsterdam: John Benjamins.

Allerton, D. J. (1978) 'Generating indirect objects in English', *Journal of Linguistics* 14(1): 21–33.

—— (2006) 'Verbs and their satellites', in B. Aarts and A. McMahon (eds), *The Handbook of English Linguistics*. Malden MA: Blackwell, pp. 146–79.

Andersen, H. (1989) 'Markedness theory—the first 150 years', in O. M. Tomić (ed.), *Markedness in Synchrony and Diachrony*. Berlin and New York: Mouton de Gruyter, pp. 11–46.

Anderson, J. M. (1997) *A Notional Theory of Syntactic Categories*. Cambridge: Cambridge University Press.

—— (2004) 'On the grammatical status of names', *Language* 80(3): 435–74.

Anderson, S. R. and Kiparsky, P. (eds) (1973) *A Festschrift for Morris Halle*. New York: Holt, Rinehart and Winston.

Andrews, A. D. (1990) 'Case structures and control in modern Icelandic', in J. Maling and A. Zaenen (eds), *Modern Icelandic Syntax*. New York: Academic Press, pp. 187–234.

Aristotle (1984) *Categories*. In *The Complete Works of Aristotle*, the revised Oxford translation, volume 1, edited by Jonathan Barnes, translated by J. L. Ackrill. Princeton NJ: Princeton University Press, pp. 3–24.

—— (1984) *Metaphysics*. In *The Complete Works of Aristotle*, the revised Oxford translation, volume 2, edited by Jonathan Barnes, translated by W. D. Ross. Princeton NJ: Princeton University Press, pp. 1552–728.

Asher, R. E. (1994a) (ed.) *The Encyclopedia of Language and Linguistics*. Oxford: Pergamon Press.

—— (1994b) 'Design features', in R. E. Asher (ed.), *The Encyclopedia of Language and Linguistics*. Oxford: Pergamon, pp. 875–7.

Bailey, C.-J. and Shuy, R. W. (eds) (1973) *New Ways of Analyzing Variation in English*. Washington DC: Georgetown University Press.

Baker, M. C. (2003) *Lexical Categories: Verbs, Nouns, and Adjectives*, Cambridge Studies in Linguistics. Cambridge: Cambridge University Press.

Ballmer, T. T. and Pinkal, M. (eds) (1983) *Approaching Vagueness*. Amsterdam: North-Holland.

Baltin, M. and Collins, C. (eds) (2001) *The Handbook of Contemporary Syntactic Theory*. Oxford: Blackwell.

Barbosa, P., Fox, D., Hagstrom, P., McGinnis, M., and Pesetsky, D. (eds) (1998) *Is the Best Good Enough?* Cambridge MA: MIT Press and MIT Working Papers in Linguistics.

Barlow, M. (2000) 'Usage, blends and grammar', in M. Barlow and S. Kemmer (eds), *Usage-based Models of Language*. Stanford CA: CSLI Publications, pp. 315–45.

—— and Kemmer, S. (eds) (2000) *Usage-based Models of Language*. Stanford CA: CSLI Publications.

Barsky, R. F. (1997) *Noam Chomsky: A Life of Dissent*. Cambridge MA: MIT Press.

Battistella, E. L. (1996) *The Logic of Markedness*. New York/Oxford: Oxford University Press.

Bauer, L. (1983) *English Word-formation*. Cambridge: Cambridge University Press.

—— (1998) 'When is a sequence of two nouns a compound in English?' *English Language and Linguistics* 2(1): 65–86.

—— (2005) 'Conversion and the notion of lexical category', in L. Bauer and S. Valera (eds), *Approaches to Conversion/Zero-Derivation*. Münster/New York/Munich/Berlin: Waxmann, pp. 19–30.

Beach, W. A., Fox, S. E., and Philosoph, S. (eds) (1977) *Papers from the Thirteenth Regional Meeting of the Chicago Linguistic Society*. Chicago IL: CLS.

Belletti, A. and Rizzi, L. (1988) 'Psych verbs and theta theory', *Natural Language and Linguistic Theory* 6(3): 291–352.

Berg, T. (2000) 'The position of adjectives on the noun–verb continuum', *English Language and Linguistics* 4(2): 269–93.

Berlin, B. and Kay, P. (1969) *Basic Color Terms: Their Universality and Evolution*. Berkeley CA: University of California Press.

Bernstein, J. B. (2001) 'The DP hypothesis', in M. Baltin and C. Collins (eds), *The Handbook of Contemporary Syntactic Theory*. Oxford: Blackwell, pp. 536–61.

Bever, T. (1975) 'Functional explanations require independently motivated functional theories', in R. E. Grossman *et al.* (eds), *Papers from the Parasession on Functionalism*. Chicago IL: CLS, pp. 580–609.

—— and Carroll, J. M. (1981) 'On some continuous properties in language', in T. Myers *et al.* (eds), *The Cognitive Representation of Speech*. Amsterdam: North-Holland. pp. 225–33.

Biber, D., Johansson, S., Leech, G., Conrad, S., and Finegan, E. (1999) *Longman Grammar of Spoken and Written English*. London: Longman.

Bjarkman, P. C. and Raskin, V. (eds) (1986) *The Real-world Linguist: Linguistic Applications in the 1980s*. Norwood NJ: Ablex.

Blevins, J. P. (2005) 'Remarks on gerunds', in C. Orhan Orgun and P. Sells (eds), *Morphology and the Web of Grammar*. Stanford CA: CSLI Publications, pp. 25–47.

Bloomfield, L. (1933) *Language*. London: George Allen and Unwin.

Bod, R., Hay, J., and Jannedy, S. (eds) (2003) 'Introduction', in R. Bod, J. Hay, and S. Jannedy (eds), *Probabilistic Linguistics*. Cambridge MA: MIT Press, pp. 1–10.

Boeckx, C. (2006) *Linguistic Minimalism: Origins, Concepts, Methods, and Aims*. Oxford: Oxford University Press.

Boersma, P. and Hayes, B. (2001) 'Empirical tests of the Gradual Learning Algorithm', *Linguistic Inquiry* 32(1): 45–86.

Boersma, P. Dekkers, J., and van de Weijer, J. (2000) 'Introduction', in J. Dekkers, F. van der Leeuw, and J. van de Weijer (eds), *Optimality Theory*. Oxford: Oxford University Press, pp. 1–44.

Bolinger, D. L. (1957) *Interrogative Structures of American English*. Publication 28 of the American Dialect Society. University of Alabama Press.

—— (1960) 'Linguistic science and linguistic engineering', *Word* 16: 374–91.

—— (1961*a*) *Generality, Gradience, and the All-or-none*. The Hague: Mouton. (Chapters 1 and 2 are reprinted in Aarts *et al.* 2004.)

—— (1961*b*) 'Syntactic blends and other matters', *Language* 37(3): 366–81.

—— (1971) *The Phrasal Verb in English*. Cambridge MA: Harvard University Press.

—— (1975) *Aspects of Language*. 2nd edn. New York: Harcourt, Brace, Jovanovich.

—— (1980) '*Wanna* and the gradience of auxiliaries', in G. Brettschneider and C. Lehmann (eds), *Wege zur Universalienforschung: Sprachwissenschaftliche Beiträge zum 60. Geburtstag von Hansjakob Seiler*. Tübinger Beiträge zur Linguistik 145. Tübingen: Gunter Narr, pp. 292–9.

Borer, H. (1990) 'V+*ing*: it walks like an adjective, it talks like an adjective', *Linguistic Inquiry* 21(1): 95–103.

Borsley, R. D. (1996) *Modern Phrase Structure Grammar*. Oxford: Blackwell.

—— and Kornfilt, J. (2000) 'Mixed extended projections', in R. D. Borsley (ed.), *The Nature and Function of Syntactic Categories*. Syntax and Semantics, volume 32. New York: Academic Press, pp. 101–31.

Bouchard, D. (1995) *The Semantics of Syntax: A Minimalist Approach to Grammar*. Chicago IL: University of Chicago Press.

Brekke, M. (1988) 'The experiencer constraint', *Linguistic Inquiry* 19(2): 169–80.

Bresnan, J. (1970) 'On complementizers: toward a syntactic theory of complement types', *Foundations of Language* 6: 297–321.

—— (1972) Theory of complementation in English syntax. PhD dissertation, MIT.

—— (1997) 'Mixed categories as head sharing constructions', in M. Butt and T. H. King (eds), *Proceedings of the LFG97 Conference*. Stanford CA: CSLI Publications, pp. 1–17.

—— and Hay, J. (2006) Gradient grammar: an effect of animacy on the syntax of *give* in varieties of English. http://www-lfg.stanford.edu/bresnan/anim-spokensyntax-final.pdf.

—— and Mugane, J. (2006) Agentive Nominalizations in Gĩkũyũ and the Theory of Mixed Categories. http://www-lfg.stanford.edu/bresnan/kikuyu-temp.pdf.

Brinton, L. J. (ed.) (2001) *Historical Linguistics 1999: Selected Papers from the 14th International Conference on Historical Linguistics*. Current Issues in Linguistic Theory 215. Amsterdam: John Benjamins.

Brown, K. and Miller, J. (eds) (1996) *Concise Encyclopedia of Syntactic Theories*. Oxford: Pergamon.

—— and —— (eds) (1999) *Concise Encyclopedia of Grammatical Categories*. Amsterdam: Elsevier.

Brugman, C. and Macaulay, M. (eds) (1984) *Proceedings of the Tenth Annual Meeting of the Berkeley Linguistics Society*. Berkeley CA: Berkeley Linguistics Society.

Bullen, H. St J. (1797) *The rudiments of English grammar.* Bury St Edmunds.

Bullokar, W. (1586) *(William Bullokar's) Pamphlet for Grammar: or rather to be said his abbreviation of his Grammar for English, extracted out of his Grammar at Large.* Oxford: Christ Church.

Burns, L. C. (1991) *Vagueness: An Investigation into Natural Languages and the Sorites Paradox.* Dordrecht/Boston/London: Kluwer.

Burton-Roberts, N. (1991) 'Prepositions, adverbs, and adverbials', in I. Tieken-Boon van Ostade and J. Frankis (eds) *Language: Usage and Description.* Amsterdam: Rodopi, pp. 159–72.

—— (1999) 'Language, linear precedence and parentheticals', in P. C. Collins and D. Lee (eds), *The Clause in English.* Amsterdam: John Benjamins, pp. 33–52.

Butt, M. and King, T. H. (eds) (1997) *Proceedings of the LFG97 conference, University of California, San Diego.* Stanford CA: CSLI Publications. Online: http://www-csli. stanford.edu/publications/LFG2/lfg97-toc.html.

Bybee, J. and Moder, C. L. (1983) 'Morphological classes as natural categories', *Language* 59(2): 251–70.

Carlson, G. (1980) *Reference to Kinds in English.* New York: Garland.

Casad, E. H. (ed.) (1996) *Cognitive Linguistics in the Redwoods: The Expansion of a New Paradigm in Linguistics.* Berlin: Mouton de Gruyter.

Chatterjee, A. (1994) *Understanding Vagueness.* Delhi: Pragati Publications.

Chiba, S. (ed.) (1988) *Aspects of Modern Linguistics.* Tokyo: Kaitakushi.

Chomsky, N. (1957) *Syntactic Structures.* The Hague: Mouton.

—— (1959) Review of Skinner (1957), *Language* 35: 26–58.

—— (1961) 'Some methodological remarks on generative grammar', *Word* 17: 219–39. (Partially reprinted in Fodor and Katz 1964, under the title 'Degrees of grammaticalness': 384–9; also partially reprinted in Aarts *et al.* 2004.)

—— (1965) *Aspects of the Theory of Syntax.* Cambridge MA: MIT Press.

—— (1970) 'Remarks on nominalization', in R. Jacobs and P. Rosenbaum (eds), *Readings in English Transformational Grammar.* Waltham MA: Ginn and Co., pp. 184–221.

Chomsky, N. (1973) 'Conditions on transformations', in S. R. Anderson and P. Kiparsky (eds), *A Festschrift for Morris Halle.* New York: Holt, Rinehart and Winston, pp. 232–86.

—— (1955/1975) *The Logical Structure of Linguistic Theory.* New York: Plenum Press.

—— (1980) *Rules and Representations.* Oxford: Blackwell. [1982 paperback edition]

—— (1981) *Lectures on Government and Binding: The Pisa Lectures.* Dordrecht: Foris.

—— (1986*a*) *Knowledge of Language: Its Nature, Origin, and Use.* New York: Praeger.

—— (1986*b*) *Barriers.* Cambridge MA: MIT Press.

—— (1992) 'A minimalist program for linguistic theory', *MIT Working Papers in Linguistics*, Occasional Papers in Linguistics 1. Cambridge MA: MIT Press. Also published in Hale and Keyser (1993) and in Chomsky (1995).

—— (1995) *The Minimalist Program.* Cambridge MA: MIT Press.

—— (1998) 'Some observations on economy in generative grammar', in P. Barbosa *et al.* (eds), *Is the Best Good Enough?* Cambridge MA: MIT Press, pp. 115–27.

Chomsky, N. (2000) *New Horizons in the Study of Language and Mind*. Cambridge: Cambridge University Press.

—— (2002) *On Nature and Language*. Cambridge: Cambridge University Press.

—— and Miller, G. A. (1963) 'Introduction to the formal analysis of natural Languages', in R. D. Luce, R. R. Bush, and E. Galanter (eds), *Handbook of Mathematical Psychology* Vol. II. New York: Wiley and Sons, pp. 269–321.

—— and Halle, M. (1968) *The Sound Pattern of English*. New York: Harper and Row.

—— and Lasnik, H. (1977) 'Filters and control', *Linguistic Inquiry* 8(3): 425–504.

Coates, J. (1971) 'Denominal adjectives: a study in syntactic relationships between modifier and head', *Lingua* 27: 160–9.

—— (1983) *The Semantics of the Modal Auxiliaries*. London: Croom Helm.

Collins, P. C. (1991) *Cleft and Pseudo-cleft Constructions in English*. London: Routledge.

—— and Lee, D. (eds) (1999) *The Clause in English: In honour of Rodney Huddleston*. (Studies in Language Companion Series). Amsterdam: John Benjamins.

Comrie, B. (1981) *Language Universals and Linguistic Typology: Syntax and Morphology*. Oxford: Blackwell.

Corrigan, R. (1989) 'Introduction', in R. Corrigan, F. Eckman and M. Noonan (eds), *Linguistic Categorization*. Amsterdam: John Benjamins, pp. 1–28.

Corrigan, R., Eckman, F., and Noonan, M. (eds) (1989) *Linguistic Categorization*. Amsterdam: John Benjamins.

Corum, C. T., Smith-Stark, C., and Weiser, A. (eds) (1973) *Papers from the Ninth Regional Meeting of the Chicago Linguistic Society*. Chicago IL: CLS.

Corver, N. and van Riemsdijk, H. (eds) (2001*a*) *Semi-lexical Categories: The Function of Content Words and the Content of Function Words*. Berlin: Mouton de Gruyter.

Corver, N. and van Riemsdijk, H. (2001*b*) 'Semi-lexical categories', in N. Corver and H. van Riemsdijk (eds), *Semi-lexical Categories*. Berlin: Mouton de Gruyter, pp. 1–19.

Covington, M. A. (1984) *Syntactic Theory in the High Middle Ages: Modistic Models of Sentence Structure*. Cambridge: Cambridge University Press.

Craig, C. (1977) *The Structure of Jacaltec*. Austin TX: University of Texas Press.

—— (ed.) (1986) *Noun Classes and Categorization: Proceedings of a Symposium on Categorization and Noun Classification. Eugene, Oregon, October 1983*. Amsterdam: John Benjamins.

Creider, C. and Hudson, R. (1999) 'Inflectional morphology in Word Grammar', *Lingua* 107: 163–87.

Cristofaro, S. (2003) *Subordination*. Oxford: Oxford University Press.

Croft, W. (1991) *Syntactic Categories and Grammatical Relations: The Cognitive Organization of Information*, Chicago and London: University of Chicago Press.

—— (2001) *Radical Construction Grammar: Syntactic Theory in Typological Perspective*. Oxford: Oxford University Press.

—— (2007) 'Beyond Aristotle and gradience: a reply to Aarts', *Studies in Language* 31(2): 409–30.

Cruse, A. (1992) 'Cognitive linguistics and word meaning: Taylor on linguistic categorization', *Journal of Linguistics* 28: 165–83.

—— and Croft, W. (2004) *Cognitive Linguistics*. Cambridge: Cambridge University Press.

Crystal, D. (1967) 'English', *Lingua* 17: 24–56. (Reprinted in Aarts *et al.* 2004.)

—— (2003) *A Dictionary of Linguistics and Phonetics*, 5th edn. Oxford/Malden: Blackwell.

Culicover, P. W. (1999) *Syntactic Nuts: Hard Cases, Syntactic Theory, and Language Acquisition*. Oxford: Oxford University Press.

—— and Jackendoff, R. (2005) *Simpler Syntax*. Oxford: Oxford University Press.

Curme, G. O. (1935) *A Grammar of the English Language*, volume II: *Parts of Speech and Accidence*. Boston MA: D. C. Heath.

Dainora, A., Hemphill, R., Luka, B., Need, B., and Pargman, S. (eds) (1995) *Papers from the Thirty-first Regional Meeting of the Chicago Linguistic Society*. Chicago IL: CLS.

Daneš, F. (1966) 'The relation of centre and periphery as a language universal', *Travaux linguistiques de Prague* 2: 9–21.

Dehé, N., and Kavalova, Y. (2006) 'The syntax, pragmatics, and prosody of parenthetical *what*', *English Language and Linguistics* 10(2): 289–320.

Dekkers, J., van der Leeuw, F., and van de Weijer, J. (eds) (2000) *Optimality Theory: Phonology, Syntax, and Acquisition*. Oxford: Oxford University Press.

Delorme, E. and Dougherty, R. (1972) 'Appositive NP constructions', *Foundations of Language* 8: 2–29.

Denison, D. (1990) 'The Old English impersonals revived', in S. Adamson *et al.* (eds), *Papers from the 5th International Conference on English Historical Linguistics*. Amsterdam: John Benjamins, pp. 111–40.

—— (1993) *English Historical Syntax*: Verbal Constructions. London: Longman.

—— (1998) 'Syntax', in S. Romaine (ed.), *The Cambridge History of the English Language*, vol 4, 1776–1997. Cambridge: Cambridge University Press, pp. 92–329.

—— (2000) 'Gradience and current change in the English NP'. Paper read at the 11th ICEHL conference, Santiago de Compostela, Spain.

—— (2001) 'Gradience and linguistic change', in L. Brinton (ed.), *Historical Linguistics 1999*. Amsterdam: John Benjamins, pp. 119–44.

Dikken, M. den (2006) *Relators and Linkers: the Syntax of Predication, Predicate Inversion, and Copulas*. Cambridge MA: MIT Press.

Dimitriadis, A., Siegel, L., Surek-Clark, C., and Williams, A. (eds) (1997) *Proceedings of the 21st Annual Penn Linguistics Colloquium*. Penn Working Papers in Linguistics 4.2. Department of Linguistics, University of Pennsylvania.

Dinneen, F. P. (ed.) (1966) *Report of the 17th Annual Round Table Meeting on Linguistics and Language Studies, GURT 1966*. Washington DC: Georgetown University Press.

Dixon, R. M. W. (1991/2005) *A New Approach to English Grammar, on Semantic Principles*. Oxford: Clarendon Press. (The second edition is entitled *A Semantic Approach to English Grammar*.)

Dummett, M. (1975/1996) 'Wang's paradox', *Synthese* 30: 301–24. (Partially reprinted in Keefe and Smith 1996: 99–118.)

Eilfort, W. H., Kroeber, P. D., and Peterson, K. L. (eds) (1985) *Papers from the Twenty-first Regional Meeting of the Chicago Linguistic Society*. Chicago IL: CLS.

Emonds, J. (1976) *A Transformational Approach to English Syntax*. New York: Academic Press.

—— (1984) 'The prepositional copula *as*', *Linguistic Analysis* 13(2): 127–44.

Emonds, J. (1985) *A Unified Theory of Syntactic Categories*. Dordrecht: Foris.

—— (1987) 'Parts of speech in generative grammar', *Linguistic Analysis* 17(1/2): 3–42.

—— (2001) 'The flat structure economy of semi-lexical heads', in N. Corver and H. van Riemsdijk (eds), *Semi-lexical categories*. Berlin and New York: Mouton de Gruyter, pp. 23–66.

Erteschik-Shir, N. and Lappin, S. (1979) 'Dominance and the functional explanation of island phenomena', *Theoretical linguistics* 6: 41–86.

Fabb, N. (1990) 'The difference between English restrictive and non-restrictive relative clauses', *Journal of Linguistics* 26: 57–78.

Fanego, T. (1998) 'Developments in argument linking in early Modern English gerund phrases', *English Language and Linguistics* 2: 87–119.

—— (2004) 'On reanalysis and actualization in syntactic change', *Diachronica* 21(1): 5–55.

Fanselow, G., Fery, C., Schlesewsky, M., and Vogel, R. (eds) (2006) *Gradience in Grammar: Generative Perspectives*. Oxford: Oxford University Press.

Fillmore, C. J., Kay, P., and O'Connor, M. C. (1988) 'Regularity and idiomaticity in grammatical constructions: the case of "let alone"', *Language* 64(3): 501–38. (Also in Kay 1997.)

—— —— Michaelis, L., and Sag, I. (forthcoming) *Construction Grammar*. Stanford CA: CSLI Publications.

Firth, J. R. (1930) *Speech*. London: Ernest Benn. (The version used here was reprinted in P. Strevens (ed.) (1964) *The Tongues of Men* and *Speech*. London: Oxford University Press.)

—— (1955) 'Structural linguistics', *Transactions of the Philological Society* 1955: 83–103.

Fodor, J. A. (1998) *Concepts: Where Cognitive Science Went Wrong*. Oxford: Clarendon Press.

—— and Katz, J. J. (eds) (1964) *The Structure of Language: Readings in the Philosophy of Language*. Englewood Cliffs NJ: Prentice-Hall.

Forbes, A. D. (2006) 'Squishes, clines, and fuzzy signs: mixed and gradient categories in the biblical Hebrew lexicon', in A. D. Forbes and D. G. K. Taylor (eds), *Foundations for Syriac Lexicography I: Colloquia of the International Syriac Language Project*. Perspectives on Syriac Linguistics 1. Piscataway NJ: Gorgias Press, pp. 105–40.

Frege, G. (1903/1997) *Grundgesetze der Arithmetik*, volume II, taken from *The Frege Reader*, ed. by M. Beaney. Oxford: Blackwell.

Fried, M. and Boas, H. C. (eds) (2005) *Grammatical Constructions: Back to the Roots*. Constructional approaches to language. Amsterdam/Philadelphia: John Benjamins.

Fuchs, C. and Victorri, B. (eds) (1994) *Continuity in Linguistic Semantics*. Amsterdam/Philadelphia: John Benjamins.

Fujimura, O. (ed.) (1973) *Three Dimensions of Linguistic Theory*. Tokyo: TEC.

García, E. C. (1967) 'Auxiliaries and the criterion of simplicity', *Language* 43(4): 853–70.

Geeraerts, D. (1989) 'Prospects and problems of prototype theory', *Linguistics* 27: 587–612.

Giegerich, H. (2004) 'Compound or phrase? English noun-plus-noun constructions and the stress criterion', *English Language and Linguistics* 8(1): 1–24.

Givón, T. (1984) *Syntax: A Functional-typological Introduction.* 2 vols. Amsterdam: John Benjamins.

—— (1986) 'Prototypes: between Plato and Wittgenstein', in C. Craig (ed.), *Noun Classes and Categorization*, Amsterdam: John Benjamins, pp. 77–102.

—— (1993) *English Grammar: A Function-based Introduction.* 2 vols. Amsterdam: John Benjamins.

—— (1995) *Functionalism and Grammar.* Amsterdam/Philadelphia: John Benjamins.

—— (2001) *Syntax: An Introduction.* 2 vols. Amsterdam: John Benjamins.

Gleason, H. A. (1955) *An Introduction to Descriptive Linguistics.* New York: Henry Holt and Co.

Goldberg, A. E. (1995) *Constructions: A Construction Grammar Approach to Argument Structure.* Chicago: University of Chicago Press.

—— (2006) *Constructions at Work: The Nature of Generalization in Language.* Oxford: Oxford University Press.

—— and Casenhiser, D. (2006) 'English constructions', in B. Aarts and A. McMahon (eds), *The Handbook of English Linguistics.* Malden MA: Blackwell, pp. 343–55.

Goodluck, H. and Rochemont, M. (eds) (1992) *Island Constraints: Theory, Acquisition and Processing.* Dordrecht: Kluwer.

Greenbaum, S., Leech, G., and Svartvik, J. (eds) (1979) *Studies in English Linguistics: For Randolph Quirk.* London: Longman.

Gries, S. Th. (2003) 'Towards a corpus-based identification of prototypical instances of constructions', *Annual Review of Cognitive Linguistics* 1: 1–27.

Groombridge, H. (1797) *The Rudiments of the English Tongue.* Bath.

Grossman, R. E., San, L. J., and Vance, T. J. (eds) (1975) *Papers from the Parasession on Functionalism.* Chicago IL: Chicago Linguistic Society.

Gruber, M. C., Higgins, D., Olson, K. S., and Wysocki, T. (eds) (1998) *Papers from the Thirty-Fourth Regional Meeting of the Chicago Linguistic Society.* Volume 2: *The panels.* Chicago IL: CLS.

Haegeman, L. (1988) 'Parenthetical adverbials: the radical orphanage approach', in S. Chiba (ed.), *Aspects of Modern Linguistics.* Tokyo: Kaitakushi, pp. 232–54.

—— (1994) *Introduction to Government and Binding Theory,* 2nd edn. Oxford: Blackwell.

—— and Guéron, J. (1999) *English Grammar: A Generative Perspective.* Oxford: Blackwell.

Haiman, J. (ed.) (1985) *Iconicity in Syntax.* Amsterdam: John Benjamins.

—— and Thompson, S. A. (eds) (1988) *Clause Combining in Grammar and Discourse.* Amsterdam: John Benjamins.

Hale, K. and Keyser, S. J. (eds) (1993) *The View from Building 20: Essays in Linguistics in Honor of Sylvain Bromberger.* Cambridge MA: MIT Press.

Halliday, M. A. K. (1961) 'Categories of the theory of grammar', *Word* 17: 241–92. (Reprinted in Halliday 2002: 37–94.)

—— (2002) *On Grammar.* Volume 1 of the collected works of M. A. K. Halliday, ed. by J. Webster. London and New York: Continuum.

Halliday, M. A. K. and Matthiessen, C. M. I. M. (2004) *An Introduction to Functional Grammar*, 3rd edn. London: Edward Arnold.

Harris, R. A. (1993) *The Linguistics Wars*. Oxford: Oxford University Press.

Harris, Z. (1951) *Structural Linguistics*. Chicago: University of Chicago Press/Phoenix Books.

—— (1957) 'Co-occurrence and transformation in linguistic structure', *Language* 33: 283–340.

Haspelmath, M. (1996) 'Word-class-changing inflection and morphological theory', in G. Booij and J. van Marle (eds), *Yearbook of Morphology 1995*. Dordrecht: Kluwer, pp. 43–66.

—— (1998) 'Does grammaticalization need reanalysis?' *Studies in Language* 22(2): 315–51.

Hawkins, J. (ed.) (1988) *Explaining Language Universals*. Oxford: Blackwell.

Hayes, B. P. (2000) 'Gradient well-formedness in optimality theory', in J. Dekkers, F. van der Leeuw, and J. van de Weijer (eds), *Optimality Theory*. Oxford: Oxford University Press, pp. 88–120.

Hockett, C. F. (1955) *A Manual of Phonology*. Baltimore: Waverly Press.

—— (1959) 'Animal "languages" and human language', in J. N. Spuhler (ed.), *The Evolution of Man's Capacity for Culture*. Detroit MI: Wayne State University Press, pp. 32–9.

Hopper, P. J. and Thompson, S. A. (1980) 'Transitivity in grammar and discourse', *Language* 56(2): 251–99.

—— and —— (1984) 'The discourse basis for lexical categories in Universal Grammar', *Language* 60(4): 703–52. (Reprinted in Aarts *et al.* 2004.)

—— and —— (1985) 'The iconicity of the universal categories "noun" and "verb"', in J. Haiman (ed.), *Iconicity in Syntax*. Amsterdam: John Benjamins, pp. 151–83.

Hopper, P. J. and Traugott, E. (1993) *Grammaticalization*. Cambridge: Cambridge University Press.

Householder, F. (1995) 'Aristotle and the Stoics on language', in E. F. K. Koerner and R. E. Asher (eds), *Concise History of the Language Sciences*. Oxford: Pergamon, pp. 93–8.

Huddleston, R. (1974) 'Further remarks on the analysis of auxiliaries as main verbs', *Foundations of Language* 11: 215–29.

—— (1976*a*) 'Some theoretical issues in the description of the English verb', *Lingua* 40: 331–83.

—— (1976*b*) *An Introduction to English Transformational Syntax*. London: Longman.

—— (1984) *Introduction to the Grammar of English*. Cambridge: Cambridge University Press.

—— (1994) 'The contrast between interrogatives and questions', *Journal of Linguistics* 30(2): 411–39.

—— and Pullum, G. (2005) *A Student's Introduction to English Grammar*. Cambridge: Cambridge University Press.

—— and Pullum, G. *et al.* (2002) *The Cambridge Grammar of the English Language*. Cambridge: Cambridge University Press.

Hudson, R. (1990) *English Word Grammar*. Oxford: Blackwell.

—— (1991) 'Double objects, grammatical relations and proto-roles', *UCL Working Papers in Linguistics* 3: 331–68.

—— (1995) 'Competence without Comp?', in B. Aarts and C. F. Meyer (eds), *The Verb in Contemporary English*. Cambridge: Cambridge University Press, pp. 40–53.

—— (1996) *Sociolinguistics*, 2nd edn. Cambridge: Cambridge University Press.

—— (2000*a*) 'Grammar without functional categories', in R. Borsley (ed.), *The Nature and Function of Syntactic Categories*. New York: Academic Press, pp. 7–36.

—— (2000*b*) 'Gerunds and multiple default inheritance', *UCL Working Papers in Linguistics* 12: 303–35. A revised version appeared as Hudson (2003).

—— (2003) 'Gerunds without phrase structure', *Natural Language and Linguistic Theory* 21(3): 579–615.

Jackendoff, R. (1977) *X-bar Syntax*. Cambridge MA: MIT Press.

—— (1983) *Semantics and Cognition*. Cambridge MA: MIT Press.

—— (1994) *Patterns in the Mind: Language and Human Nature*. New York: Basic-Books/HarperCollins.

—— (2002) *Foundations of Language: Brain, Meaning, Grammar, Evolution*. Oxford: Oxford University Press.

Jacobs, R. and Rosenbaum, P. (eds) (1970) *Readings in English Transformational Grammar*. Waltham MA: Ginn and Co.

Jacobsson, B. (1977) 'Adverbs, prepositions and conjunctions in English: a study in gradience', *Studia Linguistica* 31: 38–64.

Jakobson, R. (1959) 'Boas' view of grammatical meaning. Memoir 89', *American Anthropologist* 61.

—— (1961) 'Linguistics and communication theory', in R. Jakobson (ed.), *Proceedings of Symposia in Applied Mathematics*, vol. 12. Providence RI: American Mathematical Society, pp. 245–52.

Jaworska, E. (1986) 'Prepositional phrases as subjects and objects', *Journal of Linguistics* 22: 355–74.

Jespersen, O. (1894) *Progress in Language: With Special Reference to English*. London: Swan Sonnenschein & Co. Facsimile edition with an introduction by James McCawley. Amsterdam Classics in Linguistics 1800–1925, volume 17 (1993).

—— (1924) *The Philosophy of Grammar*, London: George Allen and Unwin Ltd.

—— (1933) *Essentials of English Grammar*, London: George Allen and Unwin Ltd.

—— (1909–1949) *A Modern English Grammar on Historical Principles*. Seven volumes. London and Copenhagen: George Allen & Unwin and Munksgaard.

Joos, M. (1950/1957) 'Description of language design', *Journal of the Acoustical Society of America* 22: 701–8; also in M. Joos (ed.) (1957) *Readings in Linguistics: The Development of Descriptive Linguistics in America 1925–56*. Washington: American Council of Learned Societies, pp. 349–56. (Reprinted in Aarts *et al.* 2004.)

Kager, R. (1999) *Optimality Theory*. Cambridge textbooks in linguistics. Cambridge: Cambridge University Press.

Kathol, A. and Bernstein, M. (eds) (1993) *Proceedings of the Eastern States Conference on Linguistics*. Ithaca NY: CLC Publications.

Katz, J. J. (1964) 'Semi-sentences', in J. A. Fodor and J. J. Katz (eds), *The Structure of Language*. Englewood Cliffs NJ: Prentice-Hall, pp. 400–16.

Kay, P. (1995) 'Construction grammar?' in J. Verschueren *et al.* (eds), *Handbook of Pragmatics*. Amsterdam: John Benjamins, pp. 171–7.

—— (1997) *Words and the Grammar of Context*. CSLI Lecture Notes 40. Stanford CA: CSLI Publications.

—— (2002) 'An informal sketch of a formal architecture for Construction Grammar', *Grammars* 5: 1–19.

—— and Fillmore, C. J. (1999) 'Grammatical constructions and linguistic generalizations: the *What's X doing Y?* construction', *Language* 75(1): 1–33.

Kayne, R. (1997) 'The English complementizer *of*', *The Journal of Comparative Germanic Linguistics* 1: 43–54.

—— (2002) On the syntax of quantity in English. MS, New York University.

Keefe, R. (2000) *Theories of Vagueness*. Cambridge: Cambridge University Press. (Chapter 1 is reprinted in Aarts *et al.* 2004.)

—— and P. Smith (1996*a*) *Vagueness: A reader*. Cambridge MA/London: MIT Press.

—— and P. Smith (1996*b*) 'Introduction: theories of vagueness', in R. Keefe and P. Smith (eds), *Vagueness: A Reader*. Cambridge MA/London: MIT Press, pp. 1–60.

Keizer, E. (2004) 'Postnominal PP complements and modifiers: a cognitive distinction', *English Language and Linguistics* 8(2): 323–50.

Keller, F. (1997) 'Extraction, gradedness, and optimality', in A. Dimitriadis *et al.* (eds), *Proceedings of the 21st Annual Penn Linguistics Colloquium*. University of Pennsylvania, pp. 169–86.

—— (1998) 'Gradient grammaticality as an effect of selective constraint re-ranking', in Gruber *et al.* (eds), *Papers from the Thirty-fourth Regional Meeting of the Chicago Linguistic Society*. Chicago IL: CLS, pp. 95–109.

—— (2000) Gradience in grammar: experimental and computational aspects of degrees of grammaticality. PhD thesis, University of Edinburgh.

Kluender, R. (1992) 'Deriving island constraints from principles of predication', in H. Goodluck and M. Rochemont (eds), *Island Constraints*. Dordrecht: Kluwer, pp. 223–58.

Koerner, E. F. K. and Asher, R. E. (eds) (1995) *Concise History of the Language Sciences: From the Sumerians to the Cognitivists*. Oxford: Pergamon.

Kornai, A. and Pullum, G. (1990) 'The X-bar theory of phrase structure', *Language* 66: 24–50.

Kortmann, B. (1997) *Adverbial Subordination: A Typology and History of Adverbial Subordinators Based on European Languages*. Berlin and New York: Mouton de Gruyter.

—— and König, E. (1992) 'Categorial reanalysis: the case of deverbal prepositions', *Linguistics* 30, 671–697.

Kruisinga, E. (1932) *A Handbook of Present-day English*, part II. 5th edn. Groningen: Noordhoff.

Labov, W. (1973) 'The boundaries of words and their meanings', in C.-J. Bailey and R. W. Shuy (eds), *New Ways of Analyzing Variation in English*. Washington DC: Georgetown University Press, pp. 340–73.

La Galy, M., Fox, R. A., and Bruck, A. (eds) (1974) *Papers from the Tenth Regional Meeting of the Chicago Linguistic Society*. Chicago IL: CLS.

Lakoff, G. (1970) *Irregularity in Syntax*. New York: Holt, Rinehart and Winston.

—— (1973a) 'Hedges: a study in meaning criteria and the logic of fuzzy concepts', *Journal of Philosophical Logic* 2(4): 458–508. Also in Peranteau, Levi, and Phares (1972), pp. 183–228.

—— (1973b) 'Fuzzy grammar and the performance/competence terminology game', in C. T. Corum, C. Smith-Stark, and A. Weiser (eds), *Papers from the Ninth Regional Meeting of the Chicago Linguistic Society*. Chicago IL: CLS, pp. 271–91.

—— (1974) 'Syntactic amalgams', in M. La Galy, R. A. Fox, and A. Bruck (eds), *Papers from the Tenth Regional Meeting of the Chicago Linguistic Society*. Chicago IL: CLS, pp. 321–44.

—— (1977) 'Linguistic gestalts', in W. A. Beach, S. E. Fox, and S. Philosoph (eds), *Papers from the Thirteenth Regional Meeting of the Chicago Linguistic Society*. Chicago IL: CLS, pp. 236–87.

Lakoff, G. (1987a) *Women, Fire, and Dangerous Things: What Categories Reveal about the Mind*. Chicago and London: University of Chicago Press. (Chapters 1 and 2 are reprinted in Aarts *et al.* 2004.)

—— (1987b) 'Cognitive models and prototype theory', in U. Neisser (ed.), *Concepts and Conceptual Development*. Cambridge: Cambridge University Press, pp. 63– 100. (Reprinted in E. Margolis and S. Laurence (eds) (1999) *Concepts*. Cambridge MA: MIT Press, pp. 391–421. References in the text are to the latter version.)

Landsberg, M. E. (1994) 'Origins of language', in Asher (ed.), *The Encyclopedia of Language and Linguistics*. Oxford: Pergamon, pp. 2886–91.

Langacker, Ronald W. (1987) *Foundations of Cognitive Grammar*, Volume 1: *Theoretical Prerequisites*. Stanford CA: Stanford University Press.

—— (1991) *Foundations of Cognitive Grammar*, Volume 2: *Descriptive Application*. Stanford CA: Stanford University Press.

Lapointe, S. G. (1993) 'Dual lexical categories and the syntax of mixed category phrases', in A. Kathol and M. Bernstein (eds), *Proceedings of the Eastern States Conference on Linguistics*. Ithaca NY: CLC Publications, pp. 199–210.

Leech, G. and Coates, J. (1979) 'Semantic indeterminacy and the modals', in S. Greenbaum, G. Leech, and J. Svartvik (eds), *Studies in English Linguistics*. London: Longman, pp. 79–90.

—— and Li, L. (1995) 'Indeterminacy between Noun Phrases and Adjective Phrases as complements of the English verb', in B. Aarts and C. F. Meyer (eds), *The Verb in Contemporary English*. Cambridge: Cambridge University Press, pp. 183–202.

—— Francis, B. and Xu, X. (1994) 'The use of computer corpora in the textual demonstrability of gradience in linguistic categories', in C. Fuchs and B. Victorri (eds), *Continuity in Linguistic Semantics*. Amsterdam: John Benjamins, pp. 57–76.

Lees, R. (1959) Review of L. Apostel, B. Mandelbrot and A. Morf *Logique, langage et théorie de l'information, Language* 35(2): 271–303.

—— (1960) Review of Bolinger (1957), *Word* 16: 119–25.

Legendre, G., Grimshaw, J., and Vikner, S. (eds) (2001) *Optimality-theoretic Syntax.* Cambridge MA: MIT Press.

Lehmann, C. (1988) 'Towards a typology of clause linkage', in J. Haiman and S. A. Thompson (eds), *Clause Combining in Grammar and Discourse.* Amsterdam: John Benjamins, pp. 181–225.

Levinson, S. C. (1983) *Pragmatics.* Cambridge: Cambridge University Press.

Lightfoot, David (1991) *How to Set Parameters: Arguments from Language Change.* Cambridge MA: MIT Press.

Lovechild, Mrs. (pseudonym of Lady Eleanor Fenn) (1798) *Parsing Lessons for Elder Pupils.* London.

Lyons, J. (1966) 'Towards a "notional" theory of the "parts of speech"', *Journal of Linguistics* 2: 209–36.

—— (1968) *Introduction to Theoretical Linguistics.* Cambridge: Cambridge University Press.

—— (1977) *Semantics,* 2 volumes, Cambridge: Cambridge University Press.

Mair, C. and Hundt, M. (eds) (2000) *Corpus Linguistics and Linguistic Theory.* Amsterdam: Rodopi.

Maling, J. (1983) 'Transitive adjectives: a case of categorial reanalysis', in F. Heny and B. Richards (eds), *Linguistic Categories: Auxiliaries and Related Puzzles.* Vol. I. Dordrecht: D. Reidel, pp. 253–89.

—— and Zaenen, A. (eds) (1990) *Modern Icelandic Syntax.* Syntax and Semantics 24. New York: Academic Press.

Malouf, R. P. (2000*a*) 'Verbal gerunds as mixed categories in Head-Driven Phrase Structure grammar', in R. D. Borsley (ed.), *The Nature and Function of Syntactic Categories.* New York: Academic Press, pp. 133–66.

—— (2000*b*) *Mixed Categories in the Hierarchical Lexicon.* Stanford CA: CSLI Publications.

Manning, C. (2003) 'Probabilistic syntax', in R. Bod, J. Hay, and S. Jannedy (eds), *Probabilistic Linguistics.* Cambridge MA: MIT Press, pp. 289–341.

Marchand, H. (1969) *The Categories and Types of Present-day English Word-formation,* 2nd edn. Munich: C. H. Beck.

Margolis, E. and Laurence, S. (eds) (1999) *Concepts: Core Readings.* Cambridge MA/London: MIT Press.

Massam, D. (1999) '*Thing is*-constructions', *English Language and Linguistics* 3(2): 335–52.

Matthews, P. (1981) *Syntax.* Cambridge: Cambridge University Press.

Matthiessen, C. and Thompson, S. A. (1988) 'The structure of discourse and "subordination"', in J. Haiman and S. A. Thompson (eds), *Clause Combining in Grammar and Discourse.* Amsterdam: John Benjamins, pp. 275–329.

McCarthy, J. J. (2001) *A Thematic Guide to Optimality Theory.* Research surveys in linguistics. Cambridge: Cambridge University Press.

McCawley, J. D. (1977) 'The nonexistence of syntactic categories'. in *Second Annual Metatheory Conference Proceedings*, Michigan State University, East Lancing, MI. Reprinted in J. D. McCawley (1982) *Thirty Million Theories of Grammar*. Chicago IL: University of Chicago Press. (Page references refer to the reprint.)

—— (1986) 'What linguists might contribute to dictionary making if they could get their act together', in P. C. Bjarkman and V. Raskin (eds), *The Real-world Linguist*. Norwood NJ: Ablex, pp. 3–18.

—— (1996) 'Generative semantics', in K. Brown and J. Miller (eds), *Concise Encyclopedia of Syntactic Theories*. Oxford: Pergamon, pp. 164–69. (Also in Asher 1994*a*).

—— (1998) *The Syntactic Phenomena of English*, 2nd edn. Chicago IL: University of Chicago Press.

Michael, I. (1970) *English Grammatical Categories and the Tradition to 1800*. Cambridge: Cambridge University Press.

—— (1987) *The Teaching of English: From the Sixteenth Century to 1870*. Cambridge: Cambridge University Press.

Miller, D. G. (2002) *Nonfinite Structures in Theory and Change*. Oxford: Oxford University Press.

Mohrman, C., Sommerfelt, A., and Whatmough, J. (eds) (1961) *Trends in European and American Linguistics 1930–1960*. Utrecht/Antwerp: Spectrum.

Monboddo, Lord J. B. (1774) *Of the origin and progress of language*. Edinburgh.

Moore, T. E. (ed.) (1973) *Cognitive Development and the Acquisition of Language*. New York: Academic Press.

Murphy, G. L. (2002) *The Big Book of Concepts*. Cambridge MA: MIT Press.

Muysken, P. (1982) 'Parametrizing the notion "Head"', *Journal of Linguistic Research* 2: 57–75.

Myers, T., Laver, J., and Anderson, J. (eds) (1981) *The Cognitive Representation of Speech*. Amsterdam: North-Holland.

Need, B., Schiller, E., and Bosch, A. (eds) (1987) *Papers from the Twenty-third Regional Meeting of the Chicago Linguistic Society*. Chicago IL: CLS.

Neisser, U. (ed.) (1987) *Concepts and Conceptual Development: Ecological and Intellectual Factors in Categorization*. Cambridge: Cambridge University Press.

Nelson, G. (ed.) (1998) *Landmarks in English Grammar: The Eighteenth Century*. London: Survey of English Usage. CD-ROM.

Neustupný, J. V. (1966) 'On the analysis of linguistic vagueness', *Travaux linguistiques de Prague* 2: 39–51. (Reprinted in Aarts *et al.* 2004.)

Newmeyer, F. J. (1986) *Linguistic Theory in America*, 2nd edn. San Diego CA: Academic Press.

—— (1998) *Language Form and Language Function*. Cambridge MA: MIT Press.

—— (2000) 'The discrete nature of syntactic categories: against a prototype-based account', in R. Borsley (ed.), *The Nature and Function of Syntactic Categories*. New York: Academic Press, pp. 221–50. (Also published as chapter 4 in Newmeyer 1998. Reprinted in Aarts *et al.* 2004.)

—— (2003) 'Grammar is grammar and usage is usage', *Language* 79(4): 682–707.

Okrent, A. and Boyle, J. P. (eds) (2000) *Papers from the Thirty-sixth Regional Meeting of the Chicago Linguistic Society.* Chicago IL: CLS.

Olofsson, A. (1990) 'A participle caught in the act. On the prepositional use of *following*', *Studia Neophilologica* 62: 23–35.

Olson, M. (1981) Barai clause junctures: toward a functional theory of interclausal relations. Dissertation, Australian National University.

Orhan Orgun, C. and Sells, P. (2005) *Morphology and the Web of Grammar: Essays in Memory of Steven G. Lapointe.* Stanford Studies in Morphology and the Lexicon. Stanford CA: CSLI Publications.

Ouhalla, J. (1991) *Functional Categories and Parametric Variation*, London and New York: Routledge.

—— (1999) *Introducing Transformational Grammar: From Principles and Parameters to Minimalism*, 2nd edn. London: Arnold.

Ozón, G. (2007) Ditransitives in English: a corpus-based study. PhD dissertation, UCL.

Palmer, F. (1979) 'Why auxiliaries are not main verbs', *Lingua* 47: 1–25.

—— (1987) *The English Verb*, 2nd edn. London: Longman.

—— (1990) *Modality and the English Modals*, 2nd edn. London: Longman.

Peranteau, P. M., Levi, J. N., and Phares, G. C. (eds) (1972) *Papers from the Eighth Regional Meeting of the Chicago Linguistic Society.* Chicago IL: CLS.

Pinker, S. (1999) *Words and Rules: The Ingredients of Language.* London: Weidenfeld and Nicolson.

Plag, I. (2006) 'The variability of compound stress in English: structural, semantic and analogical factors', *English Language and Linguistics* 10(1): 143–72.

Plath, W. (1961) 'Mathematical linguistics', in C. Mohrman, A. Sommerfelt, and J. Whatmough (eds), *Trends in European and American Linguistics 1930–1960.* Utrecht/Antwerp: Spectrum, pp. 21–57.

Pollard, C. and Sag, I. A. (1994) *Head-driven Phrase Structure Grammar.* Center for the Study of Language and Information; Chicago IL: University of Chicago Press.

Pollock, J.-Y. (1989) 'Verb movement, Universal Grammar, and the structure of IP', *Linguistic Inquiry* 20(3): 365–424.

Postal, P. (1966) 'On so-called "pronouns" in English', in Dinneen (ed.), *Report of the 17th Annual Round Table Meeting on Linguistics and Language Studies, GURT 1966.* Washington DC: Georgetown University Press, pp. 177–206.

—— (1974) *On Raising.* Cambridge MA: MIT Press.

Prideaux, G. D. (1984) *Psycholinguistics.* London: Croom Helm.

Priestley, J. (1761) *The Rudiments of English Grammar.* London. (Re-issued in Nelson 1998.)

Prince, A. and Smolensky, P. (2004) *Optimality Theory: Constraint Interaction in Generative Grammar.* Malden MA: Blackwell.

Pullum, G. (1976) 'On the nonexistence of the verb-auxiliary distinction in English', *Nottingham Linguistic Circular*, 5(2): 20–3.

—— (1985) 'Assuming some version of X-bar theory', in W. H. Eilfort, P. D. Kroeber, and K. L. Peterson (eds), *Papers from the Twenty-first Regional Meeting of the Chicago Linguistic Society.* Chicago IL: CLS, pp. 323–53.

—— (1991*a*) *The Great Eskimo Vocabulary Hoax and Other Irreverent Essays on the Study of Language*. Chicago IL: University of Chicago Press.

—— (1991*b*) 'English nominal gerund phrases as noun phrases with verb-phrase heads', *Linguistics* 29: 763–99.

—— (2002) Marginal membership in lexical categories and its implications for syntactic theory. Talk at University College London.

—— and Wilson, D. (1977) 'Autonomous syntax and the analysis of auxiliaries', *Language* 53: 741–88.

—— and Zwicky, A. M. (1991) 'Condition duplication, paradigm homonymy, and transconstructional constraints', in L. Sutton and C. Johnson (eds), *Proceedings of the Seventeenth Annual Meeting of the Berkeley Linguistic Society*. Berkeley CA: BLS, pp. 252–66.

Pulman, S. G. (1983) *Word Meaning and Belief*. London: Croom Helm.

Putnam, H. (1975/1992) *Mind, Language and Reality*. Philosophical Papers. Volume 2. Cambridge: Cambridge University Press.

Quine, W. V. (1960) *Word and Object*. Cambridge MA: The Technology Press of the Massachusetts Institute of Technology, and New York/London: John Wiley and Sons.

Quirk, R. (1965) 'Descriptive statement and serial relationship', *Language* 41(2): 205–17. (Reprinted in Aarts *et al.* 2004.)

—— (1995) 'Exploring the English genitive: a tribute to Jespersen', in R. Quirk *Grammatical and Lexical Variance in English*. London: Longman, pp. 63–77.

—— and Mulholland, J. (1964) 'Complex prepositions and related sequences', *English Studies* 45: 64–73.

—— Greenbaum, S., Leech, G., and Svartvik, J. (1972) *A Grammar of Contemporary English*. London: Longman.

——, ——, ——, and —— (1985) *A Comprehensive Grammar of the English Language*. London: Longman.

Radford, A. (1976) 'On the non-discrete nature of the verb-auxiliary distinction in English', *Nottingham Linguistic Circular*, 5(2): 8–19.

—— (1988) *Transformational Grammar: A First Course*. Cambridge: Cambridge University Press.

Reibel, D. A. and Schane, S. A. (eds) (1969) *Modern Studies in English*. Englewood Cliffs NJ: Prentice-Hall.

Rice, S. (1987) 'Towards a transitive prototype: evidence from some atypical English passives', in J. Aske, N. Beery, L. Michaelis, and H. Filip (eds), *Proceedings of the Thirteenth Annual Meeting of the Berkeley Linguistic Society*. Berkeley CA: BLS. 422–34.

Richards, I. A. (1936) *The Philosophy of Rhetoric*. London: Oxford University Press.

Riemsdijk, H. van (1998) 'Categorial feature magnetism: the endocentricity and distribution of projections', *Journal of Comparative Germanic Linguistics* 2: 1–48.

—— (2001) 'A far from simple matter: syntactic reflexes of syntax-pragmatics mis-alignments', in I. Kenesei and R. M. Harnish (eds), *Perspectives on Semantics,*

Pragmatics, and Discourse: A Festschrift for Ferenc Kiefer. Pragmatics and Beyond New Series 90. Amsterdam: John Benjamins, pp. 21–41.

Robins, R. H. (1952) 'Noun and verb in universal grammar', *Language* 28(3): 289–98.

—— (1990) *A Short History of Linguistics*, 3rd edn. London: Longman.

Romaine, S. (1998) *The Cambridge History of the English Language*, vol 4, *1776–1997*. Cambridge: Cambridge University Press.

Rosch, E. (1973*a*) 'On the internal structure of perceptual and semantic categories', in T. E. Moore (ed.), *Cognitive Development and the Acquisition of Language*. New York: Academic Press, pp. 111–44.

—— (1973*b*) 'Natural categories', *Cognitive Psychology* 4: 328–50.

—— (1975) 'Cognitive representations of semantic categories', *Journal of Experimental Psychology: General* 104: 192–233.

—— (1978) 'Principles of categorization', in E. Rosch and B. B. Lloyd (eds), *Cognition and Categorization*. Hillsdale NJ: Erlbaum, pp. 27–48. (Reprinted in Aarts *et al.* 2004.)

—— and Mervis, C. (1975) 'Family resemblances', *Cognitive Psychology* 7: 573–605.

—— and Lloyd, B. B. (eds.) (1978) *Cognition and Categorization*. Hillsdale NJ: Lawrence Erlbaum Associates.

——, Mervis, C. B., Gray, W. D., Johnson, D. M., and Boyes-Braem, P. (1976) 'Basic objects in natural categories', *Cognitive Psychology* 8: 382–439.

Rosenbach, A. (2006) 'Descriptive genitives in English: a case study on constructional gradience', *English Language and Linguistics* 10(1): 77–118.

Rosenbaum, P. S. (1967) *The Grammar of English Predicate Complement Constructions*. Cambridge MA: MIT Press.

Ross, J. R. (1969*a*) 'Adjectives as Noun Phrases', in D. A. Reibel and S. A. Schane (eds), *Modern Studies in English*. Englewood Cliffs NJ: Prentice-Hall, pp. 352–60.

—— (1969*b*) 'Auxiliaries as main verbs', in Todd (1969), 77–102.

—— (1972) 'The category squish: Endstation Hauptwort', in P. M. Peranteau, J. N. Levi, and G. C. Phares (eds), *Papers from the Eighth Regional Meeting of the Chicago Linguistic Society*. Chicago IL: CLS, pp. 316–28.

—— (1973*a*) 'A fake NP squish', in C. J. Bailey and R. W. Shuy (eds), *New Ways of Analyzing Variation in English*. Washington DC: Georgetown University Press, pp. 96–140.

—— (1973*b*) 'Nouniness', in Fujimura (ed.), *Three Dimensions of Linguistic Theory*. Tokyo: TEC, pp. 137–257. (Reprinted in Aarts *et al.* 2004.)

—— (1974) 'Three batons for cognitive psychology', in W. Weimer and D. Palermo (eds), *Cognition and the Symbolic Processes*. Hillsdale NJ: Lawrence Erlbaum Associates, pp. 63–124.

—— (1981) Nominal decay. Unpublished MS, MIT.

—— (1987) 'Islands and syntactic prototypes', in B. Need, E. Schiller, and A. Bosch (eds), *Papers from the Twenty-third Regional Meeting of the Chicago Linguistic Society*. Chicago IL: CLS, pp. 309–20.

—— (1995) 'Defective noun phrases', in A. Dainora *et al.* (eds), *Papers from the Thirty-first Regional Meeting of the Chicago Linguistic Society*. Chicago IL: CLS, pp. 398–440.

—— (2000) 'The frozenness of pseudoclefts: towards an inequality-based syntax', in A. Okrent and J. P. Boyle (eds), *Papers from the Thirty-sixth Regional Meeting of the Chicago Linguistic Society.* Chicago IL: CLS, pp. 385–426.

Russell, B. (1923/1996) 'Vagueness'. *Australian Journal of Philosophy and Psychology* 1: 84–92. (The version referred to appears in: R. Keefe and P. Smith (eds), *Vagueness*. Cambridge MA: MIT Press, pp. 61–8. Also reprinted in Aarts *et al.* 2004.)

Sag, I. A. (1973) 'On the state of progress on progressives and statives', in: C.-J. Bailey and R. W. Shuy (eds), *New Ways of Analyzing Variation in English*. Washington DC: Georgetown University Press, pp. 83–95.

Salmon, V. (1979) *The Study of Language in 17th-Century England.* Amsterdam Studies in the Theory and History of Linguistic Science III, Studies in the History of Linguistics, volume 17. Amsterdam/Philadelphia: John Benjamins.

Sapir, E. (1921/1957) *Language: An Introduction to the Study of Speech.* New York: Harcourt, Brace/Harvest Books.

Saussure, F. de (1916/1974) *Course in General Linguistics.* Translated by Wade Baskin. London: Fontana/Collins.

Schachter, P. (1976) 'A nontransformational analysis of gerundive nominals in English', *Linguistic Inquiry* 7(2): 205–41.

Schilpp, P. A. (ed.) (1974) *The Philosophy of Karl Popper.* La Salle IL: Open Court.

Schütze, C. T. (1996) *The Empirical Base of Linguistics: Grammaticality Judgments and Linguistic Methodology.* Chicago IL: University of Chicago Press.

Schwartz, S. P. (1980) 'Natural kinds and nominal kinds', *Mind* 89: 182–95.

Seppänen, A., Bowen, R. and Trotta, J. (1994) 'On the so-called complex prepositions', *Studia Anglica Posnaniensia* 29: 3–29.

Seuren, P. A. M. (1998) *Western Linguistics: An Historical Introduction.* Oxford: Blackwell.

Shibatani, M. and Thompson, S. (eds) (1996) *Grammatical Constructions: Their Form and Meaning.* Oxford: Clarendon Press.

Siegel, M. (1994) '*Such*: binding and the pro-adjective', *Linguistics and Philosophy* 17(5): 481–97.

Sivertsen, E. (ed.) (1958) *Proceedings of the Eighth International Congress of Linguists.* Oslo: Oslo University Press.

Skinner, B. F. (1957) *Verbal Behavior.* New York: Appleton Century Crofts.

Sorace, A. and Keller, F. (2005) 'Gradience in linguistic data', *Lingua* 115: 1497–524.

Spinillo, M. (2003) 'On *such*', *English Language and Linguistics* 7(2): 195–210.

—— (2004) Reconceptualising the English determiner class. PhD dissertation, University College London.

Spuhler, J. N. (ed.) (1959) *The Evolution of Man's Capacity for Culture.* Detroit MI: Wayne State University Press.

Stockwell, R. (1963) Review of Bolinger (1961*a*), *Language* 39: 87–91.

Störig, H.-J. (1959/1985) *Geschiedenis van de filosofie.* 2 volumes. Utrecht/Antwerp: Het Spectrum.

Strang, B. (1968) *Modern English Structure*, 2nd edn. London: Edward Arnold.

Sutton, L. and Johnson, C. (eds) (1991) *Proceedings of the Seventeenth Annual Meeting of the Berkeley Linguistic Society.* Berkeley CA: BLS.

Svartvik, J. (1966) *On Voice in the English Verb.* The Hague and Paris: Mouton.

Taylor, J. R. (1996) *Possessives in English: An Exploration in Cognitive Grammar.* Oxford: Clarendon Press.

—— (1998) 'Syntactic constructions as prototype categories', in M. Tomasello (ed.), *The New Psychology of Language.* Mahwah NJ: Lawrence Erlbaum, pp. 177–202.

—— (2002) *Cognitive Grammar.* Oxford: Oxford University Press.

—— (2003) *Linguistic Categorization,* 3rd edn. Oxford: Oxford University Press. (Chapter 10 of the 2nd edn is reprinted in Aarts *et al.* 2004.)

Thompson, S. A. (1988) 'A discourse approach to the cross-linguistic category "adjective"', in J. Hawkins (ed.), *Explaining Language Universals.* Oxford: Blackwell, pp. 167–185.

Tieken-Boon van Ostade, I. and Frankis, J. (eds) (1991) *Language: Usage and Description.* Amsterdam: Rodopi.

Todd, W. (ed.) (1969) *Studies in Philosophical Linguistics.* Series I. Evanston IL: Great Expectations Press.

Tomasello, M. (ed.) (1998) *The New Psychology of Language: Cognitive and Functional Approaches to Language Structure.* Mahwah NJ: Lawrence Erlbaum.

Tooke, J. H. (1786) *The diversions of Purley.* London. (The edition cited here is the 1829 edition, reprinted by Routledge/Thoemmes Press in 1993, ed. Roy Harris.)

Trask, R. L. (1993) *A Dictionary of Grammatical Terms in Linguistics.* London: Routledge.

—— (1998) Contribution to a discussion on the universality of nouns and verbs, LINGUIST List 9: 1712.

—— (1999) 'Parts of speech', in K. Brown and J. Miller (eds), *Concise Encyclopedia of Grammatical Categories.* Amsterdam: Elsevier, pp. 278–84.

Tsohatzidis, S. L. (ed.) (1990) *Meanings and Prototypes: Studies in Linguistic Categorization.* London: Routledge.

Tuggy, D. (1996) 'The thing is is that people talk that way. The question is is why?' in E. H. Casad (ed.), *Cognitive Linguistics in the Redwoods.* Berlin: Mouton de Gruyter, pp. 713–52.

Ungerer, F. and Schmid, H.-J. (1996) *An Introduction to Cognitive Linguistics.* London: Longman.

Vachek, J. (1966) 'On the integration of the peripheral elements into the system of language', *Travaux linguistiques de Prague* 2: 23–37.

Van Valin, R. D. (1984) 'A typology of syntactic relations in clause linkage', in C. Brugman and M. Macaulay (eds), *Proceedings of the Tenth Annual Meeting of the Berkeley Linguistics Society.* Berkeley CA: BLS, pp. 542–58.

Verschueren, J. (1985) *What People Say They Do with Words.* Norwood NJ: Ablex.

——, Östman, J.-O., and Blommaert, J. (eds) (1995) *Handbook of Pragmatics: Manual.* Amsterdam: John Benjamins.

Visser, F. Th. (1963–1973) *An Historical Syntax of the English Language.* 4 volumes. Leiden: Brill.

Warner, A. (1993) *English Auxiliaries: Structure and History.* Cambridge: Cambridge University Press.

Weimer, W. and Palermo, D. (eds) (1974) *Cognition and the Symbolic Processes.* Hillsdale NJ: Lawrence Erlbaum Associates.

Wells, R. (1958) 'Is a structural treatment of meaning possible?' in E. Sivertsen (ed.), *Proceedings of the Eighth International Congress of Linguists.* Oslo: Oslo University Press, pp. 654–66.

Whorf, B. L. (1956) *Language, Thought, and Reality: Selected Writings of Benjamin Lee Whorf,* ed. John B. Caroll. Cambridge MA: MIT Press.

Wierzbicka, A. (1989) 'Prototypes in semantics and pragmatics: explicating attitudinal meanings in terms of prototypes', *Linguistics* 27: 731–69.

—— (1990) ' "Prototypes save": on the uses and abuses of the notion of "prototype" in linguistics and related fields', in S. L. Tsohatzidis (ed.), *Meanings and Prototypes.* London: Routledge, pp. 347–67.

—— (1996) *Semantics: Primes and Universals.* Oxford: Oxford University Press.

Wilkins, J. (1668/1968) *An Essay Towards a Real Character, and a Philosophical Language.* London: For S. Gellibrand, and for John Martyn. Facsimile edition. London: Scolar Press.

Williamson, T. (1994) *Vagueness.* London: Routledge.

Winters, M. E. (1990) 'Toward a theory of syntactic prototypes', in S. L. Tsohatzidis (ed.), *Meanings and Prototypes.* London: Routledge, pp. 285–306.

Wittgenstein, L. (1921/1981) *Tractatus logico-philosophicus.* Translated by C. K. Ogden, with an Introduction by Bertrand Russell. London: Routledge and Kegan Paul.

—— (1953/1958) *Philosophical Investigations,* 3rd edn 1968. Translated by G. E. M. Anscombe. Oxford: Blackwell. (Partially reprinted in Aarts *et al.* 2004.)

Wurff, W. van der (1993) 'Gerunds and their objects in the Modern English period', in J. van Marle (ed.), *Historical Linguistics 1991: Papers from the 10th International Conference on Historical Linguistics.* Amsterdam: John Benjamins, pp. 363–75.

—— (1997) 'Gerunds in the Modern English period: structure and change', *The History of English* 3: 163–96.

Zadeh, L. A. (1965) 'Fuzzy sets', *Information and Control* 8: 338–53.

—— (1972) 'A fuzzy set-theoretic interpretation of linguistic hedges', *Journal of Cybernetics* 2(3): 4–34.

—— (1987) *Fuzzy Sets and Applications: Selected Papers,* ed. R. R. Yager. New York: Wiley.

Zandvoort, R. W. (1962) *A Handbook of English Grammar,* 2nd edn. London: Longman.

Ziff, P. (1964) 'On understanding "understanding utterances" ', in J. A. Fodor and J. J. Katz (eds), *The Structure of Language.* Englewood Cliffs NJ: Prentice-Hall, pp. 390–9.

Zwicky, A. (1987) 'Constructions in Monostratal Syntax', in B. Need, E. Schiller, and A. Bosch (eds), *Papers from the Twenty-third Regional Meeting of the Chicago Linguistic Society.* Chicago IL: CLS, pp. 389–401.

Names Index

Aarsleff, Hans 21 n. 6
Aarts, Bas 2, 33, 43, 45, 98, 109, 136, 149, 154, 185, 187, 205, 211 n. 5, 223
Aarts, Flor xii
Abney, Steven 125
Ackema, Peter 52, 231, 231 n. 18
Adams, Valerie xii, 134, 149–50, 187
Allerton, David J. 174
Andersen, Henning 91
Anderson, John 65–6, 102, 157, 157 n. 20, 158, 214, 214 n. 9, 217–19
Andrews, Avery D. 49
Apollonius Dyscolus 14
Apostel, L. 43 n. 4
Aristotle 1, 3, 5, 10–12, 14–15, 18, 27, 29–30, 33, 35, 37, 57, 62, 67–8, 71, 123, 131, 138, 140, 154, 157, 165, 223–5
Asher, R. E. 39

Bailey, C. -J. 55
Baker, Mark C. 19–20, 131, 136 n. 7, 239, 239 n. 22
Ballmer, Thomas T. 37
Barbosa, P. *et al.* 72
Barlow, Michael 83, 84–5, 85 n. 6
Barsky, Robert F. 48
Battistella, Edwin L. 72, 90, 91, 91 n. 13, 92–4
Bauer, Laurie 59, 131, 134, 142
Belletti, Adriana 49
Berg, Thomas 50, 54
Berlin, Brent 27, 68
Bernstein, Judy 51
Bever, Thomas 44, 57
Biber, Douglas *et al.* 66 n. 12, 127, 187
Blache, Philippe xii
Blake, William 97, 122–3, 206, 234

Blevins, James P. 76 n. 14, 144–5
Bloomfield, Leonard 17–18, 59, 63–4, 164
Boas, Hans C. 170
Bod, Rens 73
Boeckx, Cedric 45
Boersma, Paul *et al.* 72–3
Bolinger, Dwight 1, 4, 34, 39–41, 41 n. 2, 42–3, 52, 57, 86, 150, 151 n. 17, 188
Borer, Hagit 140–1
Borsley, Robert D. 33, 51
Bouchard, Denis 43–4, 71, 115–17
Brekke, Magnar 139–40
Bresnan, Joan 20, 74, 78
Bullen, Henry St. John 15, 38
Bullokar, William 15
Burnett, Lord Monboddo 15
Burns, Linda Claire 37
Burton-Roberts, Noël xii, 109, 121
Bybee, Joan 29, 69

Carlson, G. 127
Carroll, J. M. 44, 57
Casenhiser, Devin 170
Chatterjee, Amita 1 n. 1, 12 n. 3, 37
Chomsky, Noam 4, 19–23, 30, 43–51, 63, 90–3, 119, 144–5, 164–6, 170, 185, 211, 234
Chrysippus 37
Coates, Jennifer 2, 82, 85 n. 7, 129
Collins, Peter 85
Comrie, Bernard xii, 32
Corrigan, Roberta 2, 11
Corver, Norbert 51
Covington, Michael A. 15
Craig, Colette 183

Creider, Chet 78
Cristofaro, Sonia 183 n. 3
Croft, William xii, 2, 21 n. 6, 32–3, 72,
    130–1, 131 n. 4, 154 n. 19, 168, 206
Cruse, Alan 29
Crystal, David 25, 63, 102–5, 166–7, 171
Culicover, Peter W. 23, 110 n. 5, 155, 170,
    219, 221–2
Curme, George O. 62, 67, 129–30 n. 2,
    129–30

Daneš, František 58
Dehé, Nicole 241
Delorme, E. 125
Denison, David xii, 82, 87, 131–3, 187 n. 5,
    188, 213, 213 n. 7, 229, 229 n. 17
Dikken, Marcel den 211 n. 5
Dionysius Thrax 14
Dixon, R. M. W. 27 n. 10
Donatus 14–15
Dougherty, R. 125
Dummett, Michael 13

Eckman, Fred 2
Einstein, Albert 29
Emonds, Joseph 20, 21 n. 7, 22–3, 24 n. 9,
    109, 149, 154, 240
Erteschik-Shir, Naomi 48
Eubulides of Megara 1

Fabb, Nigel 121, 241
Fanego, Teresa 229 n. 17
Fanselow, Gisbert *et al.* 4, 73 n. 13
Fillmore, Charles J. 168, 170, 195
Firth, J. R. 42
Fodor, Jerry A. 122 n. 10
Forbes, A. Dean 74
Francis, Brian 180
Francis, Nelson 63
Frege, Gottlob 9, 12–13, 36
Fried, Mirjam 170
Fries, C. C. 17, 74
Fuchs, Catherine 2

Galileo 45
García, Erica C. 42
Geeraerts, Dirk 2
Giegerich, Heinz 59, 131
Givón, Talmy 2, 3, 30–1, 66, 71, 118
Gleason, H. A. 17, 165
Goldberg, Adele E. 33, 78–9, 87, 164, 168,
    170, 173, 197
Greenbaum, Sidney, *see* Quirk, R. *et al.*
Gries, Stefan Th. 174
Grimm, Jacob 17
Groombridge, H. 15
Guéron, Jacqueline 143

Haegeman, L. xii, 49, 85, 121, 143, 241
Halle, Morris 91
Halliday, M. A. K. 4, 42–3, 63
Harris, Randy A. 24, 52, 58
Harris, Zellig 46 n. 5, 165
Haspelmath, Martin xii, 87 n. 9, 226,
    226 n. 15
Hay, Jennifer 73–4
Hayes, Bruce P. 73
Hegel 45
Hill, A. A. 151 n. 17
Hockett, Charles F. 17, 39
Hopper, Paul J. 31, 87, 101, 118 n. 8, 119
    n. 9, 119–20, 160, 174, 196
Householder, Fred 68
Huddleston, Rodney 16 n. 4, 24 n. 9, 26,
    67, 99, 101 n. 2, 107, 108, 108 n. 4,
    109–10, 119, 125 n. 1, 125–31, 133, 135–6,
    136 n. 8, 137–9, 142, 144, 147, 150, 152,
    156, 158, 166–7, 171, 177–8, 183, 185,
    190–1, 197, 211, 213, 213 n. 8, 215–16, 219,
    222, 229, 233, 237–8, 240
Hudson, Richard xii, 1, 20–2, 26, 65,
    77–8, 125, 143–4, 185, 204, 213–14, 227

Jackendoff, Ray 19, 20, 44, 49–50, 62, 125,
    136, 145 n. 13, 169–70, 211 n. 5
Jacobsson, Bengt 39, 151–5, 201, 204, 236
Jakobson, R. 40, 91

Jannedy, Stefanie 73
Jaworska, Ewa 222
Jespersen, Otto 26, 28 n. 10, 62, 68, 101,
   128, 151, 187–8, 201
Jonson, Ben 15
Joos, Martin 18, 34, 39, 40, 44

Kager, René 72
Katz, Jerrold J. 47
Kavalova, Yordanka 241
Kay, Paul 27, 68, 168, 170, 195
Kayne, Richard 86, 126, 155
Keefe, Rosanna 37–8
Keizer, Evelien xii, 186
Keller, Frank 72–3
Kluender, Robert 48
König, Ekkehard 147–8, 148 n. 15, 149
Kornai, András 166
Kornfilt, Jaklin 51
Kortmann, Bernd 109, 147–8, 148 n. 15,
   149
Kruisinga, Etsko 182
Kubiński, T. 59

Labov, William 1–2, 10, 69–70, 89, 234
Lakoff, George 2, 11, 24, 27, 29–30, 58, 60,
   62, 69–70, 84, 87–8, 94, 114, 167–8, 172,
   174–5, 194
Landsberg, M. E. 39
Langacker, Ronald W. 2, 4, 11 n. 1, 26–7,
   153–4
Lapointe, Steven G. 77 n. 77
Lappin, Shalom 48
Lasnik, Howard 91
Leech, Geoffrey, *see also* Quirk, R.
   et al. 34, 82, 85 n. 7, 158–60, 180–1, 206
Lees, Robert B. 43, 43 n. 4, 44
Legendre, Geraldine 72
Lehmann, Christian 119, 121, 183
Lepschy, Giulio xii
Leskien, August 17
Levinson, Stephen C. 197 n. 6
Li, Lu 158–60, 206

Lightfoot, David W. 92
Lovechild, Mrs. (pseudonym of Lady
   Eleanor Fenn) 15
Lyons, John 10, 21 n. 6, 27, 39, 90, 136,
   138, 228

Maling, Joan 157, 215–16, 218, 219
Malouf, Robert P. 76–7, 144
Mandelbrot, B. 43 n. 4
Manning, Christopher 73–4, 146 n. 14
Marchand, Hans 149
Massam, Diane 85
Matthews, Peter 63–4, 67
Matthiessen, Christian M. I. M. 42, 182
McCarthy, John J. 72
McCawley, James D. 19, 24–5, 58, 114–15,
   130 n. 3, 133–4, 134 n. 5, 135–6, 234
Mervis, Carolyn B. 2
Meyer, Charles F. 98
Michael, Ian 11, 12, 15–16, 38
Miller, D. Gary 143, 211, 214
Miller, G. A. 46
Moder, Carol Lynn 29, 69
Monboddo, Lord James Burnett 15
Morf, A. 43 n. 4
Mugane, John 78
Mulholland, Joan 111, 176
Munro, Rob xii, 42 n. 3, 239
Murphy, G. L. 12, 69
Muysken, Pieter 166

Neeleman, Ad 52, 231, 231 n. 18
Neustupný, Jiří V. 58–60, 88, 88 n. 10, 226
Nevailainen, Terttu xii
Newmeyer, Frederick J. 18, 23–4, 51, 71,
   93–4, 112, 115–17, 158, 215, 217–18, 218
   n. 13, 226
Noonan, Michael 2

Occam, William of 10, 24, 154 n. 19
O'Connor, Mary Catherine 168
Olofson, Arne 145–6
Olson, M. 183

Ouhalla, Jamal 22, 49
Ozón, Gabriel 186

Palmer, Frank 24 n. 9, 98–9
Paradis, Carita xii
Pinkel, Manfred 37
Pinker, Steven 29–30, 51
Plag, Ingo 131
Plath, Warren 63
Plato 10, 30–1, 138
Pollard, Carl 18, 32–3, 73–4
Pollock, Jean-Yves 20
Popova, Gergana xii
Popper, Karl 17, 37, 71, 225
Postal, Paul 23–4, 125, 185, 204
Prideaux, G. D. 48
Priestley, Joseph 16
Priscian 14–15
Prost, Jean-Philippe xii, 134 n. 5
Pullum, Geofffrey K. 24 n. 9, 26, 51 n. 7,
    57, 57 n. 10, 67, 75–6, 99, 100, 101, 101 n.
    2, 107, 109–10, 115, 125 n. 1, 125–9, 131,
    133, 135–6, 136 n. 8, 137–8, 141, 141 n. 10,
    142, 144–5, 147, 150, 152, 156, 158, 165 n.
    1, 165–6, 177–8, 185, 190–1, 213, 213 n. 8,
    215–17, 219, 222, 229–30, 233, 238, 240
Pulman, S. G. 27
Putnam, Hilary 122

Quine, Willard van Orman 37
Quirk, Randolph *et al.* 2–4, 26, 34, 40, 63,
    66–7, 80, 81, 81 n. 1, 82–3, 86, 86 n. 8,
    99, 110–11, 115, 117–18, 125, 127, 143, 145,
    149, 152, 160, 176, 178, 183, 184–6, 190,
    193, 223, 223 n. 14, 229

Radford, Andrew 19, 20, 24 n. 9, 55, 56,
    56 n. 9, 57, 86, 99, 136 n. 7, 228
Ramus, Petrus 15
Richards, I. A. 37 n. 1
Riemsdijk, Henk van 51, 191
Rizzi, Luigi 49
Robins, R. H. 3, 10–11, 14–15, 17, 21 n. 6, 154

Rosch, Eleanor 1, 2, 11, 24, 28, 68–9, 87–8
Rosenbach, Anette 182
Rosenbaum, Peter S. 20, 50, 182
Ross, John Robert 4, 11, 24, 30, 46 n. 5,
    52–5, 57–8, 60–1, 83 n. 2, 94, 97, 99,
    111–14, 116–17, 122–3, 130, 156, 160, 172,
    193, 228, 235–6
Russell, Bertrand 13, 202–4

Sag, Ivan 18, 32–3, 55, 73–4
St Thomas Aquinas 15
Salmon, Vivian 28, 68
Sanctius (Francisco Sanchez) 38
Sapir, Edward 9, 39, 66
Saussure, Ferdinand de 165
Schachter, Paul 144, 230
Schillp, P. A. 37
Schleicher, August 17
Schmid, Hans-Jörg 89
Schütze, Carson T. 49, 57
Schwartz, S. P. 27
Searle, John 197
Seppänen, Aimo 177
Seuren, Pieter 3, 11 n. 2, 14
Shakespeare, William 124, 128
Shibatani, Masayoshi 170
Shuy, R. W. 55
Siegel, Laura 127
Siegel, M. 127
Skinner, B. F. 30
Smith, Peter 37
Smolensky, Paul 72
Sorace, Antonella 73
Spinillo, Mariangela xii, 16, 125, 127
Stockwell, Robert 41
Störig, H. J. 11
Strang, Barbara 134, 156, 204 n. 1
Svartvik, Jan, *see also* Quirk, R. *et al* 82,
    178–9, 179 n. 2, 193

Taylor, John R. xii, 2, 11–12, 27–8, 68–70,
    88, 88 n. 11, 89, 89 n. 12, 90, 97, 122, 160,
    167, 172–6, 181, 194–7, 234

Thompson, Sandra A. 30–2, 71, 101, 160, 170, 174, 196
Tooke, John Horne 15
Trask, R. L. 17, 21 n. 6, 143
Traugott, Elizabeth 87, 118 n. 8, 119 n. 9, 119–20
Trubetzkoy, Nikolai 91
Tsohatzidis, Savas L. 2
Tuggy, David 85 n. 6

Ungerer, Friedrich 2, 89

Vachek, Josef 58
van Riemsdijk, Henk 51–2, 191
Van Valin, R. 182–3
Varro 14
Vendler, Zeno 3 n. 2
Verner, Karl 17
Verschueren, Jef 71
Visser, Frans Th. 178, 213

Waller, Tim xii
Warner, Anthony 24 n. 9, 99
Weinberg, Steven 45
Wells, Rulon 39
Wierzbicka, Anna 2, 27 n. 10, 37, 71
Wilkins, John 28, 68
Williamson, Timothy 1 n. 1, 37
Wilson, Deirdre 24 n. 9, 57 n. 10, 99
Winters, Margaret E. 172, 193–4
Wittgenstein, Ludwig 11, 12 n. 3, 13, 29, 31, 36–7, 68
Wurff, Wim van der xii, 228–9

Xu, Xunfeng 180

Zadeh, Lofti Asker 58, 60, 62
Zandvoort, R. W. 131, 135
Ziff, Paul 47
Zwicky, Arnold M. 165, 165 n. 1, 166–7, 171

Subject Index

acceptability/grammaticality 4, 44, 73
above 161
adjectival:
   passive, *see* passive
   noun 130
adjective 105–7, 125–7, 129–38, 209–10
   central 105–7
   criteria 106
   participial 142
   transitive 157
adjective-adjective compound, *see*
       compound
adjunct 186
   obligatory predication adjunct 186
adposition 20
adprep 151
adverb 136–8
   preposing 58
   temporal 156
afraid 210
after 236
agentless passive, *see* passive
ago 110, 148
agreement phrase (AgrP) 22
alive 105–7, 209–10
all-or-none 11, 18, 40, 43, 93
almost success 137–8
although 237
amalgam 84, 187
American structuralism, *see*
       structuralism
anacoluthon 189
analogy 3, 14,
and 152, 155, 239
animate agent passive, *see* passive
annihilation vagueness, *see* vagueness
anomaly 3, 14

apo koinou 187
apposition 125
approximation vagueness, *see* vagueness
apriorism 16
Aristotelian category, *see* category
article 15
as 149, 151–2
assuming (that) 149
at 219
attended processing 31
attitudinal passive, *see* passive
Attribute Value Matrix (AVM) 168–9, 195
automated processing 31
auxiliary, *see* verb

bar level, *see* X-bar Theory
barring 148
basic level, *see* categorization, levels of
because 237
before 154, 204
besides 151–2, 236
Best Fit Principle 65, 213
Bible 12
binariness 91
Binding Theory 22, 50
blend:
   lexical 187
   syntactic 4, 41, 76, 155, 187–92
boundary 60
   case 72
   vagueness 60
boy actor 129
bridge class 63
but 151–3, 238

C-node 20, 22
Case 2, 22, 50

categorial:
  assymmetry 90, 93
  indeterminacy, *see also* gradience,
    grammatical indeterminacy 4,
    44, 73
  vagueness 4
categorization 5, 9–34
  formal 23
  levels, of 27–9, 69
    basic 27
    subordinate 27
    superordinate 27
  negative 9
category:
  Aristotelian/classical 11, 12, 29–30,
    49–50, 114, 140, 154
  empty 21–2
  conceptual 88
  disguised lexical 22–3
  dual lexical 77 n. 77
  functional 20–2, 25, 171
  fuzzy syntactic 24, 97–123
  grammatical/linguistic 15–16, 19, 25,
    29, 70, 87–9, 234–41
  grammatical kind 234
  intermediate 32
  lexical 52
  logical 25
  membership 12
  mixed 52, 76–7
  natural kind 27, 234
  nominal kind, 27, 234
  peripheral 32
  second order 22
  semantic 89
  space 53, 235–41
  substantive 21
  supercategory 19
  symbol 19
  syntactic properties 215–28
  transitory 32
  tyranny of 40
central adjective, *see* adjective

centre–periphery–transition 59–60
classical category, *see* category
clause:
  adjunct 121
  clause linking typology 121, 183
  contact 188
  embedded 121
  nominal relative 190
  relative 121
  small/verbless 149
  subordinate 121
cline 42
  lexico-grammar 42
  of constructions 168
  of nounhood 101–5
close 156–8, 219
coercion 194, 208, 232
Cognitive Construction Grammar
  (CCxG), *see* Construction
  Grammar
cognitive linguistics 2, 68–71,
  167, 194
cognitive reference point 69
colorless green ideas sleep furiously 46
colour term 68
COMP 20
competence 58
complementation 64, 74, 117, 185–6
complementizer 20–1, 155, 219–22,
  237–8, 240–1
  complementizer phrase (CP) 20
  prepositional 2, 50, 220
complement, *see also*
  complementation 186
  prepositional 2, 50, 220
  vs. adjunct 186
Complete Functional Complex
  (CFC) 119–20
complex preposition, *see* preposition
complex transitive verb, *see* verb
compound 59, 129, 131
  adjective-adjective 134
  non-possessive 181–2

passive, *see* passive
possessive 181–2
preposition, *see* preposition
conceptual:
  Conceptual Principle 23
  structure 29
concerning 148
conjunction 155
  coordinating, see also and, *but* 155,
    238–9
  deverbal 149
  subordinating 110, 155, 184–5
considering 146–7
construction 78–9, 164–71, 182
  catenative 171
  complex preposition 176–8
  Constructional Gradience (CG), *see
    also* gradience 164–98
  construction-particular rule 164
  construction-types 166
  Construction Grammar, *see* next main
    entry
  coordination-subordination 182–5
  copulative 190
  determinative + noun 170
  ditransitive 186
  fused head 191–2
  genitival 180–1
  history of notion 164–70
  interrogative 196
  intransitive 190
  it + verb + *be* + focus + *who/that*-
    clause 170
  let alone 168
  noun + noun 170
  operator + subject + verb + direct
    object 170
  passive 178–80
  P + NP + P 170
  possessive 175–6, 181–2, 195
  productive 193–4
  prototypical 193
  pseudocleft 172

resultative 169
subject-auxiliary inversion 173
subject + verb + object 170
transitive 174–5, 194, 196
V + NP + *to*-infinitive 173–4, 185–6,
  222–3
verb + direct object 170
verb + indirect object + direct object 170
way 169
what's X doing Y (WXDY) 168, 195
Construction Grammar (CxG) 32–3,
  78–9, 168–70, 195
  Cognitive Construction Grammar
    (CCxG) 33, 78–9, 168, 195–7
  Radical Construction Grammar
    (RCxG) 33, 168
  Unification Construction Grammar
    (UCxG) 168, 195
contamination 187
contiguity of grammatical
  categories 235–41
Contingent Category Hypothesis
  (CCH) 23
continuous phenomena 1
continuum 40, 42
  differentiated 40
  undifferentiated 40
  verb-adjective-noun 54
convergence 5, 225, 235–41
  strong 201, 206
  weak 206–7
conversion:
  partial 135
coordination 182–5
core 58, 91
corpus 108, 226–7
cosubordination 183
CP, *see* complementizer phrase
criterial attribute 27–8
cross-categorial generalization, *see also*
  X-bar syntax 19
c-structure 78
current change 188

decategorization 161
deep(ly) blue 133
deep verb, *see* verb
defective NP 54
defining criteria 105
degree:
   of class membership 60–2, 117,
      122–3
   of clausiness 121
   of deviance 49
   of grammaticalness 45–7, 72
   of markedness 92
   of reanalysis 147–8
   of syntactic integration 119, 192
   of typicality/representativity 122–3
   of transitivity 71, 101
   of viability 61
Derivational Theory of Complexity 48
derived nominal 144
descriptive:
   genitive, *see* genitive
   grammar, *see* grammar
desententialization 119
design of language 39–40
determiner/determinative/
      (post)determiner 125 n. 1, 125–9,
      204–5
   determiner genitive, *see* genitive
   determiner pronoun, *see* pronoun
deverbal conjunction, *see* conjunction
dimension of NP-hood 114–15
direct object 117
discourse:
   manipulable participants 31
   typological linguistics 30–2, 71–2
   vagueness, *see* vagueness
discreteness 39, 63
distributional analysis 33, 46,
      130, 156
ditransitive:
   construction, *see* construction
   prototype, *see* prototype
   verb, *see* verb

dual lexical category, *see* category
due 156–8, 219
during 148

Effects = Structure Interpretation, *see*
      prototype
either/or 19, 157
E-language 44, 46, 63, 166
embedding 121
empiricism 58
   vs. rationalism 16
   and flexibility 17
empty category, *see* category
enough 215–19
except 151–2
epiphenomenon 33, 164, 166
epistemic view of vagueness, *see*
      vagueness
essentialist definitions 33
Exceptional Case Marking (ECM) 50
exceptionlessness 3, 16
existential *there*, *see there*
Experiencer Constraint 139
external syntactic 58, 114 n. 6, 226 n. 15

Fact Deletion 53
fake NP squish, *see* squish
fallacy of categorial impurity 3
falsification 224
family resemblance 29, 36, 44
far 156–8
feature 19, 48, 50
   system 20
   Feature Cooccurrence Restriction 75
   [±strong] 51
FF(LI) 19
finite clause prototype, *see* prototype
following 145–6
for 93, 148–9, 155, 220–2, 237
form class 17
formative 19
fossilization 161
frequency 108, 193

from 187
f-structure 78
full/empty 25
fun 131–3
functional:
    category, *see* category
    grammar 42–3
    functional/typological linguistics
        2, 30–2, 71–2
fusion 126, 135, 187–92
    fused construction 189
    fused determiner-head 126
    fused head construction, *see*
        construction
    fused modifier-head 135–6
    fused relative 190
    syntactic 189
fuzzi(ness) 33, 43–4, 52, 58, 115, 124, 144,
        154, 241
    grammar, *see* grammar
    set theory 60

Galilean style 45
game (Spiel) 36–7
Generalised Phrase Structure Grammar
        (GPSG) 75
generality 40–1, 59
generative grammar, *see also*
        Transformational Grammar 19
Generative Semantics 23–5, 52–8
genitive:
    genitival construction, *see*
        construction
    descriptive 182
    determiner182
    of genitive 181
    Saxon 181
gerund 52, 75–8, 143–5, 210–14
    gerund participle 143
    gerundial (noun) 143–4
    gerundival 143
    gerundive 49, 52, 143
    gerundive nominal 50, 143–4

nominal 143
Nominal Gerund Phrase 75, 143, 230
    verbal 143
Verbal Gerund Phrases (VGP) 77
gestalt 194–5
Governing Category (GC) 22
Government-Binding Theory (GB)
        2, 49, 92, 118 n. 7, 149
gradience 1, 5, 12, 23, 30, 34–79,
        80–94
    adjective-adverb 136–8
    adjective-noun 62–3, 129–36
    adjective-preposition 156–8, 215–19
    adjective phrase-noun phrase 158–60
    adjective phrase-prepositional
        phrase 160–1
    adverb-noun 155–6
    adverb-preposition-
        conjunction 150–5
    among adjectives 105–7
    among clauses 118–21
    among nouns 101–5
    among noun phrases 54–5
    among pre-head elements 124–5
    among prepositions 101–7
    among verbs 98–101
    and related notions 80–94
    as categorial indeterminacy 4, 44
    auxiliary-main verb 55–7, 99–101
    complement-adjunct 186
    complementizer-preposition 219–22
    constructional 82, 111, 164–98
    coordination-subordination 152–5,
        182–5
    determinative-adjective 125–7
    determinative-adverb 127–9
    determinative-pronoun 125
    Intersective Constructional Gradience
        (ICG) 164, 180–92, 196
    Intersective Gradience (IG) 5, 79, 90,
        97, 121–3, 124–63, 171, 201–2,
        207–8
    linear representation of 35

gradience (*cont.*)
  noun phrase-prepositional
      phrase 161–2
  set-theoretic representation of 34–5
  Subsective Constructional Gradience
      (SCG) 164, 171–80, 196
  Subsective Gradience (SG) 5, 35, 67,
      79, 90, 93, 97–123, 142, 171, 201,
      205–206
  valency gradience 101
  verb-adjective 138–42, 214–15
  verb-adjective-noun 52–4
  verb-adverb 149–50
  verb-noun 143–5, 210–14
  verb-preposition/conjunction 145–9
gradient markedness model 92–3
Graeco-Roman classification, *see* word
      class
graft 191
grammar:
  cognitive 26–30
  descriptive 3, 25–6, 62–7, 166–7
  fuzzy 58
  literary 14
  logical 14
  non-discrete, *see also* gradience 57
  Port Royal 21 n. 6
  speculative 14–5
  traditional 22 n. 8
grammatical:
  category, *see* category
  category dependence 183
  construction, *see* construction
      (grammar)
  function 6
  indeterminacy 42, 49, 87, 158
  verb, *see* verb
grammaticality 46, 48
  discrete 44
  gradient 48
  partial 46
grammaticalization 87
Grimm's Law 17

hapax legomenon 189
happy 105–7, 209–10
hardening of categories 12
Head Driven Phrase Structure Grammar
      (HPSG) 18, 32, 76
Head Feature Convention (HFC) 75
homogeneous speech community 44
hybridity 49
  true 208, 228–33
hypotaxis 119

if 237
ICE-GB, *see* International Corpus of
      English
I(nternalised)-language 46, 63
idealization 4, 9, 23, 44
idiom chunk 116
imprecision 35–7
in 161
inanimate agent passive, *see* passive
including 146–7
indeterminacy:
  constrained 4
  grammatical 42, 49, 87, 158
  classification 37
indirect object 117
  indirect objoid 174
  indirect-objectiness 174
I-node 20, 22
intercategorial resemblance 124
intergradation 151
intermediate category, *see* category
internal syntactic 58, 114 n. 6, 226 n. 15
International Corpus of English (British
      component; ICE-GB), *see also*
      Survey of English Usage 83 n. 3,
      84 n. 5, 132
interpretive semantics 25
Intersective Constructional Gradience,
      see gradience
Intersective Gradience, *see* gradience
intransitive verb, *see* verb
inflection phrase (IP) 20, 22

Janus-agent passive, *see* passive
Junggrammatiker, *see* neogrammarian

kernel sentence 48
knowledge systematisation 9

language-internal methodological
    opportunism 131 n. 4
Law:
    of the Excluded Middle 11, 11
        n. 2, 52
    of the Excluded Third 11 n. 2
leaking 9, 66, 157
Left Dislocation 54
let alone construction, *see* construction
Lexical Functional Grammar (LFG) 78
lexicalist hypothesis 19
lexical level, *see* categorization, levels of
    lexical/grammatical 25
like 151–2, 156–8, 215–19
linguistic level 17
Literal Force Hypothesis 197
    n. 6
literary grammar, *see* grammar
logic 12–13, 39
    logical theory, *see* grammar
lumping 154 n. 19

maiden voyage (criterion) 131, 133
many 125–6, 236
margin 60
marginal:
    preposition, *see* preposition
    subordinator 149
markedness 90–4
    Markedness Theory (MT) 90–4
mathematical linguistics 63
meaning:
    vague 193–4
    'too little' 195
    'too much' 194–5
merger 83–5, 85 n. 7, 86, 187–92
messiness of language 3

methodological opportunism, *see*
    language internal methodological
    opportunism
Middle English 148
minimal categorial system 65
Minimalist Program 21, 48, 51–2, 166
mixed category, *see* category
mixing 83–6, 187–92, 212
model of universe 45
modes 15
modification 64
Modistae 14
monotransitive verb, *see* verb
morphosyntactic:
    feature 162
    properties 32, 213, 223
    test 206
multifactorial statistical techniques 174
multiple:
    analysis 86–7
    multiple default inheritance 144
must 100–101

natural kind category, *see* category
near 111, 156–8, 215, 216, 216 n. 12, 217–19,
    236
necessary and sufficient conditions 33
Negative Phrase (NegP) 22
neogrammarian 3, 16–17
NICE properties 99, 99 n. 1
nominal:
    gerund, *see* gerund
    Nominal Gerund Phrase (NGP), *see*
        gerund
    nominal kind category, *see* category
    nominal relative clause, *see* clause
    verb, *see* verb
nominalizing affix 231–2, 232 n. 19
nonagentive passives, *see* passive
non-possessive compound, *see*
    compound
not 227
notwithstanding 110, 148

noun 101–105
  as universal category 21 n. 6
  binominal 211 n. 5
  prototypical 123
  verbal 213, 213 n. 8
noun adjective 16
nouniness squish, *see* squish
noun phrase:
  noun phrasiness, *see also* gradience 54,
    112, 116
  noun phrasoid 54
now 110, 137
Number Agreement 112

objoid 174
obligatory predication adjunct, *see*
  adjunct
Occam's razor 10, 24, 154 n. 19
of-gentive, *see* genitive
off the road 161
open/closed 25
Optimality theory (OT) 72–3

P–NP–N construction, *see* construction
paradox:
  bald man 1 n. 1
  Mona Lisa 1 n. 1
  Sorites 1, 13, 35
parameter 91, 164
  head parameter 92
parataxis 64, 119
parenthetical 241
part of speech, *see* word class
partial conversion, *see* conversion
participial adjectives, *see* adjective
particle 109, 236
part of speech, *see* word class
passive, *see also* passivization 178–80
  adjectival 142
  agentless 179
  animate agent 178
  attitudinal 179
  compound 179

  emotional 179
  gradient 178
  inanimate agent passive 178
  Janus-agent passive 178
  morphology 141
  nonagentive passive 179
  pseudo-passive 178
  statal passive 178, 233
passivization, *see also* passive 98, 112
pending 146–7
performance 4, 43, 46, 58
peripheral elements 64
periphery 58, 60, 91–2
Phrase Structure Grammar 32–3, 75–7
picture noun phrase 48, 73
Pied Piping 156
portmanteau word 187
Port Royal Grammar, *see* grammar
possession gestalt 175
possessive:
  compound, *see* compound
  construction, *see* construction
post-Bloomfieldian structuralism
  17–18
PP Postposing 156
pragmatic:
  pragmatic theory of fuzziness 117
  pragmatic view of vagueness 37
Prague School 43, 50, 58–60
predicand requirement 216 n. 10
prenominal possessive, *see* possessive
prenucleus 190
preposition 107–11, 155, 219–22
  compound 107
  complex 107, 176–8
  grammatical 108
  inflected 217
  intransitive 111
  lexical 108
  marginal 110, 145
  prepositional copula 149
  Preposition Deletion 156–7
  simple 107

prepositional:
    complementizer, *see* complementizer
    copula 149
pretend 142
Principium Exclusi Tertii 18
Principles and Parameters Theory
        (P&P) 2, 21, 22, 49, 92
pro ('little pro') 21
PRO ('big PRO') 21, 50, 118 n. 7
    PRO Theorem 50
probabilistic view of language 43, 226–7
Probability Theory 73–4
progressive squish, *see* squish
pronoun:
    determiner pronoun 204 n. 1
    (in)transitive 205
    pronoun adjective 16
pronominal anaphor, *see* PRO
Property Concept Word 31
prototype 3, 27, 28, 31, 32, 35, 62, 68–9,
        78–9, 88–9, 94, 101, 107, 122, 129,
        160, 174, 193, 197
    ditransitive 174
    Effects = Structure Interpretation 69
    finite clause prototype 118–21
    prototype effects 68–9, 201
    prototype syntax, *see also*
        (Intersective) Constructional
        Gradience 172, 197–8
    Prototype Theory 68, 71, 87–90, 93
    Prototype = Representation
        Interpretation 69
provided (that) 149
pseudo- 66
    pseudocleft 172
    pseudo-passive, *see* passive

quasi- 66
    quasi-argument 50

Radical Construction Grammar (RCxG),
        see Construction Grammar
raising 53, 85, 112

    to object 185
    to subject 85, 203
reanalysis 86–7, 87 n. 9, 147–8
regarding 146, 148
relative clause, *see* clause
representation 4, 13, 202–204
restructuring 86
rich, the 134
right 110, 161, 217

Saxon genitive, *see* genitive
S-bar (S') 20
    deletion 92
scale of delicacy 42
second order category, *see* category
seeing (that) 149
semantic bleaching 159
semi- 66
    semi-auxiliary 99
    semi-determiner 127
    semi-lexical head 23
serial relationship 4, 63, 80–3
set-theoretic representation of gradience,
        see gradience
since 154 n. 19
sloppy description 4
small clause, *see* clause
Sorites:
    paradox, *see* paradox
    Sorites models 223–5
sound law 3, 16
speculative grammar, *see* grammar
Split INFL Hypothesis 20
splitting 154 n. 19
squish, *see also* gradience 4, 52, 58
    fake NP 54
    nouniness 54–5, 60, 111–17
    progressive 55
    subsquish 156
    verbal 55–7, 99–101
    well-behaved 55
Stammbaumtheorie 17
statal passive, *see* passive

stereotype 122
stochastic syntax, *see* syntax
[±strong] feature, *see* feature
strong convergence, *see* convergence
structuralism 17–18, 39, 164–6
subcategorization 73–4, 154 n. 19,
    204–5
subject-auxiliary inversion (SAI), *see*
    construction
subjunctive 240
subordinate level, *see* categorization,
    levels of
subordination 182–5
subordinator, *see* conjunction
Subsective Constructional Gradience
    (SCG), *see* gradience
Subsective Gradience, *see* gradience
substantive categories, *see* category
such 126–7, 236
supercategory, *see* category
superordinate level, *see* categorization,
    levels of
supervaluationalism 38
supposing (that) 149
Survey of English Usage, *see also*
    International Corpus of
    English 229
SYNSEM attribute 33
syntactic:
  blend, *see* blend
  category, *see* category
  construction, *see also* construction 182
  merger, *see* merger
  mimicry 136
  relic 157
syntax:
  autonomous 2
  formal 2
  stochastic 73
systemic vagueness, *see* vagueness

Tag Formation 54, 112
temporal adverbs, *see* adverb

Tense Phrase (TP) 22
tertium non datur 9
than 151–2
that 237
then 137
there 110, 115, 167, 185, 222
thin 105–107, 206, 209–10
through 161
time-stability scale 30, 71
to 187
tough-movement 54
TP, *see* Tense Phrase
trace 22
traditional grammar, *see* grammar
Transformational Grammar 18–23,
    43–52, 164–6, 185
transitive:
  adjective, *see* adjective
  construction, *see* construction
  verb, *see* verb
transitivity 71
transitory category, *see* category
true:
  argument 50
  hybridity, *see* hybridity
typological linguistics 2

under fives 161–2
undifferentiated continuum, *see*
    continuum
Unification Construction Grammar
    (UCxG), *see* Construction
    Grammar
univerbation 148
Universal Category Hypothesis (UCH)
Universal Grammar (UG) 44, 91,
    165, 171
unlike 156–8
unmarked, *see* markedness
up 161
upstairs 137
utter 105–7, 130, 206–7,
    209–10

vague meaning, *see* meaning
vagueness 1, 5, 12, 13, 35, 37, 58–60,
    202–4
  annihilation 59
  approximation 59
  boundary 204
  categorial 4
  discourse vagueness 59, 88
  epistemic view of 37–8
  logical approach to 60
  pragmatic view of 37–8
  systemic 59
  theories of 37, 59
valency 101
  valency gradience, *see* gradience
variable/invariable 25
verb-adjective noun continuum, *see*
  continuum
verb complementation, *see*
  complementation
verbal gerund, *see* gerund
Verbal Gerund Phrases (VGP), *see*
  gerund
verbal noun 213
verb 98–101
  as universal category 21 n. 6
  auxiliary 24, 57, 57 n. 10, 98–101
  deep 24
  complex transitive 185
  ditransitive 101, 185–6

  intransitive 111, 154 n. 19
  modal 55–7, 98–101
  monotransitive 101, 185–6
  nominal 213 n. 8
  of negative causation 187
  phrasal 109, 205
  transitive 101, 111, 154 n. 19
  weather 101
Verner's Law 17
viability 61, 172

wave theory 17
weak convergence, *see* convergence
weather verb, *see* verb
weighting 226
well-behaved squish, *see* squish
Wellentheorie, *see* wave theory
what's X doing Y-construction (WXDY),
  see construction
whether 237
word class 10, 14, 16–17, 19–20, 25–6, 50,
  63, 97, 102, 157, 171
  Graeco-Roman classification 38
Word Grammar 65, 77–8
working 138, 158, 214–15
worth 111, 156–8, 219

X-bar Theory 19, 25, 166

zero nominalizing affix 5